ANNUAL REVIEW OF
GERONTOLOGY AND GERIATRICS

Volume 8, 1988

Varieties of Aging

ANNUAL REVIEW OF
Gerontology and Geriatrics

Volume 8, 1988

Varieties of Aging

George L. Maddox, Ph.D.
M. Powell Lawton, Ph.D.
SPECIAL VOLUME EDITORS

SPRINGER PUBLISHING COMPANY
NEW YORK

Springer Publishing Company, Inc.
536 Broadway
New York, NY 10012

88 89 90 91 92 / 5 4 3 2 1

_____

ISBN 0-8261-6490
ISSN 0198-8794

_____

Printed in the United States of America

Contents

Orientations

The Social Distribution of Societal Resources

Some Policy Implications of Population Heterogeneity

Preface

With the appearance of Volume 8 of the *Annual Review of Gerontology and Geriatrics* it is appropriate to acknowledge the tremendously creative work of founding Editor-In-Chief Carl Eisdorfer. Dr. Eisdorfer's leadership was evident in every phase of the production of the past seven volumes. The most notable of all his contributions came in the generative phase of each, where ideas flowed in bewildering profusion, yet were processed to end up with a coherent set of chapters and authors to constitute each of the volumes. His leadership will be missed, but his continuing interest will remain expressed as he contributes in the role of Founding Editor for the continuing series.

The *Annual Reviews* of the future will build on Dr. Eisdorfer's tradition. In a field that includes so many disciplines, it would be unrealistic to represent a true cross-section of these disciplines in every volume. The series will thus continue to produce volumes that sample segments of the totality, the breadth of each segment varying over the years. The present Volume 8, for example, while it includes content of interest to health-care professionals and geriatric practitioners, samples its chapters from the segment defined by sociology, economics, and social policy. Volume 9 is in process and will represent a particularly broad segment of all gerontology and geriatrics by focusing on "clinical gerontology," based on the clinical research from geriatrics, medicine, psychiatry, exercise physiology, counseling, health service organization, and self-help. Yet another variation on the theme will come in a later volume designed to provide a scholarly presentation of the current status of a number of issues in the biology aimed toward the multidisciplinary audience for this series. Over the long range, the many faces of gerontology and geriatrics will be covered, but without slavish adherence to a formula.

The Associate Editors join me in hoping that suggestions for future directions will be provided by readers.

M. Powell Lawton
Editor-in-Chief

Introduction

Demographers, epidemiologists and historians have regularly documented the very large differences in how people age, how they experience aging, and when they die among societies and across time. The observed differences appear to be explained substantially by factors external to the individual, factors such as the stability of food supply, the provision of clean water, the adequacy of public sanitation, and the availability of effective immunization against, or medical treatment for, one or another epidemic or chronic disease. Intra-societal differences, however, are a more complex matter and a relatively less studied one.

This volume of the *Annual Review* focuses attention precisely on the neglected documentation and explanation of heterogeneity of how people grow older within a society. The society of special interest is the United States in relatively recent decades, although some of the chapters include instructive comparisons with other societies.

In the opening section, sociologist Dale Dannefer and epidemiologist Lisa Berkman orient the reader to processes of resource allocation within a society which produces and maintains a system of socioeconomic stratification. An individual's social address in a system of stratification is indexed in part by income and level of formal education achieved. But the correlates of one's social address in a society are also easily recognizable by status-related differential life expectancy, patterns of sickness and utilization of health resources, and perceptions of self as socially effective and socially integrated. Dannefer notes that gerontologists, possibly as a reflection of the immaturity of their field, have preferred to pursue broad scientific generalizations about processes of aging and about older adults; consequently they have not been sufficiently interested in documenting and explaining heterogeneity in later life. He makes a strong case for both the theoretical and practical values of differential gerontology. Gerontologists have tended to be keenly aware of the relevance and interaction of both intrinsic and extrinsic factors in determining the course of aging processes. Precisely to the extent that external factors are assumed to condition the expression and experience of aging, one might expect gerontologists to celebrate observed diversity as evidence of what happens when intrinsic biological factors are conditioned in their development and expression by sociocultural and environmental factors. And, if the present is an expression of the past, then the present anticipates the future. Can alternative futures of aging be anticipated and pursued? If aging processes are modifiable, then the answer is affirmative. Acceptance of the modifiability of aging processes logically leads to a discussion of public policy options in terms of the possible beneficial effects on achieving and maintaining well-being in later life.

Lisa Berkman illustrates the application of the perspective of social and behavioral epidemiology to the study of human aging. The tradition of epidemiology is exquisitely multidimensional and multivariate in its focus on the interaction of a host in a particular environment responding to a challenge of one sort or another. For the epidemiologist, the adequacy of an individual's response is reflected in the outcomes we describe as health or illness. Berkman is particularly interested in illustrating more than the classic finding of epidemiology that socioeconomic factors are powerful predictors of health and illness. She also reviews a broad range of new evidence about the effects of socioenvironmental and behavioral factors on the physiologic mechanisms as individuals age and the preventive and mediating effects of social support systems on the health of older adults.

In the second section of the volume, four chapters document and inter- pret the heterogeneity of the ways adults age in the United States. Fredric Wolinsky and Connie Arnold (Chapter 3) document heterogeneity in health and health-services utilization among older adults but focus specifically on the need for a new perspective in the study of this heterogeneity. It is not enough, they argue, simply to "cut the deck" by new and different ways of subclassifying older adults. Scientific evidence and explanatory models must increasingly take into consideration that many of the processes of aging in which we are interested are best conceptualized as processes and as complex multivariate interactions. Wolinsky and Arnold clearly illustrate some basic problems in the mismeasurement of variables and mis-specification of models intended to explain health and health-services utilization in later life. Age, they find in their analysis, is a weak explanatory variable. Their analysis focuses attention rather on the importance of correct assessment of health needs and the relatedness of institutional and noninstitutional care. These observations lead then to a recommendation of a "fundamental restructuring of health care" to assure uniform access to services, particularly primary- care services. They go beyond this general recommendation to argue specifi- cally that a system of national health insurance has particular merits in an aging society.

Marilyn Moon's theme in Chapter 4 is nicely captured in the subtitle, "Emerging Wealth and Continuing Hardship." It is neither possible nor particularly useful, she concludes, to try to capture the economic situations of heterogeneous older adults with aggregated data describing "the elderly." The most important conclusion about the economic situation of older adults in the contemporary United States may be the persistence of a large minority of impoverished older adults in the midst of an increasingly large minority of older adults who are relatively secure economically. The nation's perception of the economic security of older adults has changed, but not necessarily in a helpful way. The older stereotype of "the deserving poor elderly" is being challenged by the equally inadequate stereotype of "the undeserving rich elderly." Individuals born in the 1930s have been called "the good times cohort" and correctly so. This outcome, Moon reminds, reflects both favorable socioeconomic conditions and effective public policies on behalf of older adults. Subsequent age cohorts will not automatically fare as well. The policy issues to which she calls attention include the designation of a later age for normal retirement, the targeting of economically vulnerable subpopulations for special economic assistance, and relating levels of social security and welfare benefits to income and wealth after retirement.

In the other two chapters of the second section, Angela O'Rand and Neal Krause focus on two categories of older adults who usually receive special attention in discussions of differential aging—women and ethnic minorities. O'Rand's analyses of the pension acquisition process in the United States—and also in Sweden—illustrate how and why being female changes the probability of having an adequate income in retirement. What does female denote in such analyses? Least of all does being female connote an explanatory biological characteristic. More accurately, femaleness connotes a socially defined characteristic associating women with special responsibilities in families; these responsibilities, in turn, affect the probability of entry into and pursuit of a career in the types of business or industrial firms likely to have provision for adequate pensions. Interestingly, Sweden, usually considered to ignore male/female differences in pension provision, also generates more adequate pension coverage for males than for females. Differential access to adequate pension income, therefore, is not explained by being female but by being female in a society with particular expectations regarding family responsibilities and career development in particular kinds of industry or business.

Neal Krause revisits an old question in gerontology regarding how we are to understand psychological well-being and its relation to gender and ethnicity. His approach is to review indications of psychological failure as expressed in pathology and to ask why the available literature has produced such conflicting findings regarding the association between femaleness and minority status and bad outcomes in terms of psychological well-being. The conflicting findings, he concludes, flow predictably from failure to specify carefully what is indexed by the classification "female" or "minority." As the chapter by Wolinsky and Arnold noted earlier, gender and minority status are very crude ways to cut the deck of human heterogeneity. Does it matter whether women and members of a minority group are economically secure or impoverished? Does it matter whether women and members of an ethnic minority have access to different kinds and levels of social support? We have not been well served, Krause concludes, by poorly conceptualized and measured concepts and mis-specified models in gerontological research. Krause makes useful recommendations for how future research on these issues can be improved.

The third section of the volume develops and illustrates some implications of the growing awareness of heterogeneity in later life for formulating and assessing public policy options. The persistence of heterogeneity in aging populations is convincing evidence that aging processes are, to important degrees, modifiable by the differential allocation of social and economic resources over the life course. One of the most important developments in gerontology in recent decades is the rediscovery of an old maxim of experimental and clinical sciences: If you want to understand something, try to change it. This is hardly a novel conclusion in a society like the United States which is familiar with the social engineering of change and with a broad array of change agents. What is new is that such an orientation would be applied to aging processes and to older adults.

The concluding chapters on social security, planning long-term care, and options for insuring long-term care illustrate how reliable information is increasingly available for assessing public policy options and for planning geriatric services in the United States. Yet the final chapters clearly indicate that such information provides important background for decisions without dictating a single obvious choice regarding policy. In the final analysis, the formation and implementation of public policy is fundamentally an act of political intent, ingenuity, and will.

Yung-Ping Chen (Chapter 7) reviews the history and identifies a variety of stress points in the operation of the generally successful social security system of the United States. The discussion leads to recommendations for change which, in his view, would probably be beneficial. Specifically, Chen discusses continued attention to reducing systemic disadvantages of being a poor, displaced female; increasing portability of private pensions; encouraging private savings; and increasing incentives to remain in the workforce longer.

Kenneth Manton (Chapter 8) presents some very recent longitudinal evidence of the distribution of functional disability among older adults. This evidence, he argues, is critical not only for estimating the needs for long-term care services and facilities but also for estimating whether current levels of need generated by age-related disability are likely to continue. The evidence from the National Long-Term Care Surveys Manton analyzes is extraordinary because it is longitudinal and provides evidence both of disease status and estimates functional capacity; the data also make possible matching individuals in the data set to Medicaid records for purposes of estimating health care utilization and costs. Manton's analysis confirms that most older adults are not functionally disabled; he provides previously unavailable insights into the dynamics of moving into, and also out of, disablement in the later years. This chapter also provides a useful introduction to a power-ful data analytic technique increasingly encountered in gerontological and geriatric research—Grade of Membership (GOM) analysis. The chapter concludes with policy recommendations regarding the kind of care system which will be most effectively responsive to the observed heterogeneous population of older adults.

In the final chapter of the book, economist Alice Rivlin, sociologist Joshua Wiener, and their associate Denise Spence develop and illustrate the application of a population model designed to estimate the personal and social consequences of different options for insuring long-term care. They conclude that current evidence suggests a substantial minority of relatively affluent older adults, possibly 30%, can be expected to finance long-term care either by buying insurance in the market or by buying into a life-care community. For the substantial majority of older adults, they conclude, private financing of long-term care is not a realistic option. In policy discussions regarding long-term care options in the United States, two points of consensus appear to have been achieved: First, the need for long-term care has become a normal risk in later life; and second, risk pooling (public or private) is an appropriate strategy. No consensus has been reached, however, about the relative responsibility of public and private sectors for insuring long-term care. The chapter illustrates the application of a very sophisticated model for stimulating the effects of various policy options for the present through the year 2050. As long-term care moves to the topic of the national agenda over the next decade, the information in this chapter will make a useful contribution to informed public choices.

In the preparation of this volume, the editors have appreciated the consci-entious cooperation of the authors, the efficiency of Ursula Springer and her staff, and the skillful coordination of this undertaking by Betty Parker Ray.

GEORGE L. MADDOX
M. POWELL LAWTON

Contributors

Connie Lea Arnold
Department of Sociology
Texas A & M University
College Station, Texas

Lisa F. Berkman
Department of Epidemiology
  and Public Health
School of Medicine
Yale University
New Haven, Connecticut

Yung-Ping Chen
Economic Security Research
The American College
Bryn Mawr, Pennsylvania

Dale Dannefer
Graduate School of Education
  & Human Development
University of Rochester
Rochester, New York

Neal Krause
School of Public Health
University of Michigan
Ann Arbor, Michigan

Kenneth G. Manton
Center for Demographic Studies
Duke University
Durham, North Carolina

Marilyn Moon
Policy Analysis Program
American Association of
  Retired Persons
Washington, D.C.

Angela M. O'Rand
Department of Sociology
Duke University
Durham, North Carolina

Alice M. Rivlin
Economic Studies Program
The Brookings Institution
Washington, D.C.

Denise A. Spence
Economic Studies Program
The Brookings Institution
Washington, D.C.

Joshua M. Wiener
Economic Studies Program
The Brookings Institution
Washington, D.C.

Fredric D. Wolinsky
Department of Sociology
Texas A & M University
College Station, Texas

FORTHCOMING

The Annual Review of Gerontology and Geriatrics, Volume 9

PART I
Orientations

Differential Gerontology and the Stratified Life Course: Conceptual and Methodological Issues

DALE DANNEFER
UNIVERSITY OF ROCHESTER

THE IMPORTANCE OF STUDYING DIVERSITY IN AGING

Like other domains of scientific inquiry, gerontology—still a young field—has had to begin by establishing the importance of its subject matter; it has therefore focused on the power of age as a predictor variable through the assemblage of vast catalogs of age-based *generalizations.* Although age has long been recognized as an important attribute of persons and roles and as a basis of social organization, a burgeoning body of research findings now underscores the premise that age is a centrally important attribute if we wish to understand the nature of other human characteristics, whether physiological, psychological, or social. It has even been argued that age is probably the single most important predictor of other characteristics:

> Chronological age is one of the most useful single items of information about an individual if not the *most* useful. From this knowledge alone an amazingly large number of general statements or predictions can be made about his anatomy, physiology, psychology and social behavior. (Birren 1959, p. 8)

Although gerontological research has also led to the qualification and in some cases the debunking of some earlier beliefs about aging—both commonsense and scientific—the catalog of age-based generalizations continues to grow.

The focus on generalization in research on aging has been and will continue to be important. However, this focus—perhaps a necessary first

I wish to thank Elaine Dannefer, E. Anne Nelson, Marion Perlmutter, and the editors and an anonymous reviewer of the *Annual Review* for their comments and suggestions on an earlier draft. I also wish to thank E. Anne Nelson for research and bibliographic assistance.

step in the establishment of a subject matter—has not thus far been adequately complemented by systematic consideration of *diversity*, that is, of the extent to which the findings stated as central tendencies, that are often the basis for generalization actually typify the experience of concrete individuals. The distribution of a characteristic in a population is an important aspect of the accurate description of any phenomenon, and it dictates the nature of appropriate statistical manipulation of data. Thus the need to consider the range of variability on a given attribute is a fundamental principle of data analysis.

The importance of considering the distribution of a characteristic, and not just its mean or modal value, is especially great in gerontology because of the emphasis in gerontological discourse given to diversity observed within aged populations (see, e.g., Baltes, 1979; Bengtson, Kasschau, & Ragan, 1977; Botwinick & Thompson, 1968; Comfort, 1968; Dannefer, 1987; Havighurst, 1957; Kalish, 1975; Lieberman, 1965; Maddox, 1987; Maddox & Eisdorfer, 1962; Neugarten, 1964, 1982; Perlmutter, 1978; Riley, 1980; Rowe & Kahn, 1987). It is of course true that the aged are diverse if for no other reason than that, by definition, the category "aged" can span more than 35 years, including groups now distinguished as young-old, old-old (Neugarten, 1982), and, most recently, the "oldest-old" (Suzman & Riley, 1985). However, the main significance of diversity of aged persons is not as an artifact of an indiscriminate lumping of the "aged" into one category, but rather in the notion that there is great and perhaps increasing diversity among age peers, however narrowly one would want to define aged categories.

For several reasons, the idea of within-age diversity has been of special concern for those who wish to represent the interests of the aged. First, it provides a logical counterpoint to the cultural tendency to stereotype the aged, usually in a negative fashion. This counterpoint is relevant to both commonsense and theoretical images of the aged. At the broadest level, it has served to adumbrate role models for successful aging and to challenge negative images of the aged (Maddox, 1970; Neugarten, 1971b, 1982; Riley, 1980). It is indeed ironic that old people—despite their diversity—are perhaps more typecast by age, and hence implicitly assumed to be more homogeneous, than any other age category except perhaps young children. Attention to diversity has also been the basis for qualifying or rejecting efforts at forced overgeneralization, such as disengagement theory (Maddox, 1963). In addition, the diversity of the aged has implications for policy and practice, as a diverse population has a more differentiated set of resource and service-delivery needs (Butler, 1974; Crystal, 1982; Maddox, 1987; Nelson, 1982).

The competing tendencies for generalization on one hand and caution against overgeneralization on the other have created a largely unarticulated but important tension in gerontological discourse—between generalization and exception, central tendency and diversity, homogeneity and heterogeneity. This tension is reflected in a renewed emphasis on the need to attend to the relation of diversity and age in sociological (Dannefer, 1984b, 1987; Dannefer & Sell, in press; Maddox, 1987; Myers, 1985), psychological (Bornstein & Smircina, 1982; Schaie, in press), and medical (Rowe & Kahn, 1987) research. Clearly, if the extent of diversity on a given characteristic among age peers varies widely at different ages, then presenting and interpreting data in terms of central tendency differences by age distorts and oversimplifies the experience and outcomes of aging. If systematic changes in the amount of diversity is a recurrent tendency in each successive cohort of aging persons, then this tendency presents itself as an integral part of the aging process that needs to be understood and is potentially rich with implications for theory and policy.

This volume is thus a welcome and overdue effort to begin the task of organizing and systematizing our knowledge of diversity. The present chapter has six main sections. The present introductory section clarifies some points that often seem to confound discussions of diversity by drawing distinctions between (1) *intercultural and interindividual* diversity and (2) the *empirical question* of aged diversity and the issue of the *need to study* the issue. The second section discusses the *characteristics* that best illustrate the issue of diversity in human aging. The third section briefly considers some differences in the implicit *meaning* of aged diversity. The fourth section deals with assumptions of the *empirical patterning* of diversity and with the kinds of *explanatory processes* that have been advanced as assumptions or theoretical statements for these patterns. The fifth section identifies some *potential fallacies* that can arise in the analysis and interpretation of data on aged diversity. The final section briefly considers the relevance of aged diversity for *gerontological theory, policy, and practice.*

From Intercultural Diversity to Interindividual Diversity

Especially from the vantage point of those who begin with an assumption of aging as a universal or homogeneous process, the notion of differential aging has been made compelling, in part, by the considerable gerontological literature produced by anthropologists (e.g., Goody, 1976; Kertzer & Keith, 1984; Myerhoff & Simic, 1978), sociologists (Quadagno, 1982; Riley, Johnson, & Foner, 1972; Uhlenberg, 1974), and historians (e.g. Achenbaum, 1978; Demos, 1978; Fischer, 1978) documenting historical and cultural variations in the experience of aging. This work has provided notable cautions against the tendency to universalize aspects of the aging process and has been an important sensitizing force for the research and policy issues raised by diversity (Manuel, 1982; Sokolovsky, 1986).

Nevertheless, most such work will not be considered in detail in this chapter because, for the task of conceptualizing differential aging, it has been limited in three important ways. First, its main focus has been on between-group diversity (rather than within-group diversity). Cultures and historical periods are seen as differentiated, but within a given social setting differentiation is generally not conceived as an issue. Certainly the limitations of this tendency in the literature have been recognized (e.g., Kertzer & Keith, 1984), and there are some valuable exceptions to it, such as Simic's (1978) comparison of the life-course experiences of two aged Yugoslavs and Demos's (1978) observation that the apparent high status of aged New Englanders in colonial America did not extend to the aged poor.

Second, these traditions of work in anthropology, history, and comparative sociology have focused primarily on sociocultural arrangements—on the meaning and the social relations surrounding the experience of aging—rather than on the psychophysical processes of aging per se. There seems sometimes to be a tacit assumption in this literature that meaning and social relations are built on an impermeable foundation of psychophysical aging, with little acknowledgment of the ways in which such age-related changes may themselves be contextually regulated—a lesson of some recent findings that have documented cultural differences in the physiology as well as social relations of later life.

Third, these research traditions have not entailed a focus on differential aging as a conceptual or empirical problem worthy of systematic study. The recognition of diversity has been largely a byproduct of a focus on other problems. For example, theories that dispel the notion of aging as a universal experience [e.g., modernization theory (Cowgill & Holmes, 1972)] introduce the issue of diversity almost by defintion; yet they have offered little stimulus for focusing on diversity as a central problem. In sum, while comparative social-scientific perspectives have helped enormously to bring the problem of diversity to our attention, they provide only a point of denarture for the task of conceptualizing aged diversity as a phenomenon wi 1 potentially regular and systematic features.

The idea that the diversity of the aged is a phenomenon in need of explanation, and hence requiring a systematic focus of inquiry rather than an occasionally invoked caution against overgeneralization, has thus far had limited acknowledgment in gerontological research. The major paradigms that have guided the conceptualization of research on aging have either explicitly or implicitly been guided by an assumption of "normal aging"; the observed modal pattern of aging around which a distributed array of values on a given characteristic were distributed could be and were treated as error variance (Dannefer, 1984a, 1984b). The logic of statistical normality, under which diversity is seen as error variance, has sometimes led to a tendency to avoid the issue because diversity is associated with disorder, which is antithetical to scientific inquiry.

Nevertheless, more than a quarter century ago, some researchers were already cautioning that the emphasis on central tendency was of limited utility and tended to result in the neglect of important variation (Kuhlen, 1959; Maddox & Eisdorfer, 1962; Neugarten, 1964). There is little disagreement with such assertions, but there also is little evidence that they have had much effect on research and theory. As a theoretical problem, diversity has received scant attention. With a few notable exceptions (Maddox, 1964, 1965; Shock & Norris, 1966), the issue of the diversity of the aged has been addressed only infrequently in empirical analyses.

The most systematic of these earlier efforts to document diversity in aging was Maddox and Douglass's detailed longitudinal study (1974). Its empirical contribution notwithstanding, this article may be more notable for its identification of many of the substantive issues and methodological challenges posed by the issue of aged diversity as a problem for study. It offers an implicit agenda for research. In the years since, few have seriously considered the attendant challenges. A review of 23 citations of the Maddox and Douglass article found in the Social Science Citation Index revealed three instances in which researchers actually brought the issue of heterogeneity to bear on an analysis of empirical data (Hayslip, 1985; Lemke & Moos, 1981). One of these was a survey (Bornstein & Smircina, 1982) of *Journal of Gerontology* articles of 1979 and 1980, which suggested that measures of variability are seldom presented in contemporary gerontological research, and even less frequently discussed:

> It can be concluded that researchers are almost exclusively concerned about hypotheses of change or stability in "mean" behavioral performances over time; scant attention is being paid to hypotheses of change or stability in the variances associated with these performances. (p. 260)

A survey of leading gerontological journals over the last few years currently being conducted by the present author indicates that this situation has not changed. Thus the growing recognition of diversity and its possible implications has yet to find its way into the mainstream of gerontological research.

Aged Diversity as an Empirical Question in Need of Study

The recent emphasis on the need to examine diversity in aging needs to be distinguished from the assumption or claim that differences do increase with age. If aged diversity is an orderly phenomenon, the primary issue is not simply to advocate the view that the aged are indeed a diverse lot; it is to understand how the amount of diversity on a given characteristic changes over the life course and to identify the factors that influence those changes. This entails both the empirical task of developing more systematic data that describe how the extent and nature of diversity within a population change with age and the theoretical task of conceptualizing the processes and mechanisms that account for those changes.

At the same time, it should be noted that analyses conducted over the past few years have increased the body of evidence supporting the idea of increasing diversity with age. In the review noted above, Bornstein and Smircina (1982) concluded that, for many variables, the empirical evidence for increasing variability is, at best, mixed. However, recent findings from larger longitudinal or time-series data, as well as earlier findings not included in Bornstein and Smircina's review, seem to support a broad picture of generally increasing diversity on physiological (Thomae, 1985; Waldron, Nowatarski, Freimer, Henry, Post, & Witten, 1982; Wilkinson, 1986), psychological (Perlmutter, 1978; Schaie, in press), and social characteristics (Henretta & Campbell, 1976; Maddox & Douglass, 1974; Riley & Foner, 1968). Most of these studies are based on longitudinal data. Such data, some of it only recently developed as long-term longitudinal studies come to fruition, present a broadly consistent picture supporting the idea of increasing intracohort diversity with age. Several synthetic cohort analyses of income data have shown repeated patterns of increasing income inequality in successive cohorts (Mincer, 1974; Treas, 1986; see also Dannefer & Sell, in press). The finding of similar patterns of increasing divergence in successive cohorts suggests that a description of age differences only in terms of averages gives at best an incomplete picture of the nature of age-related change.

When data on divergence trajectories for time intervals earlier in the life course are considered, the same pattern of increasing divergence has also been found for school-related (Rosenbaum, 1976, 1978; Walberg & Tsai, 1983), career-related (Howard & Bray, 1988; Rosenbaum, 1984), personality (Farrell & Rosenberg, 1981), and health (Wadsworth, 1986) characteristics.

DIVERSITY OF WHAT? STUDYING DIFFERENTIAL AGING AS A GENERAL PRACTICE

A question that inevitably arises in any rather abstract discussion of diversity is "diversity of what"? Are all forms of diversity equally important? The answer obviously is no, any more than all characteristics for which we might obtain central tendency measures are equally important. A chief premise of this volume is that a fundamental shift in conceptual emphasis is needed in gerontology: the practice of describing phenomena in terms of central-tendency characteristics must be balanced by systematically attending to distributional characteristics as well. Because it has been generally neglected as a systematic problem, a general treatment of the conceptualization of diversity is warranted.

Therefore, the proper response to the question "diversity of what?" is that we should be concerned with age change in the distributional characteristics of precisely those variables about which we would want to know the central tendency and its changes with age. While this means that different researchers will presumably have "diverse interests in diversity," there are certain key health and resource characteristics that virtually everyone will agree are important to understand: central measures of health (e.g., blood pressure, lung capacity, functional mobility), psychological functioning and stimulation (e.g., from work-role demands), and resource characteristics (e.g., social-network ties, savings accounts) are of great importance for understanding both the immediate constraints and the longer-term life changes that a person experiences in his or her everyday life. Many of these covariables are precisely those for which large and longitudinal data bases are being compiled.

TWO MEANINGS OF AGED DIVERSITY

Geronotologists representing a wide variety of practical and scholarly concerns have referred to the diversity of the aged. It is therefore perhaps not surprising that the phenomenon of aged diversity—taken by itself a broad and abstract notion—has been given several substantive interpretations in the gerontological literature. At the most general level, two evaluative emphases can be identified, one positive and one negative. There is both a measure of truth and a lesson for gerontological theory in each of these views.

The more attractive view of the diversity of the aged is consistent with the often-invoked cautions against the negative stereotyping of old people: the emphasis is on the individuality of persons and the acknowledgment that the aged do not surrender their personhood on their 85th or 100th birthdays. Just as in midlife, aged individuals are unique persons. Indeed, they become more so with the accumulation of a lifetime of experience, as autobiographical accounts eloquently attest (e.g., Skinner, 1983). Maddox and Douglass point out that disengagement theory is in certain ways consistent with this emphasis, as it claims that "individuals activate preferred but suppressed conceptions of the self" (1974, p. 555) as a result of disengagement from work and family roles. Another example of this emphasis is offered by Hickey (1980, p. 81), who, in the context of critiquing the view that socialization to old age is a uniform and homogenizing experience, asserts that "social roles may be discontinuous, but people are not." Implicitly if not explicitly, one element of such a view of diversity is the self-determination of the individual to maintain a distinct and unique identity through the life course. In short, this perspective suggests that old people are more diverse than younger people because they have had more time to work at becoming individuals; they retain and cherish their individuality. Aged diversity may thus be, at least in part, a cause for celebration.

A second, less positive implication of diversity is contained in the acknowledgment that for many characteristics (whether physiological, psychological, or social) diversity reflects pathology. While many older adults retain their resilience and hence resemble typical midlife adults, others are ill, infirm, or socially isolated. This contrast is well captured in the distinction recently advanced by Rowe and Kahn (1987) between "usual" and "successful" aging. While these are not operational categories, they highlight the divergent images of the positive possibility of remaining healthy and active through advanced old age on one hand, with the decrements and illnesses that are commonly expected as part of "normal" aging on the other.

The explicit recognition of this contrast is directly relevant to the practical and policy-related issues of intervention and service delivery on one hand, and prevention on the other. With regard to service delivery, the implication is that social policies and programs for the aged should be designed to match the complex and differentiated character of the aged population. Research on nursing home residents has identified the structural contradiction between standardized institutional routines and the diverse needs and expectations of the residents (Powers, 1986). Although it has thus far received less emphasis, a potentially more far-reaching implication concerns prevention: to the extent that aged heterogeneity represents pathological conditions, preventive measures taken earlier in the life course may actually reduce diversity to some degree (Dannefer, 1987; Rowe & Kahn, 1987). Seen from this vantage point, differential aging is a consequence of differential life-course experiences, and the task of differential gerontology cannot be restricted to later life but is the task of constructing an entire theory of differentiating life-course processes that operate in each successive cohort as it ages.

AGED DIVERSITY, EMPIRICAL PATTERNS, AND LIFE-COURSE PROCESSES

The questions of prevention directs attention to the larger question to which a sustained analytic consideration of the phenomenon of aged diversity inevitably leads: How does diversity emerge? What are the underlying processes that lead to aged diversity? The immediate, intuitive notion is that individuals of the same age actually diverge and become more dissimilar from one another as they age, thus presenting a kind of radial "fanning" pattern. Aged diversity is often characterized in terms consistent with this image (e.g., Baltes, 1979; Neugarten, 1971a), and there is preliminary support for it with respect to some characteristics (Maddox & Douglass, 1974; Schaie, in press; Treas, 1986). Of course, it is not the only possible pattern, and some alternatives will be described below.

From such a perspective, diversity is the product of a lifetime of complex and systematically related experiences. The task of constructing either descriptive or theoretical accounts of how this occurs has, like research on aged diversity itself, received little systematic attention. However, some scholars have considered this issue, and both individual-psychosocial and social-structural perspectives on the production of increasing diversity have been proposed.

While few would dispute the importance of the psychology and physiology of individual persons in any account of life-course outcomes, the idea that social structure and social processes play a regulative or constitutive role in the production of aged diversity is less familiar, although no less promising. The task of testing these as competing models is complicated by the fact that they predict broadly the same outcomes. That is, a pattern of increasing intracohort diversity is predicted both by a model of psychological accentuation and by a model of social-structural differentiation. Yet the causal mechanisms, and hence the policy directions, implied by each model are quite different. Each of these basic perspectives deserves brief discussion.

Aged Diversity and the Accentuation of Individual Characteristics

The individual model is represented by the term *accentuation*: characteristics that were either present in the constitution of the organism, or else shaped early in the life course, become amplified and accentuated with the passage of time. Accentuation of early differences as a cause of divergence among age peers was noted by Adam Smith, who is quoted by Elder (1969, pp. 308–309) in a discussion touching on this point:

> When they came into the world, and for the first six or eight years of their existence, they were perhaps very much alike . . . soon after, they came to be employed in different occupations. The difference of talents comes then to be taken notice of, and widens by degrees, till at last the vanity of the philosopher is willing to acknowledge scarcely any resemblance.

The notion of accentuation has been used to describe a process of intracohort differentiation in discussions of aged diversity (Maddox & Douglass, 1974; Neugarten, 1964), in longitudinal life-course research (e.g., Clausen, 1986a; Elder, 1974; Elder & Liker, 1982), and, earlier in the life course, in research on the increasing differentiation among classmates in school or college (Feldman & Weiler, 1976; Huntley, 1965, 1967). Accentuation has typically been conceived as an interactive, psychosocial process.

The term *accentuation*, in sum, has been used to describe (1) the accentuation of stable characteristics initially present in the individual, (2) the differentiating effects of unique life experiences, and (3) the interaction of these. Each of these uses of *accentuation* deserves brief discussion.

The idea of accentuation as the coming to fruition of initial differences implies an image of fixed individual pathways that diverge with the passage of time—the inverse of railroad tracks that converge at the horizon. In gerontological research, the concept underlying the idea of aged diversity seems to entail accentuation in this sense—early differences that are accentuated with the passage of time. Schaie's (in press) notion of differential rates of development—one of the most sophisticated attempts to conceptualize increasing diversity to be found in the gerontological literature—implies the image of stable but diverging individual trajectories. Thus the path of change in a specific individual's functioning is best understood by reference to that individual's own past rather than to immediate environmental factors. The earlier social-psychological studies of accentuation effects in student values (Feldman & Newcomb, 1969; Feldman & Weiler, 1976; Huntley, 1965) also seem to be primarily oriented in terms of this general image. As Huntley described his sample of college students, ". . . the differences among the groups tend to be accentuated or sharpened over the four years" of college (1965, p. 381).

On the other hand, accentuation can be seen as a consequence of experience. Thus Neugarten (1964, p. 189) conceives of accentuation as a matter of "educational, vocational, and social events accumulat[ing] one after another to create more and more differentiated sets of experiences." This view gives a greater role to socialization and hence to the environment. Divergence and ultimately unique constellations of experience are credited with creating diversity. It is important to note, however, that the organization and dynamic properties of social systems are not an explicit part of this conceptualization—a point that distinguishes this treatment from those to be discussed in the following section.

Few would disagree that the assumption underlying the process of accentuation entails, irreducibly, an interaction between social and personal characteristics. An emphasis on such interaction has been a major emphasis of some scholars who have studied accentuation. In the first identified reference to accentuation, Allport, Bruner, and Jandorf (1941) noted the effects of stress in amplifying preexisting characteristics of war victims. The studies of the long-term effects of the Great Depression by Elder and associates offer numerous examples of such an interactive dynamic. They found that the experience of deprivation tended to accentuate both strengths and weaknesses of individuals in numerous psychological characteristics, such as assertiveness, explosiveness, and irritability. In some cases, these effects occurred in interaction with other factors, such as social class or marital strength (Elder, Liker, & Jaworski, 1984; Liker & Elder, 1983). The tendency to accentuate differences in this case was sharpened by the stressful experiences of the Depression. A later analysis of the long-term effects of the Great Depression on women showed that trajectories do not always radiate in such linear fashion; middle-class women who had been deprived during the Depression appeared to be using skills developed then to help them better cope 40 years later, when they were in their sixties and seventies (Elder & Liker, 1982); neither nondeprived middle-class women nor working-class women were able to fare so well. A similarly complex, interactive pattern is also at least hinted at in the work of Schaie and associates, who report connections between changes in life conditions and changes in the observed trajectory patterns of psychological characteristics (Gribbin, Schaie, & Parham, 1980; Schaie, in press).

Despite the identification of such interactive aspects of development, the concept of accentuation has seemed to develop with an emphasis on the extent to which these interactive processes are anchored in, and largely governed by, individual responses to circumstances. Thus Feldman and Newcomb (1969) conceive of accentuation as resulting from "personality dynamics" and "intrapersonal" processes. It is in the person's response to the interactive situation, whether positive or negative, that the tenor of subsequent experiences is decided. On the whole, of course, the probability is that positive responses will generate positive responses and negatives, negatives. In the analysis of Oakland Growth data, Clausen (1986b) notes the importance of early experiences in setting individuals on a course toward effective coping. The image of the outworking over a lifetime of such individual characteristics and interactive experiences, resulting in diversity in later life, has considerable intuitive appeal.

Aged Diversity and Socially Generated Differentiation

Most researchers who have dealt with processes such as accentuation acknowledge that the social environment plays some role in the reality they are attempting to capture. However, a fundamental theoretical distinction exists between a view of the environment as an amplifier of preexisting differences and a view of the environment as a generator of differences that may not have previously existed. In the sociology of aging, this subtle and generally unarticulated distinction has only become clarified relatively recently and is important to explicate. It is an instance of the classic tension in sociology between social-psychological and structural approaches.

In pure form, the accentuation and social-structural models may be counterposed as follows: since the accentuation model locates the mechanism of divergence within the individual's early life, no recognition of the nature of social structure in adulthood is necessary in order to understand how those earlier predispositions work themselves out. The social conditions in which adulthood and later life are lived out have only a tangential impact on the nature of adulthood and aging. Social effects are either too random, too unmeasurable, or too weak in their impact to be regarded as the primary organizer of observed intracohort diversity.

By contrast, the social-structural model locates the primary mechanisms of divergence in social practices in the everyday experience of the adult life course. Its pure form implies that even if everyone entered the adult world as identical clones, the institutionalized mechanisms of social differentiation [e.g., the creation of winners and losers among age peers in corporations (Burris, 1983; Kanter, 1977; Rosenbaum, 1984; Sørensen, 1986)] would insure that they became more diverse as they aged. It is important to note that this view not only gives importance to social forces but also regards them as nonrandom and as systematic in character.

Such social-structural processes of intracohort differentiation reflect both the stratified nature of age-specific social roles and the problems of fit between persons who are aging and the existent role structure of society (Riley et al., 1972). At least two types of such processes can readily be discerned: age-role incongruity processes and inequality-generation processes.

Age-Role Incongruity

Many age-role incongruities are produced by the interaction of compositional changes within a cohort and age-specific social norms. The prevalence of such norms is well established (Elder, 1975), extending not only to role occupancy but also to the timing and ordering or role transitions (Hogan, 1981; Marini, 1984). Employees in a firm studied by Lawrence (1984, 1985) believed that the range of employee ages at a given rank in the company was both narrower and younger than it actually was; individuals were likely to estimate the "normative age" for their own jobs to be younger than they were. Under such conditions, reified age norms create a perception of age-role incongruity where none exists, a perception that can nevertheless be "real in its consequences" (Thomas & Thomas, 1928).

Perhaps the most common example of an age-role incongruity is the case of marriage. The greater longevity of women than men has meant that in each birth cohort a growing "imbalance of persons and roles" (Riley et al., 1972) develops in the later years. Four out of five widowed persons aged 65 or older are women (Crystal, 1982). As a consequence, the normative expectation of a monogamous heterosexual marriage is rendered impossible for aged cohorts so long as societal norms stipulate (1) age-homogeneous mating, (2) older males marrying younger females, and (3) male-initiated courtship. These conditions produce, *ceteris parabus*, a mathematical guarantee that each cohort will become increasingly diverse in respect to marital status as it ages, because the normatively expected marital status is prevented from enduring by differential sex mortality. The diverse array of adaptations for the widowed spouse may include living alone, living with adult offspring or other extended family members, or living with other friends and acquaintances. Even if less commonly recognized adaptations [polygyny, lesbianism, Harold-and-Maude (older woman, younger man) marriages] were to become more widespread, unless one of these became normative it would only serve to increase diversity still further.

The problem of age-role incongruity is also brought into sharp contrast when cohorts vary significantly in size, producing a condition referred to as disordered cohort flow (Waring, 1976). Cohorts of widely different sizes strain social institutions. Presently, the strains placed on the labor market as the baby-boomers advance through early adulthood have contributed to the economic pressure that is keeping inordinate numbers of them living at home with their parents. This development probably reflects more inequality in income and creates more diversity in living arrangements in these larger cohorts than in smaller ones (Bengtson & Dannefer, 1987; see also Easterlin, 1980; Waring, 1976). These currently observed strains are likely to continue to be manifest in the later earning years and in retirement.

Independent of any tendencies toward accentuation of individual characteristics or of early life experiences, age-role incongruity thus confronts a cohort with externally imposed sources of differentiation as its members age. Demonstrating how many such issues of aging have an immediate structural component, rather than being an inevitable outcome of individual aging, has been an important contribution of the age-stratification paradigm (Riley, 1980; Riley et al., 1972).

Processes of Cumulating Advantage and Disadvantage

In the case of age-role incongruities, the increase in diversity with age is an artifact of a lack of numerical "fit" between persons and roles. In the case of cumulation of advantage, the increase in diversity is simply a result of biographical experience in a society with a stratified division of labor and institutionalized career expectations (Dannefer, 1987; Elder, 1969; Rosenbaum, 1984). As examples drawn from the occupational world suggest, the cumulative process of differentiation typically becomes translated into a process of increasing differences in advantage.

In the domain of occupational achievement, the tension described at the beginning of this section—between social-psychological and structural models—is manifest in the debate between the status-attainment and labor-market perspectives in sociology. The status-attainment perspective (see, e.g., Bielby, 1981; Campbell, 1983; Haller, 1982; Sewell, Haller, & Portes, 1969) generally uses early-life characteristics to predict later-life outcomes. The labor-market perspective (e.g. Doeringer & Piore, 1971; Hodson & Kaufman, 1982; Sørensen, 1977) argues that the socioeconomic structure of jobs and careers itself organizes the opportunities and constraints faced by individuals as they move through the life course. Since this debate centers on issues of the achievement of "worldly success" through the adult years (Featherman, 1980), its implications for aging are qutie straightforward. Sørensen (1986) has presented a lucid summary of the labor-market framework as it pertains to studies of the life course and aging.

It is the task of this section to show how an understanding of these structural realities can illuminate the issue of increasing diversity with age. The general principle of cumulation of advantage and disadvantage has long been recognized as an ubiquitous tendency in social life. Merton, drawing upon the words of Jesus in the Gospel according to Matthew ("for unto every one that hath shall be given and he shall have abundance, but from him that hath not, shall be taken away even that which he hath"), called this tendency the "Matthew effect" (1968). The present author has argued that this concept offers a useful metaphor to organize the study of social processes operating at various levels that tend to produce increasing diversity within a cohort as its members age (see Dannefer, 1987). This can be illustrated through a consideration of two analytically distinct levels, organizational processes and micro-interactional processes.

Organizational Processes and the Genesis of Diversity.   In at least some cases (e.g., within centrally controlled organizations), cumulation processes are somewhat open to modification, as they may be a consequence of the operation of humanly constructed social systems that have a built-in structural component of differentiation by age. This is not to say, of course, that the production of increasing differentiation with advancing age is necessarily a part of the planful intentions in such systems. The classic case of such an organization is the pyramidal bureaucracy, which combines powerful norms of upward mobility (Halaby & Sobel, 1979; Kanter, 1977; Lawrence, 1985) with a successively smaller number of fixed positions at each higher level (Burris, 1983). The growth of theory in areas such as labor-market structure has led to a focus on the concept of the career as dictated by the structure of the organization itself—by positional vacancies and the policies and practices that regulate who can fill them (see, e.g., Rosenbaum, 1984; Sørensen, 1986; Spilerman, 1977).

For example, the research of Rosenbaum (1984) and others on patterns of promotion and hence of life chances for employees in such structures has led to the discovery that early promotion is associated with further promotions and failure to win early promotion, with becoming sidelined. Rosenbaum terms this process "tournament mobility." Tournament mobility was initially formulated in Rosenbaum's research on track mobility patterns in high school, which appear to follow a similar dynamic: among those students who "switch tracks" across the four years of high school, all movement tends to be downward (Rosenbaum, 1976). Viewing such findings in the light of a life-course stratification perspective suggests that this may be an early version of the lifelong cumulative process that continues to work itself out at the culmination of one's worklife and on into the retirement years.

Whatever their length, such differentiated trajectories have psychological as well as social consequences. Rosenbaum finds clear consequences for intellectual development for this process: Those in the upper-level tracks gained in IQ from 10th to 12th grade, while those in the lower tracks actually lost ground in their IQ scores between 10th and 12th grade. Thus it appears that structurally imposed diversity is accompanied by increasing psychological diversity across the four years of high school (see Walberg & Tsai, 1983). In view of the findings of Kohn and Schooler and associates (1983) on the effects of work on intellectual functioning and personality, it seems plausible to hypothesize that the differentiating effects of high school are but the first installments of a lifetime of stratifying psychological as well as financial experiences.

Processes of Micro-Interaction and the Genesis of Diversity.   Research on micro-interaction processes in small groups has suggested how various sorts of interpersonal dynamics can generate or reinforce such tendencies of differentiation among cohort members as they age. The tendencies for nursing home workers to label residents as "troublemakers," "incurable," or worth spending time on; for teachers to label students as bright or dull (Gubrium & Buckholdt, 1977); for bosses and co-workers to label employees as "deadwood" or "fast trackers" (Kanter, 1977), "on time" or "behind schedule" (Lawrence, 1980, 1984) serve to implement some of the structural constraints in organizations in micro-interaction. Such constraints have been shown to produce self-fulfilling prophecies (Gubrium, 1975; Rosenthal, 1974; Rosenthal & Jacobsen, 1968) and other kinds of "benign and vicious cycles" (Clausen, 1986b; Smith, 1968) of personal development.

Accentuation, the Matthew Effect, and Empirical Research

Since both accentuation and social-structural processes can predict increasing diversity of similar sorts, they are inevitably empirically confounded. Under most conditions, they cannot be easily separated, although it is possible to approximate such an objective more closely with the growing number of longitudinal data sets and the tools now available for time-series analysis. Nevertheless, some researchers will be inclined to dismiss the distinction between the two kinds of processes with the acknowledgment that "of course, both are important." But the idea of socially generated diversity adds to the notion of accentuation several new issues of theory and policy relevance that are not part of the discussion of accentuation.

First, the social-structural perspective suggests that the production of diversity is *patterned* in ways that make it amenable to systematic study in terms of substantive processes rather than random events or probability statements, as tends to be the case under the accentuation perspective.

Second, a social-structural perspective explicitly acknowledges the independent role of social processes in generating heterogeneity. This emphasis is important because it implies that heterogeneity would develop even if there were no initial individual differences among cohort members, which leads to the question of how much of the observed "pathological diversity" could be prevented or avoided through a more humanly responsive set of social arrangements.

Putting the matter this way raises a third consideration, which has implications for public policy: If social structure does make an independent contribution to the diversity of the aged, then it may be the case that some of the pathological outcomes of differential aging can be addressed through preventive social practices and policies over the entire life course. From such a life-course perspective, the contemporary debate over the allocation of public funds between youth and the aged (e.g., Preston, 1984) would take on a new dimension. Programmatic initiatives as diverse as nutritional education and job training could help provide individuals with resources that would reduce the chance of a debilitating retirement experience. In combination with current programs that target the aged, such initiatives imply a two-pronged initiative in gerontology.

To focus constructively on such preventive aspects of life-course policy, it will be necessary to achieve a much clearer understanding of the dynamics underlying the diversity of the aged than we currently have. For example, if increasing diversity is a regular feature of cohorts with regard to a variety of characteristics, to what extent does this variety reflect intracohort stratification and to what extent is it attributable to the change in the sex ratio, since women, who are poorer and more prone to chronic ailments than men, become an increasingly greater proportion of the surviving cohort with advancing age?

Whatever the answers to these questions, it is clear that social policy can alter changes in the societal distribution of resources over the life course. For example, intracohort increases in inequality notwithstanding, the policies and programs of the last half century have clearly brought a historical trend of decreasing poverty and income inequality in income among the aged (Clark, Maddox, Schrimper, & Sumner 1984; Pampel, 1981).

The question of how diversity among adults is best explained gives a new level of salience and even urgency to cross-national research. If life-course patterns of increasing heterogeneity appear much the same in all societies (or in all segments of a given society) and in disparate historical periods, this would suggest that variation in social conditions has little influence on the development of aged diversity and that the micro-level, accentuation model is appropriate. If, on the other hand, societies seem to vary systematically and predictably in the pattern of diversity production, as they do in the age trajectories of mean values for many characteristics, this would suggest that social structure, and therefore social policies, may significantly influence the age trajectories of heterogeneity. The societal level may become a central focus for conducting "natural experiments."

Not incidentally, such research offers a key strategy for a comparative test of accentuation versus allocation perspectives on the production of aged heterogeneity (Dannefer, 1987). The logic of such a test is a simple analysis-of-variance design, comparing within-group and between-group differences: Do Sweden, the United States, and Tibet, for example, each show a similar increase in variance in hypertension, in income, and in social support with increasing age? Are the patterns observable in one cohort in each society reproduced in adjacent cohorts in that society? The strongest set of findings in support of a social-process explanation would entail marked differences in trajectories between societies and similar trajectories in successive cohorts within societies. On the other hand, a finding that trajectory patterns across societies show as much similarity as those within societies would give more support to the idea of a fairly universal psychosocial process of accentuation.

Accentuation, Social Allocation, and the Role of Chance

Although accentuation and allocation each provide a plausible account of the dynamics underlying heterogeneity production, each by itself is clearly oversimplified. Whatever role such processes play, few would claim that they could ever offer anything approaching a complete account for the phenomenon of aged heterogeneity. The age trajectories of individuals contain elements of volition, imaginative spontaneity, and chance that are not reducible to deterministic processes. As Maddox (1987) notes, luck, or chance, will remain an enduring aspect of attempts to account for the patterning of age-related phenomena, constituting a third perspective on the phenomenon of aged diversity. From the vantage point of science, however, luck represents what cannot be explained, even probabilistically. It therefore must remain the explanation of last resort. The task of social scientists is to discover the extent to which the diversity of the aged can be accounted for in terms of orderly conditions and processes. As in other domains of social science, this implies a heuristic strategy of continuing to press for the identification of patterns that have the potential of ordering the understanding of how diversity develops, even if the enterprise remains fated to a large "error term." This discussion is also relevant to concepts such as probabilistic epigenesis, which has recently been proposed as a general perspective for approaching issues of individual development and aging (Featherman & Lerner, 1985). Although such a concept may be useful in describing and predicting the path of diversity within a cohort, it appears to focus on descriptive probabilities rather than specifying the operant social and psychological processes that account for the development of diversity.

The logic underlying probabilistic epigenesis has a paradigmatic affinity to "normative development" as conceived in the lifespan framework (Baltes, 1979). In this framework, age-related characteristics are declared to be "normative" despite the assumption that they increase in variability, with the result that the dynamics underlying the divergence are not conceived as problematic and in need of analysis. As the present author has argued elsewhere (Dannefer, 1984a), this position inhibits a causal analysis and, in particular, prevents a systematic consideration of interactional aspects of the production of patterns of diversity.

The Radial Fan and Its Variants: Alternative Life-Course Trajectories of Diversity Production

As discussed thus far, aged diversity, whether a consequence of accentuation, social processes, or chance, has been depicted in terms of the simplest trajectory patterns: the steadily diverging "radial fan." Some empirical support exists for such an image vis-à-vis many characteristics (e.g., Maddox & Douglass, 1974; Rowe & Kahn, 1987; Schaie, in press; Thomae, 1985; Treas, 1986). Other chapters of this volume will discuss some of this evidence in detail. However, neither the observation that the aged are more diverse nor age-stratum comparisons (consistently showing that, for example, persons aged 75–85 are substantially more diverse than those aged 35–

45) reveal very much about the empirical course of diversity over the collective life course of an age cohort on a given characteristic.

The path of diversity over the long decades of a cohort's earlier life remains obscure, giving rise to the further question of the precise path of the phenomenon's empirical development within a cohort as the cohort ages. Does it, indeed, develop gradually through the adult years? Or does it develop suddenly, triggered by a particular age-specific event? Or does the degree of heterogeneity in a cohort fluctuate from decade to decade in the life of a cohort? This general issue is addressed briefly but elegantly in Maddox and Douglass's (1974) longitudinal analysis of diversity. It is considered in detail in a recent article by Dannefer and Sell (in press), who note that the issue of describing the path of diversity implies a potentially large number of alternative life-course trajectories of variability, of which five variations are presented in Figure 1.1.

These potential trajectories make clear that the "aged heterogeneity" question is actually a special case of the larger question of how variability within a cohort is regulated over its collective life course. Note that all of these trajectories could potentially produce an identical pattern of mean values. Perhaps it could even be said that the *constancy* trajectory is the implicit model underlying the common practice of focusing on central tendency.

These trajectories each imply different underlying processes. The processes for the radial divergence trajectory have already been discussed. The *U-shaped* trajectory is a variant on the radial divergence theme, suggested by the human-capital theory of income distribution, which proposes that income inequality is least in the middle years, a view that will be considered in more detail below. The *trigger event* trajectory, with diversity suddenly expanding around age 65, could suggest an interaction of psychological and social processes, with the institutionalized transition of retirement leading to a change in the distribution of resources or constraints. As drawn in Figure 1.1, such a trajectory might support the psychological notion that heterogeneity represents a flowering of individuality, as disengagement theory might predict (see Hickey, 1980; Maddox & Douglass, 1974). Despite the apparent trend toward greater diversity for many characteristics, a counterprocess of *convergence* may be hypothesized for some characteristics. For example, some evidence suggests a tendency, in late life, for some convergence toward a life-review process, with increased subjective attention to the past (e.g., Butler, 1963; Marshall, 1980). Convergence may also occur in advanced old age if a higher proportion of the cohort simultaneously experiences terminal drop (Maddox & Douglass, 1974). Research on dendrite length suggests that variability increases until the mid-eighties, possibly reflecting the varied lifestyles and experiences of the aged, and then converges in the late eighties and nineties (Flood, Buell, Horowitz, &

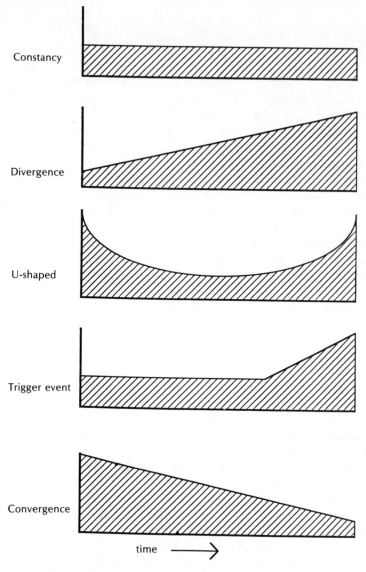

Constancy

Divergence

U-shaped

Trigger event

Convergence

time ⟶

Figure 1.1. Alternative trajectories of diversity over the life course. The vertical axis represents the amount of heterogeneity.

Coleman, 1987). Such findings are necessarily cross-sectional, since the necessary measures can only be made postmortem.

Of course, a necessary step in documenting any of these as life-course processes is longitudinal data on large samples. As noted earlier, when longitudinal data for successive cohorts show similar trajectories of variability, it becomes difficult to justify ignoring such patterns as integral aspects of the life course of a cohort. Although few analyses permit this kind of comparison, those that do—primarily studies of income patterns in cohorts—have presented at least some support for such a systematic, recurrent process in successive cohorts (Mincer, 1974; Treas, 1986). The growing number of sophisticated longitudinal data sets make such analyses—impossible until recently because of data limitations—increasingly feasible (Maddox & Campbell, 1985).

Trajectories of Variability and Levels of Analysis

Before leaving the general problems of conceptualizing differential aging and differential trajectories of variability, a final issue is raised by the possibilities of deriving different outcomes from the same data, depending on the level of analysis. For example, "homogenizing" settings or institutions (Wheeler, 1966), such as nursing homes, may create certain similarities among long-term residents on some characteristics and hence may reduce diversity within that setting. At the same time, they may contribute to increasing diversity in the larger community through the regimented differentiation of this particular subpopulation of the aged. As another example, available evidence suggests that, with respect to IQ, spouses become more similar to one another as they age, creating de-differentiation within the family, at the same time that the population at large is becoming more differentiated (Clausen 1986b; Eichorn, Hunt, & Honzik, 1981).

BETWEEN THEORY AND DATA: POTENTIAL FALLACIES IN THE STUDY OF AGED DIVERSITY

As indicated earlier, such evidence as is available tends to support the theoretical notion of a systematic and general tendency toward increasing diversity with age. However, it is at least logically possible that the phenomenon of aged diversity is entirely a consequence of factors that have nothing to do with such psychosocial or social-structural processes as have been sketched above. In order to consider fully the kinds of factors that could produce the phenomenon of the greater heterogeneity of the aged (or that could artifactually reduce it), several additional kinds of intrinsically relevant issues must be considered. This section reviews some of these issues, which can be arranged sequentially as a set of polarities: (1) cohort versus life-course processes, (2) aggregated cohort patterns versus individual-level trajectories, and (3) interindividual versus intraindividual increases in diversity.

Cohort Versus Life-Course Processes

Throughout this chapter, the assumption has clearly been that aged diversity is the result of an intracohort, life-course process—a consequence of increasing dissimilarity among age peers with the passage of time and with advancing age. However, to the extent that the evidence for this rests on cross-sectional evidence, whether in scientific articles or in geriatric practice, the same possibility for a life-course fallacy (Riley et al., 1972) exists here as it does for any other age-related characteristic. The caution offered by Maddox and Douglass (1974) regarding the inferring of life-course diversity from cross-sectional data sets still applies. In short, age differences here, as elsewhere, may reduce to cohort differences. If each succeeding cohort becomes more homogeneous, older cohorts will manifest greater diversity, even if the amount of diversity within the cohort remains absolutely stable with regard to the characteristic of interest throughout their collective life course.

There is at least one kind of historical social process that makes this more than a hypothetical possibility: the increasing bureaucratization of society, and with it the increasing institutionalization of the life course (Kohli, 1986; Meyer, 1986). Several historical studies of life-course transitions in the United States have uniformly shown increasing standardization in, for example, years of education, school leaving, labor-force entry, age at marriage, and retirement (Hogan, 1981; Marini, 1984; Modell, Furstenberg, & Hershberg, 1976; Modell, Furstenberg, & Strong, 1978). Through the same period, a trend toward reduced income inequality in succeeding cohorts also occurred. Cross-sectional comparisons thus might be expected to show a smaller amount of diversity among the young in terms of role configurations, resource availability, and other factors strictly as an artifact of cohort differences resulting from historical trends (see Dannefer & Sell, in press, for a fuller discussion of this point). Although some longitudinal research evidence supports the notion of increasing diversity as an aspect of cohort aging, other research—as well as impressions about the diversity of the aged gleaned from everyday life—is based on cross-sectional evidence. Thus, the first caveat concerns the familiar caution concerning the misinterpretation of cross-sectional data.

True Increases in Interindividual Differences Versus Intracohort Shifts

If intracohort trend data indicate that the phenomenon of aged diversity does indeed appear to be an aspect of intracohort aging, the real possibility of at least two additional kinds of fallacies exists whenever the unit of analysis is the cohort and the data do not permit the tracking of individuals longitudinally. Even subgroups cannot be tracked longitudinally in a meaningful way unless the individuals who comprise them are identified by some fixed characteristic. When no longitudinal data on individuals are available, the result is to risk committing the ecological, or aggregative, fallacy (Riley, 1963). Two problems derive from the use of data that do not follow individuals and from strategies of analysis that do not carefully trace idividual trajectories. The first of these problems is compositional, pertaining to changes in cohort membership; the second is positional, concerning shifts in relative location in the cohort.

Cohort Composition

Unless the individual is the unit of analysis and the identities of individuals are retained over time, it is quite possible for diversity to increase if death or some other mechanism selectively removes the more homogeneous elements in the subpopulation. As a simple example, if it were the case that women were generally more diverse than men on the characteristic of interest, aged diversity would be the consequence, since the members of the more diverse subpopulation survive disproportionately. An interpretation of radial divergence based on such a circumstance would constitute a compositional fallacy. Interpretations of data on cohorts in which the identity of individuals is lost, such as census data, risk such a fallacy. As Maddox and Douglass (1974) note, this point may apply even when individual identities are retained, if one's analysis does not control for selective mortality and survival. They find a decrease in diversity for 52% of the measured characteristics in the total sample between first and final observations, but an increase in diversity for 78% of the characteristics after removing those who did not survive through the last observation period. On this basis, they hypothesize that "reported decrease in variance with age is in most cases an artifact of sampling" (1974, p. 561). More generally, population mortality relentlessly tends to decrease diversity of the cohort as it ages by removing disproportionately the least healthy members.

Relative Rank of Cohort Members in the Distribution

The problem posed by the issue of relative rank is somewhat knottier. Even when an aggregated pattern of increasing divergence is found, as in the data on U.S. family income reported by Treas (1986), without individual-level data it is not possible to know the nature of individual trajectories and with individual-level data it may be difficult to describe them. The general notion of divergence, with its implication of radiating linear individual trajectories producing an aggregated pattern of increasing diversity, is clearly an over-simplification. Indeed, some pertinent theory and data suggest systematic patterns of crossover of subgroups or individuals within the cohort.

For example, human-capital theory, from which the U-shaped variant on the divergence trajectory is derived, provides a significant example with respect to earnings: those who remain in school longest start out with the lowest earnings and hence occupy the "bottom tail" of the distribution in early adulthood. However, once they enter the labor force, their earnings rapidly catch up with, pass, and continue to accelerate away from those of their peers who left school and entered the labor force earlier in the life course. Thus in this view the hypothetical U-shape derives from a criss-crossing of trajectories of two different subgroups in the population (Becker, 1975; Dannefer & Sell, in press; Mincer, 1974). More generally, panel studies of stability of position in income distribution (David & Menchik, 1984; Schiller, 1977), or of duration of time below the poverty line (Corcoran, Duncan, & Hill, 1984; Holden, Burkhauser, & Myers, 1986), indicate that some degree of less orderly shifting is a typical feature of cohort experience.

Elder and Liker's (1982) analysis, based on the Oakland Growth data, of the psychological trajectories patterns of deprived and nondeprived middle- and working-class women over a 40-year period, suggests that the most psychologically successful of these women in later life were those who had experienced deprivation during the Depression. Apparently the early experience of hardship had enabled them to develop life skills and, perhaps, inner resources that advantaged them in relation to their nondeprived peers.

These examples are not meant to suggest that the radial divergence of individuals is not a reality. Other individual-level, longitudinal analyses have found patterns resembling radial divergence—both during the school years on values (Feldman & Weller, 1976; Huntley, 1965, 1967) as well as test performance and track placement (Rosenbaum, 1976, 1978) and in the period between middle and late adulthood—for characteristics such as resource availability (David & Menchik, 1984), lifestyle (Guillemard, 1982), and health (Maddox & Douglass, 1974; Schaie, in press). Nevertheless, these crossover examples serve as cautions regarding the kinds of complexities that may underlie an aggregated cohort trajectory, whatever its shape.

Interindividual Versus Intraindividual Increases in Diversity

While the foregoing discussion has deliberately remained at an abstract level when discussing diversity, an implicit and occasionally explicit assumption has been that increasing diversity between individuals is accompanied by a clustering of correlated characteristics within individuals. The notion of cumulating advantage or disadvantage suggests that, among diverse aged individuals, the people who are ill, demoralized, and possessed of bleak life chances are the same people; the aged people who are affluent, healthy, and positively engaged are also the same people. This is not an especially controversial claim for some characteristics, such as various measures of health; and there is at least some empirical support for it in respect to the correlation between psychological and physiological variables on one hand, and lifestyle and resource variables on the other (Gribbin et al., 1980; Guillemard, 1982; Maddox & Douglass, 1974).

However, research on a variety of characteristics has suggested the notion of increased variability with age within as well as between individuals. Botwinick and Thompson (1968), and earlier Obrist (1953), report such a pattern of intraindividual change in their studies of reaction time; Hayflick and Moorhead (1961) find greater variability in cell divisions in human lung tissue from a middle-aged specimen than from a fetal one (see also Cristofalo & Stanulis, 1978). Perlmutter (1979) reports an age increase in within-subject variability in memory-test performance; and with regard to personality, a longitudinal analysis by Haan, Millsap, and Hartka (1986) reports a reduction in stability with advancing age. One possible extrapolation from such findings is the notion of a "general disorganization," or "instability," (Maddox & Douglass, 1974) as a consequence of aging itself, which could lead to greater random diversity within individuals. Such a pattern would also imply that diversity between individuals might be the random consequence of such processes. A second general possibility is that a threshold effect determines the degree of intraindividual intercorrelation. Birren, Butler, Greenhouse, Sokoloff, and Yarrow (1963) find that several kinds of characteristics are largely uncorrelated within individuals in good health, but are more interdependent in individuals in poor health. In any case, such findings call attention to the need to document carefully the relation of intraindividual as well as interindividual diversity and serve as a caution against the premature acceptance of an assumption of strongly clustered cumulative effects.

These potential fallacies hardly exhaust the list of potential methodological problems and pitfalls that confront the researcher who wishes to study diversity. A consideration of problems of measurement, such as age-specific differences in reliability, which may generate increasing diversity as an artifact, or the more general problem of how diversity itself is to be conceptualized and measured (Blau, 1977; Jasso, 1982) must remain beyond the present discussion.

Despite these important cautions, the evidence regarding increasing diversity in later life probably cannot be reduced to an epiphenomenon of data aggregation. Considerable longitudinal evidence, some of it with the individual as the unit of analysis, has already been noted. Moreover, the general effect of compositional shifts for many characteristics, such as health, is undoubtedly to remove the "bottom tail" of the distribution through mortality, thereby reducing the actual extent of diversity (Maddox & Douglass, 1974; Wilkinson, 1986). Nevertheless, careful study of the dynamics of diversity over the life course requires that these methodological factors be considered, just as they would for tracing the age trajectory of the central tendency of any characteristic in a population.

AGED DIVERSITY, GERONTOLOGICAL THEORY, AND SOCIAL POLICY

This chapter began by noting the combination of a widespread assumption of diversity in gerontological discourse, which coexists with the near eclipse of differential aging as a topic in need of empirical study. The reasons for its neglect may include the need for a new field to assert generalities, as noted earlier; they may also include the "homogenizing" and normative implications underlying paradigmatic social-science concepts, such as development and socialization (Dannefer, 1988). But prominent among the reasons for the lack of authoritative knowledge about the existence and development of aged diversity must be the lack, until very recently, of data that could be mobilized to address this question. Currently, the proliferation of large and useful longitudinal data bases on aging hold the possibility for extensive analyses of patterns of diversity at affordable cost (Maddox & Campbell, 1985).

At the same time, the issues raised above suggest that the task of adequately describing and understanding the phenomenon of diversity is a formidable research task. Since diversity is a derivative concept (in the sense that every substantive characteristic has a distribution, just as it has a central tendency value) that describes the distribution of virtually every age-related characteristic, the prospect of a systematic study of diversity fairly threatens to double the task of gerontological research. Especially in view of the potential pitfalls and complexities discussed above, one might well ask whether the payoff, in terms of empirically grounded conclusions regarding the character of and processes underlying aged diversity, would justify the costs in terms of additional data collection and analysis. There are several arguments in support of a positive answer to such a question: (1) descriptive accuracy, (2) a clearer understanding of causal processes, and (3) applications to practice and policy.

First, accurately describing the phenomenon of interest is a primary obligation of science. If increasing diversity is an integral aspect of aging, the description of age patterns and regularities only in terms of central tendency provides a distorted account of the subject matter in question.

Second, clarifying the processes that underlie descriptive outcomes is an important theoretical concern. As this entire volume makes clear, once the issue of diversity is acknowledged and squarely faced, a host of questions arise regarding the reasons for it that cannot be ignored either for theory or policy reasons. Moreover, for those committed to seeing gerontology advance as a theoretically grounded enterprise, such an integral and recurrent aspect of aging cannot go unanalyzed and unexplained. Theoretically no less than descriptively, the phenomenon of diversity poses challenges of explanation.

Third, in addition to its programmatic relevance for those concerned with service delivery to the aged, the theoretical question of the kinds of empirical processes that produce or contribute to outcomes of diversity has rather straightforward policy implications. Consider the case of family income, which Treas's (1986) analysis shows to be a regular dynamic of cohort aging for the six successive cohorts she observed. To what extent does this result from a feminization of poverty among aged surviving women, and to what extent does it reflect a generalized social-stratification process that begins early in the life course and continues into retirement for both men and women? In the former case, increasing diversity reflects something that is generated by current retirement policies; in the latter case, it is generated by the entire structure of careers. The underlying processes, and the potential policy implications of each, are quite distinct. Similar sorts of questions need to be asked in addressing ethnic differences in aging. It is at least conceivable that research on such questions could place gerontological theory in a position to contribute fresh insights to general social and psychological theory as well as to policy making—for the entire life course as well as old age.

As noted earlier, one of the key strategies for exploring intracohort trajectories of diversity is through intercohort comparisons of such trajectories within the same society over time and through comparison of different societies. If consistent patterns observed in successive U.S. cohorts show contrasting trajectories from those found in Norwegian or English cohorts, or Chinese or Israeli cohorts, such a finding would be a valuable contribution to our understanding of the possibilities and varieties of differential aging as a cohort experience and would provide valuable clues to the factors that contribute to successful and less-than-successful aging.

REFERENCES

Achenbaum, A. (1978). *Old age in the new land: The American experience since 1970.* Baltimore: Johns Hopkins University Press.

Allport, G. W., Bruner, J. S., & Jandorf, E. M. (1941). Personality under social catastrophe: Ninety life-histories of the Nazi revolution. *Journal of Personality, 10*, 1–22.

Baltes, P. B. (1979). Life-span development psychology: Some converging observations on history and theory. In P. B. Baltes & O. G. Brim, Jr. (Eds.), *Life-span development and behavior* (Vol. 2) (pp. 256-279). New York: Academic Press.

Becker, G. S. (1975). *Human capital: A theoretical and empirical analysis with special reference to education.* New York: Columbia University Press.

Bengtson, V. L., & Dannefer, F. (1987). Families, work and aging: Implications of disordered cohort flow for the 21st century. In R. Ward & S. Tobin (Eds.), *Health and aging: Sociological issues and policy directions* (pp. 256-289). New York: Springer-Verlag.

Bengtson, V. L., Kasschau, P. L., & Ragan, P. K. (1977). The impact of social structure on aging individuals. In J. E. Birren & K. W. Schaie (Eds.), *Handbook of the Psychology of Aging* (pp. 327-354). New York: Van Nostrand Reinhold.

Bielby, W. T. (1981). Models of status attainment. In D. J. Treiman & R. V. Robinson (Eds.), *Research in social stratification and mobility* (Vol. 1) (pp. 323-326). Greenwich, CT: JAI Publishing.

Birren, J. E. (1959). Principles of research on aging. In J. E. Birren (Ed.), *Handbook of aging and the individual: Psychological and biological aspects* (pp. 3-42). Chicago: University of Chicago Press.

Birren, J. E., Butler, R. N., Greenhouse, S. W., Sokoloff, L., & Yarrow, M. R. (Eds.) (1963). *Human aging: A biological and behavioral study.* Bethesda, MD: Department of Health, Education and Welfare.

Blau, P. M. (1977). *Inequality and heterogeneity.* New York: Free Press.

Bornstein, R., & Smircina, M. T. (1982). The status of the empirical support of the hypothesis of increased variability in aging populations. *The Gerontologist, 22,* 258-260.

Botwinick, J., & Thompson, L. W. (1968). A research note on individual differences in reaction time in relation to age. *Journal of Genetic Psychology, 112,* 73-75.

Burris, B. (1983). *No room at the top: Underemployment and alienation in the corporation.* New York: Praeger.

Butler, R. N. (1963). The life review: An interpretation of reminiscence in the aged. *Psychiatry, 26,* 65-76.

Butler, R. N. (1974). *Why survive? Being old in America.* New York: Harper.

Campbell, R. T. (1983). Status attainment research: End of the beginning or beginning of the end? *Sociology of Education, 56,* 47-62.

Clark, R., Maddox, G. L., Schrimper, R., & Sumner, D. (1984). *Inflation and the economic well-being of the elderly.* Baltimore: Johns Hopkins University Press.

Clausen, J. (1986a, September). *Early adult choices and the life course.* Paper presented at the annual meeting of the American Sociological Association, New York.

Clausen, J. (1986b). *The life course: A sociological perspective.* Englewood Cliffs, NJ: Prentice-Hall.

Comfort, A. (1968). Physiology, homeostasis, and aging. *Gerontologia, 14,* 224-234.

Corcoran, M., Duncan, G., & Hill, M. (1984). The economic fortunes of women and children: Lessons from the panel study of income dynamics. *Signs, 10*(2), 232-248.

Cowgill, D. O., & Holmes, L. (1972). *Aging and modernization.* New York: Appleton-Century-Crofts.

Cristofalo, V. J., & Stanulis, B. M. (1978). Cell aging: A model system approach. In C. E. Finch & G. B. Moment (Eds.), *The biology of aging*. New York: Plenum.

Crystal, S. J. (1982). *America's old age crisis*. New York: Basic Books.

Dannefer, D. (1984a). Adult development and social theory: A paradigmatic reappraisal. *American Sociological Review, 49*, 100-116.

Dannefer, D. (1984b). The role of the social in life-span development, past and future: Rejoinder to Baltes and Nesselroade. *American Sociological Review, 49*, 847-850.

Dannefer, D. (1987). Aging as intracohort differentiation: Accentuation, the Matthew effect, and the life course. *Sociological Forum, 2*, 211-236.

Dannefer, D. (1988). What's in a name? An account of the neglect of variability in theories of aging. In J. E. Birren & V. L. Bengtson (Eds.), *Theories of aging: Psychological and social perspectives on time, self, and society* (pp. 356-384). New York: Springer.

Dannefer, D., & Sell, R. R. (in press). Age structure, the life course and aged heterogeneity: Prospects for theory and research. *Comprehensive Gerontology.*

David, M., & Menchik, P. L. (1984). Nonearned income, income instability and inequality: A life-cycle interpretation. In S. Sudman & M. Spaeth (Eds.), *The collection and analysis of economic and consumer behavior data: In memory of Robert Ferber* (pp. 53-73). Chicago: University of Illinois Press.

Demos, J. (1978). Old age in early New England. In J. Demos & S. S. Boocock (Eds.), *Turning points* (pp. 5248-5287). Chicago: University of Chicago Press.

Doeringer, P., & Piore, M. (1971). *Internal labor markets and manpower analysis*. Lexington, MA: Heath Lexington.

Easterlin, R. (1980). *Birth and fortune*. New York: Basic Books.

Eichorn, D., Hunt, J., & Honzik, M. (1981). *Present and past in middle life*. New York: Academic Press.

Elder, G. H., Jr. (1969). Occupational mobility, life patterns and personality. *Journal of Health and Social Behavior, 10*, 308-323.

Elder, G. H., Jr. (1974). *Children of the great depression*. Chicago: University of Chicago Press.

Elder, G. H., Jr. (1975). Age differentiation and the life course. In A. Inkeles (Ed.), *Annual review of sociology* (Vol. 1) (pp. 165-190). Palo Alto, CA: Annual Reviews.

Elder, G. H., Jr., & Liker, J. K. (1982). Hard times in women's lives: Historical influences across forty years. *American Journal of Sociology, 88*, 241-269.

Elder, G. H., Jr., Liker, J. K., & Jaworski, B. J. (1984). Hardship in lives: Depression influences from the 1930s to old age in postwar America. In K. McKluskey & H. Reese (Eds.), *Life-span developmental psychology: Historical and generational effects* (pp. 161-201). Orlando, FL: Academic Press.

Farrell, M. P., & Rosenberg, S. D. (1981). *Men at midlife*. Boston: Auburn House.

Featherman, D. L. (1980). Schooling and occupational careers: Constancy and change in worldly success. In O. G. Brim, Jr. & J. Kagan (Eds.), *Constancy and change in human development* (pp. 675-738). Cambridge, MA: Harvard University Press.

Featherman, D. L., & Lerner, R. M. (1985). Ontogenesis and sociogenesis: Problematics for theory and research about human development and socialization across the life span. *American Sociological Review, 49,* 659–676.

Feldman, K. A., & Newcomb, T. M. (1969). *The impact of college on students.* San Francisco: Jossey-Bass.

Feldman, K. A., & Weiler, J. (1976). Changes in initial differences among major-field groups: An exploration of the "accentuation effect." In W. H. Sewell, R. Hauser, & D. L. Featherman (Eds.), *Schooling and achievement in American society* (pp. 373–407). New York: Academic Press.

Fischer, D. H. (1978). *Growing old in America.* New York: Oxford University Press.

Flood, D. G., Buell, S. J., Horowitz, G. J., & Coleman, P. D. (1987). Dendritic extent in human dentate gyrus granule cells in aging and senile dementia. *Brain Research, 402,* 205–216.

Goody, J. (1976). Aging in non-industrial societies. In R. H. Binstock & E. Shanas (Eds.), *Handbook of aging and the social sciences* (pp. 117–129). New York: Van Nostrand Reinhold.

Gribbin, K., Schaie, K. W., & Parham, I. A. (1980). Complexity of life style and maintenance of intellectual abilities. *Journal of Social Issues, 36,* 47–61.

Gubrium, J. F. (1975). *Living and dying at Murray Manor.* New York: St. Martin's.

Gubrium, J. F., & Buckholdt, D. R. (1977). *Toward maturity.* San Francisco: Jossey-Bass.

Guillemard, A. M. (1982). Old age, retirement, and social class structure: Toward an analysis of the structural dynamics of the latter stage of life. In T. K. Hareven & K. J. Adams (Eds.), *Aging and life course transitions: An interdisciplinary perspective* (pp. 221–243). New York: Guilford.

Haan, N., Millsap, R., & Hartka, E. (1986). As time goes by: Change and stability in personality over fifty years. *Psychology and Aging, 1,* 220–232.

Halaby, C. N., & Sobel, M. E. (1979). Mobility effects in the workplace. *American Journal of Sociology, 85,* 385–417.

Haller, A. O. (1982). Reflections on the social psychology of status attainment. In R. M. Hauser, D. Mechanic, A. O. Haller, & T. S. Haller (Eds.), *Social structure and behavior: Essays in honor of William Hamilton Sewell* (pp. 3–28). New York: Academic Press.

Havighurst, R. J. (1957). The social competence of middle-aged people. *Genetic Psychological Monographs, 56,* 297–375.

Hayflick, L., & Moorhead, D. S. (1961). The serial cultivation of human diploid cell strains. *Experimental Cell Research, 25,* 585–621.

Hayslip, B. (1985). Idiographic assessment of the self in the aged. *International Journal of Aging, 20,* 293–311.

Henretta, J. C., & Campbell, R. T. (1976). Status attainment and status maintenance: A study of stratification in old age. *American Sociological Review, 41,* 981–992.

Hickey, T. (1980). *Health and aging.* Monterey, CA: Brooks/Coles.

Hodson, R., & Kaufman, R. L. (1982). Economic dualism: A critical review. *American Sociological Review, 47,* 727–739.

Hogan, D. P. (1981). *Transitions and social change.* New York: Academic Press.

Holden, K. C., Burkhauser, R. V., & Myers, D. A. (1986). Income transitions at older stages of life: The dynamics of poverty. *Gerontologist, 26*, 292–297.

Howard, A., & Bray, D. W. (1988). *Managerial lives in transition: Advancing age and changing times.* New York: Guilford Press.

Huntley, C. W. (1965). Changes in study of values scores during the four years of college. *Genetic Psychology Monographs, 71*, 349–383.

Huntley, C. W. (1967). Changes in values during the four years of college. *College Student Survey, 1*, 43–48.

Jasso, G. (1982). Measuring inequality. *Sociological Methods and Research, 10*, 303–326.

Kalish, R. A. (1975). *Late adulthood: Perspectives on human development.* Monterey, CA: Brooks/Cole.

Kanter, R. (1977). *Men and women of the corporation.* New York: Basic Books.

Kertzer, D. I., & Keith, J. (Eds.). (1984). *Age and anthropological theory.* Ithaca, NY: Cornell University Press.

Kohli, M. (1986). Social organization and subjective construction of the life course. In A. B. Sørensen, F. Weinert, & L. Sherrod (Eds.), *Human development: Multidisciplinary perspectives* (pp. 271–292). Hillsdale, NJ: Erlbaum.

Kohn, M. L., & Schooler, C. (1983). *Work and personality: An inquiry into the impact of social stratification.* Norwood, NJ: Ablex.

Kuhlen, R. G. (1959). Aging and life adjustment. In J. E. Birren (Ed.), *Handbook of aging and the individual* (pp. 852–897). Chicago: University of Chicago Press.

Lawrence, B. S. (1980). The myth of the midlife crisis. *Sloan Management Review, 21*, 35–49.

Lawrence, B. S. (1984). Age-grading: The implicit organization time table. *Journal of Occupational Behavior, 5*, 23–35.

Lawrence, B. S. (1985). *New wrinkles in the theory of age: Demography, names and employee preferences.* Working paper, UCLA School of Management, Los Angeles.

Lemke, S., & Moos, R. H. (1981). The supra-personal environments of sheltered care settings. *Journal of Gerontology, 36*, 233–243.

Lieberman, M. (1965). Psychological correlates of impending death: Some preliminary observations. *Journal of Gerontology, 20*, 181–190.

Liker, J. K., & Elder, G. H., Jr. (1983). Economic hardship and marital relations in the 1930s. *American Sociological Review, 48*, 343–359.

Maddox, G. L. (1963). Activity and morale: A longitudinal study of selected elderly subjects. *Social Forces, 42*, 195–204.

Maddox, G. L. (1964). Disengagement theory: A critical evaluation. *The Gerontologist, 4*, 80–83.

Maddox, G. L. (1965). Fact and artifact: Evidence bearing on disengagement theory from the Duke Geriatrics Project. *Human Development, 8*, 117–130.

Maddox, G. L. (1970). Themes and issues in sociological theories of human aging. *Human Development, 13*, 17–27.

Maddox, G. L. (1987). Aging differently. *The Gerontologist, 27*(5), 557–564.

Maddox, G. L., & Campbell, R. (1985). Scope, concepts, and methods in the study of aging. In R. Binstock & E. Shanas (Eds.), *Handbook of aging and the social sciences* (pp. 3–31). New York: Van Nostrand Reinhold.

Maddox, G. L., & Douglass, E. (1974). Aging and individual differences: A longitudinal analysis of social, psychological, and physiological indicators. *Journal of Gerontology, 29,* 555–563.

Maddox, G. L., & Eisdorfer, C. (1962). Some correlates of activity and morale among the elderly. *Social Forces, 40,* 254–260.

Manuel, R. (Ed.). (1982). *Minority aging: Sociological and social psychological issues.* Westport, CT: Greenwood Press.

Marini, M. M. (1984). Age and sequencing norms in the transition to adulthood. *Social Forces, 63,* 229–244.

Marshall, V. W. (1980). *Last chapters: A sociology of aging and dying.* Belmont, CA: Wadsworth.

Merton, R. K. (1968). *Social theory and social structure* (enlarged ed.). New York: Free Press.

Meyer, J. (1986). The institutionalization of the life course and its effect on the self. In A. B. Sørenson, F. E. Weinert, & L. R. Sherrod (Eds.), *Human development: Interdisciplinary perspectives* (pp. 199–216). Hillsdale, NJ: Lawrence Erlbaum Associates.

Mincer, J. (1974). *Schooling, experience and earnings.* New York: National Bureau of Economic Research.

Modell, J., Furstenberg, F., & Hershberg, T. (1976). Social change and transitions to adulthood in historical perspective. *Journal of Family History, 1,* 7–32.

Modell, J., Furstenberg, F., & Strong, D. (1978). The timing of marriage in the transition to adulthood: Continuity and change. *American Journal of Sociology, 84,* 120–150.

Myeroff, B. G., & Simic, A. (Eds.). (1978). *Life's career-aging.* Beverly Hills, CA: Sage.

Myers, G. (1985). Aging and worldwide population change. In R. Binstock & E. Shanas (Eds.), *Handbook of aging and the social sciences* (pp. 173–198). New York: Van Nostrand Reinhold.

Nelson, D. W. (1982). Alternative images of old age as the basis for policy. In B. L. Neugarten (Ed.), *Age or need?* (pp. 131–169). Beverly Hills, CA: Sage.

Neugarten, B. L. (1964). A developmental view of adult personality. In J. E. Birren (Ed.), *Relations of development and aging* (pp. 176–208). Springfield, IL: Charles C. Thomas.

Neugarten, B. L. (1971a). Adaptation and life cycle. *Journal of Geriatric Psychiatry, 3,* 1–28.

Neugarten, B. L. (1971b). Grow old along with me! The best is yet to be. *Psychology Today, 5,* 45–49, 78.

Neugarten, B. L. (1982). *Age or need: Public policies and older people.* Beverly Hills, CA: Sage.

Obrist, W. D. (1953). Simple auditory reaction time in aged adults. *Journal of Psychology, 35,* 259–266.

Pampel, F. C. (1981). *Social change and the aged: Recent trends in the United States.* Lexington, MA: Lexington Books.

Perlmutter, M. (1978). What is memory aging the aging of? *Developmental Psychology, 14,* 330–345.

Perlmutter, M. (1979). Age differences in the consistency of adults' associative responses. *Experimental Aging Research, 5*(6), 549-553.

Powers, B. A. (1986, October). *Social networks of elderly institutionalized people.* Paper presented at the fourteenth annual meeting of SAGE, Ellenville, NY.

Preston, S. (1984, December). Children and the elderly in the U.S. *Scientific American, 251*(6), 44-49.

Quadagno, J. (1982). *Old age in early industrial society.* New York: Academic Press.

Riley, M. (1963). *Sociological research: Vol. 1. A case approach.* New York: Harcourt Brace Jovanovich.

Riley, M. W. (1980). Age and aging: From theory generation to theory testing. In H. B. Blalock, Jr. (Ed.), *Sociological theory and research: A critical appraisal* (pp. 339-348). New York: Free Press.

Riley, M. W., & Foner, A. (1968). *Aging and society: Vol. 1. An inventory of research findings.* New York: Sage.

Riley, M. W., Johnson, M., & Foner, A. (1972). *Aging and society: Vol. 3. A sociology of age stratification.* New York: Sage.

Rosenbaum, J. (1976). *Making inequality: The hidden curriculum of high school tracking.* New York: Wiley-Interscience.

Rosenbaum, J. (1978). The structure of opportunity in school. *Social Forces, 57,* 236-256.

Rosenbaum, J. E. (1984). *Career mobility in a corporate hierarchy.* New York: Academic Press.

Rosenthal, R. (1974). Covert communication in the psychological experiment. In P. L. Wuebben, B. C. Straits, & G. I. Schulman (Eds.), *The experiment as a social occasion.* Berkeley, CA: Glendessay Press.

Rosenthal, R., & Jacobsen, L. (1968). *Pygmalion in the classroom.* New York: Holt, Rinehart & Winston.

Rowe, J. W., & Kahn, R. L. (1987). Human aging: Usual and successful. *Science, 237,* 143-149.

Schaie, K. W. (in press). Individual differences in the rate of cognitive change in adulthood. In V. L. Bengtson & K. W. Schaie (Eds.), *Adult development: The search for meaning.* New York: Springer.

Schiller, B. R. (1977). Relative earnings mobility in the United States. *American Economic Review, 67,* 926-941.

Sewell, W. H., Haller, A. O., & Portes, A. (1969). The education and early occupational attainment process. *American Sociological Review, 34,* 82-92.

Shock, N. W., & Norris, A. H. (1966). Aging and variability. *Annals of the New York Academy of Sciences, 134,* 591-601.

Simic, A. (1978). Winners and losers: Aging Yugoslavs in a changing world. In B. G. Myeroff & A. Simic (Eds.), *Life's career-aging* (pp. 77-105). Beverly Hills, CA: Sage.

Skinner, B. F. (1983). Intellectual self-management in old age. *American Psychologist, 38,* 239-244.

Smith, B. (1968). Competence and socialization. In J. A. Clausen (Ed.), *Socialization and society* (pp. 270-319). Boston: Little Brown.

Sokolovsky, J. (1986). Ethnicity, culture and aging: Do differences really make a difference? *Journal of Applied Gerontology, 4*, 6–17.

Sørensen, A. B. (1977). The structure of inequality and the process of attainment. *American Sociological Review, 42*, 965–978.

Sørensen, A. B. (1986). Social structure and mechanisms of life-course processes. In A. B. Sørensen, F. Weinert, & L. Sherrod (Eds.), *Human development: Multidisciplinary perspectives* (pp. 177–197). Hillsdale, NJ: Erlbaum.

Spilerman, S. (1977). Careers, labor market structure, and socioeconomic achievement. *American Journal of Sociology, 85*, 551–593.

Suzman, R., & Riley, M. (1985). Introducing the "oldest old." *Health and Society, 63, 177–*186.

Thomae, H. (1985, July). *Multiple stress experience and belief systems: A psychological approach to the conceptualization of patterns of aging.* Paper presented at the 13th International Congress of Gerontology, New York.

Thomas, W. I., & Thomas, D. M. (1928). *The child in America.* New York: Knopf.

Treas, J. (1986, March). *Postwar perspectives on age and inequality.* Paper presented at the annual meeting of the Population Association of America, San Francisco.

Uhlenberg, P. (1974). Cohort variation in family life cycle experience of United States females. *Journal of Marriage and the Family, 36*, 284–292.

Wadsworth, M. E. J. (1986). Serious illness in childhood and its association with later life achievement. In R. G. Wilkinson (Ed.), *Class and health* (pp. 50–74). London: Cambridge University Press.

Walberg, H. J., & Tsai, S-L. (1983). Matthew effects in education. *American Educational Research Journal, 20*, 359–373.

Waldron, I., Nowatarski, M., Freimer, M., Henry, J. P., Post, N., & Witten, C. (1982). Cross-cultural variation in blood pressure: A quantitative analysis of the relationships of blood pressure to cultural characteristics, salt consumption and body weight. *Social Science and Medicine, 16*, 419–430.

Waring, S. (1976). Social replenishment and social change: The problem of disordered cohort flow. *American Behavioral Scientist, 19*, 237–256.

Wheeler, S. (1966). The structure of formally organized social settings. In O. G. Brim & S. Wheeler (Eds.), *Socialization after childhood* (pp. 51–116). New York: Wiley.

Wilkinson, R. E. (Ed.). (1986). *Class and health.* London: Cambridge University Press.

CHAPTER 2

The Changing and Heterogeneous Nature of Aging and Longevity: A Social and Biomedical Perspective

LISA F. BERKMAN

DEPARTMENT OF EPIDEMIOLOGY,
YALE SCHOOL OF MEDICINE

Much attention has recently been focused on the "rectangularization" of the mortality curve in the United States and other developed counties with the message that we, as a nation, have achieved maximum life expectancy and should turn our attention from increasing it further to improving health status, functioning, and what has become termed "active life expectancy." While this is a noble goal, it assumes that we are a homogeneous group of Americans keeping pace with one another in this lofty achievement. It ignores the great heterogeneity found in the U.S. population with regard to life expectancy and conditions related to it.

Heterogeneity in the rate and way older people age is now understood to be very great. In some instances, differences among people of the same age may be greater than those attributed to chronological age differences. In fact, differences in longevity and even improvements in physiologic function among birth cohorts of men and women recently turning 65, 75, or 85 years of age, compared to people reaching those ages decades ago, suggests even more profound heterogeneity in aging processes and mortality risk than we previously thought (Rosenwaike, Yaffe, & Sagi, 1980; Siegal, 1980). For instance, simply focusing on life expectancy for people who are 65 or 80 shows that, at the turn of the century, life expectancy for a person 65 years old was 11.9 years. By 1978, life expectancy for a 65-year-old was 14 years for white males, 18.4 years for white females, 14.1 for nonwhite males, and

This work was supported by the MacArthur Foundation Research Program on Successful Aging and by Contract N01-AG-0-2105 from the National Institute on Aging. The author thanks Drs. B. Singer, C. Finch, and J. Rowe for helpful comments and suggestions made during the preparation of this manuscript.

18 years for nonwhite females. Even life expectancy at 80 has improved since the turn of the century, when it was 5.3 years. In 1978, it was 6.7 for white males and 8.8 for white females (Guralnik & Fitzsimmons, 1986). Data from cohorts of men and women in Sweden show that physiologic declines in such functions as immunocompetence, which were once observed to occur when a person reached his or her sixties, do not occur in recent cohorts until they are in their late eighties, delaying a decline in "normal aging" by decades (Svanborg, 1986). In the United States, adult height and the rate at which children grow have increased (Angel 1976; Van Wierigen, 1978), sexual maturity comes at earlier ages, and menopause occurs at progressively later ages (Frommer, 1964; Tanner, 1962).

Improvements in cardiovascular mortality in the past several decades account for some of the improvements in life expectancy. Changes may also reflect broad-based improvements in standards of living (Berkman & Breslow, 1983; McKeown, 1976; Rosen, 1975) as well as changes in early childhood exposures to infectious diseases and malnutrition. These improvements in life expectancy, however, by and large predate large-scale immunization programs, which affect the health of those born in the 1940s and 1950s, since even the most recent cohorts now reaching 65 were born in the 1920s. Comparisons of morbidity and mortality risk across sociocultural and ethnic groups, a major topic of this chapter, further challenge our assumptions regarding what we think of as "normal aging." A simple example regarding blood pressure elevation with age illustrates the point. In developed countries, on a population basis, blood pressure, especially systolic pressure, increases on average with age, both among different birth cohorts and among individuals over time (NCHS, 1977; Svarsdudd & Tibblin, 1980). However, although the data are not entirely convincing, blood pressure levels in some less developed communities do not seem to rise, or do not rise so steeply with age, and there are individuals who remain relatively stable over time (Epstein & Eckoff, 1967; Oliver, Cohen, & Neel, 1975; Truswell, Kennelly, Hansen, & Leer, 1972). Blood pressure elevations occurring with age are strongly related to initial levels, with those populations with the lowest initial levels manifesting the smallest increases over time (Miall & Lovell, 1967; Svardsudd & Tibblin, 1980). These data, at variance with our general belief that increases, especially in systolic blood pressure, reflect some normal aging experience, challenge us to question whether such changes (while they might be "normative" in a statistical sense) are inevitable or part of some intrinsic process. Furthermore, "normality" in the sense of "average" may still entail considerable health risk—in this case, cardiovascular mortality. If such increases are not an inevitable part of aging, they should be considered open to modification (see Rowe & Kahn, 1987, for a discussion of this issue of usual versus successful aging).

Among population subgroups, heterogeneity is most manifest in longevity, age of onset of diseases typically associated with old age, and rates of biological, physical, and cognitive functional decline. It is least pronounced in maximum lifespan, an observation suggesting biologically or genetically programmed lifespan limits. Such broad heterogeneity in many aging processes indicates that they are influenced to some extent by environmental, behavioral, or genetic conditions, which themselves are highly variable. Conversely, such processes are not *wholly determined* by some species-specific "internal clock" that regulates the rate of decline or change of such processes similarly in all humans. The determination of the rate of aging by intrinsic or extrinsic conditions is not likely to be an either/or situation, but one in which changes in health status, functioning, and longevity clearly associated with chronological age are determined by both intrinsic and extrinsic conditions.

The aim of this chapter is to identify some behavioral and socioenvironmental conditions that appear to influence the way and rate at which people age and die. Information on this issue is most plentiful on the relationships between behavioral conditions and mortality risk (which may be translated into the prospect of longevity). Behavioral and psychosocial influences on physical and cognitive function and performance are not yet as clearly identified, since much research in this area is currently still in progress. However, it is remarkable how pervasive the influences of some psychosocial conditions appear to be with many outcomes associated with advancing age, even in areas where evidence is relatively sparse. This is an extremely important area to investigate, since functional abilities, in terms of physical and cognitive performance, are among the most important health-related outcomes to the elderly and ones that show enormous heterogeneity in range of function on a population basis (Cornoni-Huntley, Brock, Ostfeld, Taylor, & Wallace, 1986). The conditions discussed specifically in this chapter are (1) social factors related to socioeconomic status and race and (2) psychosocial factors involving social isolation, lack of support, and loneliness.

The perspective of this chapter, in which the focus is on *variability* in aging and longevity, is particularly compatible with epidemiology, since investigators in this field have not tended to focus research efforts on identifying normative changes with age but rather have chosen to examine variations in risk among people of the same age. In other words, the question most often asked by epidemiologists concerns which conditions, in addition to chronological age, play a role in determining longevity and onset of chronic disease and functional decline. Biologic age represents not only the intrinsic aging of the organism but also the accumulated exposures to hazardous or health-promoting conditions acquired over a lifetime of interaction with the environment.

The chapter is divided into three sections. In the first two sections, evidence is reviewed on the association of a particular behavioral or psychosocial condition with an array of outcomes, particularly risk of mortality, in relation to socioeconomic, ethnic, and age differences. Several issues are addressed regarding the observation that risk factors related to mortality in middle age may lose potency and have a diminished effect in old age. Where this loss of power or actual crossover in risk is observed, it is important to determine whether it is the result of a selection process in which there is a loss of susceptible individuals in the aging population (i.e., hardy, less vulnerable older people survive and thus comprise a selected cohort) or whether the same conditions actually lose their impact and are less stressful to an older person. There are also many reasons to suspect that the older person is *less* resilient to stressors and may be more vulnerable to psychosocially stressful conditions. Therefore, an examination of the changing magnitude of effect of any risk factor with age is a critical part of this chapter. Finally, the physiologic pathways that might mediate the relationship between psychosocial conditions and mortality are examined.

SOCIOECONOMIC AND ETHNIC DIFFERENCES IN LIFE EXPECTANCY AND FUNCTIONING

An individual's chance of surviving to old age and functioning without serious limitations and chronic conditions is strongly related to his or her socioeconomic position, level of education, and race. A wealth of material indicates that those in lower social classes and with less education are at increased mortality risk from most major causes of disease (Comstock & Tonascia, 1977; Kitagawa & Hauser, 1973; Marmot, Rose, Shipley, & Hamilton, 1978; Nagi & Stockwell, 1973; Salonen, 1982; Syme & Berkman, 1976) have a higher prevalence and incidence of many diseases and injuries (Devesa & Diamond, 1980, 1983; Diehl, Rosenthal, Hazudar, Comeaux, & Stern, 1985; Lapidus & Bengtsson, 1986; NCHS, 1983), and have a higher case-fatality from diseases (Dayal, Polissar, & Dahlberg, 1985; Linden, 1969; Lipworth, Abelin, & Connelly, 1970; Ruberman, Weinblatt, Goldberg, & Chaudhary, 1984), even when the incidence of the disease does not show increased risk with being in a lower socioeconomic position (e.g., breast cancer) (Dayal, Power, & Chui, 1982). People in lower social classes also have more disability days, functional impairments, and hospitalizations (NCHS, 1982, 1985, 1987). Almost all studies of cognitive function reveal that people with less education do worse on tests of mental status (Berkman, 1986; Folstein, Anthony, Parhead, Duffy, & Gruenberg, 1985; Holzer, Tischler, Leaf, & Myers, 1984; Kittner et al., 1986; Pfeiffer, 1975), although the association between education and dementia is not at all established nor is there evidence showing a decline in cognitive functioning related to educational level (White, Cartwright, Cornoni-Huntley, & Brock, 1986). In addition, because blacks in the United States experience almost all the disadvantages of lower socioeconomic status (SES), they are typically at increased risk of acquiring most conditions and have shorter life expectancy than whites (Kitagawa & Hauser, 1973).

Studies in which biomedical conditions have been considered jointly in analyses with socioeconomic factors generally show that the associations between social class and mortality risk are independent and are largely not mediated by standard cardiovascular risk factors, such as blood pressure, cholesterol, or obesity, or other general health practices, such as cigarette smoking, alcohol consumption, or physical activity (Lapidus & Bengtsson, 1986; Marmot et al., 1978; Salonen, 1982). Thus socioeconomic position per se, poverty, and the cluster of hazardous environmental and psychosocial conditions embedded in being in lower social classes might be thought of as an influence on aging in humans. It is certainly one of the factors that most clearly differentiates groups of men and women in terms of their long-term survival and their level of functioning and fitness. In terms of life expectancy at age 25, for those with 0–4 years of education, life expectancy is 43.9 years for men and 46.8 years for women, compared to 47.1 and 56.4 years for men and women respectively with some college education (Kitigawa & Hauser, 1973).

This apparently consistent although poorly understood and complex phenomenon is clear enough until people reach the age of 65. Thereafter, it becomes less clear-cut; findings are fewer and harder to interpret, leading one to suspect that in some respects a fundamentally different set of issues may be involved, for instance, the relationship between education and mortality changes among older cohorts of men and women in a national study done by Kitagawa and Hauser (1973). Among white men, standardized mortality ratios (SMR) for all causes reveal a negative gradient in relation to years of education only for those aged 25–64. White men 65 and older show no gradient whatever. Analysis by cause reveals a continued gradient with education for only two major causes: (1) influenza and pneumonia and (2) accidents. Among white women, a somewhat stronger negative gradient is observed in the group aged 25–64 than in the older group, but the latter still reveals a definite negative association between SMR and education. Other data using socioeconomic level of city tracts and age (Antonovsky, 1967) reveal a negative gradient in SMRs, which weakens among older age groups. However, unlike the data on education, the relationship never quite disappears even in a group of people aged 75 and older.

Over the last few years, more data have become available on SES and age; however, they too are inconsistent. Data from a 17-year mortality follow-up from the Alameda County Study (Kaplan, Seeman, Cohen, Knudsen, &

Guralnik, 1987) show that neither race nor socioeconomic position (SEP) predict mortality in those aged 60 and over, although both do for younger age groups. In this study, socioeconomic position was measured by total household income adjusted for household size, a measure the investigators argue could lead to substantial misclassification for those who are retired, since it may not be an accurate reflection of lifetime income differences.

In another analysis involving a comparison of respondents living in a federally designated "poverty area" with those not living in a "poverty area," results reveal substantial differences in risk among middle-aged men and women that virtually disappear among those 65 and older (Haan, Kaplan, & Camacho, 1987). Residence in a poverty area is a measure of socioeconomic position that incorporates a number of ecologically defined social and physical environmental charcteristics, including area income, employment status, education, ethnicity, and housing conditions.

On the other hand, data from a British Office of Population and Census Survey (OPCS) longitudinal study of men in England and Wales (Fox, Goldblatt, & Jones, 1985) show that occupation *before* retirement continues to predict mortality for those who died over the age of 75. In this study, steady gradients in mortality are observed for those in age categories under 65, 65–74, and 75 and over. Standardized mortality ratios range from 66 to 124, 68 to 109, and 73 to 116 for those in the highest to lowest occupation in the three respective age groups. This one and a half to twofold increase in risk is a powerful finding, since occupation before retirement (generally a good indicator of socioeconomic status in Great Britain) was classified from 1971 census data and related to mortality risk from 5–10 years later. By analyzing deaths that did not immediately follow the census (in the first five-year period), the investigators argue they have minimized short-term selection biases in which those who were ill in 1971 were likely to report being in less skilled occupations as a result of their illness. As the duration of follow-up lengthens, this study will provide increasingly important results.

Another study in England, of employed middle-aged men, shows that occupational grade (classified in ways similar to the OPCS longitudinal study) is related to mortality risk independently of risk factors for cardio-vascular and other chronic diseases, for example, obesity, cigarette smoking, alcohol consumption, and blood pressure (Marmot, et al., 1978). Other studies have also shown that standard cardiovascular risk factors generally do not account for a large part of the association between education and ischemic heart disease or all-cause mortality (Salonen, 1982, Haan et al., 1987).

Is there an easy way to summarize these findings? The answer must be no, although we should not lose sight of the forest for the trees. Demonstrably, as stated at the beginning of this chapter, almost any indicator of social class is related to health status in terms of mortality risk, incidence of disease or survival, and disability and cognitive performance from birth through middle age. The real question is *why*. Furthermore, why do findings and generalizations across studies and countries become less consistent for the elderly? Of paramount importance is a conceptualization of what conditions we mean to capture in a definition of social class.

A useful definition of social class or social position proposed by Max Weber (1946) is based on three dimensions: class, status, and power. These three dimensions cover (1) economic bases implying ownership and control of resources, (2) status in terms of prestige in the community, and (3) power in a political sense (Liberatos, Link, & Kelsey, in press). Social status is important because it implies access to goods, resources, and information acquired through social contacts and monetary resources. Practically, almost all studies of social class have measured it by levels of education, income, or occupation. Such measures of social class may, of course, not be directly related to mortality for the above reasons; they may relate more indirectly because social class is so closely linked to other risk-related behaviors or conditions, such as malnutrition, noxious environmental exposures, smoking, obesity, psychological processes, and other stressful conditions. In addition, class has been associated with the development of particular values and coping styles (Kohn, 1977).

Two studies illustrate reductions in the strength of associations between SES and biomedical conditions achieved when specific psychosocial factors are added in the first study. In the first study, occupational status is found to be related to the level of fibrinogen in a group of men who were employed in the Department of Environment, a part of the British Civil Service. When characteristics related to the nature of the job (level of control, job latitude, flexibility, support) are added to the analyses, they explain a substantial portion of the association between occupational status and fibrinogen. This finding suggests that part of the reason type of employment is related to fibrinogen may be because of the job characteristics of those in lower levels of employment that involve little control and latitude for choice, low demand for involvement, and little support.

In another study by Ruberman and associates (1984) concerning mortality in men enrolled in the B-Blocker Heart Attack Trial (BHAT), men with little education are at increased mortality risk following hospitalization for acute myocardial infarction. When two other psychosocial conditions, social isolation and "stress," are included in analyses, educational differences are greatly reduced. Unfortunately, the measure of "stress" is confounded by not only a measure of distress regarding major life events but also whether an individual was working in a low-status job, a major indicator of social class. Nevertheless, by exploring specific dimensions of psychosocial experiences related to social class, these investigators point to a promising area of investigation in which interventions may be planned and proxy indicators are substituted for a more in-depth, explanatory set of conditions.

The convergence of black–white mortality rates in later life parallels the decreased risk found in some studies of social-class differentials in mortality and points out again lack of homogeneity in elderly populations. Data from several national studies show that blacks have higher age-specific mortality rates than whites from birth through middle age; thereafter, the white age-specific mortality rates match and then usually surpass the black rates by age 75 or so (Kitagawa & Hauser, 1973; Manton, 1982; Manton, Poss, & Wing, 1979; Thornton and Nam, 1972). This phenomenon is often referred to as the black–white mortality crossover (Manton, 1982). Most studies in which this crossover has been observed are based on cross-sectional data from different birth cohorts. Criticisms of these studies have often been based on the likelihood of biased age reporting because blacks tend to overestimate their ages or because there are errors in reporting race in census enumeration.

Recently, however, longitudinal studies of elderly and/or middle-aged men and women from different U.S. communities report similar results based on longitudinal data of the same individuals over time. Wing, Stallard, Hames, and Tyroler (1985), in a study of coronary-heart disease in middle-aged and older men in Evans County, Georgia, report that blacks who survive to very old age have greater life expectancies than do whites. Similar data are reported from Alameda County in a 17-year follow-up (Kaplan, Seeman, Cohen, Knudsen, & Guralnik, 1987). And preliminary findings from another cardiovascular study, the Charlestown Heart Study, report a black-white crossover.

It is noteworthy that most of these studies have compared blacks and whites who are not homogeneous to each other with regard to major risk factors for disease. Thus we must resort to such aggregate population characteristics as prevalence of smoking, alcohol consumption, diabetes, and hypertension to speculate if middle-aged blacks are more likely than whites to smoke or have diabetes and consequently to have higher rates of disease in middle age, leaving a relatively risk-free population at very old ages. Since some of the longitudinal studies—in particular, the Evans County Study—have longitudinal data on individuals, thsee hypotheses could be explored directly without resorting to ecological-level data. Such analyses would be extremely valuable.

Explanations for risk reduction among older men and women based on socioeconomic and racial factors that are clearly associated with poor health consequences in middle age most often focus on selection factors that operate to bring more resilient people into older age cohorts. For many conditions it is argued that (1) mortality during early and middle age differentially eliminates people who are less "fit," leaving more "fit" survivors in older age categories who are less vulnerable to the condition posing the risk (perhaps because of some genetic or constitutional predisposition), and/or (2) since people with the highest level of risk do not survive to old age, there is a reduced *range* of risk for a particular condition (e.g., those who are most impoverished or have the highest blood pressures die in middle age). This latter point may apply to severe biomedical risks, such as familial hypercholesterolemia, that take their greatest toll in middle age; but it does not seem adequate to explain many reductions or changes in risk since, in general, there are many people in the highest risk categories. For instance, older cohorts are comprised of many people who are in lower SES groups, who are black, who are longtime smokers or heavy alcohol consumers, or who are overweight.

It is interesting that most explanations for the apparent contradictions noted above suggest the findings have to do with some kind of bias in selection and hence are simply artifactual. Rarely have explanations focused on *substantive* reasons for the occurrence of risk reductions; that is, why older people faced with the same condition respond differently. Consider, for example, the situation with regard to socioeconomic status and the black–white crossover.

Perhaps social position or status continues to be an important determinant of poor health in old age; but the indicators by which we measure status may change with age, depending on the social or cultural milieu in which the person lives. While income, education, and occupation may be good indicators of social class in both the hierarchical sense and in terms of access to goods and resources in middle age, they may not be accurate reflections of social position and its relative advantages in old age. In old age, social position may be determined by where one stands relative to one's peers according to different criteria (e.g., leadership in voluntary activities rather than lifetime occupation) or where one is relative to where one *was* throughout the working years. Access to goods and services may not be so closely tied to income, since informal networks may provide resources that were bought in earlier times. Furthermore, access to adequate housing, food, and medical care may be federally subsidized for many older Americans. Thus one might speculate that although the concept of social status and position remains important throughout the life cycle, the indicators of the position change. This may be especially true in the United States and less true in Great Britain, where social class is more fixed and less variant and people in general are less mobile.

Such a reformulation of the meaning of social position in later life could also explain black–white mortality crossovers, since one might argue that older black Americans attain higher status within their families and communities as they age, whereas whites fall relatively more in status as they grow old. Blacks might be expected to do better relative to whites, who may experience more "relative deprivation" according to this formulation. According to this alternative formulation, only our *indicators* of social class are wrong, not the underlying concept. To the extent that indicators continue to predict health outcomes (as in the case of men in England and Wales), they continue to reflect the correlates and consequences of being in a particular social position in society. If the indicators lose potency, they may be moving further and further away from what we intend to measure. This perspective calls for a new approach, one in which new indicators of status, reflecting the current social position of the older person, are created. These measures may be less closely linked to paid employment and more related to standing in a local community, informal resources that provide goods and services and formal care, and subsidized housing. This alternative approach would also greatly benefit work on socioeconomic indicators of health status in general, since the greatest need in this area is to understand what it is about social class that is so important to health and well-being.

SOCIAL NETWORKS, SOCIAL SUPPORT, AND WIDOWHOOD

People are very different with regard to the degree to which they maintain social connections and give and receive support. This heterogeneity is strongly related to mortality risk for reasons that are not clearly understood. Because there are now numerous reviews on this topic focused on the elderly (Minkler, 1985) as well as on people of all ages (Berkman, 1984; Cohen & Syme, 1985; House, Umberson, & Landis, 1987), this evidence will not be reviewed in depth here. Rather, it is more interesting to examine whether the risks associated with isolation and lack of support change with age and whether certain types of ties become more or less important to people as they age. Attention will also be given to the mechanisms by which psychosocial situations might influence aging and longevity.

While the importance of social relationships that provide intimacy and a sense of attachment and belonging has been recognized for some time (Bowlby, 1958; Durkheim, 1951), a host of recent prospective epidemiologic studies (Berkman & Syme, 1979; Blazer, 1982; House, 1982; Kaplan et al., in press; Orth-Gomer et al., 1988; Schoenbach, Kaplan, Fredman, & Kleinbaum, 1986; Welin et al., 1985) have shown that various measures of social ties and connections are related to an individual's chance of dying. In the Alameda County Study (Berkman & Syme, 1979), men and women ($N = 4725$) who lacked close friends and relatives, were unmarried, and did not belong to church-related groups or maintain other group affiliations (or who maintained very limited contact in one of these domains) were 2.3 (for men) or 2.8 (for women) times as likely to die in a nine-year follow-up as those who reported many contacts. When controlling for other factors—including age, race, SES, and health practices and conditions such as cigarette smoking, alcohol consumption, obesity, level of physical activity, and baseline functional status and chronic conditions—the relative risks were still over 2 (Berkman & Breslow, 1983). Another study in Tecumseh, Michigan ($N = 2754$), reported by House, Robbins, and Metzner (1982), shows a similar strength of positive association for men, but not for women, between social connectedness/social participation and mortality risk over a 10–12 year period. An additional strength of this study was the ability of the investigators to control for some biomedical predictors assessed from physical examination (e.g., cholesterol, blood pressure, respiratory function). In the same year, Blazer (1982) reported similar results from an elderly sample of men and women in Durham County, North Carolina. He compared three measures of social support and attachment: (1) self-perceived impaired social support, including feelings of loneliness, (2) impaired social roles and attachments, and (3) low frequency of social interaction. The relative risks for dying associated with these three measures was respectively 3.4, 2.0, and 1.9.

In the last few years, results from several more studies have been reported, one from a study in the United States and three from Scandinavia. Using data from Evans County, Georgia ($N = 2059$), Schoenbach and associates (1986) used a measure of social contacts modified from the Alameda County Study and found risks to be significant in older men and women even when controlling for biomedical and sociodemographic risk factors. In Sweden, Welin, Tibblin, and associates (1985) show that in different cohorts of men born in 1913 and 1923 in the Göteborg study, social isolation proved to be a risk factor for dying, independent of age and biomedical risk factors. A recent report by Orth-Gomer and Johnson (1987) is the only study besides the Alameda County one to report significantly increased risks for women who have been socially isolated. Finally, in a study of 13,301 men and women in Eastern Finland, Kaplan and associates (in press) have shown that an index of social connections almost identical to the Social Network Index used in Alameda County predicts mortality risk for men but not for women, independent of standard cardiovascular risk factors.

To summarize, people who lack social ties, who feel lonely, or who do not have a confidant are at increased mortality risk. The relative risks comparing those with no or few contacts with those who have many contacts is usually over 2, although relative risks vary substantially among subgroups of the population. Relative risks generally are greater for men than for women and for whites than for nonwhites. With a few exceptions (Schoenbach, Seeman, Kaplan, Knudsen, Cohen, & Guralnik, 1986), investigators have not examined whether risks vary by age group.

CHANGING RISK WITH AGE

In spite of the lack of systematic investigation in this area (and unlike the conflicting evidence relating SES to mortality among different age groups), the evidence on different age-related risks is relatively consistent across studies. For instance, the widowed, single, and divorced have higher mortality rates than those who are married (Durkheim, 1951; Ortmeyer, 1974; Price, Slater, & Haver, 1971). The association between widowhood and increased morbidity and mortality is particularly striking. Maddison and Viola (1968), Marris (1958), and early studies by Parkes (1964) indicate that widows, especially in the first year following bereavement, report many more complaints about their health, both mental and physical, and believe they have sustained a lasting deterioration to their health. The relationship between widowhood and increased mortality risk from a wide variety of diseases has been reported in studies using vital statistics (Cox & Ford, 1964; Kraus & Lilienfeld, 1959; McNeil, 1973; Young, Benjamin, & Wallis, 1963) and in cohort studies (Clayton, 1974; Gerber, Rusualman, Hannon, Battin, & Arkin, 1975; Parkes, Benjamin, & Fitzgerald, 1969; Rees & Lutkins, 1967; Ward, 1976).

In one of the only studies to examine the long-term effects of widowhood on men and women of different ages, Helsing and Szklo (1981) report risks are greatest for men aged 55–64 and 65–74. For men aged 75 and over there are virtually no differences in survival between widowed and married men. In men under the age of 55, widows have a worse survival experience than married men, but the differences are not significant (in large part because of a smaller number of deaths). In this study, in contrast to most others, the period of increased risk was not confined to the initial months or first year after the death of a spouse but was apparent for a long period (5–10 years) after the death. These data suggest a diminution of risk among the older group of people in the study but a strong and enduring influence on mortality risk among middle-aged and younger-old people. As suggested by Neugarten (1970), this may be explained by the fact that events may be less stressful when they are seen as "on-time" and are normative rather than unexpected (making them less stressful to older individuals). In this study, women who were widowed show no increase in mortality risk in any age group. This finding has been reported by others, even when large numbers of widows have been studied. Furthermore, the differences in mortality risk for men who were widowed persist after adjustments for smoking, education, age at first marriage, church attendance, and a proxy indicator of socioeconomic status (number of bathrooms in domicile).

A recent important study by Seeman and associates (1987) provides further support for a lessening of risk associated with marital status as people age. In an analysis of 17-year mortality from Alameda County, these investigators examine four components of an index of social networks previously shown to be associated with 9-year mortality risk (Berkman & Syme, 1979). They find that among middle-age people 60 years of age or younger, not being married is a statistically significant predictor of 17-year mortality. For those 60 and over there is no increase in risk associated with being single, widowed, or divorced. In contrast, a measure of contacts with close friends and relatives is more predictive of mortality risk in older age groups and is a significant predictor of mortality in those over 60. Membership in church-related groups is associated with significantly lower mortality in all age groups except those aged 50–59. Membership in other voluntary organizations is not a strong predictor of mortality risk in any age group.

A composite index of all four components of social networks and involvement (i.e., contacts with friends and relatives, marital status, church-group membership, other group affiliations) is a significant predictor of mortality in all four age groups, with no substantially different risk appearing in any one age group. The relative risk (hazards) from four Cox proportional hazards models are 2.5 for those aged 38–49, 1.6 for those aged 50–59, 1.5 for those aged 60–69, and 1.7 for those aged 70 and over. These risks are adjusted for age within 10-year age categories, sex, race, and baseline health status. When behavioral and psychological factors are added to the model (e.g., smoking, physical activity, relative weight, eating breakfast, depression, and perceived health status), the risks drop to 2.0, 1.4, 1.3, and 1.5 respectively. Risks for the youngest and oldest groups remain statistically significant.

Two other studies of men in Evans County, Georgia (Schoenbach et al., 1986), and older men and women in Durham County, North Carolina (Blazer, 1982), also reveal the enduring importance of social ties other than those with a spouse to the health of the elderly. Thus there is a small but consistent body of evidence suggesting that the impact of the loss of a spouse decreases as people grow older and this becomes a more normative experience, whereas relationships with close friends and relatives take on added importance for older groups of men and women. Since there is not a wealth of replicated work in this area, one might be tempted to argue that the effects of social isolation or lack of support are equal across age groups; however, it is notable that there is not a single study showing decreasing risks associated with social isolation among aging cohorts.

To summarize, the consistent findings of this diverse social epidemiologic work are that individuals in positions of lower status, or those who are isolated, disconnected, and lack intimacy and a sense of belonging to a larger community, have an increased mortality risk. The evidence indicates that, while these factors are often related to each other in many situations, when they occur as distinguishable and separate entities, they typically confer independent risks. Most importantly for investigating the effects of these psychosocial conditions in relation to aging or among the elderly, the underlying constructs of status and intimacy, which remain important throughout the life cycle, may have different components and have different meaning as people grow older. For instance, while education may be an excellent indicator of social status in middle age or in very stable societies, it may lose power as a status indicator among the elderly or in societies where status can shift over time. Similarly, although marital status may be an important indicator of intimacy and the presence of a confidant among middle-aged people, it may not be an accurate reflection of intimacy and caring among very old people, especially among very old women, for whom the normative experience is *not* to have a spouse. Research on life-course issues requires a perspective in which investigators recognize the changing meaning of constructs, since the indicators of constructs may change over time. An alternative interpretation is that these indicators may be accurate reflections of the construct but that, as people age, the constructs themselves lose meaning or power for elderly persons because they are confronted with other more threatening conditions or have access to unspecified resources that may be called upon. Since there is almost no biological evidence that older people respond to difficult circumstances more adaptively than do younger people, it is important to examine these shifts in predictability with age carefully. Furthermore, understanding such shifts in the elderly would be useful in interpreting research on mortality in young and middle-aged populations.

BIOLOGICAL PATHWAYS LEADING
FROM SOCIAL CONDITIONS TO MORTALITY

Large community-based epidemiologic studies as well as data from national sources have documented rather clearly the links between lack of social ties, widowhood, lower social status, and increased mortality risk. These studies have not, however, been so enlightening in explaining *why* or how various social conditions might produce deleterious health outcomes. In fact, most work in this area has proceeded by excluding certain conditions that could produce bias in these studies and spuriously elevate risks. Presently, we know quite a bit about conditions that do not explain the observed associations but very little about the biological mechanisms that *do* explain why conditions in the social environment might cause elevations in mortality risk.

Inferences drawn from epidemiologic studies might be useful in guiding the search for biological mechanisms. First, one of the common threads running through nearly all the published studies is the broad array of diseases and causes of death associated with lower SES, social isolation, and loneliness. Most studies reveal elevations in risk for a number of major causes of death. Second, cardiovascular risk factors (such as blood pressure, serum cholesterol, and obesity) and other behavioral risk factors (such as cigarette smoking, alcohol consumption, and physical activity) are only weakly, and usually nonsignificantly, related to assessments of social isolation, networks, or support (Berkman, Marmot, Spuhler, Markowe, & Bulpitt, in press). The strongest of these associations, however, is between social isolation and blood pressure (Knox, Theorell, Svensson, & Waller, 1985; Strogatz & James, 1986).

Using these two findings as guides, investigators may speculate that social networks and support influence mortality risk (and therefore longevity) by influencing an important factor in longevity—the rate of aging of the organism. Following this line of reasoning, one would hypothesize that, for instance, social isolation or lack of support is a biologically extrinsic but chronically stressful condition to which the organism responds by aging faster. These conditions would also then be associated with age-related morbidity and functional impairment. Thus the cumulative conditions that tend to occur in very old age are accelerated. Conversely, it is possible to conceive of social support and the intimacy and sense of belonging and worth related to being embedded in a social network as protective and in some way(s) retarding the way the organism ages, postponing the onset of a wide variety of presumptively age-related disorders. A *specific* disease or disorder is not, of course, typically determined exclusively by social conditions but by a multitude of genetic, or constitutional, factors or other lifelong exposures. The timing of the onset, rate of progression, or outcomes of a disease process may be determined to a significant extent by psychosocial conditions.

There is also an alternative possibility of central interest to gerontological research. One of the hallmarks of aging is an organism's loss of ability to respond to stresses or challenges in an adaptive way, so that homeostasis is maintained within safe bounds and/or physiological processes return to normal within the same time period that they do in younger animals (Shock, 1977; Timiras, 1972). According to this perspective, social conditions or stressors do not actually accelerate or retard the rate of various aging processes but act on an already vulnerable, less resilient aging organism by way of neuroendocrine and immune response and of kidney or cardiovascular function. Such a biological process might explain increased risk for some older people exposed to equivalent stressors. This is not, however, useful in explaining the equivalent risks observed across age groups associated with particular social phenomena. Furthermore, such an explanation is inconsistent with documented *decreases* in the effects of some risks with age (e.g., bereavement, black–white mortality crossovers). However, the mediating effects of physiological pathways are consistent with the wide diversity and lack of specificity of observed health outcomes associated with psychosocial factors.

It is also possible that age-related changes influenced by intrinsic and extrinsic factors such as those discussed above do not have serious clinical consequences in the absence of specific diseases. However, once a specific disease is superimposed on an already vulnerable individual, the age-related changes may have a major impact on the clinical presentation and course of disease. Lakatta (1983) provides an excellent discussion of this issue in relation to age-related changes in cardiovascular performance. Similarly, Sacher (1977) has indicated that to date most chemical and physical treatments that prolong life expectancy do so by governing an organism's vulnerability to disease or death. While this is a conceptually neat and appealing explanation, it is predicated on our ability to differentiate age-related changes in nondiseased people from changes associated with disease per se. While this distinction is possible for some physiologic systems and some diseases, for many others it poses a somewhat artificial distinction. Many age-related changes are actually manifestations of early diseases states or vice versa; hence many disease states are exaggerations or complications of conditions we associate with aging (e.g., atherosclerosis, osteoporosis, carbohydrate intolerance).

What is the evidence that socioenvironmental conditions or stressors can influence physiologic changes, which are often, at least implicitly, conceptualized as part of "normal aging"? Some data are available on interrelated systems that have been found to be responsive to stress and are likely to be related to important age-related health outcomes and diseases. Systems related to one another and capable of influencing disease processes in exceptionally broad ways are the neuroendocrine system and the immunological system.

THE NEUROENDOCRINE SYSTEM AND STRESS

Endocrine responsivity to psychological and physiological stress has been studied in both animals and humans for the past 30 or so years. Because the literature in this area is vast, only a few studies that are of particular interest to age-related experiences will be discussed. Readers are referred to excellent chapters in a volume by Elliott and Eisdorder (1982). Mason (1968a, b), in an early and integrative review of this topic, draws on the work of Cannon (1932, 1939) and Selye (1950) to suggest that endocrine regulation is very likely to be organized on a broad basis and that multiple endocrine systems, including sympathoadrenal medullary systems as well as pituitary-adrenal cortical activity, might participate in endocrine responses to psychologically stressful stimuli.

In a study by Hofer, Wolf, Friedman, and Mason (1972), bereaved parents of children with leukemia were followed from the last stages of illness to several years after the death of their children. The neuroendocrine responses of the parents were studied to see how they responded to temporally more extended stressful situations (more analogous to the environmental situations confronting the elderly). In this study, the most remarkable finding was that parents who initially (during their children's illness) had 17-hydroxycorticosteroid output below the mean had increased excretion rates months after the loss of their child; in contrast, those with high pre-loss excretion values showed a significant decrease in rates during the postloss period. This heterogeneous response pattern would have been totally obscured had the investigators lumped the two groups together, since the average for the total group suggested *no* change in corticosteroid excretion. These findings indicate that how people respond to a stressor, in this case the illness and death of a child, may be more important in understanding neuroendocrine responses than the stressor per se. It also indicates that there is considerable heterogeneity in the way people react both psychologically and physiologically to an extremely stressful situation.

Another informative study on coping with severe illness and bereavement, this time in spouses, again shows considerable heterogeneity in how people react to spousal illness and loss. Jacobs, Mason, Kosten, Brown, and Ostfeld (1984) found heterogeneity, in terms of severity of depressive symptoms, to be associated with urinary free cortisol excretion, revealing an association between age and cortisol excretion that is enhanced among people with severe depressive symptoms. Jacobs and associates studied 51 middle-aged and elderly men whose spouses were hospitalized with a life-threatening illness. Two months after the hospitalization or death of the spouse, respondents were interviewed and three 24-hour urine samples were collected. When the investigators examined the association between age and free cortisol, a strong positive relationship was found only for those people with high depression scores. This finding is similar to that reported by Asnis and colleagues (1981), in which age was positively associated with cortisol levels among depressed people. Most importantly, the evidence suggests that the age/cortisol association is evident *only* when the system is challenged by severe stress responses (depression), not *merely* exposure to a particular stressful condition.

Similar patterns have been observed for biomedical challenges such as glucose tolerance tests and attainment of upright position from a supine position. Rowe and Troen (1980) have suggested that when older people are exposed to such challenges, they have, for instance, a norepinephrine level that has a higher peak and is sustained for a longer time following the challenge than younger people do. Eventually, since older people are exposed to such challenges frequently in their daily lives, this may lead to a sustained or prolonged response or hyperadrenergic state (Rowe & Troen, 1980).

These studies have parallels in the aging research on neuroendocrine response to stress in animals. Sapolsky, Krey, and McEwen (1983) show that while aging rats have slightly elevated levels of basal corticosterone, by far the most remarkable change with age is the impaired capacity of the older rates to adapt to and recover from stress. In a series of experiments, old and young rats exposed to cold or immobilization stress reacted initially in the same way, with dramatic increases in corticosterone; but after 90 minutes, and even up to 150 minutes after exposure, the young rats had returned to basal levels while the aged rats still maintained very high levels due to continued secretion rates. In another set of experiments, Meany and associates (Meany, Aitken, Bodnoff, Iny, & Sapolsky, 1985; Meany, Aitken, Van Berkel, Bhatnager, & Sapolsky, 1988) found that rats handled during the postnatal period also showed faster adrenocortical recovery from stress than did nonhandled rats. These results look very simliar to those comparing young and old rats. Furthermore, the aged rats who were not handled showed an age-related rise in basal glucocorticoid levels that was not apparent among the aged handled rats. The findings suggest that the cumulative exposure to glucocorticoids over the lifespan was greater in the nonhandled compared with the handled rats. Hippocampal cell loss and cognitive impairment were also much more pronounced in the aged nonhandled rats. The results indicate that experiences involving environmental stimulation influence the way rodents react to stress and perhaps account for some of the variability observed among aging animals and humans as well.

The implication for humans of stress research using animals is that age differences in neuroendocrine response in the absence of stress or challenge are minimal compared to those that are manfiest under more trying circumstances. The last experiments noted above illustrates how an environmental condition, handling during the early life of the rat, retards a response to stress that is identified with a condition we think of as illustrating "normal aging." The evidence suggests that such response patterns are not entirely intrinsically determined. This finding is of importance because, if we conceive of the way in which an organism recovers from stress as part of biological aging, it illustrates the extent to which patterns of adaptation are environmentally regulated. Importantly, in this case the environmental condition is not a stressor but a behavior that under natural conditions would be related to intimate, nurturant behavior and would protect against maladaptive responses to other, unrelated stressors.

Henry (1982) has further suggested that repeated swings in neurohormonal levels during such times when usual feedback response is overridden eventually can give way to a sustained disorder. However, more data are needed to confirm this observation since, in some cases, the research relating the effects of acute stressors to those of chronic stressors suggests that some adaptation to chronic stress may occur in some situations (Zigmond & Harvery, 1970). On the other hand, several studies show that long-term environmental manipulations aimed at reducing stress and anxiety in laboratory mice may produce large decreases in corticosterone and delayed onset of mammary tumors in virally exposed mice (Riley, 1975). Sapolsky and Donnelly (1985) show in another experiment that stress accelerates the rate of tumor growth in aged rats and that corticosterone in young rats produces tumor growth similar to rates observed in older rats, suggesting endocrine regulation of tumor growth in vulnerable rats. Visintainer, Volpicelli, and Seligman (1982) also show that among rats exposed to inescapable shock—a condition mimicking the psychological states of helplessness, loss of control, and depression—21% of them rejected tumors, compared to 63% of those given escapable shock. These results imply that lack of control over stressors, not shock per se, impeded tumor rejection. In another area of research on health effects of stress, DeKosky, Scheff, and Cotman (1984) have reported that elevated corticosterone levels are related to reduced axon sprouting in aged animals. Axon sprouting is potentially associated with cognitive function. Thus experiments in which rats are exposed to chronic and often uncontrollable stress suggest that these long-term stressors are not necessarily related to adaptive responses but do have pathological consequences under some conditions.

As evidence grows about the effects of stress, there is also a hint (although evidence is conflicting) that specific psychosocial factors may be differentially related to specific neuroendocrine mechanisms. Although multiple systems and multiple circumstances are often not tested simultaneously, a notable exception is a study by Dimsdale and Moss (1980) that compares elevations in plasma catecholamines produced by physical exertion in contrast to public speaking. Norepinephrine increased more than twice as much during physical exertion as during speaking, but epinephrine increased about three times more for speaking than for exercise. Such differences in human responses require us to be extremely cautious in drawing inferences about humans using evidence from laboratory animals exposed to various physical and psychological stressors. In another study, Lundberg and Frankenhaeuser (1980), using a sample of college students in a variety of experimental settings, concluded that a vigilance task experienced as both effortful and distressing induced an increase in both cortisol and epinephrine. A self-paced controllable task that required effort but was not experienced as distressing induced an increase in epinephrine but a decrease in cortisol. Thus environmental conditions seen as distressing or challenging can have specific effects on pituitary-adrenal or sympathetic-adrenal systems. Cortisol was suppressed in conditions of high controllability and predictability and elevated under conditions of distress.

Henry (1982), citing this work as well as the work of others, indicates that emotions involving dejection, loss of mastery, and distress in contrast to elation and attachment activate adrenal-cortical responses (cortisol), whereas the sympatho-adrenal systems (norepinephrine and epinephrine) are activated by more traditional fight/flight responses involving, variously, anger, anxiety, and relaxation. However, much more work needs to be done in identifying psychosocial states that have different outcomes and have specific effects on neuroendocrine systems.

To summarize this diverse body of evidence, one notes first that both chronological age and specific psychosocial or behavioral conditions influence how animals and humans respond to stress. In humans, a state of depression accentuates the association between age and a neuroendocrine response to stress. In animals, age and certain behaviors lead to maladaptive, delayed, and incomplete recovery from stress. Some neuroendocrine responses are related to tumor growth, axon sprouting, and cognitive impairment. Most troublesome in these various findings is the inability to extrapolate from animal experiments to humans or from human studies to animal experiments in order to increase our understanding of what constitutes a stressful experience and how stress is mediated by the organism. For instance, social isolation, which would appear to be a stressful experience for humans, judging from epidemiologic work, may or may not invoke a stress response in a mouse, depending on the social organization of the species (Brain, 1975). Furthermore, much animal work in the laboratory uses physical stressors as stimuli, but some evidence from humans indicates that they may respond differently to physical (e.g., exercise) in contrast to psychological stressors. Thus, to make maximum progress in understanding stress, as a factor in mortality, investigators working with laboratory animals and those working with humans under observational or experimental conditions must be cautious in extrapolating evidence from one area to another and would do well to communicate carefully with one another in order to build models that are truly parallel.

IMMUNOCOMPETENCE AND STRESS

There is now a rapidly growing literature on the effects of various psychological phenomena and immune response. For recent reviews see Borysenko and Borysenko (1982), Jemmott and Locke (1984), Rogers, Dubey, and Reich (1979), and a related volume by Locke and associates (1985). Many early studies in this field focused on relatively minor infectious diseases, such as upper respiratory tract infections (Hinkle, 1974; Meyer & Haggerty, 1962), and in some studies the influence of stress on illness versus reporting illness could not be clearly distinguished (Jacobs, Spilken, & Norman, 1969).

While immune function is a complex and multidimensional phenomenon in which various responses are regulated by different sets of conditions, much progress has been made in the last decade on actual changes in specific aspects of immune function or rates of seroconversion and severity of disease. For instance, Kasl, Evans, and Niederman (1979) showed that academic pressure among West Point cadets was related to seroconversion for infectious mononucleosis and to severity of clinical disease following. Jemmot and Locke have reviewed a series of other papers focusing on immunocompetence and stress among students and children (1984).

In focusing on immune system response to stresses encountered in middle-aged and older people, a series of studies have suggested interesting changes in immune function among bereaved people and those who are severely depressed. In one of the initial studies of immune functioning and bereavement, Bartrop, Lockhurst, Lazarus, Kiloh, and Penny (1977) found that bereaved spouses had diminished lymphocyte function in the months *preceding* the death of their spouse when compared to age, sex, and race-matched controls. These differences in lower lymphocyte response to mitogenic stimulation were not apparent two weeks after the death of the spouse. However, in another study, Schleiffer, Keller, Camerino, Thornton, and Stein (1983) compared immunologic functioning of men whose wives had terminal breast cancer and found that *after* bereavement the men had significantly lower T and B lymphocyte responses to various mitogens when compared to prebereavement status. Since there was no control group or determination of basal level of response in this study, it cannot be determined whether the prebereavement response levels were already altered. However, both these studies provide initial evidence that aspects of humoral and cell-mediated immunity are altered around the time of bereavement.

Schleiffer and colleagues have also shown that people who are severely depressed have a lower absolute number of T and B cells and lower lymphocyte stimulation responses to mitogens (Schleiffer, Keller, Myerson, Raskin, & Davis, 1984). This altered response, however, is confined to those hospitalized for depression and is not found in outpatients or other inpatients (Schleiffer, Keller, Siris, Davis, & Stein, 1985). In another study of psychiatric inpatients, Kiecolt-Glaser et al. (1984a) reported that people who scored high on a loneliness scale had significantly higher levels of urinary cortisol, a poorer T-lymphocyte response to phytohemagglutinin, and lower levels of natural killer-cell activity.

In pursuing the link between loneliness and impaired immune response, Kiecolt-Glaser, Garner, Speicher, Penn, and Glazer (1984b) found that cellular immune response, measured by natural killer-cell activity, is related to loneliness among medical students. Blood was drawn twice from 75 first-year medical students one month before final exams and on the first day of exams. Natural killer-cell activity declined from the first to the second time period, and students with high scores on scales of stressful life events and loneliness had significantly lower levels of natural killer-cell activity. High loneliness scorers also have significantly higher Epstein-Barr virus (EBV) antibody titer than lower scorers (Glazer, Kiecolt-Glaser, Speicher, & Holliday, 1985). This finding is significant in light of the findings by Kasl and associates (1979) and because EBV antibody titers may reflect cellular immune mechanisms involved in the regulation of latent infections.

Such studies cumulatively are provocative and indicate a mechanism by which such experiences as bereavement, social isolation, and loneliness might influence disease risks. Furthermore, much laboratory work relates adrenocortical hormones to immune response (Claman, 1977; Coquelin & Gorski, 1984; Monjan, 1981), providing a potential link between much of the literature reviewed in the previous section on stress responses and neuroendocrine function. It has been frequently hypothesized that environmental stressors, including psychosocial ones, have these effects by influencing neuroendocrine responses, which in turn influence a number of physiologic functions ranging from immune function to carbohydrate metabolism and cardiac function.

PROSPECTS AND PROBLEMS

Humans, even in developed countries where life expectancy is increasing at advanced ages, remain a heterogeneous lot. Age-related diseases and physiological changes we have come to think of as part of "normal aging" do not affect all people in the same way, nor do all individuals experience the same changes as they reach the same age. Heterogeneity, at least in terms of mortality risk, varies by level of social isolation and integration as well as by social status. Furthermore, the differences in morbidity and mortality risks between people in different social positions has not decreased in the last decades even though overall life expectancy has improved. If such heterogeneity in the rate of decline in physiological function, in risk of acquiring diseases, and in the risk of dying are modifiable by experimental procedures, or if they vary by environmental conditions in observational studies, we must question the degree to which such changes are intrinsic and hence inevitable and irreversible. The perspective taken here is that many of these presumptively age-related functions and risks are determined, to some extent, by the socioenvironmental circumstances of individuals.

While the epidemiologic evidence linking lower social status and social isolation to increased mortality risk is sound and consistent across a wide variety of studies in different populations, there are a number of issues that make linking such social circumstances to differential effects of aging processes and subsequently to differential morbidity and mortality risk problematic. Clarifying this linkage might well be considered a priority area for further research if we are to understand more fully the influence of psychosocial conditions on aging. A number of specific suggestions can be made:

1. A major concern in future research is to clarify the change in risk from middle to old age and to relate differential risk to social experiences. In many of the studies reported, relative risks decrease in magnitude in the oldest age group. As indicated earlier, there is little biological plausibility to the idea that older people confronted with the same stressful condition react in more optimal ways than do middle-aged people. Therefore, either investigators are no longer capturing the essence of the social experience they intend with the traditional indicators available or older people bring some unknown resources to bear on otherwise difficult situations. The possibility that classical indicators of social status (e.g., primarily lifetime occupation or education) designed to measure prestige or status among middle-aged, working groups lose their close association with social status in the elderly is an intriguing possibility. It is important to develop new measures of social stratification for the elderly, or at least to consider ways that stratification shifts over the life course. Similarly, marital status may no longer tap a sense of intimacy or social integration for older people as widowhood becomes a normative experience.

2. In drawing inferences from experimental studies of animals in which "stressors" have linked to neuroendocrine or immunologic changes, the "stressor" often appears largely irrelevant to any human stress we know of based on observational studies. We are hard pressed to extrapolate findings from animal studies to humans; and some evidence suggests we must be extremely cautious, since real differences in responses to specific stressors may occur in both animals and humans. Furthermore, experimental studies of humans often use samples that bear little resemblance to typical at-risk populations, again making it difficult to generalize to elderly populations. Findings from studies of conveniently available medical students, college sophomores, and healthy, well-educated volunteers could be considerably strengthened by replications in middle-aged and older samples representative of their communities. In general, animal research based on experimental laboratory models and observational studies of humans (and animals living under field conditions) can inform each other much better than they currently do. Often published reports on the same substantive area are not collated, resulting in a loss of useful information to investigators in all fields. In the long run, we, as gerontologists, need to develop strategies by which animal and human investigations on specific issues are co-ordinated in such a way that extrapolation from animals to humans is possible.

3. Epidemiologists and other investigators involved in large-scale observational studies of humans often have a difficult time specifying psychological and/or biological pathways by which social circumstances influence mortality risk. On the other hand, scientists conducting laboratory experiments often do not know whether the stress response they are studying is capable of causing clinically relevant disease. For instance, changes in immunocompetence (e.g., natural killer-cell activity, mitogen response) or catecholamine levels are likely to be important mediating mechanisms between psychosocial conditions and disease or death, but they are not important health outcomes in their own right. Ultimately, we need a body of evidence, both experimental and observational, that reveals the processes and pathways by which extrinsic socioenvironmental conditions influence aging processes and/or disease states and ultimately mortality. The needed assessment of stressors must be realistic if interventions are to be planned on a social level. The outcomes of interest must be consequential, not trivial, in terms of functioning and/or morbidity and mortality. And if the findings are to be trusted, they must identify biologically plausible pathways linking external events to biomedical outcomes. By extending the limits of traditional boundaries in future research, we can achieve such goals.

4. A knowledge of what it is specifically about a stressful experience that is deleterious to health is critical if we are to plan interventions. At this time we do not know whether risk related to some social characteristics (e.g., poverty) in middle or old age is simply a reflection of an early experience during childhood (e.g., malnutrition) or whether it is related to current or accumulated exposure. Interventions involving alteration of the social circumstances in order to clarify effects may be beneficial if the risk is related to current exposure or (2) if it is not too late to affect culminating long-term exposures (as with smoking). Clearly, interventions among elderly persons will do little to change past exposure to some factors (e.g., malnutrition during childhood). In some instances, the specific etiological reason social class or some other social variable is associated with morbidity or mortality may be so difficult to discern that only an intervention will be able to test various hypotheses. For example, Finch (1976) has proposed that attempts to influence aging in one or another way may fail if there is a critical period for a specific intervention that has passed. Thus only certain aging phenomena may be accessible to intervention in adulthood, especially in the elderly adult. Other interventions may be effective only during infancy or puberty. It is important to note, however, that some psychosocial interventions have been performed on elderly subjects (Arnetz, Theorell, Levi, Kallner, & Eneroth, 1983; Kiecolt-Glaser et al., 1985) with intriguing results, suggesting that at least some component of risk associated with the psychosocial phenomenon reflects current and modifiable exposure.

5. Finally, our knowledge linking psychosocial phenomena to outcomes other than acute physiological responses or mortality remains extremely limited. Among the elderly, the most important areas of concern regarding

possibly beneficial interventions in physical and cognitive functioning and in chronic debilitating diseases (e.g., diabetes, cardiovascular and cerebrovascular disease, Alzheimer's disease, Parkinson's disease, arthritis). We have almost no information about the role psychosocial factors play in the incidence, progression, or fatality of these major diseases and disabilities.

This chapter began with the idea that focusing on active life expectancy as a desirable general outcome in later life might lead us to ignore the great heterogeneity that is evident in differential functioning and life expectancy of older adults. Ultimately, we need to return to such outcomes and make the explanation of functional heterogeneity a major objective of research in aging.

REFERENCES

Angel, J. L. (1976). Colonial to modern skeletal change in the U.S.A. *American Journal of Physical Anthropology, 45,* 723-735.

Antonovsky, A. (1967). Social class, life expectancy, and overall mortality. *Milbank Memorial Fund Quarterly, 45,* 31-73.

Arnetz, B., Theorell, T., Levi, L., Kallner, A., & Eneroth, P. (1983). An experimental study of social isolation of elderly people: Psychoendocrine and metabolic effects. *Psychosomatic Medicine, 45,* 395-406.

Asnis, G. M., Sachar, E. J., Halbreich, V., Nathan, R. S., Novacenko, H., & Ostrow, L. C. (1981). Cortisol secretion in relation to age in major depression. *Psychosomatic Medicine, 43,* 235-242.

Bartrop, R. W., Lockhurst, E., Lazarus, L., Kiloh, L. G., Penny, R. (1977). Depressed lymphocyte function after bereavement. *Lancet, 1,* 834-836.

Berkman, L. F. (1984). Assessing the physical health effects of social networks and social support. *Annual Review of Public Health, 5,* 413-432.

Berkman, L. F. (1986). The association between educational attainment and mental status examinations. *Journal of Chronic Disease, 39,* 171-174.

Berkman, L. F., Breslow, L. (1983). *Health and ways of living: The Alameda County Study.* New York, Oxford University Press.

Berkman, L. F., Marmot, M. G., Spuhler, T., Markowe, H. L. J., & Bulpitt, C. J. (in press). Social support, grade of employment and some biological and behavioral risk factors for chronic disease: Findings from the Whithall Department of Environment Study of London Civil Servants. Manuscript submitted for publication.

Berkman, L. F., & Syme, S. L. (1979). Social networks, host resistance, and mortality: A nine year follow-up study of Alameda County residents. *American Journal of Epidemiology, 109,* 684-694.

Blazer, D. (1982). Social support and mortality in an elderly community population. *American Journal of Epidemiology, 115,* 684-694.

Borysenko, M. & Borysenko, J. (1982). Stress, behavior, and immunity: Animal models and mediating mechanisms. *General Hospital Psychiatry, 4,* 59-67.

Bowlby, J. (1958). The nature of the child's ties to his mother. *International Journal of Psychoanalysis, 39,* 350–373.

Brain, P. (1975). What does individual housing mean to a mouse. *Life Sciences, 16,* 187–200.

Cannon, W. B. (1932). *The wisdom of the body.* New York: Norton.

Cannon, W. B. (1939). The William Henry Welch Lectures. II. Homeostasis in senescence. *Journal of Mount Sinai Hospital N.Y., 5,* 598–606.

Clayton, P. J. (1974). Mortality and morbidity in the first year of widowhood. *Archives of General Psychiatry, 30,* 747–750.

Cohen, S., & Syme, S. L. (1985). *Social support and health.* New York: Academic Press.

Comstock, G. W., & Tonascia, J. A. (1977). Education and mortality in Washington County, Maryland. *Journal of Health and Social Behavior, 18,* 54–61.

Cornoni-Huntley, J., Brock, D. B., Ostfeld, A. M., Taylor, J. O., & Wallace, R. B. (1986). *Established populations for epidemiologic studies of the elderly: Resource data book* (NIH Publication No. 86-2443.) Washington, DC: U.S. Government Printing Office.

Cox, P. R., & Ford, J. R. (1964). The mortality of widows shortly after widowhood. *Lancet, 1,* 163.

Dayal, H. H., Polissar, L., & Dahlberg, S. (1985). Race, socioeconomic status, and other prognostic factors for survival from prostate cancer. *Journal of the National Cancer Institute, 74,* 1001–1006.

Dayal, H. H., Power, R. N., & Chui, C. (1982). Race and socioeconomic status in survival from breast cancer. *Journal of Chronic Disease, 35,* 675–683.

DeKosky, S. T., Scheff, S. W., & Cotman, C. W. (1984). Elevated corticosterone level: A possible cause of reduced axon sprouting in aged animals. *Neuroendocrinology, 38,* 33–38.

Devesa, S. S., & Diamond, E. L. (1980). Association of breast cancer and cervical cancer incidences with income and education among whites and blacks. *Journal of the National Cancer Institute, 65,* 515–528.

Devesa, S. S., & Diamond, E. L. (1983). Socioeconomic and racial differences in lung cancer incidence. *American Journal of Epidemiology, 118,* 818–831.

Diehl, A. K., Rosenthal, M., Hazuda, H. P., Comeaux, P. J., & Stern, M. P. (1985). Socioeconomic status and the prevalence of clinical gallbladder disease. *Journal of Chronic Disease, 38,* 1019–1026.

Dimsdale, J. E., & Moss, J. (1980). Plasma catecholamines in stress and exercise. *Journal of the American Medical Society, 243,* 340–342.

Durkheim, E. (1951). *Suicide.* New York: Free Press.

Elliott, G. R., & Eisdorfer, C. (Eds.). (1982). *Stress and human health: Analysis and implications of research.* New York: Springer.

Epstein, F. H., & Eckoff, R. D. (1967). The epidemiology of high blood pressure. In J. Stamler, R. Stamler, & T. N. Pullthan. *The epidemiology of hypertension* (pp. 155–166). New York: Grune & Stratton.

Finch, C. E. (1976). The regulation of physiological changes during mammalian aging. *The Quarterly Review of Biology, 51,* 49–83.

Folstein, M., Anthony, J. C., Parhead, I., Duffy, B., Gruenberg, E. M. (1985). The meaning of cognitive impairment in the elderly. *Journal of American Geriatrics Society*, *33*, 228–235.

Fox, A. J., Goldblatt, P. O., & Jones, D. R. (1985). Social class mortality differentials: Artefact, selection or life circumstance. *Journal of Epidemiology and Community Health*, *39*, 1–8.

Frommer, D. J. (1964). Changing age of menopause. *British Medical Journal*, *2*, 344–351.

Gerber, I., Rusualem, R., Hannon, N., Battin, D., & Arkin, A. (1975). Anticipatory grief and widowhood. *British Journal of Psychiatry*, *122*, 47–51.

Glaser, R., Kiecolt-Glaser, J. K., Speicher, C. E., & Holliday, J. E. (1985). Stress, loneliness and changes in herpesvirus latency. *Journal of Behavioral Medicine*, *8*, 249–260.

Guralnik, J., & Fitzsimmons, S. C. (1986). Aging in America: A demographic perspective. *Geriatric Cardiology*, *4*, 175–183.

Haan, M., Kaplan, G. A., & Camacho, T. (1987). Poverty and health: Prospective evidence from the Alameda County Study. *American Journal of Epidemiology*, *125*(6):989–998.

Helsing, K., & Szklo, M. (1981). Mortality after bereavement. *American Journal of Epidemiology*, *114*, 41–52.

Henry, J. P. (1982). The relation of social to biological processes in disease. *Social Science and Medicine*, *16*, 369–380.

Hinkle, L. E. (1974). The effect of exposure to cultural change, social change and changes in interpersonal relationships on health. In B. S. Dohrenwend & B. P. Dohrenwend (Eds.), *Stressful life events: Their nature and effects* (pp. 9–44). New York: Wiley.

Hofer, M. A., Wolff, C. T., Friedman, S. B., & Mason, J. (1972). A psychoendocrine study of bereavement. Part I. 17-hydroxycorticosteroid excretion rates of parents following death of their children from leukemia. *Psychosomatic Medicine*, *34*, 481–491.

Holzer, C. E., Tischler, G. L., Leaf, P. J., & Myers, J. K. (1984). An epidemiologic assessment of cognitive impairment in a community population. *Research in Community and Mental Health*, *4*, 3–32.

House, J. S., Umberson, D., & Landis, K. (in press). Structures and process of social support. *Annual Review of Sociology*, *14*.

Jacobs, M. A., Spilken, A., & Norman, M. (1969). Relationship of life change, maladaptive aggression, and upper respiratory infection in male college students. *Psychosomatic Medicine*, *31*, 31–44.

Jacobs, S., Mason, J., Kosten, T., Brown, S., & Ostfeld, A. (1984). Urinary-free cortisol excretion in relation to age in acutely stressed persons with depressive symptoms. *Psychosomatic Medicine*, *46*, 213–221.

Jemmott, J. B., & Locke, S. (1984). Psychosocial factors, immunologic mediation and human susceptibility to infectious diseases: How much do we know. *Psychosocial Bulletin*, *95*, 78–108.

Kaplan, G. A., Salonen, J. T., Cohen, R. D., Brand, R. J., Syme, S. L., & Puska, P.

(in press). Social connections and mortality from all causes and cardiovascular disease: Prospective evidence from Eastern Finland. *American Journal of Epidemiology.*

Kaplan, G. A., Seeman, T. E., Cohen, R. A., Knudsen, L., & Guralnik, J. (1987). Mortality among the elderly in the Alameda County Study: Behavioral and demographic risk factors. *Ameican Journal of Public Health, 77,* 307-312.

Kasl, S. V., Evans, A. S., Niederman, J. C. (1979). Psychosocial risk factors in the development of infectious mononucleosis. *Psychosomatic Medicine, 41,* 445-466.

Kiecolt-Glaser, J. K., Garner, W., Speicher, C. E., Penn, G., & Glaser, R. (1984a). Psychosocial modifiers of immunocompetence in medical students. *Psychosomatic Medicine, 46,* 7-14.

Kiecolt-Glaser, J. K., Ricker, D., Messick, G. J., Speicher, C. E., Garner, W., & Glaser, R. (1984b). Urinary cortisol, cellular immunocompetency, and loneliness in psychiatric inpatients. *Psychosomatic Medicine, 46,* 15-24.

Kiecolt-Glaser, J. K., Glaser, R., Williger, D., Stout, J., Messick, G., Sheppard, S., Ricker, D., Romisher, S. C., Briner, W., Bonnell, G., & Donnerberg, R. (1985). Psychosocial enhancement of immunocompetence in a geriatric population. *Health Psychology, 4,* 25-41.

Kitagawa, E. M., & Hauser, P. M. (1973). *Differential mortality in the United States: A socioeconomic epidemiology.* Cambridge, MA: Harvard University Press.

Kittner, S. J., White, L. R., Farmer, M. E., Wolz, M., Kaplan, E., Moses, E., Brody, J. A., & Feinleib, M. (1986). Methodologic issues in screening for dementia: The problem of education adjustment. *Journal of Chronic Diseases, 39,* 163-170.

Knox, S. S., Theorell, T., Svensson, J. C., & Waller, D. (1985). The relation of social support and working environments to medical variables associated with elevated blood pressure in young males: A structural model. *Social Science and Medicine, 21,* 525-531.

Kohn, M. (1977). *Class and conformity: A study of values* (2nd ed.). Chicago: University of Chicago Press.

Kraus, A. S., & Lilienfeld, A. M. (1959). Some epidemiologic aspects of the high mortality rate in the young widowed group. *Journal of Chronic Diseases, 10,* 207-210.

Lakatta, E. G. (1983). Determinants of cardiovascular performance: Modification due to aging. *Journal of Chronic Diseases, 36,* 15-30.

Lapidus, L., & Bengtsson, C. (1986). Socioeconomic factors and physical activity in relation to cardiovascular disease and death: A 12-year follow-up of participants in a population study of women in Gothenburg, Sweden. *British Heart Journal, 55,* 295-301.

Liberatos, P., Link, B. G., & Kelsey, J. L. (in press). The measurement of social class in epidemiology. *Epidemiologic Reviews.*

Linden, G. (1969). The influence of social class on the survival of cancer patients. *American Journal of Public Health, 59,* 267-274.

Lipworth, L., Abelin, T., & Connelly, R. R. (1970). Socio-economic factors in prognosis of cancer patients. *Journal of Chronic Disease, 23,* 105-116.

Locke, S., Ader, R., Besedovsky, H., Hall, N., Solomon, G., & Strom, T. (1985). *Foundations of psychoneuroimmunology.* New York: Aldine.

Lundberg, U., & Frankenhaeuser, M. (1980). Pituitary-adrenal and sympathetic-adrenal correlates of distress and effort. *Journal of Psychosomatic Research, 24,* 125–130.

Maddison, D., & Viola, A. (1968). The health of widows in the year following bereavement. *Journal of Psychosomatic Resources, 12,* 297–306.

Manton, K. G. (1982). Temporal and age variation of United States black/white cause-specific mortality differential: A study of the recent changes in the relative health status of the United States black population. *The Gerontologist, 22,* 170–179.

Manton, K. G., Poss, S. S., & Wing, S. (1979). The black/white mortality cross-over investigation from the perspective of the components of aging. *The Gerontologist, 19,* 291–300.

Markowe, H. L. J., Marmot, M. G., Shipley, M. J., Bulpitt, C. J., Meade, T. W., Stirling, Y., Vickers, M. V., & Semmence, A. Fibrinogen: A possible link between social class and coronary heart disease. *British Medical Journal, 241,* 1312–1314.

Marmot, M. G., Rose, G., Shipley, M., & Hamilton, P. J. S. (1978). Employment grade and coronary heart disease in British civil servants. *Journal of Epidemiology and Community Health, 32,* 244–249.

Marris, R. (1958). *Widows and their families.* London: Routledge & Kegan Paul.

Mason, J. (1968a). A review of psychoendocrine research on the pituitary-adrenal cortical system. *Psychosomatic Medicine, 30,* 576–591.

Mason, J. (1968b). The scope of psychoendocrine research. *Psychosomatic Medicine, 30,* 565–575.

McKeown, T. (1976). The role of medicine: Dream, mirage, or nemesis? London: Nuffield Provincial Hospitals Trust.

McNeil, D. N. (1973). Mortality among the widowed in Connecticut. Unpublished master's thesis, Yale University, New Haven, CT.

Meany, M., Aitken, D., Bodnoff, S., Iny, L., & Sapolsky, R. (1985). The effects of postnatal handling on the development of the glucocorticoid receptor systems and stress recovery in the rat. *Progress in Neuro-psychopharmacology and Biological Psychiatry, 9,* 731–734.

Meany, M. J., Aitken, D. H., VanBerkel, C., Bhatnagar, S., & Sapolsky, R. M. (1988). Effect of neonatal handling on age-related impairments associated with the hippocampus. *Science, 239,* 766–768.

Meyer, R. J., & Haggerty, R. J. (1962). Streptococcal infections in families. *Pediatrics, 29,* 539–549.

Miall, W. E., & Lovell, H. G. (1967). Relation between change of blood pressure and age. *British Medical Journal, 1,* 660–664.

Minkler, M. (1985). Social support and health of the elderly. In S. Cohen & S. L. Syme (Eds.), *Social support and health* (pp. 199–218). New York: Academic Press.

Monjan, A. A. (1981). Stress and immunity: Studies in animals. In R. Ader (Ed.), *Psychoneuroimmunology* (pp. 185–194). New York: Academic Press.

Nagi, M. H., & Stockwell, E. G. (1973). Socioeconomic differentials in mortality by cause of death. *Health Services Report, 88,* 449–456.

National Center for Health Statistics. (1977). Blood pressure levels of persons 6–74 years of age in the United States. In J. Roberts (Ed.), *Vital and health statistics* (Series 11, No. 203). [DHEW Publication No. (HRA) 78-1648]. Washington, DC: U.S. Government Printing Office.

National Center for Health Statistics. (1982). *Health: United States 1982.* [DHHS Pub. No. (PHS) 83-1232]. Washington, DC: U.S. Government Printing Office.

National Center for Health Statistics. (1983). *Current estimates from the National Health Interview Survey.* Washington, DC: Department of Health and Human Services.

National Center for Health Statistics. (1985). *Health characteristics according to family and person income* (Series 10, No. 147). Washington, DC: Department of Health and Human Services.

National Center for Health Statistics. (1987). *Disability days* (Series 10, No. 158). Washington, DC: Department of Health and Human Services.

Neugarten, B. (1970). Adaptation and the life cycle. *Journal of Geriatric Psychiatry, 4,* 71–100.

Oliver, W. J., Cohen, E. L., & Neel, J. V. (1975). Blood pressure, sodium intake, and sodium related hormones in the Yanomamo Indians, a "no-salt" culture. *Circulation, 52,* 146–151.

Orth-Gomer, K., & Johnson, J. (1987). Social network interaction and mortality: A six year follow-up of a random sample of the Swedish population. *Journal of Chronic Diseases, 4,* 944–957.

Ortmeyer, C. (1974). Variations in mortality, morbidity, and health care by marital status. In C. F. Erhardt & J. E. Berlin (Eds.), *Mortality and morbidity in the United States* (pp. 159–188). Cambridge, MA: Harvard University Press.

Parkes, C. M. (1964). The effects of bereavement on physical and mental health: A study of the medical records of widows. *British Medical Journal, 2,* 274–279.

Parkes, C. M., Benjamin, B., & Fitzgerald, R. G. (1969). Broken heart: A statistical study of increased mortality among widowers. *British Medical Journal, 1:*740–743.

Pfeiffer, E. (1975). A short portable mental status questionnaire for the assessment of organic brain deficit in elderly patients. *Journal of American Geriatrics Society, 23,* 443–441.

Price, J. S., Slater, E., & Hare, E. H. (1971). Marital status of first admissions to psychiatric beds in England and Wales in 1965 and 1966. *Social Biology, 18,* 574–594.

Rees, W. P., & Lutkins, S. G. (1967). Mortality of bereavement. *British Medical Journal, 4,* 13–16.

Riley, V. (1975). Mouse mammary tumors: Alteration of incidence as apparent function of stress. *Science, 189,* 465–467.

Rogers, M., Dubey, D., & Reich, P. (1979). The influence of the psyche and the brain on immunity and disease susceptibility: A critical review. *Psychosomatic Medicine, 41,* 147–164.

Rosen, G. (1975). Preventive medicine in the United States: 1900–1975. New York: Science History Publications.

Rosenwaike, I., Yaffe, N., & Sagi, P. (1980). The recent decline in mortality of the extreme aged: An analysis of statistical data. *American Journal of Public Health, 70*, 1074–1080.

Rowe, J., & Kahn, R. (1987). Human aging: Usual and successful. *Science, 237,* 143–149.

Rowe, J. W., & Troen, B. R. (1980). Sympathetic nervous system and aging in man. *Endocrine Reviews, 1,* 167–179.

Ruberman, W., Weinblatt, E., Goldberg, J., & Chaudhary, B. (1984). Psychosocial influences on mortality after myocardial infarction. *New England Journal of Medicine, 311,* 552–559.

Sacher, G. (1977). Life table modification and life prolongation. In C. Finch & L. Hayflick (Eds.), *The handbook of the biology of aging* (pp. 582–638). New York: Van Nostrand Reinhold.

Salonen, J. T. (1982). Socioeconomic status and risk of cancer, cerebral stroke, and death due to coronary heart disease and any disease: A longitudinal study in eastern Finland. *Journal of Epidemiology and Community Health, 36,* 294–297.

Sapolsky, R., & Donnelly, T. M. (1985). Vulnerability to stress-induced tumor growth increases with age in rats: Role of glucocorticoids. *Endocrinology, 117,* 662–666.

Sapolsky, R. M., Krey, L. C., & McEwen, B. S. (1983). The adrenocortical stress-response in the aged male rat: Impairment of recovery from stress. *Experimental Gerontology, 18,* 55–64.

Schleiffer, S. J., Keller, S. E., Camerino, M., Thornton, J. C., & Stein, M. (1983). Suppression of lymphocyte stimulation following bereavement. *Journal of the American Medical Association, 250,* 374–377.

Schleiffer, S. J., Keller, S. E., Myerson, A. T., Raskin, M. J., Davis, K. L., & Stein, M. (1984). Lymphocyte function in major depressive disorder. *Archives of General Psychiatry, 41,* 484–486.

Schleiffer, S. J., Keller, S. E., Siris, S. G., Davis, K. L., & Stein, M. (1985). Depression and immunity: Lymphocyte function in ambulatory depressed patients, hospitalized schizophrenic patients, and patients hospitalized for herniorrhaphy. *Archives of General Psychiatry, 42,* 129–133.

Schoenbach, V. J., Kaplan, B. H., Fredman, L., & Kleinbaum, D. G. (1986). Social ties and mortality in Evans County, Georgia. *American Journal of Epidemiology, 123,* 577–591.

Seeman, T. E., Kaplan, G., Knudsen, L., Cohen, R., & Guralnik, J. (1987). Social network ties and mortality among the elderly in the Alameda County Study. *American Journal of Epidemiology, 126,* 714–723.

Selye, H. (1950). *Stress.* Montreal: ACTA.

Shock, N. (1977). Systems integration. In C. Finch & L. Hayflick (Eds.), *The biology of aging* (pp. 639–665). New York: Van Nostrand Reinhold.

Siegal, J. (1980). Recent and prospective demographic trends for the elderly population and some implications for health care. In S. G. Haynes & M. Feinleib (Eds.),

Second conference on the epidemiology of aging. (DHHS NIH Publication No. 80-969) (pp. 289–314). Washington, DC: U.S. Government Printing Office.

Strogatz, D. S., & James, S. A. (1986). Social support and hypertension among blacks and whites in a rural, southern community. *American Journal of Epidemiology, 124,* 949–956.

Svanborg. (1986). Personal communication.

Svarsdudd, K., & Tibblin, G. (1980). A longitudinal blood pressure study. Change of blood pressure during 10 years in relation to initial values. The study of men born in 1913. *Journal of Chronic Diseases, 33,* 627–636.

Syme, S. L., & Berkman, L. F. (1976). Social class, susceptibility and sickness. *American Journal of Epidemiology, 104,* 1–8.

Tanner, J. (1962). *Growth at adolescence.* New York: Oxford University Press.

Thornton, R. G., & Nam, C. B. (1972). The lower mortality rates of nonwhites at older ages. An enigma in demographic analyses. *Research Report in Social Science, 11,* 1–8.

Timiras, P. S. (1972). *Developmental physiology and aging.* New York: Macmillan.

Truswell, A. S., Kennelly, B. M., Hansen, J. D. L., & Lee, R. B. (1972). Blood pressures of the Kung bushmen in northern Botswana. *American Heart Journal, 85,* 5–12.

Van Wierigen, J. C. (1978). Secular growth changes. In F. Falkner & J. M. Tanner (Eds.), *Human growth: 2. Postnatal growth* (pp. 307–332). New York: Plenum.

Visintainer, M. S., Volpicelli, J., & Seligman, M. P. (1982). Tumor rejection in rats after inescapable or escapable shock. *Science, 216,* 437–439.

Ward, A. W. (1976). Mortality of bereavement. *British Medical Journal, 1,* 700–702.

Weber, M. (1946). Class status, and party. In H. H. Gerth & C. W. Mills (Eds.), *From Max Weber: Essays in sociology* (pp. 180–195). New York: Oxford University Press.

White, L. R., Cartwright, W. S., Cornoni-Huntley, J., & Brock, D. (1986). Geriatric epidemiology. *Annual review of gerontology and geriatrics,* Volume 6 (pp. 215–309). New York: Springer Publishing.

Wing, S., Stallard, E., Hames, L., & Tyroler, H. A. (1985). The black/white mortality cross-over: Investigation in a community-based cohort. *Journal of Gerontology, 40,* 78–84.

Young, M., Benjamin, B., & Wallis, C. (1963). The mortality of widows. *Lancet, 2,* 454–457.

Zigmond, M., & Harvey, J. (1970). Resistance to central norepinephrine depletion and decreased mortality in rats chronically exposed to electric foot shock. *Journal of Neuro-Visceral Relations, 31,* 373–381.

PART II

The Social Distribution of Societal Resources

CHAPTER 3

A Different Perspective on Health and Health Services Utilization

FREDRIC D. WOLINSKY, PH.D.
DEPARTMENT OF SOCIOLOGY AND
DEPARTMENT OF HUMANITIES IN MEDICINE,
TEXAS A&M UNIVERSITY
and
CONNIE LEA ARNOLD
DEPARTMENT OF SOCIOLOGY,
TEXAS A&M UNIVERSITY

For more than a decade gerontologists interested in health and health behavior have called for the recognition of the marked heterogeneity that exists in these areas (e.g., Bloom & Soper, 1980; Butler, 1975; Evashwick, Rowe, Diehr, & Branch, 1984; Haug, 1981; Kovar, 1977, 1986; Shanas & Maddox, 1985; Soldo & Manton, 1985; Wan & Arling, 1983; Wolinsky & Coe, 1984), and a thoughtful examination of the most recent federal government publication on the subject supports their call (Havlik et al., 1987). These observations about heterogeneity (1) are consistent with both theory and research, (2) suggest a number of methodological problems, and (3) have important implications for public policy. We will illustrate all three points, devoting a separate section of this chapter to each.

The first section involves the epidemiology of differential health and health services utilization. In it we discuss the latent assumption of homogeneity in the literature, including as illustrative examples the use of limited age, living arrangements, and ethnicity categorizations. Then we review the trend toward the heterogeneity perspective, including such matters as differentiating heavy from moderate from low users of services and examining the consistency of their utilization patterns over time. The first section con-

This work was supported in part by grants to Dr. Wolinsky from the National Institute on Aging (K04-AG00328 and R01-AG06618). The views and opinions expressed in this paper are those of the authors and should not be construed as representing the official position or policy of the National Institute on Aging or Texas A&M University.

cludes with a review of the evidence for differential health and health services utilization across various age and ethnic groups taken from a pooled analysis of the 1976 to 1984 Health Interview Surveys (HISs).

The second section of the chapter focuses on methodological issues in studying health and health services utilization. We begin with measurement issues, including the differences in meaning and interpretation between objective and subjective measures of health status, and between contact, volume, episode, and recency measures of health services utilization. We then turn to modeling issues, including the differences between categorical versus metric analyses, limited versus saturated models, as well as the functional forms of various predictive equation systems. To illustrate the importance of these issues for public policy recommendations, this section concludes with a multivariate analysis of health and health behavior, using the data taken from the pooled HISs once again.

The final section focuses on the policy implications that differential health and health services utilization have for Medicare. Based on the multivariate results, we join the cause of those who call for a shift to need-based rather than chronological age-based criteria for service eligibility. Similarly, we also join those who call for the expansion of covered services to include social and other nonmedical needs. Where we differ with most others, however, is in our call for the replacement of the current system by a uniform national health insurance program of basic and catastrophic coverage for individuals of all ages. The cornerstone of such a system would be the primary care physician, acting as both health care manager and gate-keeper.

THE EPIDEMIOLOGY OF DIFFERENTIAL HEALTH AND HEALTH SERVICES UTILIZATION

In beginning her landmark paper, which was directed toward a public health and not a gerontological audience, Kovar (1977, p. 4) eloquently addressed the homogeneity assumption head-on:

It would be a mistake to think of the elderly as a homogeneous population. As a group, they are more likely than younger persons to suffer from multiple, chronic, often permanent conditions that may be disabling, but the majority are living active lives—many of them in their own households. The range in health status is just as great in this age group as in any other, even though the proportion of persons who have health problems increases with age and a minor health problem that might be quickly alleviated at younger ages tends to linger. Aging is a process that continues over the entire lifespan at differing rates among different persons.

The rate of aging varies among populations and among individuals in the same population. It varies even within an individual because different body systems do not age at the same rate.

Kovar's observations underscore the paradox in which gerontologists studying the health and illness behavior of the elderly have for so long themselves been ageist, albeit unintentionally so, toward their subjects. And if Binstock (1985) and Marshall (1986) are correct, the increasing focus on the oldest-old (i.e., those 85 years of age and older) that has been stimulated in part by the National Institute on Aging [via major, special funding programs (see Suzman & Riley, 1985; Suzman & Willis, 1988)] may actually intensify the problem. Binstock and Marshall fear that the data now coming to light on the oldest-old will result in new stereotypes that serve only to generate and reinforce anxieties about age-group conflicts over the allocation of health services. As two notable examples, consider the increasing popularity of the phrase *intergenerational equity* in discussions about the economic implications of the rising dependency ratio and the growing ethical debate on what "ought" be expected to do for the very old (Callahan, 1987).

The Age Homogeneity Assumption

And how did this problem get its start? It probably began with the enactment of the enabling legislation for Social Security, which somewhat arbitrarily established a chronological age marker for eligibility. Ever since, largely due to the power of inertia, there has been a tendency to characterize the elderly as that apparently homogeneous group of persons aged 65 or over. This makes one wonder how markedly different gerontology and geriatrics would be had that enabling legislation specified an age percentile marker for eligibility. In 1930, age 65 marked the 95th percentile in the age distribution. By 1986, however, the chronological age that marked the 95th percentile had risen to 75.

From the health and health behavior perspective, the homogeneity assumption appears to have been somewhat tacitly accepted in much of the literature prior to the early 1970s. By then the changing demographic dynamics had resulted in an increasing number of persons over age 65 who were healthy, active, and clearly not wards of the state. This, of course, diminished the analytic utility of the term *elderly*. Rather than accept outright the heterogeneity of the elderly population, gerontologists embraced Neugarten's (1974) suggestion that a new distinction be made between the young-old and the old-old, in which the latter embody the traditional characterizations of the "elderly." Unfortunately, too many geronotologists failed to grasp Neugarten's main point and simply began to compare and contrast the two age groups (see Snider, 1981); that is, they merely cut the deck of elderly individuals into two piles. The reasons, we believe, lie in the immaturity of the field, its descriptive rather than analytic orientation, and convenience. In any event, the result has been only a subtle shift in the adherence to the homogeneity assumption from studying the health and illness behavior of *the* elderly, to comparing and contrasting that of the young-old and the old-old, and now, to comparing and contrasting that of the young-old, the old-old, and the oldest-old.

And even when other factors have been introduced to account for within-group variance in health and health behavior, the focus [despite the claims of Shanas and Maddox (1985) to the contrary] has been more on recutting the deck along another dimension (as in a limited, contingency table approach) rather than on recognizing the underlying heterogeneity of individuals. For example, consider the manner in which living arrangements and ethnicity have been introduced. With regard to the former, it has generally been assumed that elderly individuals who live alone are more likely to view themselves as being in poorer health and to use more health services than their counterparts who live with others. A variety of reasons are given, all of which relate to the broad theme of social support, including its emotional, instrumental, and affirmational dimensions (see Antonucci, 1985; Krause, Chapter 6, this volume). And there is a growing body of evidence that not only substantiates these claims but also views the effects of widowhood to be spurious when living arrangements are considered (see Cafferata, 1988; Homan, Haddock, Winner, Coe, & Wolinsky, 1986).

But where has the introduction of living arrangements into the study of health and health behavior led us? Unfortunately, it has only introduced another dichotomous factor (living alone versus with others) with which to cut the deck. It has not focused attention on the more important conceptual issue, which involves the dynamics of change in the convoy of social support over the life course (Antonucci & Akiyama, 1987; Kahn, 1979; Kahn & Antonucci, 1980), and their effects on health and health behavior. Indeed, all of these studies make the simplifying assumption that current living arrangements are both stable and the cause (rather than the effect) of social-support levels and their sequelae. The end result is that the spirit, if not the letter, of the homogeneity assumption remains fundamentally intact.

The introduction of ethnicity to the study of health and health behavior has also been a relatively recent phenomenon, despite longstanding evidence in the social sciences of its critical importance (Jackson, 1967). Indeed, Jackson (1985) has been reluctant to review comprehensively the ethnogerontological literature because of its "largely descriptive and inconclusive nature" (p. 264). The typical treatment of ethnicity initially involved a focus on white subjects, avoiding the issue altogether by excluding nonwhites from the analysis. This approach explicitly assumed whites to be culturally homogeneous and nonwhites to be different, yet culturally homogeneous as well.

During the late 1960s and early 1970s, the exclusion of nonwhite subjects from the study of health and health services utilization was recognized by gerontologists as too limiting, and a new approach emerged. This awareness of the unsatisfactory exclusion of nonwhites resulted in reliance on an equally unsatisfactory racially based dichotomization, with whites compared and contrasted with blacks and nonwhite/nonblack individuals excluded from the analysis [see Jackson (1985) for a detailed review]. By the late 1970s the increasing interest in the Hispanic subpopulation resulted in the expansion of the racially based dichotomy into a racially based trichotomy: whites, blacks, and Hispanics. Unfortunately, the implicit assumption of homogeneity within each of the three groups continued, despite substantial evidence for the existence of cultural heterogeneity [especially within the Hispanic group (cf. Andersen, Lewis, Giachello, Aday, and Chiu, 1981)]. Indeed, even Jackson (1985) ultimately falls into the Hispanic homogeneity trap, assuming the marked cultural diversity within this group to be relatively unimportant.

Most recently there have been several plans to disaggregate the Hispanic category, at least into its own tripartite division of Puerto Rican–Americans, Cuban-Americans, and Mexican-Americans (*Report of the Secretary's Task Force on Black and Minority Health*, 1985; Schur, Bernstein, & Berk, 1987; Travino & Moss, 1984; Wolinsky, Aguirre, & Keith, 1986a). These authors argue that there is more (albeit unidentified) cultural heterogeneity than homogeneity among Hispanics and that this, in turn, results in different patterns of health and health services use. And the evidence for the differential health behavior that they present is rather convincing. For example, Travino and Moss (1984) have shown that the annual rate of physician utilization ranges from a low of 6.6 among Puerto Rican elderly to a high of 10.8 among Cuban elderly. And Schur and associates (1987) have shown that among those with a usual source of care, 83.2% of Cubans receive their care in a doctor's office, compared to 48.9% of Puerto Ricans.

Despite the advances this disaggregation of the Hispanic group provides for our understanding of the health and health behavior of the elderly, it really only serves to cut the deck into a few more piles. That is, it does not further our understanding of ethnically related cultural differences. Rather, it merely subdivides what was once considered to be one homogeneous Hispanic subpopulation into three different, but presumably internally homogeneous, subpopulations. And it is important to note that this is based not on theory but on the convenience of national origin information in the data. It is the heterogeneity within each of these Hispanic subpopulations that needs to be explained, perhaps by the introduction of measures of ethnic identification or self-conception (see Saenz & Aguirre, 1988).

These three illustrations (i.e., limited age, living arrangements, and ethnicity characterizations) make our point. Research that takes heterogeneity explicitly into account has come about only in the past two decades. Moreover, despite growing evidence and logic to the contrary, the latent homogeneity assumption has not yet been effectively cast off. Rather, what has emerged is somewhat analogous to a risk-factor mentality, in which limited categorical factors [also including sex, education, and economic status (Federal Council on Aging, 1981)] are introduced in an epidemiological fashion in the hope of identifying a small number of subpopulations, each of which is relatively homogeneous in its health and health behavior. In so doing, the spirit, if not the letter, of the latent homogeneity assumption lives on.

The Emergence of a Different Perspective

Perhaps among the more clear and recent challenges to the homogeneity assumption are the growing reliance on multivariate analytic techniques and the application to the elderly of conceptual and empirical models developed for the nonelderly. The former more explicitly recognize the heterogeneity of health and health behavior within the elderly population, and the latter place that heterogeneity among the elderly on a par with the heterogeneity traditionally found among the nonelderly population. The results reported in the literature have demonstrated the utility of these approaches (Branch et al., 1981; Coulton & Frost, 1982; Evashwick et al., 1984; Eve, 1982, 1984; Eve & Friedsam, 1980; Haug, 1981; Russell, 1981; Stoller, 1982; Wan & Arling, 1983; Wan & Odell, 1981; Wolinsky & Coe, 1984; Wolinsky et al., 1983).

Indeed, these studies find that although health status is clearly the most important determinant of health services use, most of the variation remains unexplained. This is consistent with the findings from comparable studies of the nonelderly population, underscoring the fact that the health and health behavior of the elderly is not more homogeneous than that of the young. Quite the contrary, the fact that these models explain a little less of the variation in the use of health services by the elderly, as contrasted to the nonelderly, suggests that more (not less) heterogeneity exists among older Americans.

But perhaps the most important aspect of these challenges are their emphases on the conceptual and statistical elaboration of relationships. This denotes a different perspective, directed more toward the explanation of the health and health behavior of elderly *individuals* rather than the characterization of various *subpopulations*. We cannot emphasize enough the importance of this new perspective. As the number of factors included in these models increases, it becomes clear that the individual is *the* critical ingredient in the analysis. Indeed, numerous factors underscore the importance of individual differentiation. Whereas one can erroneously assume that certain social groups are homogeneous in some aspect of their behavior, that same assumption cannot be made for individuals.

Unfortunately, the differentiation issue is not quite as straightforward as it may seem. There are limits to how far we can go in the pursuit of modeling heterogeneity. Technically, we are constrained by the available degrees of freedom. These technical limitations, however, are easily enough overcome by reliance on large-scale surveys. It is the conceptual constraints that are actually the most limiting. The purpose of statistical analysis, after all, is to reveal and summarize shared patterns of behavior in the data. Therefore, it is impossible to avoid some amount of aggregation (and typing) if we are to reveal and summarize those shared behavior patterns. Ultimately, then, we are left with optimizing the trade-off between statistical aggregation and individual assessment. It should be clear from the above discussion that, to date, research on the aged's health and health services utilization has erred on the side of aggregation.

Two more focused issues about the health and health behavior of the elderly, which have also explicitly confronted the homogeneity assumption, albeit in a different way, have surfaced during the 1980s. These issues involve (1) the recognition that the amount of health services used by elderly individuals ranges along a continuum from heavy to moderate to low and (2) the examination of the consistency of elderly individuals' utilization patterns over time. Work on the former is important for two reasons. One is that standard predictive models of health services utilization have been shown to fare more poorly when heavy users (defined as those above the 95th percentile in the distribution) are included in the analysis without adjustment, as opposed to when their utilization levels are artificially constrained to be more moderate [i.e., truncated at the 95th percentile (see Wolinsky & Coe, 1984)]. This suggests that both the reasons for and their priority of importance in determining health services utilization differ between heavy and nonheavy users. And those differences have salient implications for the study of health and health behavior, including the possibility that all health services utilization by heavy users is fundamentally nondiscretionary (i.e., disease-, doctor-, or delivery-system generated, and appropriately so); if this is indeed the case, then health education and cost-containment efforts directed at both heavy users and their providers are not likely to be successful.

The other reason that the identification of heavy users is important focuses on disconfirming the assumption of homogeneity among the elderly by establishing that the basis for their (heavy users') homogeneity is not age. In a remarkable explanation of the 1980 National Medical Care Utilization and Expenditure Survey, Berki and associates (1986) classified separately high, low, and moderate users of hospital, physician, and prescription drug services. They found that:

> Both univariate and multivariable analyses [of all ages combined] show that the most important distinguishing characteristics of high users of any of the three medical services are poor health status, severe functional limitations, and the presence of multiple medical conditions—most importantly cancer, cardiac disorders, musculoskeletal diseases, respiratory diseases, and injuries and poisonings. Almost all high-volume users of every service category (88 percent for hospital days, 89 percent for ambulatory visits, and 94 percent for prescribed medications) had at least three different diagnostic conditions reported during the year. (Berki et al., 1986, p. 1)

Thus it is not the elderly per se who are high users of health services, but those with multiple and severe health problems (see also Kovar, 1986).

Berki and associates (1986) also demonstrated what a remarkably small segment of the noninstitutionalized population are high users, as well as how much their health care costs. High users of hospital care represent 1.7% of the population but account for 54.4% of all hospital days; high users of ambulatory services represent 4.5% of the population but account for 32.3% of all ambulatory visits; and high users of prescription drugs represent 5.9% of the population but account for 32.9% of all prescription acquisitions. At the other end of the extreme, low users of health services represent 17% of the population but account for only 3.3% of all ambulatory visits.

Clearly, then, heavy users represent the greatest drain on the health care delivery system. But besides being severely ill, who are these heavy users? More often than not, they are people in the process of dying. Indeed, Lubitz and Prihoda (1984) have shown that a very large proportion of Medicare expenditures occur during the recipient's last year of life. As a result, the issue of heavy users was initially viewed as an aging problem because (1) it emerged from analyses of Medicare expenditure data and (2) the elderly have higher mortality rates. Recently, however, Roos, Montgomery, and Roos (1987) have taken the issue a step further by using data from the Manitoba Longitudinal Study of Aging to disentangle the effects of aging from those of dying. They conclude that:

> In Manitoba as in the United States, hospital utilization markedly increases in a short period before death, dying has a greater impact on utilization than age per se, and small numbers of individuals consume a disproportionate amount of care. Also . . . very elderly decedents spend somewhat fewer days in [the] hospital and make fewer physician visits than those dying at younger ages. . . . [Thus] the time between onset of illness and death may be shorter for older decedents. (Roos et al., 1987, p. 253)

Moreover, Roos and associates found a substantial number of individuals in all age groups, including the elderly, whose deaths did not result in significant health care expenditures. Therefore, the homogeneity assumption fails to apply even to the special case of the dying elderly (see also Kovar, 1986).

The intriguing combination of high health care costs and marked heterogeneity in utilization patterns among the elderly has focused interest on a related issue. Over time, are there consistently high or low users of health services, and if so, how might they be characterized? Because this question can only be addressed by using data from large-scale, longitudinal surveys, no definitive answers are presently available (Mossey, Havens, & Wolinsky, in press). Nonetheless, preliminary reports from the Manitoba study (Mossey & Shapiro, 1985) indicate that about 60% of the noninstitutionalized elderly, including both those who were alive at the end of the study and those who died during it, were rather consistent (i.e., within four visits, annually) in their use of physician services for six or more of the eight years of data collection. Moreover, even though more of the decedents had consistently high rates of physician utilization (seven or more visits annually) as compared to the survivors (21.5% versus 14.2%), an equivalent proportion of them (about 20%) were consistently very low users (zero to two visits) even during their last year of life. Thus these data suggest that a relatively small proportion of the elderly are consistently heavy users of health services.

But who are these consistent users? Using multivariate logistic regression analyses and standard indicators taken from the behavioral model of health services utilization (Andersen, 1968), Mossey and associates (in press) were unable to differentiate consistent from inconsistent users. They were, however, able to discriminate between levels of utilization among the consistent users. The need for health care [measured by the illness scale (see Mossey & Roos, 1987)] accounted for 54% of the variance among the survivors and 63% of the variance among the decedents. All of the other factors combined added less than 4% to the explained variance. Indeed, the effect of age was not statistically significant among the survivors, and it had only a marginal (and negative) effect among the decedents. As a result, Mossey and associates conclude that consistently high use reflects ill health and consistently low use reflects good health, period.

Taken together, these studies of heavy versus nonheavy and consistent versus inconsistent users of health services make a most important point. There is sufficiently compelling evidence to drive gerontologists away from their traditional reliance on chronological age as *an* important, if not *the* most important, factor in their research. As a variable, age simply has very limited predictive utility for the analysis of data on health and health services utilization. Failure to recognize and comprehend the implications of this limited explanatory power only serves to maintain artificially the latent homogeneity assumption.

Evidence of the Heterogeneity of Health and Health Services Utilization

We conclude this section with a review of the empirical evidence demonstrating the differential health and health services utilization among the elderly. Because of the increasing availability of comprehensive data on the elderly in general (see Havlik et al., 1987), and on the oldest-old in particular (see Cornoni-Huntley et al., 1985), we limit ourselves to a brief overview of the health and health behavior data available from pooling individuals aged 45 or over who resided in any of the 31 largest SMSAs in the 1976 to 1984 HISs. The HISs were pooled in order to provide a sufficient number of cases for stable parameter estimates within a variety of subpopulations, and the analysis was limited to individuals in the largest SMSAs so that contextual data on the nature of the communities and their health care delivery systems could subsequently be incorporated from the Area Resources File (see Wolinsky et al., 1986a).

Table 3.1 contains, by various age groups (for comparative purposes), the percentage reporting their health to be excellent or good, the percentage with chronic conditions causing limitations in everyday activities, the percentage with one or more days of restricted activity due to health reasons during the preceding two weeks, the percentage with one or more days of bed disability due to health reasons during the preceding two weeks, the percentage having one or more physician visits during the preceding year (among those with doctor visits), the number of physician visits during the preceding year, the percentage having one or more hospital episodes during the preceding year, the number of nights spent in the hospital during the preceding year (among those with hospital episodes), and the percentage having one or more visits to a dentist during the preceding year.

As expected, there is a perfectly consistent, monotonic pattern when age (columnar) comparisons are made for all four health status measures. The older the age group, the poorer the average health status. Also as expected, there is a generally consistent pattern when age comparisons are made for the five health services utilization measures. The older the age group, the higher the average health services utilization. The two exceptions involve physician and dental contact. For the former, only the oldest-old break the pattern, with their physician contact rates dropping off by about 2%. This is consistent with previous reports (see Soldo & Manton, 1985; Wolinsky, Arnold, & Nallapati, in press; Wolinsky, Mosely, and Coe, 1986b), suggesting the possibility of the onset of a significant alteration of health behavior among octo- and nonagenarians. The dental contact rates monotonically decline across age groups. This, too, is consistent with previous reports. It has, however, recently been shown to be the result of cohort succession rather than an effect of the aging process (see Wolinsky & Arnold, in press).

Table 3.1 Health and Health Services Utilization Data from the 1976 to 1984 Health Interview Surveys for Elderly Persons Living in the 31 Largest SMSAs, by Age Group.

Age group	Percent in excellent or good health	Percent with limited activity days	Percent with restricted activity days	Percent with bed disability days	Percent with physician contact	Average number of physician visits	Percent with hospital contact	Average number of hospital nights	Percent with dental contact
65 & over	71.0	40.3	15.8	7.4	79.6	5.64	17.6	2.72	45.3
45–54	84.6	17.2	12.4	6.3	72.5	4.27	10.0	1.16	69.0
55–64	77.2	26.8	14.3	6.8	75.3	4.88	11.9	1.60	62.4
65–74	72.0	36.0	14.9	6.9	78.7	5.36	16.1	2.42	50.2
75–84	69.5	44.6	17.0	7.9	81.5	6.00	19.4	3.13	39.2
85 & over	68.1	61.1	18.4	9.8	80.3	6.58	22.8	3.79	25.2

Because of the large number of cases, all of the differences shown in Table 3.1 are statistically significant well beyond conventional probability levels. This should not, however, be taken as support for an age-graded homogeneity assumption. To underscore that fact, Table 3.2 shows comparable data broken down further by sex and ethnicity. As indicated, within each age group there are remarkable (and statistically significant) differences in both health and health behavior between the sexes and across the ethnic categories. And comparable breakouts based on a variety of other factors also yield marked differences, as will be reflected in the multiple regression analysis of these data that concludes the next section. Thus there can be no doubt about the heterogeneity of the health and health services utilization of the elderly.

METHODOLOGICAL ISSUES IN STUDYING HEALTH AND HEALTH SERVICES UTILIZATION

Although there can be no doubt about the heterogeneity of the elderly's health and health services utilization, there are a number of methodological problems that limit our understanding of it. In general, these problems may be grouped into two categories: measurement issues and modeling issues. Two or three examples will suffice to illustrate each category. This section will conclude with a multiple regression analysis of the pooled HIS data demonstrating the importance of these issues for public policy.

Measurement Issues

One of the most frequently discussed measurement issues involves the distinction between objective and subjective indicators of health status. Shanas and Maddox (1985, p. 701) have succinctly identified the essence of this distinction:

> In practice, health in the aged is usually defined in one of two ways: in terms of the presence or absence of disease, or in terms of how well the older person functions or his general sense of "well being." A definition of health in terms of pathology or disease states is commonly used by health personnel, particularly physicians. . . . Such a judgment is often described as "objective" . . . . An alternative way to define health among the elderly is based not on pathology or disease states, but on level of functioning. . . . Thus the things that old persons can do, or think they can do, are useful indicators of both how healthy they are and the services they will require or seek.

Table 3.2 Health and Health Services Utilization Data from the 1976 to 1984 Health Interview Surveys for Elderly Persons Living in the 31 Largest SMSAs, by Age Group, Sex, and Ethnicity.

Age, sex, and ethnic group	Percent in excellent or good health	Percent with limited activity days	Percent with restricted activity days	Percent with bed disability days	Percent with physician contact	Average number of physician visits	Percent with hospital contact	Average number of hospital nights	Percent with dental contact
AGE: 45–54									
Puerto Rican males	68.6	29.9	20.5	13.6	69.7	7.91	16.3	2.42	47.2
Puerto Rican females	52.9	34.5	27.0	16.6	79.9	8.91	16.9	2.10	56.4
Cuban males	86.4	12.6	4.5	2.5	63.3	2.70	7.5	.59	58.7
Cuban females	78.5	16.7	9.7	5.7	76.8	5.52	11.0	.90	67.9
Mexican-American males	84.5	13.1	9.6	5.0	55.5	3.63	6.8	.79	52.9
Mexican-American females	77.2	19.0	13.9	7.9	71.2	6.02	9.2	.63	63.9
Black males	74.0	22.5	13.5	6.9	69.1	4.89	10.6	1.92	51.0
Black females	66.4	25.6	19.5	10.8	80.5	6.01	12.1	1.70	53.4
Anglo males	88.0	15.8	9.9	4.9	67.4	3.34	9.1	1.08	70.5
Anglo females	87.1	15.9	13.1	6.5	77.1	4.58	10.3	1.04	73.8
AGE: 55–64									
Puerto Rican males	55.7	37.1	19.4	9.7	73.4	6.64	15.3	4.41	45.6
Puerto Rican females	53.9	42.3	30.8	19.2	80.1	8.99	12.8	2.69	49.0
Cuban males	82.0	22.4	8.1	4.4	66.5	5.04	12.4	1.48	50.9
Cuban females	71.1	33.2	13.9	7.5	78.1	6.78	10.7	1.57	56.5
Mexican-American males	70.7	28.4	14.5	6.2	61.1	4.49	11.1	1.64	47.1
Mexican-American females	64.6	32.4	19.1	9.5	70.8	5.61	11.3	0.94	52.9
Black males	61.5	37.9	18.4	9.2	74.7	6.26	15.0	2.78	48.2
Black females	57.4	38.0	23.1	11.9	81.9	7.33	12.8	1.95	45.1
Anglo males	80.3	26.5	12.0	5.2	73.2	4.40	12.4	1.67	64.0
Anglo females	79.7	24.0	14.5	7.0	76.8	4.75	11.0	1.34	65.8

(*continued*)

Table 3.2 *continued*

Age, sex, and ethnic group	Percent in excellent or good health	Percent with limited activity days	Percent with restricted activity days	Percent with bed disability days	Percent with physician contact	Average number of physician visits	Percent with hospital contact	Average number of hospital nights	Percent with dental contact
AGE: 65–74									
Puerto Rican males	62.9	46.8	17.7	11.3	83.9	6.76	14.5	1.97	47.7
Puerto Rican females	58.9	46.6	24.7	13.7	90.4	11.33	11.0	2.01	32.7
Cuban males	71.2	30.5	14.4	7.6	76.3	4.85	12.7	1.54	45.2
Cuban females	51.5	37.4	22.2	9.9	85.4	8.38	17.5	1.91	37.9
Mexican-American males	64.1	40.6	18.8	10.9	64.1	5.14	14.8	2.01	41.8
Mexican-American females	54.4	39.1	23.1	9.5	83.4	8.70	19.5	2.24	35.2
Black males	54.9	49.8	19.7	10.2	72.2	6.32	19.8	3.41	32.7
Black females	54.6	43.8	24.0	12.0	80.8	7.66	17.9	3.16	31.1
Anglo males	74.6	36.3	12.0	5.4	76.7	4.79	17.1	2.67	51.8
Anglo females	74.2	33.6	15.2	7.0	80.3	5.32	15.0	2.09	53.5
AGE: 75–84									
Puerto Rican males	40.0	60.0	30.0	20.0	80.0	14.10	20.0	3.40	16.7
Puerto Rican females	26.3	73.7	47.4	42.1	84.2	12.33	36.8	5.37	11.1
Cuban males	60.0	40.0	15.6	4.4	84.4	8.14	20.0	1.20	29.0
Cuban females	65.5	48.3	8.6	0.0	93.1	5.95	13.8	1.38	38.7
Mexican-American males	60.8	45.1	15.7	5.9	76.5	5.37	15.7	1.73	29.7

Mexican-American females	55.4	56.8	32.4	10.8	83.8	6.41	17.6	2.08	22.0
Black males	60.1	50.0	19.2	10.4	75.9	6.90	23.5	4.66	20.9
Black females	54.8	55.2	26.6	12.9	82.5	9.90	17.7	2.98	28.2
Anglo males	70.6	44.5	13.2	6.4	79.5	5.17	21.2	3.61	39.1
Anglo females	71.3	43.1	18.1	8.2	82.8	6.04	18.3	2.83	41.7
AGE: 85 and over								
Puerto Rican males	20.0	100.0	40.0	40.0	80.0	2.80	0.0	0.0	25.0
Puerto Rican females	71.4	42.9	0.0	0.0	71.4	3.86	14.3	2.14	20.0
Cuban males	100.0	0.0	0.0	0.0	50.0	6.00	50.0	3.50	0.0
Cuban females	57.1	71.4	0.0	0.0	85.7	6.36	21.4	2.00	10.0
Mexican-American males	55.6	66.7	44.4	22.2	100.0	11.44	22.2	1.11	50.0
Mexican-American females	47.8	69.6	34.8	17.4	87.0	13.10	39.1	3.13	8.3
Black males	47.2	69.8	18.9	11.3	77.4	9.08	18.9	4.04	5.3
Black females	61.2	68.2	24.8	14.0	79.1	7.20	15.5	4.43	10.1
Anglo males	71.2	56.8	15.8	8.9	79.1	7.27	25.4	4.35	27.3
Anglo females	68.7	61.9	18.8	9.7	80.9	6.02	22.2	3.52	26.5

Although the two approaches are not irreconcilable, neither are they iso-morphic in their implications for understanding the health and health services utilization of the elderly.

On the one hand, the objective (or medical model-based) indicators are more accurate reflections of the physiological dimension of health status, including signs, test results, and diagnosed disease entities. On the other hand, the subjective (or functional model-based) indicators are more accurate reflections of the individual's perception of and response to his or her physiological state. Thus the objective indicators may be considered more accurate measures of the "need" for health care, while the subjective indicators may be considered more accurate measures of the "demand" for health care (Feldstein, 1983).

This distinction (need versus demand) has important implications for studying health services utilization (Wolinsky, 1988). For example, if the health service under study is discretionary (e.g., initial visits to the doctor), then the subjective measures are more likely to have greater explanatory power. If, however, the health service under study is nondiscretionary (e.g., hospitalization rates), then the objective measures are more likely to have greater explanatory power. In circumstances where the discretionary nature of the health service under study is somewhat mixed (e.g., annual physician utilization rates), then both types of measures are likely to be predictive but neither is likely to dominate. Thus the selection of health services utilization studies as well as the comparison of results across studies using different measures.

Mechanic (1979) has taken this issue a step further. In trying to reconcile the divergent findings of the two major schools of health services utilization studies, he argues that:

A major difficulty in surveys of health is the inadequacy of questionnaire indicators of illness and health status. Although questions on perceived health status, symptoms, chronic disease, and restricted activity are commonly asked, these usually reflect a complex pattern of illness perception and behavior that goes beyond the narrower conceptual definition of morbidity that researchers would, ideally, like to measure. (Mechanic, 1979, p. 390)

At the root of Mechanic's argument is the notion that subjective measures of health status represent the channeling of available data on the individual's physiological health state through his or her ontological being (i.e., what an individual defines to be his or her existence, including what is personally important and relevant). As a result, these subjective indicators (whether they be responses to questions about perceived health status or self-reports of symptoms or conditions) are more measures of health behavior than they are of health status. That is why these measures are more predictive of health services utilization than are other psychosocial or organizational factors.

Moreover, this pattern of findings suggests that the use of subjective (or functional) measures of health status, especially those obtained through social surveys, is inappropriate for establishing morbidity levels. Because one's ontological being derives from social processes, the rational calculus used to channel the available physiological data is relative to the individual's sociocultural and experiential heritage. As Mechanic notes, these underlying social processes account for why

> persons with similar complaints behave so differently and why the same person with comparable symptoms at various times chooses to seek medical care on one occasion, but not on another. (1979, p. 394)

These social processes also explain why some physiological signs or bodily changes become available data regarding one's health state (i.e., are perceived to exist by the individual and are then recognized and classified as symptoms) and some do not (Mechanic, 1980).

Another important issue is the way in which health services utilization is measured. Of particular interest is the unit of analysis employed (Andersen & Newman, 1973). Among the more frequently used are contact, volume, episode, and recency measures. Contact measures indicate whether or not a particular service was used during a defined catchment period. For example, Tables 3.1 and 3.2 contain measures of physician and hospital contact during the preceding year. These data indicate whether an individual saw a physician or spent a night in the hospital. Thus contact measures focus more on access to the health service in question than on the amount of consumption. Accordingly, one would expect sociocultural and other background factors to exhibit their greatest impact on contact measures.

In contrast, volume measures indicate how many services were used during this catchment period. Typical examples (see Tables 3.1 and 3.2) include the number of physician visits or nights spent in the hospital during the preceding year. Thus volume measures focus on consumption levels, implicitly assuming some degree of access already existed. Accordingly, one would expect health status and the characteristics of the health care delivery system to exhibit their greatest impact on volume measures.

It would seem prudent, therefore, for any analysis of health services utilization to employ both contact and volume measures for each type of health behavior under study. The results should then be compared and contrasted in order to better understand individual-level barriers to, and delivery system-level catapults for, health services utilization (Wolinsky, 1988). In addition, because volume measures implicitly assume access exits, analysis of such measures should be restricted to those who have made contact (see Schur et al., 1987; Wolinsky, Coe, Mosely, & Homan, 1985). It is, after all, only logical to exclude nonusers from the analysis when the question is how much utilization occurred. The question of whether utilization occurred, of course, is addressed in the analysis of contact measures.

Episode measures take the notion of contact and volume one step forward by norming them to the emergence and sequelae of the illness event. That is, the catchment period becomes defined not in chronological time, but rather in terms of the illness episode. The advantage here is that more meaningful comparisons can be made because the utilization (whether in terms of contact or volume measures) is episode-specific. For example, given the same illness episode, do different individuals have equal likelihood of contacting a physician? And among individuals with contact, does everyone receive the same number of visits? The disadvantage lies in the increased complexities of data collection. Few individuals experience the same symptom episodes in any given catchment period, even though most experience some symptoms.

Recency measures of health services utilization are another matter. Frequently they take the form of asking respondents how long it has been since they went to a doctor. This involves several problems. One is that the categories seldom have equal intervals, with the two least recent categories typically being (1) five or more years ago and (2) never. This makes the interpretation of product-moment-based analyses (e.g., regression) problematic, because it clearly violates a variety of the underlying statistical assumptions (such as interval-level measurement, homoscedasticity, and multivariate normal distributions).

A second problem with recency measures involves the disjuncture between their catchment period and those of the independent variables that are used to predict them. Using current characteristics of the individual (especially factors like income, morale, living arrangements, and health status) to predict health services utilization that occurred five or more years ago defies logic, unless, of course, one assumes that these characteristics are stable over reasonably long segments of the life course. And that assumption appears untenable, given the extant literature. Note that to a considerably lesser extent the length of the catchment period can also be problematic for contact and volume measures, especially in terms of data aggregation and causal process issues (see Mechanic, 1979).

Perhaps the most important problem with recency measures, however, is interpreting them. Although to some extent these measures capture an element of contact (access), a meaningful characterization of access can become rather obscured, depending on the number and breadth of the catchment categories. Volume is not measured and illness episodes are not identified. Since it is difficult to fathom exactly what the analysis of recency measures tells us about health services utilization, recency measures should probably not be used.

Modeling Issues

After the measures of health status and services utilization have been selected, one is confronted with a variety of options for modeling their analysis. Three related issues involved in making those selections warrant special attention. These are the differences between (1) categorical versus metric analyses, (2) limited versus saturated models, and (3) the functional forms of various predictive equation systems. In discussing the first we shall rely on the traditional measure of perceived health status used in social survey research as our example. Respondents to health surveys are typically asked whether they would rate their health status as excellent, good, fair, or poor.

To be sure, the perceived health status question elicits very important information from the respondent. It initiates the process by which available data on the individual's physiological health state is channeled through his or her ontological being. Because the resulting definition of the situation has validity and meaning for the respondent, the only practical question is how that information is used by researchers in their statistical modeling. Most of the time the response categories are assigned numeric values ranging from 1 to 4, representing the metric (internalized) coding procedures associated with regression analyses (see Branch et al., 1981; Evashwick et al., 1984; Wolinsky & Coe, 1984).

But does the metric coding of perceived health status optimally exploit the elicited information, or is it even legitimate? We answer negatively to both questions. The metric coding approach assumes that the difference between any two contiguous response categories is of equal importance for the outcome measure, such as physician utilization. It seems unlikely, for example, that the difference between reports of excellent versus good health has as much effect as the difference between reports of good versus fair health. The former captures more subtle differences between being in peak form versus not having any health problems, while the latter captures the recognition that something is not right with one's health. Unfortunately, the metric coding of the question about perceived health status conceptually and statistically obscures these important distinctions. In order to more fully capture these distinctions (and more fully maximize the effects of the categorical contrasts), the measure of perceived health status should be dichotomized as excellent or good versus fair or poor (see Schur et al., 1987; for an excellent review of the construction, use, and power of dummy variables, see Polissar & Diehr, 1982). This issue also applies to a variety of other categorical measures that are frequently treated as metric indices.

The second issue focuses on the use of limited versus saturated (i.e., fully specified, multivariate) analytic models. Having gone to some length to dispel the homogeneity assumption, and in the process noting the emergence of multivariate modeling focusing on the importance of the individual and his or her characteristics and traits, our call here for more saturated analytic models should come as no surprise. In addition to the logical demands that stem from the heterogeneity assumption, however, the assessment of the net or unique effects of each factor of interest requires more saturated modeling.

Consider, for example, the case of assessing the net effects of widowhood on physician utilization and the contradictory evidence regarding this relationship. Consistent with the longstanding belief that widowhood has a profound (but perhaps impermanent) effect on the surviving spouse (Hyman, 1983), studies had, until recently, typically reported that widowed individuals go to the doctor and the hospital more often than married individuals (see Verbrugge, 1979). More recent work by Cafferata (1988) and Homan and associates (1986), however, reports that this is not the case.

The discrepancy between these two sets of studies is explained not so much by changes (which may or may not have occurred) in the effects of widowhood over time but by changes in the way in which health services utilization has been modeled. Failing to control for living arrangements (i.e., whether the surviving spouse lived alone), the earlier studies attributed the observed differences in physician utilization to the effects of widowhood. In contrast, after controlling for living arrangements, the more recent studies found widowhood had no net effect. These studies attributed the observed differences in physician utilization to living alone.

The third modeling issue involves the functional form of the predictive equation system. There are two points to be considered here. These are the additivity and nonreciprocity assumptions of most modeling procedures (e.g., regression analysis). The additivity assumption holds that the effects of any particular factor (such as social supports) on health services utilization does not depend on the value of any other factor (such as gender or ethnicity). If it does, then regression analysis will result in biased estimates of the parameters of the analytic model unless the appropriate statistical interaction terms are introduced or the analyses are conducted separately within groups and the results compared across groups.

There is good evidence, both conceptual and empirical, suggesting that the effects of many of the factors used to predict health services utilization differ for men and women (Verbrugge, 1985) and for whites and blacks (Keith & Ellis, 1987). Moreover, such statistical interaction is likely to occur when other outcomes are examined as well (see Krause, Chapter 6, this volume). Nonetheless, one seldom finds either the inclusion of the appropriate statistical interaction terms or the comparison of separate analyses across groups (see Mutran & Ferraro, in press). As a result, our confidence in the effects of one or another variable on the use of health services, as reported in the literature, must be somewhat discounted.

The other point about the functional form of predictive equation systems concerns the nonreciprocity assumption. In addition to assuming that there is no statistical interaction among the predictors, regression (and other) analyses assume that there is no reciprocal causation between any two or more factors in the model. If there is, it, too, leads to biased estimates of the model's parameters. This problem is far more difficult to resolve and requires the use of two-stage rather than ordinary least squares (OLS) regression techniques (see Heise, 1975).

Although the problematic reciprocal relationships may involve independent variables only (e.g., income and morale), both independent and dependent variables (e.g., morale and health status), or dependent variables only (e.g., physician and hospital utilization), we wish to underscore the last. In particular, we find the failure to statistically consider the interplay between physician and hospital utilization to be remarkable, especially given the consensus found in the conceptual literature about their relationship. As a result, little is known about how the consumption of one alters the potential for the use of the other (see Mutran & Ferraro, in press). Given the increasing interest in substitution hypotheses (cf. Wolinsky et al., 1986b), a continued aversion to nonreciprocal modeling techniques would seem ill advised.

A Multiple Regression Analysis of the HIS Data

A detailed, complex regression analysis that takes all of the above issues into simultaneous consideration is well beyond the scope of this chapter. Indeed, it has not yet been attempted in the literature. Therefore, what we briefly present next are the results of applying an additive, nonreciprocal, saturated model of health and health services utilization to the pooled HIS data. This is sufficient to demonstrate the basic importance of the conceptual and methodological issues described above for public policy concerning the health and health care of elderly Americans.

The standard multivariate approach that we have selected is Andersen's (1968) behavioral model of health services utilization, which has frequently been applied to the special case of the elderly (see Branch et al., 1981; Coulton & Frost, 1982; Evashwick et al., 1984; Eve, 1982, 1984; Eve & Friedsam, 1980; Mossey et al., in press; Mutran & Ferraro, in press; Stoller, 1982; Wan & Arling, 1983; Wan & Odell, 1981; Wolinsky & Coe, 1984; Wolinsky et al., 1983, 1988). It defines the use of health services as a function of the predisposing, enabling, and need characteristics of the *individual*.

Predisposing characteristics reflect the fact that some individuals have a greater propensity than others to use health services and that these propensities may be predicted by various characteristics prior to the onset of specific illness episodes. Typical indicators include age, marital status, living arrangements, race, education, and labor-force participation. Enabling characteristics reflect the fact that while some individuals may be predisposed to use health services, they will not unless they are able to do so. Typical indicators include family income, place of residence, and having a telephone (because in the HIS, telephone contacts with a physician are considered as visits). Need characteristics reflect the individual's perceived or evaluated health status, which is viewed as the basic and direct stimulus for health services utilization given appropriate levels of the predisposing and enabling characteristics. Typical indicators include self-assessed health status and the extent of activity limitations due to health conditions.

In the analyses reported in Table 3.3, the predisposing and enabling characteristics were coded as follows. Sex, widowhood, living arrangements, labor-force participation, place of residence, and having a telephone were coded as dummy variables (i.e., 0 or 1), with the presence of the trait described indexed as unity. Education was coded in the actual number of formal years attained, and income was coded in thousands of (1979 constant) dollars. A set of dummy variables was constructed to represent age, with the near-elderly (i.e., ages 45–64) as the reference (or omitted) category. Thus the effects of each of the age dummy variables represent the difference between being in that age group versus being near-elderly. A set of dummy variables was also constructed to represent ethnicity, with Anglos being the reference category.

A note on the dichotomous nature of several of the dependent variables is in order at this point. We used ordinary least squares (OLS) regression techniques to estimate the parameters of the behavioral model, because extensive research has clearly shown that when the split of a dichotomous dependent variable is within the 0.25/0.75 (and probably even the 0.10/0.90) range, OLS yields results quite comparable to logistic regression or discriminant function analyses (see Cleary & Angel, 1984). And in these data, the splits are generally within these acceptable boundaries (the principal exception being bed disability days). Standard statistical techniques were used to assess the remaining assumptions of the OLS techniques (see Lewis-Beck, 1981).

There are two very important patterns in the results shown in Table 3.3. Both have considerable significance for public policy concerning the health and health behavior of elderly Americans. First, despite the large number of variables used in these predictive equations, very little of the variance was explained (i.e., the R^2 levels range from .056 to .142). Although both better measurement of the independent and dependent variables and more complex modeling techniques (as described above) might well result in moderate increments to the R^2 levels, the majority of the health and health behavior remains (and likely will remain) unexplained. This underscores the remarkable heterogeneity of the health and health services utilization of elderly Americans. Simply stated, if there were homogeneity within various subpopulations and sub-subpopulations, then the R^2 levels reported here would have been closer to unity than to zero. But that is clearly not the case. Therefore, the continuation of a risk-factor approach to health policy for the elderly is unlikely to prove effective.

The second important pattern in the results shown in Table 3.3 involves the effects of the predisposing, enabling, and need characteristics. Although the need characteristics are the most important predictors of use, there are three reasons why this should not be mistakenly construed as evidence for the equitable nature of the health care delivery system. First and foremost (and as indicated above), the majority of the variance in health services utilization was unexplained. Thus it is not yet certain why elderly Americans use or do not use health services. Second, although the direct effects of the predisposing and enabling characteristics on use are relatively modest, many of them are both statistically and substantively meaningful. And these indicate the existence of both economic (e.g., income and employment status) and noneconomic (e.g., gender and ethnicity) barriers to access. Third, the predisposing and enabling characteristics explain about as much of the variance in the health status measures as they (the health status measures) do for the utilization measures. Thus the predisposing and enabling factors also have indirect effects on use through their direct effects on health status. In sum, it would be erroneous to portray these results as indicative of equity in the health and health care of elderly Americans.

The effects of the dummy variables representing the age groups also deserve special (but necessarily brief) mention here. Dental contact is the only outcome measure for which being in each successive age group consistently has a significantly greater impact (i.e., poorer health or greater use). Elsewhere we have clearly shown this exception to be a cohort, not an aging, effect (Wolinsky & Arnold, 1988). For the remaining outcomes, the effects of age group are quite varied, demonstrating both the inconsistency and limited utility of chronological age as a linear predictor of health and health services utilization. For example, those aged 65–74 and 85–94 are equally disadvantaged in terms of activity limitations relative to the near-elderly, while their counterparts aged 75–84 are significantly less disadvantaged. Those aged 65–74 report significantly lower perceived health status than their near-elderly counterparts, while the older elderly report significantly higher perceived health status. Among those who have seen a physician in the past year, only those aged 95 and over have significantly different volumes of utilization, and they see the doctor less often. And among those who have been hospitalized in the past year, the near-elderly, the young-old, and the oldest-old have comparable numbers of hospital episodes.

Table 3.3 Unstandardized Regression Coefficients for the Predisposing, Enabling, and Need Characteristics on the Health and Health Services Utilization Indicators.

	Limited activity	Good health	Bed disability	Restricted activity	Physician contact	Hospital contact	Dental contact	Volume of physician visits	Volume of hospital nights
PREDISPOSING									
Female	-.082[d]	.039[d]	.014[d]	.026[d]	.071[d]	-.012[d]	.051[d]	.238[d]	-.417[d]
Widowed	.036[d]	-.009[a]	.005[a]	.009[a]	.001	.002	-.066[d]	.118[d]	.294[a]
Lives alone	-.012[b]	.045[d]	.008[c]	.027[d]	.019[d]	.008[a]	.077[d]	.286[d]	.328[d]
Education	-.007[d]	.014[d]	.001[c]	.001[b]	.006[d]	.000	.029[d]	-.008	-.063[d]
Employed	-.230[d]	.166[d]	-.014[d]	-.021[d]	.004	-.021[d]	.009[a]	-.544[d]	-.673
Age 65–74	.042[c]	-.023[d]	-.011[d]	-.014[d]	.021[d]	.000	-.020[d]	.043	.188
Age 75–84	.009[d]	.031[d]	-.033[d]	-.052[d]	.056[d]	.019[d]	-.060[d]	.014	.465[c]
Age 85–94	.042[d]	.048[d]	-.034[d]	-.055[d]	.082[d]	.038[d]	-.114[d]	.039	.613[c]
Age 95 or more	.186[d]	.052[d]	-.029[d]	-.076[d]	.049[d]	.053[d]	-.227[d]	-.317[b]	.483
Puerto Rican Americans	.034[a]	-.091[d]	.060[d]	.058[d]	.062[d]	.005	.036	.819[d]	.696
Cuban Americans	-.044[d]	-.005	-.009	-.023[a]	.030[a]	-.001	.001	.576[d]	-.444

Mexican Americans	$-.047^d$	.009	.005	.009	$-.045^d$	$-.017^a$	$.045^d$	$.211^a$	-1.316^d
Black Americans	$.046^c$	$-.105^d$	$.013^d$	$.015^d$	$.032^d$	$-.004$	$-.063^d$	$.399^d$	.204
ENABLING									
Lives in Central city	.002	$-.021^d$	$.004^a$	.003	$-.008^b$	$-.010^d$	$-.007$	$.205^a$	.070
Income	$-.006^d$	$.008^d$	.000	$.000^a$	$.004^d$	$.001^d$	$.009^d$	.003	.013
Telephone	$-.016^a$	$.025^c$	$-.016^c$	$-.008$	$.082^d$	$.016^a$	$.078^d$	.076	$-.111$
NEED									
Limited activity			$.076^d$	$.180^d$	$.149^d$	$.111^d$	.003	2.063^d	1.818^d
Good health			$-.095^d$	$-.157^d$	$-.092^d$	$-.111^d$	$.039^d$	-1.973^d	-1.380^d
INTERCEPT	.599	.382	.138	.225	.512	.165	.027	5.418	9.059
R^2	.132	.121	.069	.137	.056	.067	.142	.190	.114
N	97,346	97,346	97,346	97,346	97,346	97,346	67,124	74,427	12,695

$^a p \leq .05$
$^b p \leq .01$
$^c p \leq .001$
$^d p \leq .0001$

POLICY IMPLICATIONS

We now turn to a consideration of the implications that the heterogeneity of health and health services utilization and the methodological problems involved in measuring and modeling that heterogeneity have for public policy. Four important points emerge from the preceding discussion. The first is that there is a demonstrably marked heterogeneity in the health and health behavior of elderly Americans.

Second, health status has been consistently shown to be the single most important determinant of health services utilization, whether among the elderly population as a whole, among heavy users, or among low users. To be sure, the literature clearly indicates that of the variance in health behavior that can be explained, the vast majority is accounted for by the direct effects of measures of health status, with chronological age contributing relatively little. And this leads directly to the third point. Regardless of which predictive model is used or where the sample is drawn from, the amount of variance in the use of health services that can be explained is modest. Most applications of the behavioral model to the special case of the elderly account for less than 25% of the variance in their health services utilization.

But it is the fourth point that is the most troubling. It involves the possibility that the measurement and modeling issues may play a significant role in points two and three above. With regard to the dominance of the relationship between health status and the use of health services (point two), the subjective nature of functional health status measures makes them inappropriate for use in evaluating the equitable nature of the health care delivery system. In discussions of this equitable distribution of health care, the perception of illness is not a satisfactory substitute for the fact of illness. What has been demonstrated to date is that the consumption of health services is primarily a function of the demand, as distinct from the need, for them.

What are the implications of these four points for public policy about the health and health care of the elderly? Despite the limitations of the available knowledge base, we believe that there is sufficiently compelling evidence to warrant a fundamental restructuring of the American health care delivery system. Indeed, we believe [much like Davis (1985)] that the time has come to abandon both (1) the risk-factor approach for the allocation of health care benefits and (2) the tradition of "pragmatic incrementalism" in American public policy (see Binstock, 1985). Although the likelihood of such a momentous change may not be great (Estes & Newcomer, 1983), it must be considered.

The foundation for such a new system would consist of four basic elements. First and foremost would be a shift to a need-based from the present chronological age-based criterion for service eligibility. To be sure, we are not the first to make this call (see especially Binstock, 1985; Neugarten, 1974, 1979, 1982). Nor are we likely to be the last. Nonetheless, given the remarkable evidence for the heterogeneity of the health and health behavior of the elderly, the time for a need-based health care policy has come.

Second, the range of covered services must be expanded to include institutional and noninstitutional long-term care. This would provide the elderly with access to much-needed but not presently reimbursable social and other nonmedical services that are pertinent to achieving and maintaining good health (see Cantor & Little, 1985). The salience of such an expansion will become even more critical as the nature of the illness burden continues to change in the coming decades (see Soldo & Manton, 1985). Moreover, such a policy shift would explicitly recognize the essential and well-established interplay among the physiological, psychological, and social dimensions of health (see Shanas & Maddox, 1985).

Third, the restructuring of the American health care delivery system must be based on a national health insurance (NHI) plan. And that NHI plan must be uniform, mandatory, and involve all age groups. Further, it should provide both basic and catastrophic coverage but include no frills (such as cosmetic surgery, in vitro fertilization, or more than one preventive checkup annually—all of which could be covered under private, supplemental plans, if desired). Such an NHI plan is necessary if we are to have a truly equitable health care delivery system (see Fuchs, 1974) and avoid the fractious effects of dispassionate ageism and tabloid thinking (see Binstock, 1985).

Fourth, the primary care physician must become the cornerstone of such a new health care delivery system, accepting the responsibility and being given the authority for functioning as both manager and gatekeeper for the health care needs of his or her panel of patients. In order to ensure the integrity of such a scheme, in terms of both quality assurance and cost containment, a system of checks and balances would be necessary. This would likely include the provision of fiscal incentives and peer review for physicians and consumer affairs commissions for the public.

The four basic elements that we propose for restructuring the American health care delivery system have received only the briefest treatment here. Indeed, we have consciously avoided specifics in order to focus on the broader, more important themes. Nonetheless, the intent of our proposal and the rationale that undergirds it should be reasonably clear. Both too much and not enough are known about the health and health behavior of the elderly to continue current public policies. New directions, regardless of how unconventional they may be, must be considered in pursuing the goal of a health care delivery system that is equitable for everyone. The four basic elements outlined above are offered to stimulate such consideration.

REFERENCES

Andersen, R. M. (1968). *A behavioral model of families' use of health services.* Chicago: Center for Health Administration Studies.

Andersen, R., Lewis, S., Giachello, A., Aday, L. A., & Chiu, G. (1981). Access to medical care among the Hispanic population of the southwestern United States. *Journal of Health and Social Behavior, 22,* 78–89.

Andersen, R., & Newman, J. (1973). Societal and individual determinants of medical care utilization in the United States. *Milbank Memorial Fund Quarterly, 51,* 95–124.

Antonucci, T. C. (1985). Personal characteristics, social support, and social behavior. In R. H. Binstock & E. Shanas (Eds.), *Handbook of aging and the social sciences* (2nd ed.) (pp. 94–128). New York: Van Nostrand Reinhold.

Antonucci, T. C., & Akiyama, H. (1987). Social networks in adult life and a preliminary examination of the convoy model. *Journal of Gerontology, 42,* 519–527.

Berki, S., Lepkowski, J., Wyszewianski, L., Landis, J. R., Magilavy, M. L., McLaughlin, C., & Murt, H. (1986). *High-volume and low-volume users of health services: United States, 1980* (DHHS Publication No. 86-20402). Washington, DC: U.S. Government Printing Office.

Binstock, R. H. (1985). The oldest old: A fresh perspective or compassionate ageism revisited. *Milbank Memorial Fund Quarterly, 63,* 420–451.

Bloom, B. S., & Soper, K. A. (1980). Health and medical care for the elderly and aged population: The state of the evidence. *Journal of the American Geriatrics Society, 28,* 451–455.

Branch, L., Jette, A., Evashwick, C., Polansky, M., Rowe, G., & Diehr, P. (1981). Toward understanding elders' health service utilization. *Journal of Community Health, 7,* 80–92.

Butler, R. N. (1975). *Why survive? Being old in America.* New York: Harper & Row.

Cafferata, G. L. (in press). Marital status, living arrangements, and the use of health services by elderly persons. *Journal of Gerontology, 43.*

Callahan, D. (1987). *Setting limits: Medical goals in an aging society.* New York: Simon & Schuster.

Cantor, M., & Little, V. (1985). Aging and social care. In R. H. Binstock & E. Shanas (Eds.), *Handbook of aging and the social sciences* (2nd ed.) (pp. 745–781). New York: Van Nostrand Reinhold.

Cleary, P. D., & Angel, R. (1984). The analysis of relationships involving dichotomous dependent variables. *Journal of Health and Social Behavior, 25,* 334–348.

Cornoni-Huntley, J. C., Foley, D. J., White, L. R., Suzman, R., Berkman, L. F., Evans, D. A., & Wallace, R. B. (1985). Epidemiology of disability in the oldest old: Methodologic issues and preliminary findings. *Milbank Memorial Fund Quarterly, 63,* 350–376.

Coulton, C., & Frost, A. (1982). Use of social and health services by the elderly. *Journal of Health and Social Behavior, 23,* 330–339.

Davis, K. (1985). Health care policies and the aged: Observations from the United

States. In R. H. Binstock & E. Shanas (Eds.), *Handbook of aging and the social sciences* (2nd ed.) (pp. 727–744). New York: Van Nostrand Reinhold.

Estes, C. L., & Newcomer, R. J. (1983). *Fiscal austerity and aging: Shifting government responsibility for the elderly.* Beverly Hills: Sage.

Evashwick, C., Rowe, G., Diehr, P., & Branch, L. (1984). Factors explaining the use of health care services by the elderly. *Health Services Research, 19,* 357–382.

Eve, S. B. (1982). Use of health maintenance organizations by older adults. *Research on Aging, 4,* 179–203.

Eve, S. B. (1984). Age strata differences in utilization of health care services among adults in the United States. *Sociological Focus, 17,* 105–120.

Eve, S. B., & Friedsam, H. (1980). Multivariate analysis of health care services utilization among older Texans. *Journal of Health and Human Resources Administration, 3,* 169–191.

Federal Council on Aging. (1981). *The need for long term care: Information and issues.* Washington, DC: U.S. Government Printing Office.

Feldstein, P. J. (1983). *Health care economics* (2nd ed.). New York: Wiley.

Fuchs, V. (1974). *Who shall live? Health economics and social change.* New York: Basic Books.

Haug, M. R. (1981). Age and medical care utilization patterns. *Journal of Gerontology, 36,* 103–111.

Havlik, R. J., Liu, B. M., Kovar, M. G., Suzman, R., Feldman, J. J., Harris, T., & Van Nostrand, J. (1987). *Health statistics on older persons, 1986* (DHHS Publication No. 87-1409). Washington, DC: U.S. Government Printing Office.

Heise, D. (1975). *Causal analysis.* New York: Wiley.

Homan, S. M., Haddock, C. C., Winner, C. A., Coe, R. M., & Wolinsky, F. D. (1986). Widowhood, sex, labor force participation, and the use of physician services by elderly adults. *Journal of Gerontology, 41,* 793–796.

Hyman, H. (1983). *Of time and widowhood.* Durham, NC: Duke University Press.

Jackson, J. J. (1967). Social gerontology and the Negro: A review. *The Gerontologist, 7,* 168–178.

Jackson, J. J. (1985). Race, national origin, ethnicity, and aging. In R. H. Binstock & E. Shanas (Eds.), *Handbook of aging and the social sciences* (2nd ed.) (pp. 264–303). New York: Van Nostrand Reinhold.

Kahn, R. L. (1979). Aging and social support. In M. Riley (Ed.), *Aging from birth to death* (pp. 77–91). Boulder, CO: Westview.

Kahn, R. L., & Antonucci, T. C. (1980). Convoys over the life course: Attachment, roles, and social support. In P. Baltes & O. Brim (Eds.), *Life-span development and behavior* (pp. 253–286). New York: Academic Press.

Keith, V. K., & Ellis, S. (1987, August). *Utilization of health services by the black and white elderly.* Paper presented at the annual meeting of the Society for the Study of Social Problems, Chicago.

Kovar, M. G. (1977). Health of the elderly and use of health services. *Public Health Reports, 92,* 9–19.

Kovar, M. G. (1986). Expenditures for the medical care of elderly people living in the community in 1980. *Milbank Memorial Fund Quarterly, 64,* 100–132.

Lewis-Beck, M. S. (1981). *Applied regression*. Berkeley: Sage.

Lubitz, J., & Prihoda, R. (1984). Use and costs of Medicare services in the last years of life. In *Health, U.S., 1983* (DHHS Publication No. 84-1232). Washington, DC: U.S. Government Printing Office.

Marshall, V. (1986). Personal communication.

Mechanic, D. (1979). Correlates of physician utilization: Why do major multivariate studies of physician utilization find trivial psychosocial and organizational effects? *Journal of Health and Social Behavior, 20*, 387-396.

Mechanic, D. (1980). The experience and reporting of common physical complaints. *Journal of Health and Social Behavior, 21*, 146-155.

Mossey, J. M., Havens, B., & Wolinsky, F. D. (in press). The consistency of formal health care utilization. In M. Ory & K. Bond (Eds.), *Aging and the use of formal health services*. New York: Tavistock Publications.

Mossey, J. M., & Roos, L. (1987). Using claims to measure health status: The illness scale. *Journal of Chronic Diseases, 40* (Suppl. 1), 41-54.

Mossey, J. M., & Shapiro, E. (1985). Physician use by the elderly over an eight-year period. *American Journal of Public Health, 75*, 1333-1334.

Mutran, E., & Ferraro, K. J. (in press). Medical need and use of health services among older adults: Examination of gender and racial differences. *Journal of Gerontology, 43*.

Neugarten, B. L. (1974). Age groups in American society and the rise of the young old. *Annals of the American Academy of Political and Social Science, 415*, 187-198.

Neugarten, B. L. (1979). Age or need entitlement. In J. Hubbard (Ed.), *Aging: Agenda for the eighties* (pp. 48-52). Washington, DC: Government Research Corporation.

Neugarten, B. L. (1982). Policy for the 1980s: Age or need entitlement? In B. L. Neugarten (Ed.), *Age or need?* (pp. 19-32). Beverly Hills: Sage.

Polissar, L., & Diehr, P. K. (1982). Regression analysis in health services research: The use of dummy variables. *Medical Care, 20*, 959-974.

Report of the Secretary's Task Force on Black and Minority Health. (1985). Washington, DC: U.S. Government Printing Office.

Roos, N. P., Montgomery, P., & Roos, L. L. (1987). Health care utilization in the years prior to death. *Milbank Memorial Fund Quarterly, 65*, 231-254.

Russell, L. (1981). An aging population and the use of medical care. *Medical Care, 19*, 633-643.

Saenz, R., & Aguirre, B. E. (1988). Mexican descent and ethnic self-conception. Mimeo, Department of Sociology, Texas A&M University, College Station, Texas.

Schur, C. L., Bernstein, A. B., & Berk, M. (1987). The importance of distinguishing Hispanic subpopulations in the use of medical care. *Medical Care, 25*, 627-641.

Shanas, E., & Maddox, G. L. (1985). Health, health resources, and the utilization of care. In R. H. Binstock & E. Shanas (Eds.), *Handbook of aging and the social sciences* (2nd ed.) (pp. 697-726). New York: Van Nostrand Reinhold.

Snider, E. L. (1981). Young-old versus old-old and the use of health services: Does the difference make a difference? *Journal of the American Geriatrics Society, 29*, 354-358.

Soldo, B. J., & Manton, K. G. (1985). Changes in the health status and service needs of the oldest old: Current patterns and future trends. *Milbank Memorial Fund Quarterly*, *63*, 286–323.

Stoller, E. P. (1982). Patterns of physician utilization by the elderly: A multivariate analysis. *Medical Care*, *20*, 1080–1089.

Suzman, R., & Riley, M. W. (1985). Introducing the "oldest old." *Milbank Memorial Fund Quarterly*, *63*, 177–186.

Suzman, R., & Willis, D. (Eds.). (1988). *The oldest old*. New York: Oxford University Press.

Travino, F. M., & Moss, A. J. (1984). *Health indicators for Hispanic, black, and white Americans* (DHHS Publication No. 84-1576). Washington, DC: U.S. Government Printing Office.

Verbrugge, L. M. (1979). Marital status and health. *Journal of Marriage and the Family*, *41*, 267–285.

Verbrugge, L. M. (1985). Gender and health: An update on hypotheses and evidence. *Journal of Health and Social Behavior*, *26*, 157–177.

Wan, T. T. H., & Arling, G. (1983). Differential use of health services among disabled elderly. *Research on Aging*, *5*, 411–431.

Wan, T. T. H., & Odell, B. G. (1981). Factors affecting the use of social and health services among the elderly. *Ageing and Society*, *1*, 95–115.

Wolinsky, F. D. (1988). *The sociology of health: Principles, practitioners, and issues* (2nd ed.). Belmont, CA: Wadsworth.

Wolinsky, F. D., Aguirre, B. E., & Keith, V. M. (1986a). Ethnicity, aging, and the use of health services (DHHS Project Proposal R01-AG06618). Mimeo, Department of Sociology, Texas A&M University, College Station, Texas.

Wolinsky, F. D., & Arnold, C. L. (in press). A birth cohort analysis of dental contact among elderly Americans. *American Journal of Public Health*, *78*.

Wolinsky, F. D., Arnold, C. L., & Nallapati, I. V. (in press). Explaining the declining rate of physician utilization among the oldest-old. *Medical Care*, *26*(5).

Wolinsky, F. D., & Coe, R. M. (1984). Physician and hospital utilization among noninstitutionalized elderly adults: An analysis of the health interview survey. *Journal of Geronotology*, *39*, 334–341.

Wolinsky, F. D., Coe, R. M., Miller, D. K., Prendergast, J. M., Creel, M. J., & Chavez, M. N. (1983). Health services utilization among the noninstitutionalized elderly. *Journal of Health and Social Behavior*, *24*, 325–337.

Wolinsky, F. D., Coe, R. M., Mosely, R. R., & Homan, S. M. (1985). Veterans' and nonveterans' use of health services: A comparative analysis. *Medical Care*, *24*, 1358–1371.

Wolinsky, F. D., Mosely, R. R., & Coe, R. M. (1986b). A cohort analysis of the use of health services by elderly Americans. *Journal of Health and Social Behavior*, *27*, 209–219.

CHAPTER 4

The Economic Situation of Older Americans: Emerging Wealth and Continuing Hardship

MARILYN MOON

PUBLIC POLICY INSTITUTE

AMERICAN ASSOCIATION OF RETIRED PERSONS

The image of the economic well-being of our older citizens is changing in America. No longer are the elderly universally viewed as needy. The absolute growth of incomes and wealth of persons aged 65 and over and their gains made relative to younger families have increasingly become the subject of articles in the media (see, e.g., Peterson, 1987). A new stereotype may be emerging of America's elderly as an affluent and perhaps even greedy group. The image of the elderly is changing from the deserving poor to the undeserving rich.

Like most stereotypes, this view overstates the case. As a society, we have made great strides in improving the economic status of many of our older citizens. Public programs for income security have played a major role in these gains. But progress does not come evenly. Aging differently affects the economic status of older Americans. Income and wealth of those aged 65 and over reflect choices made early in life and events beyond the control of individuals. Individuals' choices about education, career paths, and levels of savings are determinants of well-being for which we hold people accountable, although many would choose differently with the benefit of hindsight. Still other events—such as the state of the economy, the death of a spouse, and health status of the survivors—may also affect the resources that families bring to their later years.

Together these influences determine the level of living that can be achieved by our older citizens. But they do so in ways that do not evenly affect the outlook for each family or individual; indeed, systematic differences in outlook occur among groups of the population, such as minorities and women.

The dichotomy between the wealthiest and the poorest older Americans creates new challenges and belies the notion that we have conquered problems of economic security for this age group. A better understanding of the sources of the dichotomy and implications for the future can help shape more realistic public policy. With or without that better understanding, however, programs directly affecting the well-being of senior citizens will be subjected to scrutiny for possible reductions or modifications. The troubled fiscal situation of the federal government and the fragility of the economy in the late 1980s will likely drive much of the impetus for change. But such policy changes would then reshape the outlook for the economic status of future generations of senior citizens. Government policy plays a critical role in the economic well-being of persons aged 65 and older.

This chapter explores what we know about the basic progress that has been made, how the distribution of income differs among the elderly, and what the observed difference in income imply for consumption and well-being. Tracing the reasons for such change can help in understanding the future outlook. The chapter then concludes with a discussion of how public policy that affects economic status may also change over time.

OUTLINING THE BASIC PROGRESS

Economic statistics on income and poverty rates for those aged 65 and over and for a limited number of additional demographic subgroups are regularly available from published reports of the Bureau of the Census (1987a, b). But detailed analyses, more finely disaggregating the data and trying to explain their meaning, have been undertaken by a large number of researchers interested in the economics of aging. An excellent survey of some of these early studies can be found in Clark, Kreps, and Spengler (1978). In general, these studies indicate that in recent years the average level of economic well-being of the elderly has improved substantially. These improvements can be seen particularly in the incomes and wealth of families and individuals aged 65 and older. But to comprehend fully the ability of elderly individuals to meet their needs, it is crucial to look beyond averages and understand the diversity of the resources of this group. A number of researchers have begun to counsel caution in generalizing about the elderly as a whole (Quinn, 1987; Smeeding, 1986).

General Trends in Well-Being

Incomes for those aged 65 and older have risen steadily, from an average in 1970 of $8,029 per capita (in 1984 dollars) to $11,118 in 1984. This represents a gain of nearly 30% in the purchasing power of this age group. Moreover, between 1980 and 1984 the elderly's rate of income growth outstripped increases in income for other, younger subgroups of the population. While average before-tax incomes for elderly families still lag behind those of younger families, after adjusting for differences in family size and tax liabilities, the disposable (after-tax) per capita incomes of older Americans compare favorably with those of the young. In fact, some researchers have claimed that the overall well-being of the elderly now is on a par with or even exceeds that of younger families (Danziger, van der Gaag, Smolensky, & Taussig, 1984; Smeeding, 1986).

In addition to this steady rise in average incomes, rates of poverty among the elderly have declined in recent years. The share of the elderly in poverty dropped from 25% in 1968 to 12.4% in 1986. In 1982, for the first time, the rate of poverty among the elderly was lower than that for the rest of the population, and that gap has widened since then. The largest declines in poverty rates for the elderly occurred before 1975, however (Bureau of the Census, 1987a).

Some researchers have gone further and suggested that poverty rates are even lower (Smeeding, 1982) when the benefits of noncash programs are taken into account in computing rates of poverty. Such analyses have even prompted some policy analysts to declare poverty an issue of the past for persons aged 65 and over (Anderson, 1978). The greatest impact on reducing poverty by this method comes when health expenditures by Medicare and Medicaid are added to income. Since the elderly are very heavy users of health care services, their rates fall the most, leading to the peculiar result that the sicker you are, the better off you are financially. Moreover, because no adjustments are made to the poverty threshold measure to take into account differences in health needs by various age groups, this method of adding health benefits to income is particularly problematic when used to compute poverty rates (Moon, 1979).

But not all the statistics on the elderly are as rosy as the picture painted thus far. While it is perfectly correct to say that the elderly as a group have shown impressive gains, that is not the same as arguing that each elderly individual experienced such gains. For example, some of the increase in well-being associated with comparisons of mean incomes across time reflects the changing composition of the elderly. Each year individuals turning age 65 join the "elderly" category, and the incomes of these individuals have tended on average to be higher with each succeeding year. This has been particularly true of income from Social Security, largely because of rising average wages over time for those paying into the system. At the other end of the age distribution, persons dying each year are likely to have lower average incomes than the group just turned 65. Thus even if there were no real (inflation-adjusted) growth in incomes of individual elderly persons each year, these demographic changes would yield steady improvements in reported average income levels (Moon, 1987).

Such improvements may be deceptive if they lead policy makers to conclude that each individual enjoys the average increase in income each year. For example, comparing census data between 1979 and 1984 shows that the average income of unmarried women aged 65–69 increased by 47.5% over the five-year period. On the other hand, comparing the incomes of those aged 65–69 in 1979 to those aged 70–74 in 1984 shows only a 13.5% increase in income. Individuals within the elderly population display much slower rates of income growth than does the group as a whole. These differences are captured in rates of poverty as well (see Table 4.1). Poverty declines more slowly when tracking a particular cohort than when looking at all those over age 65.

When considering year-to-year changes in measures such as poverty, additional care must also be taken in interpreting the numbers. For poverty, changes in the *number* of poor elderly over time may be more instructive than the poverty rate.

If the average income gains mainly reflect increases in the number of higher-income persons turning 65 rather than income gains for all, the poverty rate would fall faster than the number of people below the poverty line. That is, all the "new" elderly would raise the denominator used to calculate the poverty rate but not change the numerator. Indeed, this is at least partially the case. The number of elderly persons in poverty has been dropping since 1980, but at a slower pace than suggested by the decline in the poverty rate. Moreover, the number of poor elderly in 1986 was higher than the number of poor in 1973 (Bureau of the Census, 1974, 1987a).

To fully understand the overall economic status of the elderly, it is also crucial to note that many of our older citizens are clustered just above the official poverty lines (Ruggles & Cullinan, 1985). That is, the poverty line for a single elderly individual was $5,255 in 1986, and 125% of that threshold would be $6,569. In 1986, 3.5 million individuals aged 65 or over were listed as poor. Another 2.2 million have incomes of no more than 25%

Table 4.1 Rate of Poverty among Unmarried Women Aged 65 and Over, 1969–1984.

Age group of unmarried women	Year			
	1969	1974	1979	1984
All aged 65 and over	35.9%	24.4%	23.5%	20.6%
Aged 65 to 69 in 1969	28.5	22.6	23.9	21.6
Aged 65 to 69 in 1974	[a]	23.2	21.5	21.4

[a]Not available.

Source: Bureau of the Census, *Current Population Surveys*, 1970, 1975, 1980, and 1985.

Table 4.2 Proportion of the Elderly Below Selected Income Thresholds, 1969–1986.

Year	Poverty threshold	Percent of the elderly below: 125% of poverty	150% of poverty
1969	25.1	35.2	43.3
1975	15.3	25.4	34.9
1980	15.7	25.7	34.4
1983	14.1	22.5	30.2
1986	12.4	20.5	28.0

Source: Ruggles & Cullinan (1985).

above the poverty threshold. And if the poverty line is raised to 150% of the poverty threshold, 28% of the elderly—about 8 million persons—had very limited incomes. A large portion of the elderly remain in the "near-poor" category; they have not "escaped" very far above the poverty level (see Table 4.2). Declines in these near-poor categories have also occurred at a slower pace than for the standard poverty threshold measures. Overall, when the elderly become poor, they are unlikely to escape this classification over their lifetimes (Ruggles, 1987).

Smeeding (1986) has focused particular attention on this just-above-poverty category—a group he calls the "tweeners." Such individuals are ineligible for means-tested programs and are particularly vulnerable to any economic hardships. A severe illness, for example, could wipe out the fragile economic base of these older Americans. These individuals are more likely to be old and members of minority groups. Actually, this vulnerable group now includes some individuals below the poverty thresholds, since Supplemental Security Income and Medicaid eligibility do not cover all the poor.

The Distribution of Income

Another way of looking at the well-being of the elderly is to focus on the distribution of incomes across this group. In this way, it is possible to get a more sensitive view than when using only an average income level or a poverty rate. The elderly's income is widely dispersed, as shown in Table 4.3, which divides the elderly into income quintiles (fifths of the population sorted by level of income) after controlling for differences in family size over time. If income were evenly distributed, each quintile would have equal incomes. As shown here, however, the bottom fifth of all elderly households had incomes of $4,267 on average in 1984, or an amount about one-ninth the size of the average for the top 20% of all elderly families (derived from Radner, 1987).

Table 4.3 Average Income of the Elderly by Quintile, 1984.

Quintile	Average income[a]
1	$ 4,267
2	7,238
3	11,047
4	16,914
5	36,646
All elderly units	$15,238

[a]Income levels have been adjusted for differences in household size.

Source: Radner (1987).

Table 4.3 graphically illustrates the wide range of income levels associated with the elderly. Again, these findings belie the stereotype that the elderly are alike. A substantial number of older Americans continue to have very low incomes despite the enormous size of the Social Security program and increases in other income sources. And, as already noted, some have high income levels by anyone's standards.

Moreover, in recent years the pattern of income growth has increased this dispersion rather than lessened it. The benefits of rising average incomes have *not* been evenly shared across the elderly population (Moon & Sawhill, 1984). While growth between 1967 and 1979 was disproportionately greater for the lowest income groups, the opposite was true between 1979 and 1984 (see Figures 4.1 and 4.2) (Radner, 1987). While all quintiles experienced a growth in real income since 1979, the higher-income elderly groups did disproportionately better. And since the base that the lowest quintile of the elderly start from is so small, the dollar gap between those at the bottom and the top increases even more dramatically. For example, families in the lowest quintile had an increase in real income of $517 on average, as compared to a much larger $6,710 increase for elderly families in the top quintile between 1979 and 1984.

Income Differences by Demographic Group

Disparities in economic status can also be seen in groups divided by sex, race, age, and other demographic characteristics, again underscoring how differently individuals age. For example, the very old have incomes that are lower on average in each quintile of the income distribution than when all those aged 65 and over are included (Moon, 1985). And women living as

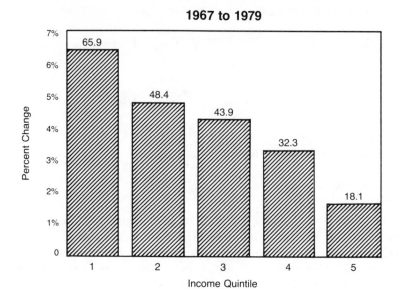

Figure 4.1. Income growth by quintile, 1967 to 1979.

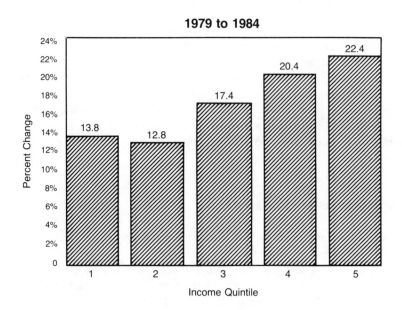

Figure 4.2. Income growth by quintile, 1979 to 1984.

unrelated individuals have incomes that are only about 71% of those of their male counterparts in each quintile. In particular, the case of older women deserves additional scrutiny.

Women

Like all older Americans, women have experienced gains in average incomes and life expectancies. Increases in women's life expectancies mean that discussions of aging—particularly as regards the very old—are also implicitly discussions of women. Between 1970 and 1982, the number of women over the age of 65 in the United States grew from 11.6 million to 16 million—a 38% increase. Moreover, the number of women aged 75 and over grew 50% during the same period. Women continue to outlive men, thus increasing as a share of the elderly population as well.

Superficially, these facts would suggest that today's and tomorrow's elderly women can look forward to both a long life and a financially secure retirement. However, for many that is not likely to be the case. Women are more likely to have incomes that place them at the lower end of the income scale than are men. The ratio of older women to older men in poverty is 2.46 to 1, as compared to the much lower 1.49 ratio of women to men overall (Moon, 1987). Poverty rates are higher for adult women of all age groups than for men, so it should not be surprising that such disadvantages carry over for older women as well. Indeed, in many ways the problems of women span the generations, suggesting that in explaining poverty and income differences, the important distinctions relate to gender, not generational, differences.

When still married, women as well as men have a much lower chance of being in poverty. But the rates are dramatically higher for unmarried women. Increasingly, researchers have focused on the special problems of widows, noting their significantly lower incomes (Morgan, 1986; Ross, Danziger, & Smolensky, 1987). Moreover, the poverty rates for unmarried women (largely widows) do not seem to increase with age (Moon, 1987). But many of these studies look only at cross-sectional evidence and may distort some of the findings.

Recent work by Burkhauser, Holden, and Myers (1986) suggests that because of the way the census asks family-composition and income questions, women widowed during the income year are asked to report only their *own* incomes, even though their husbands may have been alive and had considerable amounts of income during much of the period. Consequently, when panel data are examined, incomes tend to show a dramatic fall and then a subsequent recovery. What is not known is how much of this is a statistical aberration and how much may be a legitimate problem of income loss during the transition to widowhood. Moreover, this implies that cross-sectional comparisons—by age group, for example—may be somewhat distorted, since older widows are more likely to have been widowed for a number of years and are beyond the problem with reporting income in the first year after widowhood. Even after considering possible overstatement of poverty for this group, however, Burkhauser and associates (1986) conclude that poverty rates double when women move from being married to being widowed.

Minorities

To a large extent, gains for the elderly as a whole have not been felt by minority families and individuals. Poverty rates for elderly minorities continue to be much higher than those for whites, and the numbers of minority poor among the elderly have remained quite constant over time. In addition to the number of such persons below the poverty level, even more are near-poor. That is, if 125% of the poverty threshold is the indicator used, the number of low-income minority elderly is triple that of the official number of poor. Unlike women, whose risks of being poor change dramatically with their living arrangements, all types of minority households are likely to be poor. In a study of economic hardship, Cook and Kramek (1986) found that the black elderly are about twice as likely as the white elderly to report being unable to buy needed food and medical care and being unable to pay rent or being evicted.

Even above the poverty lines, incomes of black and Hispanic elderly persons are below that of white families. And regarding asset incomes and private pensions, the disparities are particularly great.

Across-the-board improvements such as increased Social Security benefits have not been sufficient to alleviate the problems of the minority elderly. These retirement benefits are low because of below-average wages and salaries of many minority individuals over their entire working lives. It will take many years before improvements in earnings will result in higher incomes for future retired minorities. Two recent articles on the future prospects for prosperity among the black and Hispanic elderly conclude that much remains to be done to raise earnings during the working years for these groups (Torres-Gil, 1986; Watson, 1986).

The Oldest-Old

In the last few years, increasing attention has been directed to the oldest of our citizens. Whether the cutoff is age 75, age 80, or age 85, studies have shown that incomes and resources are lower for these groups (Radner, 1987; Yeas & Grad, 1987). In addition, the oldest-old are more likely to live alone, to be frail, and to need additional supportive or medical services (see the discussion of consumption below). Also, we often lose track of these individuals when they enter institutions—dropping them from surveys that look at economic well-being. Thus we are likely to understate the size of the problem of financial well-being for these older senior citizens and for the elderly as a whole.

A recent series of articles in the *Milbank Memorial Fund Quarterly* focused exclusively on this group (see, for example, Atkins, 1985; Torrey, 1985). Torrey found that the incomes of people aged 85 and older is 36% less than the income of people aged 65–69. She was able to determine the incomes of institutionalized persons, finding that incomes of this subgroup aged 85 and over was $3,493 in 1980, or about two-thirds of the income level of all those aged 85 and over and less than half the income level of all persons aged 65 and over.

Other Contributors to Well-Being

Wealth

Another indicator of well-being for the elderly is the wealth they have accumulated over their lifetimes. On average, older individuals tend to have increasing amounts of liquid and other assets from which to draw. Many of the elderly continue to save and accumulate resources over their lifetimes, often for the purpose of protecting themselves against unexpected medical or other expenses (Mirer, 1979). Consequently, such resources should also be considered when examining economic status.

Table 4.4 displays some intriguing statistics on the asset holdings of families headed by persons of different ages. As expected, older Americans hold substantially more wealth than do young families and individuals. After age 55, many Americans have been able to accumulate savings. Home ownership rises dramatically at a much earlier age.

One of the more striking findings in this table is the difference between mean and median amount of liquid and financial assets, however. Effectively, the mean is brought up by a small number of individuals at the top of the distribution who have extremely large asset holdings. The median, which indicates what the family halfway up the distribution has in holdings, is much lower. For example, half of all families with heads aged 65–74 who have financial assets have holdings under $10,000, even though the average is $30,000. Thus for the typical elderly family, the capacity to finance extraordinary medical expenses from savings would be quite limited. From other studies, it is also known that those with higher incomes are also likely to be those with higher assets and that wealth, particularly liquid assets, is much more unevenly distributed than income (Wolff, 1987). Wealth thus exacerbates the inequality in resources among the elderly.

Table 4.4 Financial Assets and Home Ownership of Households Holding Such Assets, by Age Group.

Age of head (years)	Percent of households owning liquid assets	Liquid assets of those households holding such assets[1]		Total financial assets of households holding such assets[2]		Percent of households with home ownership	Net equity of home owner[3]	
		Mean	Median	Mean	Median		Mean	Median
Under 25	81	$ 1,970	$ 600	$ 2,650	$ 750	10	$18,870	$13,780
25–34	87	4,270	1,200	7,960	1,510	40	32,640	27,770
35–44	91	8,910	3,000	14,410	3,750	66	52,070	40,600
45–54	89	14,830	3,310	23,010	4,130	75	64,470	50,000
55–64	91	25,440	7,430	54,950	9,340	73	73,580	55,000
65–74	88	30,670	9,680	65,340	11,400	69	63,570	45,000
75 and over	76	26,480	7,890	37,060	10,350	57	47,760	40,000

[1]Liquid assets include checking accounts, savings accounts, money market accounts, certificates of deposit, IRA and Keogh accounts, and savings bonds.
[2]Financial assets include liquid assets plus stocks, other bonds, nontaxable holdings (municipal bonds and shares in certain mutal funds), and trusts.
[3]Nonfarm home owners.

Source: Council of Economic Advisors (1985).

Another interesting finding of Table 4.4 is the difference in assets between the young-old (those aged 65–74) and the old-old (families headed by someone aged 75 or older). Average and median holdings are substantially lower for the older group. Such families, who are more likely to be subject to higher medical care costs, have fewer resources to use.

Finally, home ownership among the elderly is not as widespread as often believed. The proportion of households with such assets is lower than during the prime earning years, and for the oldest families is at a level below that for those aged 35–44. Net equity in owned homes is also lower.

On balance then, while the elderly do have greater resources than other age groups, there is strong reason to be wary of characterizing all the elderly as well-off in terms of such assets. As with incomes, the wealthiest elderly families are undoubtedly in very strong economic positions, but within this age group a great deal of diversity in levels of well-being remains. Wealth holdings for middle-income families are likely to be dominated by an owned home—an asset that is often excluded when considering resources that could be used to meet routine expenses. More liquid assets are heavily concentrated among a small proportion of the elderly, and that inequality in the distribution of resources has been increasing over time, not decreasing. Another interesting time trend on wealth holdings is that the traditional relative advantage of the elderly as compared to other groups is also declining somewhat (Wolff, 1987).

Help from Relatives

Another resource that may be available to the elderly is help from other family members, usually adult children. In recent years, older persons have become more likely to live alone, but that does not mean that they have severed close ties with their families (Shanas, 1979). Indeed, in periods of illness, the elderly often receive financial or informal support from and may even move in with their children.

Measuring the value of the "insurance" that such relationships provide is difficult, however. Only a small minority of the elderly now report receiving help from relatives (CEA, 1985). But what is missed by such a measure is the *potential* for such help should the need arise. The increasing independence of the elderly from other relatives may suggest that such help could occur in circumstances where the need is extraordinary, such as for long-term maintenance care for the frail elderly.

Such aid is also likely to be very unevenly distributed across the population, reflecting the relative economic status of both the elderly and their relatives, relationships with family members, and health status (Moon, 1977). Elderly families with low incomes may not receive aid if their relatives are also poor, for example. Thus while it is difficult to ascertain how benefits would vary by income of the elderly, it is unlikely that such help could be relied on for many of the elderly with low levels of resources.

WHAT THIS WEALTH BUYS

Older Americans use their incomes to buy different combinations of goods and services than do younger families. The needs of older persons vary, particularly with regard to housing and health. Moreover, since resources also vary between the young and the old, expenditures on basic necessities loom larger for some groups than others.

General Consumption Expenditures

A recent study by Lazer and Shaw (1987) examines how older Americans spend their incomes, using the 1984 Consumer Expenditure Survey. They subdivided people into 55-to-64, 65-to-74, and 75-and-over age groupings (see Table 4.5). In actual dollars, the oldest group spent considerably less on housing than did the population as a whole or the younger elderly groups. But because incomes are also substantially lower for this group, the share of income it spends on housing (35.1%) is considerably more. Spending on health care shows a progressively higher absolute and proportional spending pattern by age. This oldest age group spends 13.6% of out-of-pocket income on health care and insurance, as compared to 4.3% health care spending across all households. Among the various categories of spending,

Table 4.5 Average Annual Expenditures of Older Households, 1984.

Expenditure category	Households headed by persons aged		
	55-64	65-74	75+
Food	$3,602	$2,714	$1,865
Housing	6,195	4,562	3,767
Apparel	1,136	657	331
Transportation	4,435	2,926	1,409
Health care	1,065	1,360	1,458
Contributions	874	681	800
Personal insurance	2,481	711	225
All Other[a]	2,475	1,427	863
Total	$22,264	$15,038	$10,718

[a]Other includes entertainment, personal care, reading, education, and miscellaneous.
Source: Lazer & Shaw (1987).

health care ranks second (behind housing) for those aged 75 and over. For ages 55–64, in contrast, spending on food, transportation, and personal insurance also exceeds health spending. The group aged 65–74 spends, in absolute dollars, nearly as much on health care and a little more on housing, but incomes are also 50% higher than for the group aged 75 and over. Finally, health-spending differences are even more dramatic if viewed on a per capita basis, since household size declines progressively with age (as household spending on health increases).

Health Care Expenditures

It should not be surprising, then, that spending on health care among the elderly has received special attention. Despite the introduction of Medicare (for those 65 and over) and Medicaid (for those with low incomes) in 1965, the percent of own income spent on health care by persons over age 65 is at an all-time historic high and projected to increase further (Varner, 1987). Indeed, this prospect is often the only consumption issue mentioned when people provide analyses of economic status for older Americans. Incomes have risen rapidly for this age group, but out-of-pocket health costs have simply risen faster.

While some analysts stress the benefits from Medicare and Medicaid to the well-being of the elderly, it is also critical to look at the remaining burdens, particularly on those with modest incomes. Analyses of the acute care portion of these expenses reveal considerable burdens on those with low or moderate incomes. Feder, Moon, and Scanlon (1987) estimate that in 1986 elderly persons with a hospital stay and incomes of less than $10,000 spent 18.3% of income, on average, out of their own pockets for acute health care services. Since this is an average, it understates the level of burden of a considerable minority of this group. Smeeding, in his study of "Tweeners" (1986), stressed the low rates of private health insurance purchased by this group, which leave them vulnerable to very high potential health care liabilities.

Expenditures on Long-Term Care

As serious as these considerations are, the costs of long-term care hold the potential for even more devastating reductions in economic status for older families. These costs are even harder to work with, however, because institutionalized individuals are generally not included in surveys that capture income or expenditures. Thus, the out-of-pocket costs of the Lazer/Shaw study cited above are unlikely to include these expenses. An individual will pay, on average, more than $22,000 for a year's stay in a nursing home (Doty, Liu, & Wiener, 1985). Medicare pays virtually nothing, and Medicaid will only cover these costs once an individual has spent down all his or her assets. Then the spouse remaining in the community will likely be impoverished as a condition of Medicaid eligibility.

Ironically, the likelihood of incurring costs from both acute and long-term health care rises steadily with age—in reverse proportion to ability to pay. Again, it is the elderly woman living alone who is most at risk of needing long-term care services (Doty et al., 1985). Moon and Smeeding (in press) are not optimistic about the ability of many of the current generation of older Americans to afford long-term care or private insurance aimed at protecting this group. And the outlook for the future is not particularly reassuring. Rivlin and Wiener (1988) suggest that only a minority of older families will ever be able to afford to protect themselves against long-term care expenditures.

TRACING THE REASONS FOR CHANGE
IN ECONOMIC WELL-BEING

Rising well-being over time has occurred for many reasons. For individuals, economic status after age 65 depends on a combination of events and choices, only some of which were truly under their own control. Across a lifetime, people make decisions about whether to invest in themselves with education and training, whether to save and invest, and, more recently, whether to have families. They are also subject to a broad range of unforeseen events that can have enormous consequences. For example, the sizes of their own cohort group and those that precede and follow them surely affect economic status. Changes in technology affect the pace of growth in our economy and the relative values of different types of goods and services and the occupations associated with producing them. The hardships imposed by illness and injury can also change dramatically the financial outcomes at retirement.

As a consequence it would be very hard to predict what the level of living of an individual will be at retirement by looking at that person at age 20 or even at age 40 or 50. Indeed, studies that have tried to predict financial success from one generation to another often find very poor correlations. That is, parents' financial success is often not a good predictor of the financial well-being of the children (see, for example, Jencks, 1972; Taubman, 1976).

It is instructive, however, to look at sources of income received by different groups for clues about where growth has come from and what the prospects are for the future of that cohort and those to come.

Sources of Income

The growth in incomes of the elderly in recent years does not stem from only one source; rather, most sources of incomes for the elderly have grown substantially. Changes that have occurred in the share of income from various sources offer insight into why the incomes of the elderly have grown so rapidly and whether such growth can be expected to continue. For example, over the last 20 years Social Security benefit increases have played a key role, although as a share of total income that role has grown little since 1975. The most dramatic growth has occurred in asset incomes, such that this source accounts for a much larger share of the elderly's income than in 1962. These and other income sources are shown in Figure 4.3, which compares income shares from various sources between 1962 and 1984 (Yeas & Grad, 1987).

The dramatic decrease in the contribution of wage and salary income has meant that the elderly enjoy considerable protection from periods of high unemployment. But it also means loss in ability to adjust income to changing needs over time.

The old fears about the ravages of inflation are not as critical as before the introduction of Social Security cost-of-living adjustments (COLAs). Indeed, Clark, Maddox, Schrimper, and Sumner (1984) go even further and argue that the elderly were not on average harmed by inflation over the period from 1969 to 1974. They found, for example, that even pensions were often subjected to ad hoc adjustments that afforded some inflation protection. But the data for this analysis ended before the high rates of inflation of the late 1970s, which did coincide with increases in poverty rates.

Since 1980, benefits of lower inflation have helped more than the high rates of unemployment have hurt this population subgroup, accounting for strong average growth across most of the sources of income. Indeed, lower rates of inflation enhance a number of sources of income for the elderly. First, because of the way that Social Security is adjusted for inflation, there is a lag in the yearly increase. That is, the cost-of-living adjustment reflects the rate of inflation over a one-year period prior to the actual adjustment date. In periods of rising inflation, the elderly usually fall a little behind in real benefit growth (such as in the late 1970s). But in a period such as the years 1980 to 1984, in which the rate of inflation abated each year, the elderly "catch up." For example, the cost-of-living adjustment in July 1980 was 14%, but inflation for that calendar year was just over 11%. Similar gains in inflation-adjusted benefits were made in succeeding years as well. In fact, these gains were large enough to more than offset the negative effects of receiving only a six-month cost-of-living adjustment in 1984 (legislated as part of the Social Security amendments of 1983). Average inflation-adjusted Social Security benefits to the elderly rose by 10% between 1980 and 1984

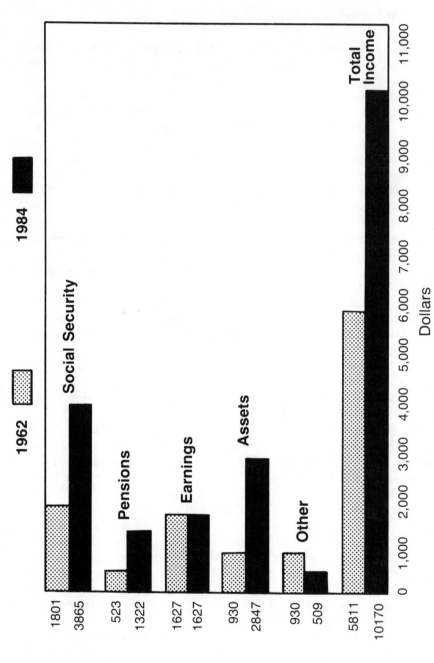

Figure 4.3. Shares of income by source, 1984.

118

(Moon, 1985). If, on the other hand, inflation rises again, benefits will lag behind the cost-of-living and the elderly will be worse off. The choice of beginning and ending dates for comparisons is thus critical.

Another income source likely benefiting from lower inflation has been private pensions, which are not automatically protected against periods of rapid price increases. Although real pension incomes showed little growth over this period, they might actually have declined if inflation had remained high. In addition, for higher-income elderly households, high inflation-adjusted interest rates in the last several years have meant rapid growth in income from assets. In fact, asset income was the fastest-rising component of income for the elderly between 1980 and 1984 (Moon & Sawhill, 1984). And Figure 4.3 demonstrates how important income from assets has been over the period from 1962 to 1984 (Yeas & Grad, 1987).

Sources of income also vary by age group within the elderly population (Yeas & Grad, 1987). For the oldest-old, Social Security and property income account for nearly four-fifths of annual incomes (see Table 4.6). Earnings, on the other hand, are much more important for the younger elderly. But since incomes steadily decline with age as well, dollar amounts of Social Security benefits to the youngest age group are nearly as large as those to the oldest age group, although they account for a much smaller share of total income. The oldest-old have lower incomes and less flexibility to adjust their incomes over time for needs such as health care expenses.

If we looked instead at source of income by level of income of families and individuals, only then would various forms of cash assistance show up

Table 4.6 Sources of Income for the Elderly by Age Group, 1982[a].

Income source	Age group			
	65–67	68–72	73–79	80+
Earnings	35%	29%	9%	4%
Asset income	18	24	30	31
Social Security	28	38	44	48
Public assistance	1	1	1	2
Pensions[b]	14	14	13	10
Other	4	4	3	5
Median income (1984 dollars)	$15,170	$13,627	$11,071	$9,853

[a]These findings are listed by "aged units," defined as either a married couple living together, at least one of whom is age 65 or older, or an individual 65 or older who does not live with a spouse. Income of other family members is excluded from the calculation.
[b]This category includes both public and private pensions.

Source: Grad (1984).

as significant over time. Supplemental Security Income (SSI) has become a less and less important contributor to well-being—in part because of the rising incomes of those aged 65 and over. But another important factor is the low participation rate in SSI by the elderly. Warlick (1982) speculated that those who had little to gain were unlikely to participate. Since state supplements under SSI have deteriorated throughout the 1980s, it is not unreasonable to assume that this may be continuing to discourage individuals from participating (Beedon & Nathan, 1988).

Life Events

Major changes in economic status also occur after individuals age—often in connection with a major life event such as widowhood, a health crisis, or retirement. We know much less about these situations, however, because so little of the data available to us follows individuals through time. A number of researchers have used panel data, particularly the Retirement History Survey (RHS), to begin to analyze the importance of these events.

Recent work by Holden, Burkhauser, and Feaster (1987) using the RHS finds that incomes remain remarkably stable over a 10-year period unless some major life event has occurred. Otherwise, incomes do not seem to erode over time. Moreover, widowhood seems to place individuals at greater risk of poverty than does retirement. Since most individuals receive a reasonable replacement of earnings from Social Security and pensions, only about 5% are at risk of falling into poverty. It is the widow who is most likely to suffer a greater risk of poverty.

On the other side of the equation, new work with the Survey of Income and Program Participation (SIPP) also demonstrates that once poor, those over 65 are more likely to remain poor than their younger counterparts for a 12-month period (Ruggles, 1987). In fact, if measured according to this "persistently poor" standard, elderly persons' poverty rate is higher than that of the population as a whole.

PROSPECTS FOR THE FUTURE

The future economic status of the elderly will depend on many unknown factors. Life expectancy, health status, age at retirement, savings behavior, the overall health of the economy, and public policy changes will all play a role. The first two of these factors, all of which are affected by source of income, are discussed in Chapter 8 of this volume and will not be considered in detail here. Many of these determinants of well-being are beyond an individual's control as well as predictive abilities. As a society, however, what happens in the public policy arena can be affected if not controlled; such control directly affects over a third of the incomes of our senior citizens and indirectly, a much larger proportion. Thus after looking at possible future trends, this chapter concludes with an analysis of the policy options that are likely to help shape the future economic status of the elderly.

Trends for the Future

If the trends of the last decade were simply taken as projections into the next, we would expect to see continued steady growth in average incomes of elderly persons, continued improvement relative to the working population, and a general trend toward somewhat lower poverty rates. In turn, we could also expect higher levels of assets and less reliance on relatives among those aged 65 and over.

Indeed, recent evidence from the 1950–1980 censuses (Ross, Danziger, & Smolensky, 1984) and from wealth surveys taken between 1962 and 1984 (Wolff, 1987) indicate that the next generation of elderly—that is, those born between 1920 and 1935, who will reach age 65 between 1985 and 2000—will be even better off than today's elders. This age group (aged 25–40 in 1960) has had the good fortune to be in their prime working years during the period of maximum earnings growth of the halcyon 1960s, to find the value of their homes soaring during the inflation of the 1970s, and to be in the maximum liquid asset position to capture most fully the high real interest rates and stock market boom of the early to middle 1980s. Individuals born in the 1930s have been dubbed the "good times" generation by demographer Carl Harter.

There are several reasons for caution in making blanket pronouncements about our ever-rising well-being, however. First, the rate of growth of Social Security benefits is likely to slow somewhat in the near future. Second, income from private pensions, which has shown rapid growth in recent years, now seems to be leveling off. Third, the changing age composition of elderly adults will also affect the extent to which incomes grow over time. If the elderly population grows more as a result of longer lifespans than because of new entrants to the 65-and-over category, income growth will tend to be slower. Finally, recent experience suggests that changes in well-being among the elderly relative to the nonelderly are sensitive to the trade-off between inflation and unemployment.

Growth by Source of Income

The rapid rate of growth in inflation-adjusted Social Security benefits through the 1970s and early 1980s was related to a dramatic increase in benefits in 1973 and to the so-called double-indexing flaw in benefit calculations that increased benefits to new retirees at an unusually rapid rate. The last group of retirees to be affected by the double-indexing flaw were born in 1916. (For about five years, beneficiaries retiring after the 1972 Social Security amendments benefited from an unintentional formula change that effectively provided them a windfall.) Some analysts have consequently argued that new awards will not continue to rise each year, as has been the case in the past. Indeed, in May 1984 new awards for men averaged *less* than those for current beneficiaries. But these statistics do not yet show a clear trend; they are also affected by such factors as the size of the cost-of-living adjustment relative to wage increases in the years just before retirement. If the growth in new awards does indeed begin to slow, however, this factor alone could have an important impact on growth in the elderly's relative economic well-being, since Social Security accounts for more than one-third of total income for persons aged 65 and over.

Private pensions have expanded rapidly in recent years, reflecting not only higher awards over time but also an expansion in the proportion of retired individuals receiving such pensions. On average, however, private pension income is still less than 10% of the elderly's total income. The growth in this latter component is expected to level off in the near future and remain an important income source for only a minority of the elderly. Further growth in coverage by private pensions is expected to move at a slower pace, since much of the growth in employment in the United States is now in the service sector, and that is an area where fringe benefits tend to be less generous on average than in manufacturing (Chen, 1985). Consequently, average income growth will not be as rapid in the future from this source of income.

Demographic Influences

For the next 10 years, growth in the proportions of persons aged 65 and over will be concentrated in the over-85 category, reflecting increased life expectancies. Individuals turning 65 will have been born in the 1920s, a period when birth rates were relatively low. And, of course, in the next decade after that, the very small Depression generation will result in even fewer new entrants to the "elderly" category. For example, between 1990 and 2000, the population between the ages of 65 and 74 will *decline* by 2.6% while the 85-and-over group will grow nearly 30% (Doty et al., 1985). Thus the very old will grow as a proportion of the elderly, and their lower average incomes are likely to help hold down overall rates of growth in income as compared to the 1970s. These oldest Americans are least likely to work, and their pension, Social Security, and other incomes are unlikely to increase markedly over time.

The State of the Economy

Finally, a return of high rates of inflation could place some strains on the elderly's economic status. Although many are protected, at least to some degree, by various types of cost-of-living adjustments (COLAs), the uncertainty created by high rates of inflation and lags in COLAs can cause hardships for some of the elderly. For example, between 1980 and 1984, an elderly individual's Social Security benefits rose about 5% in real terms (even accounting for the delay in the COLA passed in the Social Security amendments of 1983) because the lags in the adjustment process worked in their favor in a period of declining inflation. If inflation rates were again to rise steadily, the adjustment would move in an opposite direction and many elderly would experience a decline in real incomes. The impact of such declines would vary dramatically across elderly households. Those with low incomes tend to rely very heavily (if not exclusively) on income from Social Security, so any deterioration in that benefit is particularly hard on them.

The stock market crash of October 19, 1987, suggests that the long period of rising stock prices may have come to an end. A period of increased uncertainty about investing and saving may cause some of the elderly to at least *feel* worse off and place particular burdens on those in the process of retiring. If the market continues to be very uncertain over time, workers with defined contribution plans will find it difficult to make retirement decisions without placing themselves at considerable risk.

The negative effects of high rates of unemployment, on the other hand, take much longer to affect the elderly. Individuals who endure long spells of unemployment or end up in lower-paying jobs as a result of the economy will face reduced Social Security benefits when they retire. In periods of high unemployment, workers are also more likely to retire early, taking reduced benefits. Such consequences have little perceptible effect immediately on the elderly but may have very important consequences over the longer term.

Thus in the near future the status of the elderly will likely be more sensitive to whether high rates of inflation return and less sensitive to economic decline or stagnation—unless such a decline tempts Congress and the administration to reduce Social Security or Medicare benefits. The difficulty in predicting economic conditions into the future or of assessing their cumulative impacts over time suggests that it is very difficult to confidently predict the well-being of any group over time. On balance, however, some of the factors contributing to high rates of growth in average incomes for the elderly can be expected to slow in the future. This does not imply that elderly adults will be worse off than now; indeed, the overall well-being of persons aged 65 and over will likely continue to rise.

The Distribution of Income

These changes also suggest that the disparity in incomes within the 65-and-over age group is likely to worsen. The status of the oldest-old is particularly vulnerable, since these seniors depend on income sources, such as Social Security, that rise slowly (even with full cost-of-living adjustments). Historically, income from earnings and assets rises faster than the Consumer Price Index (CPI). Moreover, current public policy suggests that programs aiding those with lower incomes are unlikely to expand. Young elderly, particularly those still in the labor force, will do better than their older, poorer counterparts.

Finally, the distribution of incomes across families of all ages has become increasingly unequal since the mid-1970s (Moon, 1985). Incomes of families at the top of the income distribution have grown at a faster rate than those of lower- and moderate-income families. This pattern suggests that inequality in income of the elderly is likely to continue for the indefinite future as these individuals age. The findings of greater concentration in wealth holdings reported above also raise questions about whether this trend will continue and whether further inequality in total well-being is likely.

Another important unknown in how we view the well-being of the elderly is their status relative to other groups. Although predicting growth for the elderly is difficult in and of itself, it is even harder to predict how such growth will compare with income changes for younger working families. If the trends discussed here hold and the economy experiences relatively rapid real growth in the next decade, the status of the elderly relative to the young could again decline. More likely, however, is that the economic position of the elderly will stabilize relative to their younger counterparts. This relative status of the elderly is likely to be important in any political debates over who should pay for Medicare, since many of the potential policy alternatives involve trade-offs between burdens on the old and burdens on the young.

Overall, the outlook appears to continue to be good for the elderly, although future improvements are likely to come at a slower pace than in recent years.

Future Policy Options

Over time, the increasing diversity in the economic status of older Americans may contribute to the perception of a need for changing publicly provided income-support programs for older adults. But the elderly's dependence on public benefits varies dramatically. And since the poor are the most dependent, the differences between rich and poor among the old may become further exaggerated unless decisions about public programs are made with great care. For example, in the fall of 1987 advocates of freezes in the Social Security COLA sometimes argued that since older Americans were doing better than the young, cutbacks would not be painful. Such claims rest on the new stereotype of a uniformly affluent older population. But since Social Security constitutes a much higher share of income for lower-income individuals than for those who truly are well-to-do, the burdens would fall disproportionately on those least able to absorb the cuts.

The important challenge for policy thus will be to address this diversity in a meaningful way. Some policies have begun to do so. For example, taxation of Social Security benefits as part of the 1983 amendments represented a change aimed only at individuals with relatively high incomes from all sources. Similarly, the Tax Reform Act of 1986 offered the lowest tax relief to higher-income seniors—a group that has historically enjoyed low tax liability. Finally, the catastrophic insurance legislation passed by Congress in 1988 will charge a significant income-related premium, which will reduce substantially the overall subsidy provided to high-income beneficiaries of Social Security.

Thus some redress of preferential treatment for those with higher incomes has been occurring. A careful analysis of posttax income growth in the last half of the 1980s may result in quite a different view of the role of government benefits in the well-being of our wealthier, older citizens. We are likely to see a trend toward higher tax contributions by this group relative to government benefits received.

How might future policy changes deal with economic diversity in improved targeting of benefits? The answer to this question is not easy, particularly since there is considerable difference between what may be appealing in theory and what may work in practice. Several examples of different approaches are discussed below.

It will become increasingly appealing to subdivide the "elderly." Indeed, to some extent that has already been occurring, with new attention paid to the oldest-old. And the special needs of some groups, such as widows, may command attention. Finally, some policy makers and analysts propose a dramatic shift from a social insurance to a welfare model in public programs. Each of these possible approaches are briefly discussed below.

Changing the Concept of the Aged

It is now common parlance to subdivide individuals aged 65 and over into the young-old and the old-old, although the specific dividing line remains blurred. The justification for subdividing the elderly into two or more groups stems from specific needs and concerns of the older group. In other areas we have begun to think about raising the original age at which people are thought to be "elderly." Eligibility for full benefits for Social Security will rise from age 65 to age 67 in 2022. And the recent debate about the reauthorization of the Older Americans Act included consideration of whether the age cutoff for receiving services should be raised from 60 to 70. These new age requirements implicitly seek to reduce benefits or limit eligibility over time.

The justification for many of these new age distinctions rests largely on the increased life expectancy of older persons. But a complicating factor not always taken into account is the question of whether health status is also improving for older Americans. And here the evidence suggests that longer lives are not necessarily healthier lives (Poterba & Summers, 1985). Since that is the case, a two-year increase in life expectancy does not necessarily imply that age of retirement or eligibility for special programs ought automatically to be advanced by two years as well. Moreover, the old issue of diversity arises again here. While many individuals are in vigorous health at age 65, others are not.

What about targeting enhanced benefits to the oldest-old? Again, the question arises of whether such efforts will truly achieve their goals of providing income or other support for the most vulnerable group. On average, such individuals are not as well off as their younger counterparts. But why should age itself trigger special benefits? Cost-of-living adjustments and the savings behavior of at least the current generation of elderly suggest that individuals' incomes do not deteriorate very much over time, absent some major event, such as widowhood (Holden, Burkhauser, & Feaster, 1987). And although ill health or death of a spouse are more likely to occur at advanced age, it is the event, not the age, that is the trigger. Indeed, young widows are more likely to be in poverty than older ones. Why, then, not use some other indicator, such as marital status?

Changing Programs to Recognize Special Groups

The particular problems of some groups have been noted earlier; not all the elderly have benefited equally over time. Thus one direction that future policy changes could take would be to single out some groups for special treatment. Unmarried women (or widows) are the most likely candidates.

Efforts to improve the status of older women are likely to center on public programs, such as Social Security and Supplemental Security Income. Older women are very dependent on Social Security, and they are unlikely to be able to increase their earnings, or their asset or pension incomes, over time.

Although Social Security benefits for unmarried women in 1984 were nearly equal to those for unmarried men, this source of income may not continue to offer such full support in the future. The high incidence of divorce restricts the degree to which women's benefits are based on their spouses' incomes—which tend to be higher. Moreover, the Social Security Administration also reports that for the first time in many years, the primary insurance amount that women have earned—their basic entitlement on their own earnings records—is falling. Although the causes are not yet known, the formula for calculating benefits now uses more potential labor-force years, placing women who leave the labor force for a time at a severe disadvantage; that is, they are more likely to have "zero" years added to the calculations. Moreover, the continued low earnings of women relative to men also likely contributes to the low basic benefits.

A period of temporary benefit enhancements rights after the death of a spouse—and perhaps associated with health care costs for that spouse—might help some widows who find themselves only temporarily in need. Extension of Social Security at the couple's combined level for several months might provide some security in a transition period, for example.

For women likely to experience extended or permanent periods of poverty, changes in widows' benefits under Social Security might be considered. Similarly, young widows who are not yet eligible for Social Security may be particularly at risk. For example, SSI's basic guarantee is lower for individuals than for couples. If this policy were changed to bring all single beneficiaries up to the poverty line, a substantial number of widows could be helped. Such targeted options also have costs, however, and might only be offered over time if other benefits were reduced.

Here the choices might be very much like those provided in various earnings-sharing proposals. Unless very expensive "hold-harmless" provisions are provided that prevent anyone from losing ground, or unless benefits are phased in over a long period of time, earnings-sharing proposals often result in many losers as well as gainers under Social Security. And, ironically, some of the losers could be widows or other unmarried women (Congressional Budget Office, 1985).

Additional Income-Relating of Benefits

A third area of possible increased benefit targeting of Social Security and Medicare would increasingly make these programs subject to increased income-relating of benefits. Of course, Social Security has always had a benefit structure meant to target proportionately more benefits on those with low earnings. And, as mentioned above, many recent policy changes in these social insurance programs have extended this targeting further: for example, taxation of Social Security benefits and the new income-related premium for Medicare catastrophic insurance.

Will we move further in this direction? Those who see the payroll tax as increasing too fast and those who would like to cut further the federal budget are likely to maintain strong pressures to increase taxation of Social Security (and perhaps Medicare) benefits, change the benefit formula under Social Security, or institute further premium changes under Medicare tied to the income tax (see, for example, Peterson, 1987).

These efforts could result in a more equal distribution of incomes over time to older adults. And if the goal is to provide a basic income floor from the federal government, income-relating is a surer way of achieving goals than policy changes based on, for example, age or gender—at least *in theory.*

The downside of such arguments is the fear of erosion of support for the most popular and stable programs in the federal government. One has only to compare the status of Medicare with that of Medicaid to understand why many fear putting programs for the elderly more on a welfare footing. Both of these programs began at the same time, and both were intended to provide access to health care for particular subgroups of the population. Medicaid, however, is seriously underfunded, causing major problems in attracting physicians willing to serve patients and jeopardizing access to those who are eligible. And Medicaid is serving a more restricted group all the time; less than half the poor are even eligible (Holahan & Cohen, 1986). Certainly there are other factors to be considered here, but a welfare approach tends to be very unpopular in the United States and could dramatically change the support for Medicare and Social Security. Subtle changes in these programs, such as changing Social Security's benefit formula, for example, might be the best way to walk the line between improved targeting and eroded support.

CONCLUSIONS

The diversity in the economic status of the current generation of older Americans and the uncertainty about the rapidity of progress over time suggest that it is more important than ever to avoid unnecessary stereotypes. Viewing elderly adults as the undeserving rich rather than the deserving poor could encourage a reduction in public commitment to programs such as Social Security and Medicare. But it is the success of these programs that to a considerable degree accounts for the progress in the economic status of the elderly—particularly at the lower end of the economic scale. Erosion of these programs over time would likely turn back the clock on improvements in economic status and further exacerbate the differences between the rich and the poor among the old.

REFERENCES

Anderson, M. (1978). *Welfare.* Stanford, CA: Hoover Institution.

Atkins, G. L. (1985). The economic status of the oldest old. *Milbank Memorial Fund Quarterly/Health and Society, 63,* 395–419.

Beedon, L., & Nathan, S. (1988). SSI: State supported benefits to individuals age 65 and over living independently. Washington, DC: American Association of Retired Persons.

Bureau of the Census. (1970). *Money income and poverty status of families and persons in the U.S.: 1969* (Series P-6, 189). Washington, DC: U.S. Government Printing Office.

Bureau of the Census. (1974). *Money income and poverty status of families and persons in the U.S.: 1973* (Series P-6, 189). Washington, DC: U.S. Government Printing Office.

Bureau of the Census. (1975). *Money income and poverty status of families and persons in the U.S.: 1974* (Series P-6, 189). Washington, DC: U.S. Government Printing Office.

Bureau of the Census. (1980). *Money income and poverty status of families and persons in the U.S.: 1979* (Series P-6, 189). Washington, DC: U.S. Government Printing Office.

Bureau of the Census. (1985). *Money income and poverty status of families and persons in the U.S.: 1984* (Series P-6, 189). Washington, DC: U.S. Government Printing Office.

Bureau of the Census. (1987a). *Money income and poverty status of families and persons in the U.S.: 1986* (Series P-6, 189). Washington, DC: U.S. Government Printing Office.

Bureau of the Census. (1987b). *Money income of households, families, and persons in the United States: 1986* (Series No. 156, p. 60). Washington, DC: U.S. Government Printing Office.

Burkhauser, R. V., Holden, K. C., & Myers, D. A. (1986). Marital disruption and poverty: The role of survey procedures in artificially creating poverty. *Demography, 23,* 621–631.

Chen, Y-P. (1985). Economic status of the aging. In R. Binstock & E. Shanas (Eds.), *Handbook of aging and the social sciences* (2nd ed.) (pp. 641–665). New York: Van Nostrand Reinhold.

Clark, R., Kreps, J., & Spengler, J. (1978). Economics of aging: A survey. *Journal of Economic Literature, 16,* 919–962.

Clark, R., Maddox, G., Schrimper, R., & Sumner, D. (1984). *Inflation and the economic well-being of the elderly.* Baltimore: Johns Hopkins University Press.

Congressional Budget Office. (1985). *Report on earnings sharing implementation study.* Washington, DC: U.S. Government Printing Office.

Cook, F. L., & Kramek, L. M. (1986). Measuring economic hardship among older Americans. *The Gerontologist, 26,* 38–47.

Council of Economic Advisors (CEA). (1985). Economic status of the elderly. *Economic Report of the President.* Washington, DC: U.S. Government Printing Office.

Danziger, S., van der Gaag, J., Smolensky, E., & Taussig, M. (1984). Income transfers and the economic status of the elderly. In M. Moon (Ed.), *Economic transfers in the United States* (pp. 239–273). Chicago: University of Chicago Press.

Doty, P., Liu, K., & Wiener, J. (1985). An overview of long term care. *Health Care Financing Review, 6*, 69–78.

Feder, J., Moon, M., & Scanlon, W. (1987). Nibbling at catastrophic costs. *Health Affairs, 6*, 5–19.

Grad, S. (1984). *Income of the population 55 and over, 1980* (Social Security Administration Publication No. 13-11871). Washington, DC: U.S. Government Printing Office.

Holahan, J., & Cohen, J. (1986). *Medicaid: The trade off between cost containment and access to care.* Washington, DC: Urban Institute Press.

Holden, K. C., Burkhauser, R. V., & Feaster, D. J. (1987). The timing of falls into poverty after retirement: An event-history approach. Mimeo, University of Wisconsin.

Holden, K. C., Burkhauser, R. V., & Myers, D. A. (1986). Income transitions at older stages of life: The dynamics of poverty. *The Gerontologist, 26*, 292–297.

Jencks, C. (1972). *Inequality: A reassessment of the effect of family and schooling in America.* New York: Basic Books.

Lazer, W., & Shaw, E. (1987). How older Americans spend their money. *American Demographics, 9*, 36–41.

Mirer, T. (1979). The wealth-age relation among the aged. *American Economic Review, 69*, 435–443.

Moon, M. (1977). *The measurement of economic welfare: Its application to the aged poor.* New York: Academic Press.

Moon, M. (1985). *Poverty among elderly women and minorities.* Washington, DC: Urban Institute Discussion Paper.

Moon, M. (1987). *Economic issues facing a growing population of older women.* Washington, DC: AARP Issue Brief.

Moon, M., & Smeeding, T. (1989). *Care of tomorrow's elderly; Encouraging private initiatives and reshaping public programs.* American Enterprise Institute, University Press of America.

Moon, M., & Sawhill, I. (1984). Changes in income distribution. In J. Palmer & I. Sawhill (Eds.), *The Reagan record* (pp. 317–347). Cambridge, MA: Ballinger.

Moon, M. (1979). The incidence of poverty among the aged. *Journal of Human Resources, 14*, 211–221.

Morgan, L. A. (1986). The financial experience of widowed women: Evidence from the LRHS. *The Gerontologist, 26*, 663–668.

Peterson, P. (1987). The morning after. *The Atlantic Monthly*, pp. 43–69.

Poterba, J., & Summers, L. (1985, May). *Public policy implications of declining old-age mortality.* Paper presented to the Brookings Conference on Retirement and Aging, Washington, DC.

Quinn, J. (1987). The economic status of the elderly: Beware of the mean. *Review of Income and Wealth, 33*, 62–83.

Radner, D. (1987). Money incomes of aged and nonaged family units, 1967–84. *Social Security Bulletin, 50,* 9–28.

Rivlin, A., & Wiener, J. (1988). *Reforming long-term care: Who will pay for us when we are old and gray.* Washington, DC: The Brookings Institution.

Ross, C. M., Danziger, S., & Smolensky, E. (1987). Interpreting changes in the economic status of the elderly, 1949–1979. *Contemporary Policy Issues, 5,* 98–112.

Ruggles, P. (1987). The economic status of the low-income elderly: New evidence from the SIPP. Washington, DC: The Urban Institute.

Ruggles, P., & Cullinan, P. (1985). *The contribution of transfer payments to the incomes of the elderly.* Paper prepared for The Urban Institute, Washington, DC.

Shanas, E. (1979). Social myth as hypothesis: The case of the family relations of old people. *The Gerontologist, 19,* 3–9.

Smeeding, T. (1982). *Alternative methods for valuing in-kind transfer benefits and measuring their impact on poverty* (Technical Report No. 50, Bureau of the Census). Washington, DC: U.S. Government Printing Office.

Smeeding, T. (1986). Nonmoney income and the elderly: The case of the "tweeners." *Journal of Policy Analysis and Management, 5,* 707–724.

Smeeding, T., & Straub, L. (1986). Health care finance among the elderly: Who really pays the bills? *Journal of Health Politics, Policy and Law, 12,* 35–52.

Taubman, P. (1976). The determinants of earnings: Genetics, family and other environments. *American Economic Review, 66,* 858–870.

Torrey, B. B. (1985). Sharing increasing costs of declining income: The visible dilemma of the invisible aged. *Milbank Memorial Fund Quarterly/Health and Society, 63,* 377–394.

Torres-Gil, F. (1986). An examination of factors affecting future cohorts of elderly hispanics. *The Gerontologist, 26,* 140–146.

Varner, T. (1987). Catastrophic health care costs for older Americans. (AARP Issue Paper No. 8702). Washington, DC: American Association of Retired Persons.

Warlick, J. (1982). Participation of the aged in SSI. *Journal of Human Resources, 17,* 236–260.

Watson, W. H. (1986). Crystal ball gazing: Notes on today's middle aged blacks with implications for their aging in the 21st century. *The Gerontologist, 26,* 136–139.

Wolff, E. (1987). Estimate of household wealth inequality in the U.S., 1962–1983. *Review of Income and Wealth, 33,* 231–256.

Yeas, M., & Grad, S. (1987). Income of retirement aged persons in the United States. *Social Security Bulletin, 50,* 5–14.

CHAPTER 5

Convergence, Institutionalization, and Bifurcation: Gender and the Pension Acquisition Process

ANGELA M. O'RAND

DUKE UNIVERSITY

INTRODUCTION

Worldwide problems related to inflation, growing economic interdependence, and shifting demographic structures are requiring that social welfare policies be scrutinized and reorganized. In response to these problems, the 1970s and 1980s have witnessed much legislative and market-based redistributive activity in Western Europe and the United States, particularly in the areas of health, family maintenance, and pension provision. In all areas of social welfare, legislative and market-based strategies are reconsidering the "artificial separation between 'public' and 'private'" (Rainwater & Rein, 1983, p. 112).

The specific concern of this chapter is how the integration of public and private social welfare strategies is stratifying men's and women's lives and therefore their relative access to and acquisition of retirement income. Pension provision systems comprise the major category of welfare policy, both private and public, across societies. As such, these systems exemplify the major social arrangements that impinge on men's and women's increasingly extended adult lives and on their relative economic well-being in later life.

This is a revised version of a paper titled "Gender and the Pension Acquisition Process," presented at the National Science Foundation Invited Conference on "Life Course, Family and Work: Research and Policy," Oslo, Norway, February 8–13, 1986. The research was supported by NIH grant 2T 32 AG00029 to the Duke University Center for Aging and Human Development and NIH grant AG02136 to the author.

The examination of this process will focus on how historically contrasting welfare systems—the United States and Sweden—nevertheless yield similar gender outcomes in the pension provision system. The analysis will begin with a brief overview of the major hypotheses that have been proposed in the literature to explain the development of modern welfare states. Then, the pension acquisition system of the United States will be highlighted, especially as it contrasts and coincides with the pension entitlement systems of Sweden and other Scandinavian states. How this process interacts with the household division of labor will receive special attention. The implications and prospects of the public–private integration process will then be considered.

Convergence, Institutionalization, and Bifurcation

Titmuss (1969) provided the seminal formulation of ideal types of social welfare in modern societies. He proposed that three major categories of welfare system organization prevailed: social welfare, fiscal welfare, and occupational welfare. The first two are primarily public (or state-driven), with social welfare characterized as universalistic and fiscal welfare, as categorical. The former takes the form of collective interventions to meet the common entitlements of all individuals or citizens regardless of need (as in the example of public education), while the latter takes the form of interventions to alleviate the special needs associated with social categories (for example, particular states of dependency attached to childhood, old age, and "domestic service"). The fiscal welfare system is thus the quintessential model of the "safety-net" benefit program.

Occupational welfare, on the other hand, is private, with the allocative and distributive mechanisms embedded in the employment sector, not the state. The historical roots of this system are embedded in such contexts as the "welfare work" system of American industry (Jacoby, 1985) and the paternalistic managerial practices of Japan (Higgins, 1981). Here social insurance is a private commodity, acquired by employees through service in the workplace. And retirement benefits are earned (saved) through private personal (e.g., life insurance and bank savings) or private collective (e.g., union or company pensions and employee profit-sharing) schemes (Van Gunsteren & Rein, 1985), not allocated as universal entitlements [e.g., basic pension benefits to all who reach age 65 regardless of employment history (Forsberg, 1986)].

The worldwide integration of these public and private social welfare models in recent years is generating at least three major hypotheses regarding the developing welfare states of the West. The first proposes that a worldwide *convergence* of welfare systems is underway (Hage & Hanneman, 1980; Rainwater & Rein, 1983; van Gunsteren & Rein, 1985). According to this argument, more private- (employment-) centered systems like those of the United States and Japan have moved in recent years toward greater (though limited) public initiative and regulation in mandating welfare benefits, while more public-centered systems like those in Europe, particularly in Sweden, are undergoing "reprivatization" (Higgins, 1981; Wilensky, 1976), with a growing public encouragement via tax policies for the development of private insurance schemes. This notion of convergence, of course, departs in a significant way from traditional modernization theories of the welfare state (see especially Wilensky, 1975), which once emphasized a more linear development of these systems out of economic, technological, and demographic pressures (Pampel, 1981). The new convergence theory suggests a more episodic and nonlinear view.

The second hypothesis is that the integration of the public and the private is occurring through a process of *rationalization* that is *institutionalizing the life course* (Graebner, 1980; Mayer & Muller, 1986). Here the argument is that the modern welfare state operates primarily on *rules of temporal order*, which sequentially program the parameters of individual lives and control the succession of cohorts through the major institutional domains (family, economy, and polity). The proclivity of welfare states for establishing orderly and calculable criteria for the distribution and allocation of social roles leads to predictable patterns in the age-grading of the life course (Kohli, 1986a). During the period of economic or market participation of individual lives, the industrial enterprise also constrains individual time with industrial time constraints (Kohli, 1986b). Thus, for example, the retirement system is best conceived as a rule structure regulating the timing and duration of employment (Graebner, 1980), the temporally regulated acquisition of and eligibility for pensions (O'Rand & MacLean, 1986), and the sequential orchestration of cohort flow through the employment sector (DeViney & O'Rand, in press).

The third proposes that a *bifurcated structure* of social welfare is being sustained and reproduced among modern welfare states (Quadagno, 1987a, b, 1988). According to this argument, the linkage of public and private welfare strategies produces a structure that provides private insurance for the (political) majority and public assistance for the (political) minority, following the Pareto-optimality principle that "as some persons become better off, no one should be worse off" (Bell, 1976, p. 270). Thus the growing feminization of poverty in Western welfare states is being shaped and reproduced by the simultaneous extension of relatively more public assistance to women, on the one hand, and relatively more private insurance to men, on the other (David & Land, 1985; Pearce & McAdoo, 1981; Scott, 1984).

All three hypotheses provide a framework for examining a major outcome of developing welfare policies in the West—gender stratification in retirement. This outcome has come about as public and private programs have developed in the post-World War II period in ways that have institutionalized the life courses of men and women and reinforced their relative statuses in the private (primarily employment and household) and public (governmental program) sectors.

Life-course patterns in work and family are highly interdependent with private and government pension provision and related social welfare programs. As such, work and family role sequences have come to be *institutionalized* within the constraints of gender-based benefit status designations, such as widowhood (Achenbaum, 1986; O'Rand, 1983), and employee benefit system coverage, participation, and eligibility criteria, such as continuous service requirements (O'Rand & MacLean, 1986; Quadagno, 1987a; Schulz, 1985). Consequently, differential patterns of economic dependence (Myles, 1984), the timing of retirement (O'Rand & Henretta, 1982a), and the relative socioeconomic statuses of men and women before and after retirement (George, Fillenbaum, & Palmore, 1984; O'Rand and Landerman, 1984) are highly contingent on public- (Social Security) and labor-market-based (private and government retirement system) plan participation and benefit eligibility structures.

THE CONVERGENCE OF ACQUISITION AND ENTITLEMENT

Over the past 50 years, the employment-based public and private "occupational welfare system" in the United States (Titmuss, 1969) has developed along several dimensions to stratify gender groups over the life course and, thereby, to create (and recreate) gender-related patterns of economic dependency and risk for poverty in the older population. Specifically, the extension of gender-specific benefits in the public sector in combination with gender-related opportunities for pension acquisition in the private sector has constructed and reinforced life-course patterns among men and women that determine their relative economic well-being upon retirement.

The following analysis examines features of the pension acquisition system in the United States that differentiate men's and women's opportunities and outcomes. First, the pension acquisition system of the United States is briefly contrasted with the alternative European entitlement system, in keeping with Titmuss's more general typology (1969) of the occupational versus social welfare models. Then the labor-market and public components of the U.S. system are examined, respectively, as parallel institutions whose benefit structures have come to differentiate men's and women's retirement outcomes.

The pension acquisition system, which has been dominant in the United States, can be contrasted with what can be termed pension entitlement systems, which have dominated some other industrial societies. Table 5.1 outlines the major features of these alternative systems in ideal typical form. They must be viewed only as ideal types, since, historically, industrial societies that conform more with one type than another still often share some common features and can vary over time in their specific structures as a result of legislation as well as economic and political change. Moreover, the convergence hypothesis described earlier suggests further that modern welfare systems are becoming more rather than less alike (Hage & Hanneman, 1980; Higgins, 1981; van Gunsteren & Rein, 1985).

Comparison of the U.S. pension system with those in other industrialized countries accentuates the equity-based character of the U.S. welfare system as a whole (Graebner, 1980; Quadagno, 1988). This system tends to provide pensions more readily and systematically for selected elements of the employed population, often with pluralistic (multitiered) sources for retirement benefits from the state (e.g., Social Security), private collective units (e.g., firm and labor-union pension plans), and private personal savings mechanisms (e.g., individual IRAs, life insurance, annuities, bank savings) (see U.S. Department of Health, Education and Welfare, 1978; van Gunsteren and Rein, 1985). Retirement benefits are based on employer-worker contribution regimens in which benefits are equivalent to earnings-based contributions, following a calculus based primarily on a criterion of equity, or distributive justice. This principle, which Achenbaum (1986) argues exists in constant tension with the principle of adequacy, has firm ideological roots

Table 5.1 Ideal Types of Pension Provision in the Welfare State.

Major Features	Two ideal types	
	Acquisition	Entitlement
Organizing principle	Equivalence	Solidarity
Pension coverage	Employed	Universal
Dominant sector	Private	Public
Welfare policy structure	Occupational welfare system with fiscal welfare as safety-net system	Social welfare system
Health coverage	Employed/insured	Universal
Family allowances	Indigent	Universal
Dependence	Particularistic needs assessment	"Natural" dependence of population categories
Gender differentiation	Occupational	Patriarchal

in welfare capitalism (Quadagno, 1988). Therefore, upon retirement the pension changes from savings to income and thus replaces earnings. Earnings replacement (also referred to as income maintenance) is the operational definition of equity-based equivalence (see Table 5.1).

Pensions are typically one element of a larger welfare system covering health and family-related needs, all of whose elements stem from the employment domain where these benefits are acquired ("earned") by workers on behalf of themselves and/or their dependents or beneficiaries. Such systems were named "occupational welfare systems" by Titmuss (1969) because of the allocative role of the employment sector. However, these systems are often accompanied by what he termed "fiscal welfare systems," otherwise known as "safety-net" benefit programs, which operate according to state-developed "needs-assessment" criteria. Thus in the United States, for example, Supplemental Security Income (SSI) for the needy retired and Aid to Families with Dependent Children (AFDC) for the indigent child complement (not substitute for) work-related occupational welfare. As such, safety-net programs supplement or augment the occupational welfare system to benefit populations that fall outside the employment sectors.

Such programs arise out of what Quadagno (1967a, b) has referred to as the "bifurcated structure" of American "exceptionalism," where social insurance exists for the majority and social assistance for the poor. Yet close examination of alternative ("nonexceptional") systems reveals similar bifurcation. In the American case, the occupational sector has a dominant role in determining the primary access to retirement benefits. Populations excluded from occupational coverage become eligible for public benefits. In European social welfare systems, the public sector provides baseline universal support for all citizens, which is then augmented by occupational-sector benefits drawn from employment careers (Pampel & Park, 1986). The result is similar, with general inequality in retirement incomes based ultimately on employment histories—the exception being that broader-based social welfare, covering health, housing, and related family maintenance costs in addition to income support, diminishes the relative risk for poverty when compared with the American case (Heidenheimer, Hector, & Adams, 1983; Higgins, 1981; O'Rand, 1984; Pearce, 1978; Wilson, 1979).

The alternative form of welfare system is not anchored in the private sector and, thus, is not restricted to the employed population (see Table 5.1). Instead, *entitlement systems* are based on a solidarity principle—as opposed to equity-based equivalence—that endorses initially the right to universal coverage for all citizens, without particularistic needs-assessments required (van Gunsteren & Rein, 1985). Great Britain and the Scandinavian countries (particularly Sweden) most closely approach this form. Benefits such as "flat rates," *Volkpensions*, and "transition allowances" are manifestations of this type. Thus in Sweden every citizen's entitlement to a basic pension at age 65, without requisite earnings records or means tests, stands in stark contrast to private pension benefits and Supplemental Security Income (SSI) in the United States.

Moreover, national supplemental pension schemes in Sweden, which are based on pensionable (earned) income (called ATP schemes), are characterized largely by *employer contributions only* toward pension savings (Forsberg, 1986). In the United States, employee contributions typically match employer contributions, following different formulas for private defined-contribution and defined-benefit plans as well as for Social Security, with few exceptions (Schulz, 1985). The basic pension in Sweden serves as a "benefit floor" for the national supplemental pension (ATP), which is based on earnings records; as such, the latter scheme is equivalent to U.S. Social Security without employee contribution criteria. Yet minimum tenure (years of continuous service) requirements for the attainment of full earnings-related benefits mirror private-sector service requirements in the American case. All in all, social welfare strategies increase opportunities for maintaining lifetime income levels, yet inequalities are similarly produced by participation in market employment over the life course.

Publicly organized social welfare in these countries is further characterized by more universal access to health and family benefits (Day, 1978; Forsberg, 1986; Heidenheimer et al., 1983; Pampel & Weiss, 1983). Entitlement systems are not as likely to view health, old-age, and child care as private privileges and responsibilities; instead, they tend to see them as "natural dependencies" (Titmuss, 1969) to be provided for collectively and universally. Accordingly, the risks for poverty by such naturally dependent or vulnerable groups are minimized. Comparisons of Sweden with the United States and other European countries reveal that its retirement, health, and family benefits system produces average income levels that place its population, including women across all age groups, well above poverty thresholds (Nordic Statistical Secretariat, 1981; Valocchi, 1986).

The relative heterogeneity of the older population across these two systems needs further study. However, one might expect, following the conceptual scheme outlined in Table 5.1, that gender differences, for example, are mediated by different factors. In the acquisition system, divergent occupational and earnings histories among the employed population (men and women alike) are primary factors in retirement and opportunity, with family roles differentiating men's and women's work patterns. Labor-force participation, occupational segregation, and labor-market organization all strongly regulate pension acquisition (O'Rand, 1986).

Alternatively, differences between gender categories in entitlement systems are more likely to be based strictly on what can be termed "patriarchal" criteria, that is, on state-determined social definitions of gender-specific rights. Instances of this pattern might include differential entitlement statuses for (1) male heads of households and wives, (2) widows and widowers, or (3) divorced women and divorced men.

Yet even in the United States, where occupational criteria are primary factors in the pension acquisition process, patriarchal criteria have been issues in both the private employment sector (with respect to sex-segregated mortality tables defining contribution/benefit levels and to "joint/survivor options" in pension planning) and the public sector [where the rights of divorced spouses to each other's Social Security benefits were redefined in the 1983 amendments to the Social Security Act (Boaz, 1987; U.S. Senate, 1986)].

In Sweden, the provision of income-based pension supplements (ATP) integrates the occupational with the patriarchal by increasing male workers' access to greater pension incomes. Moreover, the recent introduction of private supplemental pension schemes (ITP/STP) brings with it greater gender stratification. Table 5.2 reports average public and private pension benefits for men and women aged 65 and over in Sweden in 1982 (from Statistics Sweden, 1985, p. 47). Here the pattern of gender stratification is clear. Women are relatively more dependent on the public basic pension and ATP schemes, whereas men are three times more likely to have access to work-based forms of pension savings (ITP/STP). The integration of the public and the private yields a bifurcated structure, with women in the lower-benefit public system and with men having greater access to the higher-benefit private system.

In sum, the pension provision system of the United States is organized primarily around the employment system. Thus the opportunity structure

Table 5.2 Average Pension Benefit by Type of Pension in Sweden in 1982 for Women and Men 65 and Older (in SEK, Swedish kronor).

Type of pension	Women ($N = 790,100$)		Men ($N = 599,400$)	
	SEK	%	SEK	%
Basic pension only	24,100	42	24,700	10
Basic pension + ATP*	28,300	29	37,600	39
Basic pension + ATP + ITP/STP*	41,000	10	59,700	33
Basic pension + ATP + civil service pension	48,600	11	67,100	13
Basic pension + ATP + local government pension	42,900	8	62,400	5
Total	31,300	100	48,700	100

*ATP = national pension scheme.
ITP/STP = supplemental pension schemes derived from private sector.
Source: Statistics Sweden (1985, p. 47).

for retirement produces heterogeneity primarily on the basis of the occupational and earnings histories of men and women and their respective relations of dependence on each other based on separate work and family roles.
Yet even in the greater entitlement system of Sweden, retirement income is
based on the integration of public and private (employment) systems. As
such, gender stratification follows the same form there, though the rate of
poverty is lower. Accordingly, private and public pension benefit systems
are inextricably intertwined in the designation of benefit opportunities and
benefit rights and in the regulation of family- and work-role sequences
during adulthood.

Bifurcation and Institutionalization
in the Occupational Pension Structure
of the United States

Employee pensions are unequally available to workers in the United States;
whereas Social Security covers above 95% of the workforce, only 55% of the
workforce at any one time over the past 20 years have been covered by a
pension (Schulz, 1985). Pension coverage rates vary considerably across
industries (O'Rand, 1985a, b; O'Rand & Henretta, 1982a), across (and
within) firms in the same industries (O'Rand & MacLean, 1986), and across
occupational markets (O'Rand, 1986). These structural constraints are particularly problematic in the U.S. context, where pension acquisition is tied
to work history and market location. As employer- or union-provided work
benefits, private pensions and other employee benefits are rewards for
attachment to the workplace that are not universally available to all
workers. As such, they are structural factors that differentiate the opportunity structure for retirement saving among workers and that shape the
worklives or careers of workers who find such benefits, when they are
available, to be incentives for long-term job attachment (O'Rand, 1986;
O'Rand & MacLean, 1986).

Along these lines, the pension acquisition process is best conceptualized
as a narrowing opportunity structure for retirement saving by workers.
Figure 5.1 portrays this opportunity (or risk) structure as a punctuated
selection sequence. The selection sequence consists of successive employment events, that is, work in a firm providing pension *coverage* followed by
participation in the pension plan according to temporal rules of eligibility
(age) and service (tenure) until *vesting* (eligibility for a benefit) is achieved
and final *benefit receipt* occurs at "normal" retirement age. This event- and
time-graded process (Featherman & Lerner, 1985) nonrandomly allocates
individuals from the general population, beginning with worker status and
ending with final pension benefit receipt.

At successive phases of this population process, segments of the working population are at risk for exclusion as a result of life-course (chiefly family), firm-related, industrial, and social policy factors. Worker/nonworker status (level I in Figure 5.1) systematically selects from the population. Women are two-thirds as likely as men to be working at any one time in the United States. Similarly, black men, men and women over age 65, and selected regional and migrant categories are less likely to be working as a result of structural unemployment, temporary economic setbacks, inadequate education or training, personal factors, or discrimination in employment.

Among the working population, selection into a pension-covered job (level II in Figure 5.1) is also nonrandom. About half of all workers at any one time have employers (or unions) who provide coverage, and then always for full-time workers only (Beller, 1981; O'Rand & MacLean, 1986). The likelihood of pension coverage in a job is increased by location in the public (governmental) and core private (monopoly) sectors (O'Rand & Henretta, 1982a), large firm size (O'Rand, 1986; Schulz, Leavitt, & Kelley, 1979), and unionization (or professionalization) (O'Rand, 1986; Slavick, 1966).

Not all workers in firms with pension coverage participate in these plans (level III in Figure 5.1); nor do all participants eventually meet final participation (age and continuous service), or vesting, criteria (level IV in Figure 5.1). Chief among the factors that exclude workers from participation is part-time work status, which by plan-participation criteria is excluded. Other participation criteria also may discourage participation, especially if worker contributions to plans are required.

Plans vary considerably in their rule structures and participation criteria (O'Rand & MacLean, 1986; Slavick, 1966). These rules typically define age, or service, or some combination of both criteria to establish eligibility for participation, final receipt of benefits, levels of partial and full benefits tied to vesting schedules, and retirement timing. And while legislation during the past decade has sought to standardize these criteria by limiting age and service requirements to minimum standards, variations persist across firms and even within firms that offer different plans to different subgroups of workers (O'Rand & MacLean, 1986).

Gender is another important factor in plan participation (O'Rand, 1985a). Women are less likely to be participating in a pension plan, even after the effects of selection into plan coverage and part-time work are taken in account. Similarly, women who are participating have not, on average, participated as long (measured in years) as men in pension plans. The pension plan-participation phase of the acquisition process is perhaps the most rule-regulated, yet the most variable, structure across firms (O'Rand & MacLean, 1986; Slavick, 1966). Age, continuous service, and employee contribution criteria are so variable as to defy easy description. In this labyrinth of rules, women are particularly disadvantaged.

Figure 5.1. Analysis sequence for patterns of pension acquisition.

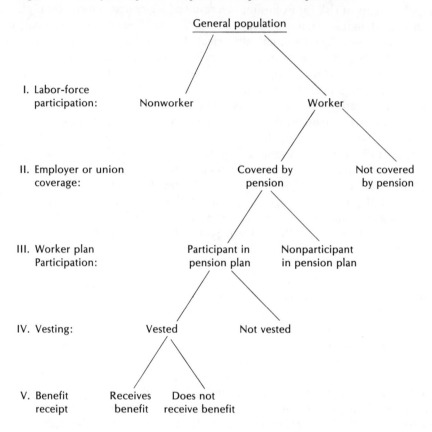

Figures 5.2 and 5.3 display predicted average years of pension participation by age in the U.S. working population in 1979. The data come from the *Current Population Survey* in May of that year, when a special supplement on pension coverage and participation was added to the survey (U.S. Bureau of the Census, 1982). The graphs are plotted polynomial regressions that predict (logged) average years of pension participation by age (with its linear, quadratic, and cubic components included to capture nonlinear properties of these distributions) *and* by the hazard for noncoverage. The hazard variable is a predicted probability of noncoverage by a pension that serves to control for sample selection bias (Berk, 1983; Heckman, 1980). Since nearly half of the sample of workers is lost when only covered workers can be examined for their participation patterns, a selection on the dependent variable is likely. The hazard variable is predicted from a set of variables defining worker characteristics and firm and sectoral locations

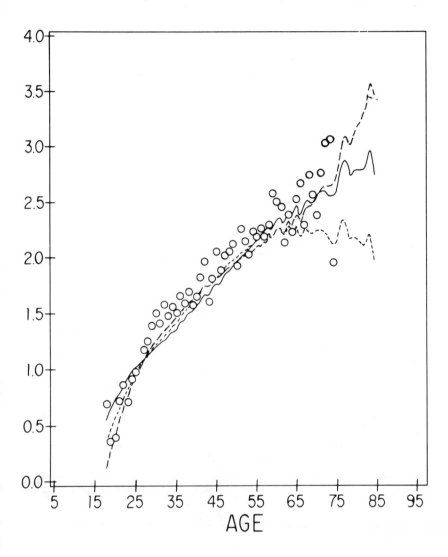

Figure 5.2. Predicted average logged years participation in current pension with linear, quadratic, and cubic components of polynomial for women workers in U.S. by age in 1979. *Solid line*: linear; *short dashed line*: quadratic; *longer dashed line*: cubic; *open circles*: age-mean.

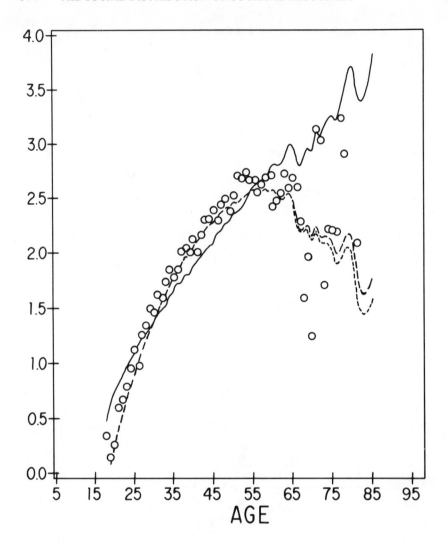

Figure 5.3. Predicted average logged years participation in current pension with linear, quadratic, and cubic components of polynomial for men workers in U.S. by age in 1979. *Solid line*: linear; *short dashed line*: quadratic; *longer dashed line*: cubic; *open circles*: age-mean.

that influence the likelihood of pension coverage. The variables predicting the hazard are listed in the footnote to Table 5.3, and the equations that generated Figures 5.2 and 5.3 are reported in Table 5.3.

In 1979, about 55% of the workforce was in pension-covered employment, but only 38% was participating in a pension plan. The rates of plan participation for men and women were 44% and 30%, respectively. Examination of Figures 5.2 and 5.3 shows that women, on average, have fewer years of pension participation when compared with men across age. Also, the rate of increase in average years of participation by age is higher for men, particularly after the age of 30, when the two sets of curves diverge significantly.

Another notable difference between the two patterns is the curvilinearity after age 55. Men's years of pension participation level off between ages 45 and 55, then drop somewhat dramatically—probably as early retirement occurs in this group and as "first" pensions have become vested in and "second" pensions are still maturing (O'Rand, 1985a). Women, on the other hand, do not demonstrate the same level of drop-off, though a significant quadratic component of the distribution exists (refer to Table 5.3 for polynomial tests). It is more likely that successive age groups of women are participating in "first" pensions and, on average, have to "catch up" in the vesting schedule at later ages, thus limiting early retirement patterns. It is

Table 5.3 Weighted Polynomial Regression of Average Years Pension Participation on Age Controlling for Sample Selection Bias among Working Women and Men in 1979.

	Power polynominal regression coefficients						
Equations	Intercept +	Hazard^a +	Age +	Age^2 +	Age^3	R^2	p
Women ($N = 3417$)							
Linear	.406	−.994	.038			.285	<.0001
Quadratic	−.389	−.962	.079	−.001		.291	<.0001
Cubic	−2.146	−.968	.217	−.004	.000	.294	<.0001
Men ($N = 6358$)							
Linear	.315	−1.312	.047			.370	<.0001
Quadratic	−1.887	−1.214	.160	−.001		.407	<.0001
Cubic	−2.118	−1.213	.178	−.002*	.000**	.407	<.0001

^{a}The hazard variable is the predicted probability of *noncoverage* by a pension estimated on the total CPS sample ($N = 26044$) using the following variables as predictors: age, age 65 or more, race, gender, number of children under 18 living in household, government worker, core private sector worker, unionized, part-time worker, and firm size. The hazard variable controls for sample selection bias in the analysis of pension participation patterns of covered workers.
Note: All coefficients are significant at p <.001 except for *p <.01 and **p is not significant.

also highly likely that cohort effects are operating in a way that favors younger cohorts of women—between ages 25 and 55—in their access to pension coverage and in their more sustained work histories.

Pension coverage opportunities and work histories are highly associated with these participation rates. Table 5.4 summarizes these associations by describing average coverage, participation, and job attachment rates across age groupings. Men are more likely than women to be working in jobs with pension coverage during the middle years (ages 31–44, 45–54, and 55–64), to have participated longer in a pension plan, and to have been working longer for the same employer.

We probably know least of all what factors affect final vesting in private pensions (level IV of Figure 5.1), especially after holding constant the risk for noncoverage. Since vesting is defined by tenure or service criteria within the firm (or to a plan that is portable across firms) (O'Rand & MacLean, 1986), interdependent job attachment and pension participation patterns are directly influential.

Public policy has addressed the protection of workers' vested claims to pensions in which they have participated and has sought to regulate the fiduciary bases of pension funds, especially in the private sector. While the Employee Retirement Income Security Act (ERISA) of 1974 sought to standardize vesting schedules and tenure requirements, considerable variation across plans continues. ERISA worked to eliminate exceedingly long-

Table 5.4 Pension Coverage, Plan Participation, and Job Attachment Levels of Five Age Groups of Women and Men Workers in 1979.

	Women					
	18–30 (4,373)	31–44 (3,334)	45–54 (1,738)	54–64 (1,310)	65+ (316)	Total (11,071)
% Covered by employer	.52	.55	.57	.52	.24	.53
% Participating in plan[a]	.22	.36	.42	.41	.14	.32
Mean years participation[b]	3.78	6.86	10.80	13.38	16.80	7.96
Mean years with employer[b]	3.34	6.26	9.89	12.64	12.43	7.05
	Men					
	18–30 (5,261)	31–44 (4,682)	45–54 (2,574)	55–64 (1,952)	65+ (504)	Total (14,973)
% Covered by employer	.52	.64	.62	.58	.25	.57
% Participating in plan[a]	.29	.53	.54	.50	.13	.44
Mean years participation[b]	3.93	8.92	16.02	17.43	15.76	10.60
Mean years with employer[b]	3.70	8.61	15.02	17.58	14.96	9.74

[a]Percentage based on all workers, not only on pension-covered workers.
[b]Average based only on workers participating in pension plans.

term (25 years or more) vesting schedules and rigid, often excessive, requirements for "continuous" service that discriminated against workers whose service was interrupted by layoffs or such personal needs as childbirth (Treynor, Regan, & Priest, 1976). Both these obstacles had hampered successful vesting for workers with more discontinuous careers and low-status jobs. Women have benefited particularly by this legislation.

Still, despite this legislation and despite the fact that over half of the labor force has been in pension-covered employment on an annual basis over the past decade, only 40% of men and 20% of women have actually retired since 1980 with private or government (non–Social Security) pension benefits (Beller, 1981; Root, 1985). This has left women overwhelmingly dependent on Social Security, considered a safety-net income transfer program. U.S. women's pattern of relative dependence on Social Security alone mirrors almost exactly Swedish women's dependence on the basic pension (see Table 5.2). U.S. women are four times more likely than men to be exclusively dependent on Social Security (U.S. Senate, 1986). U.S. women over age 65 are also at a 70% higher risk of poverty after retirement when compared with men in the same age group (O'Rand, 1984; U.S. Senate, 1986), a pattern less observable in European social welfare states, which offer support for health, housing, and other needs of older populations besides minimum income (Heidenheimer et al., 1983; Nordic Statistical Secretariat, 1981; Valocchi, 1986).

All in all, access to pension savings structures is the primary route to income maintenance in retirement, the primary focus of the U.S. welfare system. These structures operate both as rewards for sustained commitments to firms and pension plans and as incentives to remain with particular jobs in order to achieve vested status in a pension plan (O'Rand, 1985a, b). As such, pensions—like earnings—are important labor-market factors that differentiate the labor force across age groups and stratify the older population into income groups. They serve both to compensate labor attachment patterns and to encourage their maintenance. They produce heterogeneity in the work and retirement populations, particularly of the sort that places women at a distinct disadvantage for participating in and eventually receiving their own "earned" benefits.

The Public Extension of Gender-Specific Benefits and the Institutionalization of the Life Course

The equity-based pension acquisition system of the United States thus presents women with a sequence of increasing risks for dependency or poverty in old age, particularly with respect to the acquisition of their own benefits. Paradoxically, the Social Security system both corrects and exacerbates this outcome. On the one hand, one can summarize the history of the Social Security old-age insurance system as the history of the growth of women's benefits. The "pragmatic incrementalism" (Achenbaum, 1986) of the public retirement system has included a succession of (categorical) benefit extensions to women relatively more than to men. Beginning with the 1939 amendments to the original Social Security Act of 1935, which introduced survivors' benefits, a half-century of providing for women's dependent economic status can be chronicled in successive amendments to the act. Spousal benefits were introduced, steadily increased, and progressively made more widely available for a decade and a half after World War II; the amendments of 1946, 1957, 1958, and 1960 all expanded spousal benefits by "technically adjusting" their levels, conditions, and timing. And during this period, *spouse* was synonymous with *wife* (Achenbaum, 1980).

The 1960s were highlighted by the initiation and implementation of health (Medicare) benefits. The 1972 amendments to the Social Security Act further benefited women in at least three ways: (1) the eligibility age for widow's benefits was pulled back to age 60, permitting early retirement for some women (O'Rand & Henretta, 1982a); (2) benefits were indexed to cost-of-living increases (a policy implemented in Sweden 20 years earlier); and (3) Supplemental Security Income (SSI), a safety-net program for the indigent elderly, was enacted. All three changes improved women's benefit status. The widow's benefit change accelerated some women's access to their deceased husbands' benefits earlier than their husbands could have received them as retirees. The CPI indexing adjusted fixed benefits to changing living costs, which at minimum prevented lower-benefit recipients from slipping further into economic dependence. Indeed, this benefit adjustment, in conjunction with the implementation of SSI, is hailed as primarily responsible for having lowered the poverty rate among the elderly, including older women, by 1980 (Achenbaum, 1986).

Finally, the 1983 amendments capped more than 40 years of the extension of women's benefits by making divorced spouses eligible for 50% of their previous spouses' benefits if the marriage had lasted at least 10 years— legislation specifically focused on women's vulnerability after divorce as "displaced homemakers."

Thus women's disadvantage as workers in the private pension acquisition process has been offset in many ways by their "protection" as spouses and homemakers. However, the other outcome of these gender-specific extensions has been to reaffirm and reinforce women's dependent status in retirement. In these ways, gender roles across adulthood have been shaped and constrained by the occupational welfare system. The temporal ordering of public status sequences (e.g., from spouse to eligible divorced beneficiary) and the catgorical extension of rights to dependent benefits (e.g., access to widow's benefits earlier than normal retirement age) have contributed to the gender-related institutionalization of the life course.

Household Roles and the Pension Acquisition System

The institutionalization of the life course is influenced not only by employment- and government-related welfare structures. It is actually the product of the interaction between these structures and traditional household (family) arrangements, which are gender-based (England & Parkas, 1985). Childbearing/rearing roles particularly constrain women's labor-market attachments (Fuchs, 1986) and, consequently, their pension participation patterns (O'Rand, 1985a). And though these gender-based roles are reinforced and constrained by policy structures, they have independent effects on cohort patterns of pension acquisition.

Childbearing, for example, has persistent net effects on the timing of retirement among women; each child increases the chance of later rather than earlier retirement among those women who ever work (O'Rand & Henretta, 1982a). Number of children has no effect on men's retirement schedules. Childbearing also influences the dollar amounts of both Social Security and private and government pension benefits that women acquire as workers, with dollar amounts from private pension sources decreasing relatively more with each child than those from Social Security (O'Rand & Landerman, 1984). Men's benefit amounts are not influenced by number of children.

Childbearing also affects retirement patterns indirectly, through its influences on work history. First, the midlife work attachment patterns of both wives and unmarried women on the threshold of retirement are influenced by children (O'Rand & Henretta, 1982b). Women with fewer children are more likely in the 15 years before retirement age to exhibit continuous work histories rather than interrupted or nonwork ones. Similarly, number of children predicts entry patterns into the full-time labor force among women; midlife career entry (first full-time job after age 35), for example, is strongly influenced by childbearing (O'Rand & Henretta, 1982a). And though the long-term trend during this century is toward early entry and sustained lifetime work attachment among women (Masnick & Bane, 1980), delayed patterns of career entry have not disappeared.

Both interrupted and delayed work history patterns, along with other limited work history patterns, directly constrain the pension acquisition process by (1) selecting women into jobs without pension coverage, that is, part-time jobs or work in retail and service sector firms without pension programs, (2) slowing their progress toward pension vesting, and (3) depressing their earnings levels and, consequently, their pension benefit levels after retirement. Here we find the consequential *intersection of occupational role structures and the household division of labor* that shapes ultimate retirement outcomes. Accordingly, family roles act in conjunction with pension structures (both public and private) to determine the sources and levels of retirement dollars that provide opportunities for early retirement.

Finally, late-life family transitions, as well as earlier childbearing patterns, affect retirement timing. The transition to widowhood among older women can either accelerate or delay their retirement. The primary source of this variation is economic status. Widows who become entitled to their husbands' benefits from public sources, such as Social Security, and from retirement savings in private pensions and other assets—both of which usually exceed their own earnings-related retirement benefits—have the option of early retirement (O'Rand & Henretta, 1982a). However, the loss (or impending loss) of a spouse can also propel women back into the labor force or result in their remaining there after the normal retirement age (O'Rand, 1984). In short, family-related life-course transitions interact with economic status to predict retirement patterns.

CONCLUSIONS

Worldwide patterns of convergence, institutionalization, and bifurcation in welfare structures are stratifying men's and women's lives in old age. Women's retirement statuses across varying forms of welfare states are remarkably similar. Women move, paradoxically, from relatively greater economic dependence on the private household system and its division of labor in early life to relatively greater dependence on public programs in later life. Such a pattern, resulting from the integration of public and private employment and retirement systems, exists across societies. And though change appears to be a constant feature of all welfare states, persistent gender differences suggest a special dynamic worthy of our attention.

The traditional social welfare systems of Western Europe have provided a higher "floor" of support, based on a principle of entitlement, that, on average, diminishes the risk for poverty among vulnerable populations, especially older women. Higher benefits in the form of transfer payments, health and housing benefits, and other family entitlements insulate older women from the potential shocks of retirement. However, the higher floor is attached to a bifurcated structure of lifetime opportunities and benefits that is isomorphic with that in the United States.

The organization of pension provision systems provides an important context for the study of family, work, and the life course. Retirement is the last major status transition in the life course. It is conditioned by lifetime patterns of family and work that are themselves regulated by social policies related to employment, health and family care, and retirement savings. The comparative study of the life course within these different systems is an important part of the agenda before us.

The U.S. pension provision system is a complex, interdependent system of public (Social Security) and private pension acquisition rule structures that have come not only to institutionalize the timing of retirement, but also to shape the adult life courses of men and women long before retirement age is reached. Pensions are not only deferred lifetime rewards for work; they are also employer- and state-provided incentive structures whose age and service rules systematically and cumulatively differentiate gender-related opportunities. The private pension opportunity structure can be conceived as a sequence of risks for workers with cumulative effects on final retirement outcomes. Pension rule structures pertaining to participation and eligibility act as age- and time-graded subsystems embedded within the event-graded pension acquisition sequence of the worker's career.

The public (Social Security) system, on the other hand, is more universally available to all workers and to nonworkers. Its impact on men's and women's lives is nevertheless paradoxical. It compensates for women's limited access to private pension acquisition; but in the process of extending largely gender-specific Social Security benefit entitlements to women and disadvantaged groups, it has contributed to the institutionalization of women's economically dependent status in old age.

A chief outcome of the constraints of pension acquisition systems on human lives is gender-related heterogeneity in retirement well-being. Women are at higher risk for declines in economic well-being in retirement than men, particularly for poverty. Policies directed at correcting the private-sector practices hold the greatest promise for redressing inequities in the U.S. pension acquisition system. Beginning with the Employee Retirement Income Security Act (ERISA) of 1974, a decade of private pension reform has attempted to reduce some of the hazards of the pension acquisition process. ERISA set boundaries on age and service criteria that had systematically worked to women's disadvantage. The Tax Equity and Fiscal Responsibility Act of 1982 (TEFRA) was enacted to correct for discriminatory benefit payment structures in firms and to decrease the risks faced by workers in small firms, which, as a group, are less likely to provide or to be fiscally capable of maintaining equitable pension systems. Finally, the Retirement Equity Act (1984) has further adjusted age, survivor, and divorced benefit rules in private plans to eliminate even more factors discriminating against women as benefit recipients: the age of 21 has been set as the minimum for pension plan participation; survivors' benefits in the private sector have received more protection than in the past; and divorce rules based on equal-share principles like thos embedded in the 1983 amendments to the Social Security Act have been extended to men and women alike.

The general thrust of recent legislative activity in the United States is toward greater integration of public- and private-sector arrangements for the welfare of older populations in ways that compensate for the asymmetrical effects of an occupationally anchored bifurcation of retirement income sources. To the extent that European social welfare systems are being rearranged to augment the role of private-sector programs, while continuing to maintain public-sector programs as entitlements, a worldwide convergence of welfare systems may indeed continue—and may move toward a more equitable treatment of men and women in old age.

REFERENCES

Achenbaum, W. A. (1986). *Social Security: Visions and revisions.* Cambridge, England: Cambridge University Press.

Bell, D. (1976). *The cultural contradictions of capitalism.* New York: Basic Books.

Beller, D. (1981). Coverage patterns of fulltime employees under private retirement plans. *Social Security Bulletin, 44,* 3–11.

Berk, R. A. (1983). An introduction to sample selection bias. *Social Science Research, 11,* 301–340.

Boaz, R. F. (1987). The 1983 amendments to the Social Security Act: Will they delay retirement? A summary of the evidence. *The Gerontologist, 27,* 151–155.

David, M., & Land, H. (1985). Sex and social policy. In H. Glennerster (Ed.), *The future of the welfare state: Remaking social policy* (pp. 138–156). London: Heinemann.

Day, L. H. (1978). Government pensions for the aged in 19 industrialized countries: Demonstration of a method for cross-national evaluation. *Comparative Studies in Sociology, 1,* 217–234.

DeViney, S., & O'Rand, A. M. (in press). Gender-cohort succession and retirement among older men and women, 1951–1984. *Sociological Quarterly.*

England, P., & Farkas, G. (1985). *Households, employment and gender.* New York: Aldine.

Featherman, D. L., & Lerner, R. M. (1985). Ontogenesis and sociogenesis: Problematics for theory and research about development and socialization across the lifespan. *American Sociological Review, 50,* 659–676.

Forsberg, M. (1986). *The evolution of social welfare policy in Sweden.* Stockholm: The Swedish Institute.

Fuchs, V. R. (1986). Sex differences in economic well-being. *Science, 232,* 459–464.

George, L. K., Fillenbaum, G., & Palmore, E. (1984). Sex differences in the antecedents and consequences of retirement. *Journal of Gerontology, 39,* 364–371.

Graebner, W. (1980). *A history of retirement.* New York: Yale University Press.

Hage, J., & Hanneman, R. A. (1980). The growth of the welfare state in Britain, France, Germany and Italy: A comparison of three paradigms. *Comparative Social Research, 3,* 45-70.

Heckman, J. (1980). Sample selection bias as a specification error with an application to the estimation of labor supply functions. In S. P. Smith (Ed.), *Female labor supply: Theory and estimation* (pp. 206-248). Princeton, NJ: Princeton University Press.

Heidenheimer, A., Heclo, H., & Adams, J. (1983). *Comparative public policy: The politics of social choice in Europe and America.* New York: St. Martin's.

Higgins, J. (1981). *States of welfare: A comparative analysis of social policy.* New York: St. Martin's.

Jacoby, S. (1985). *Employing bureaucracy: Managers, unions and the transformation of work, 1900-1945.* New York: Columbia University Press.

Kohli, M. (1986a). The world we forgot: A historical review of the life course. In V. W. Marshall (Ed.), *Later life: The social psychology of aging* (pp. 271-303). Beverly Hills: Sage.

Kohli, M. (1986b). Social organizaton and subjective construction of the life course. In A. B. Sorensen, F. E. Weinert, & L. R. Sherrod (Eds.), *Human development and the life course: Multidisciplinary perspectives* (pp. 271-292). Hillsdale, NJ: Erlbaum.

Masnick, G., & Bane, M. J. (1980). *The nation's families: 1960-1990.* Cambridge, MA: Joint Center for Urban Studies of MIT and Harvard University.

Mayer, K. U., & Muller, W. (1986). The state and the structure of the life course. In A. B. Sorenson, F. E. Weinert, & L. R. Sherrod (Eds.), *Human development and the life course: Multidisciplinary perspectives* (pp. 217-246). Hillsdale, NJ: Erlbaum.

Myles, J. (1984). *Old age in the welfare state.* Boston: Little Brown.

Nordic Statistical Secretariat. (1981). *Social security in Nordic countries.* Stockholm: Author.

O'Rand, A. M. (1983). Loss of work role and subjective health assessment in later life among men and unmarried women. *Research in the Sociology of Education and Socialization, 5,* 265-286.

O'Rand, A. M. (1984). Women. In E. Palmore (Ed.), *Handbook on the aged in the U.S.* (pp. 125-142). Homewood, IL: Greenwood.

O'Rand, A. M. (1985a, August). *Age, job attachment and pension acquisition among women and men.* Paper presented at the annual meeting of the American Sociological Association, Washington, DC.

O'Rand, A. M. (1985b). The hidden payroll: Employee benefits and the structure of workplace inequality. *Sociological Forum, 1,* 657-683.

O'Rand, A. M., & Henretta, J. C. (1982a). Delayed career entry, industrial pension structure and retirement in a cohort of unmarried women. *American Sociological Review, 47,* 365-373.

O'Rand, A. M., & Henretta, J. C. (1982b). Midlife work history and retirement income. In M. Szinovacz (Ed.), *Women's retirement: Policy implications of recent research* (pp. 25-44). Beverly Hills: Sage.

O'Rand, A. M., & Landerman, L. R. (1984). Women's and men's retirement income status: Early family role effects. *Research on Aging, 6*, 25–44.

O'Rand, A. M., & MacLean, V. M. (1986). Labor markets, pension rule structure, and retirement benefits for long-term employees. *Social Forces, 65*, 224–240.

Pampel, F. C. (1981). *Social change and the aged: Recent trends in the United States.* Boston: Little Brown.

Pampel, F. C., & Park, S. (1986). Cross-national patterns and determinants of female retirement. *American Journal of Sociology, 91*, 932–955.

Pampel, F. C., & Weiss, J. A. (1983). Economic development, pension policies, and the labor force participation of aged males: A cross-national, longitudinal approach. *American Journal of Sociology, 89*, 350–372.

Pearce, D. (1978). The feminization of poverty: Women, work and welfare. *Urban Social Change Review, 11*, 1–36.

Pearce, D., & McAdoo, H. (1981). *Women and children: Alone and in poverty.* Washington, DC: Center for National Policy Review.

Quadagno, J. (1987a). Women's welfare benefits and American exceptionalism. *Comparative Historical Sociology Newsletter* IV, p. 4.

Quadagno, J. (1987b). Theories of the welfare state. *Annual Review of Sociology, 13*, 109–128.

Quadagno, J. (1988). *Labor's rights in the welfare state: The transformation of old age security.* Chicago: University of Chicago Press.

Rainwater, L., & Rein, M. (1983). The growing complexity of economic claims in welfare societies. In *Evaluating the welfare state: Social and political perspectives* (pp. 111–129). New York: Academic Press.

Root, L. S. (1985). Employee benefits and social welfare: Complement and conflict. *The Annals of the American Academy of Political and Social Science, 479*, 101–118.

Schulz, J. H. (1985). *The economics of aging* (3rd ed.). Belmont, CA: Wadsworth.

Schulz, J. H., Leavitt, T. D., & Kelley, L. (1979). Private pensions fall short of preretirement levels. *Monthly Labor Review, 28*, 32–40.

Scott, H. (1984). *Working your way to the bottom: The feminization of poverty.* London: Pandora.

Slavick, F. (1966). *Compulsory and flexible retirement in the American economy.* Ithaca, NY: Cornell University Press.

Statistics Sweden. (1985). *Women and men in Sweden: Facts and figures.* Stockholm: Author.

Titmuss, R. M. (1969). *Essays on the welfare state.* London: Allen and Unwin.

Treynor, J. L., Regan, P. J., & Priest, W. W., Jr. (1976). *The financial reality of pension funding under ERISA.* Homewood, IL: Dow Jones–Irwin.

U.S. Bureau of the Census. (1982). Current Population Survey, May 1979. *Survey of pension plan coverage.* ICPSR, Ann Arbor: University of Michigan, 1982.

U.S. Department of Health, Education and Welfare. (1978). *Social Security programs throughout the world 1977* (Research Report No. 50, Social Security Administration, Office of Research and Statistics). Washington, DC: U.S. Government Printing Office.

U.S. Senate. (1986). *Developments in aging: 1986: Vol. 1. A report of the Special Committee on Aging.* Washington, DC: U.S. Government Printing Office.

Valocchi, S. M. (1986). Welfare policy and stratification outcomes in Great Britain, West Germany, and Sweden. In R. V. Robinson (Ed.), *Research in social stratification and mobility: A research annual* (Vol. 5) (pp. 283–320). Greenwich, CT: JAI Press.

van Gunsteren, H., & Rein, M. (1985). The dialectic of public and private pensions. *Journal of Social Policy, 14,* 129–149.

Wilensky, H. L. (1975). *The welfare state and equality: Structural and ideological roots of public expenditures.* Berkeley: University of California Press.

Wilensky, H. L. (1976). *The 'new corporatism,' centralization and the welfare state.* Beverly Hills, CA: Sage.

Wilson, D. (1979). *Welfare state in Sweden.* London: Heinemann Educational Books.

CHAPTER 6

Gender and Ethnicity Differences in Psychological Well-Being

NEAL KRAUSE
SCHOOL OF PUBLIC HEALTH
AND
THE INSTITUTE OF GERONTOLOGY,
THE UNIVERSITY OF MICHIGAN

This chapter reviews evidence on gender and racial differences in psychological well-being and presents a framework that can be used to explain why such differences exist. At the onset, it may be helpful to define how the phrase *psychological well-being* will be used, because gerontologists have included a diverse array of constructs under the general rubric of well-being.

As George (1981) notes, measures of well-being run the gamut from indicators of life satisfaction and morale to indicators of psychiatric disorder. This chapter will be concerned only with well-being as measured by indicators of psychiatric health. Scales measuring this type of well-being assess such symptoms as anxiety, tension, depression, and fear. The discussion below will focus on mild or moderate symptoms of psychiatric disorder as well as clinical cases of psychiatric disorder as they would be diagnosed by a psychiatrist. Accordingly, the term *psychological disorder* will be used to identify mild or moderate symptoms, while the phrase *psychiatric disorder* will be reserved for discrete diagnoses or clinical cases. For the sake of simplicity, the general term *disorder* will be used to refer to both psychological and psychiatric disorder.

During the past several decades, researchers have conducted a considerable number of studies in the general population that focus on gender and racial differences in psychological and psychiatric disorders (for reviews of this research, see Neighbors, 1984; Weissman, 1987). Essentially, these researchers have hypothesized that women experience more disorder than men (Gove & Tudor, 1973) and that nonwhites suffer from more disorder than whites (Dohrenwend & Dohrenwend, 1970). Similar hypotheses have been developed by gerontologists, who have attempted to determine whether these gender and racial differences extend into late life (e.g., Feinson, 1987; Palmore, Nowlin, & Wang, 1985).

It has seemed plausible to hypothesize that women and minority group members are at higher risk for disorders because they occupy disadvantaged social positions; they are more likely than others to experience poverty and discrimination (Feinson, 1987; Schultz, 1985). Yet despite the seemingly sound theoretical basis for such predictions, findings from empirical studies on gender and racial differences in rates of disorders are equivocal, especially with regard to race. Although many studies find racial differences in rates of psychological and psychiatric disorder, these differences tend to disappear once the effects of social class are controlled statistically (e.g., Comstock & Helsing, 1976). Similarly, there appears to be some disagreement as to whether elderly women suffer from more disorder than elderly men. Some researchers find that older women are at greater risk (e.g., Weissman et al., 1985), while other investigators fail to observe significant differences (e.g., Blazer & Williams, 1980). These equivocal results clearly warrant investigation.

The discussion that follows will provide a framework that may be useful for resolving at least some of the problems presented in existing literature. The chapter concentrates on three issues. First, two methodological factors that may be largely responsible for the current contradictory findings will be identified and discussed. The first factor involves the appropriateness of using gender and race as proxy measures for experiences that people encounter in these disadvantaged social positions; the second factor involves the measurement of psychological and psychiatric disorder. Second, existing research will be reviewed critically. Current findings will be examined, with particular attention to the samples and methods used to generate them. Emphasis will be placed on showing how existing findings can contribute to further theoretical development. Finally, it will be argued that the life-stress perspective can provide a useful framework for resolving existing contradictory findings and for generating useful hypotheses for future research. Differential rates of disorder will be attributed to both increased exposure to life stressors and to greater vulnerability to their effects. Differences in the social-support process among disadvantaged social groups will be examined as one factor contributing to this differential vulnerability.

METHODOLOGICAL AND CONCEPTUAL ISSUES

As Bohrnstedt (1983) and others have argued, measurement is a *sine qua non* of science. But good measurement is predicated upon sound conceptualization. Any attempt to make valid causal inferences will fail unless researchers give careful attention to delineating the constructs they hope to measure. Nevertheless, many investigators have ignored these basic principles in studying gender and racial differences in psychological and psychiatric disorder and in measuring or conceptualizing both the independent and dependent variables used in their studies. Problems in both of these areas can be illustrated briefly.

Conceptualizing Gender and Race

As typically used in the social and behavioral sciences, gender and race are proxy measures that stand for the experiences people encounter in these roles or social-status positions. If researchers fail to appreciate this fully, two problems tend to result: they treat gender and race as self-sufficient explanatory variables and they tend to overlook the linkages between these proxy measures and other indicators that come closer to assessing the experiences of disadvantaged women and minority group members. Consequently, investigators often fail to exploit the full potential of available data.

At best, gender and race only approximate an individual's social location. The slippage between what we wish to indicate and what we are actually indicating by these concepts can lead to an inaccurate or incomplete view of the role played by gender and race in the genesis of disorder. Although these proxy measures stand for experiences that people are *likely* to encounter, being a member of a minority group or being a woman does not guarantee that such experiences will always be encountered.

A simple example may help clarify this point. As discussed earlier, a number of researchers suspect that low income (i.e., poverty) is largely responsible for the higher rates of psychological disorder among minority group members. However, not all minority group members are poor. In fact, evidence provided by Schultz (1985) indicates that while the overall income of elderly blacks is less than that of elderly whites, there is still considerable variation in income within elderly black populations. Therefore, when an analysis focuses exclusively on the direct effects of race on disorder, race and poverty tend to be confounded.

The resolution of this problem is straightforward: if poverty, not race, is the likely causal factor, researchers must measure what they are really after. Instead of relying solely on a proxy measure such as race to represent those causal aspects of disadvantaged social positions that increase rates of disorder, these experiences must be assessed directly. However, researchers must make an effort to link suspected causal factors directly with measures of gender and race. Investigators need appropriate causal models. Viewed in the context of the example provided above, the goal of causal modeling would not be merely to determine whether race or income exerts the greatest effect on disorder. Instead, the purpose of this approach would be to show that race is associated with poverty, which in turn affects disorder. In this manner, a researcher is able to indicate how race affects disorder. All too often, however, investigators merely examine the direct association of race and disorder while controlling for the effects of income. These analyses frequently reveal that the direct effect of income on disorder is significant, while nonsignificant findings are observed for the direct effects of race. Based on these findings, researchers conclude inappropriately that race is not an important determinant of psychological disorder.

Problems in the Conceptualization and Measurement of Disorder

Three issues will be examined briefly in this section: The first involves potential advantages associated with the study of specific types of disorder; the second concerns problems with the reliability and validity of existing measurement scales; and the third involves the use of existing scales for different racial and gender groups.

Researchers have used three broad categories of instruments to measure disorder: (1) global rating scales that assess nonspecific symptoms of mild psychological disorder, such as the Langner 22-Item Scale (Langner, 1962); (2) scales that assess specific forms of psychological disorder but do not attempt to make clinical diagnoses, such as the Center for Epidemiological Studies Depression Scale (CES-D) (Radloff, 1977); and (3) indexes that attempt to identify cases of specific psychiatric disorders, such as the Diagnostic Interview Schedule (DIS) (Robins, 1986).

Research focusing on specific kinds of psychological or psychiatric disorders may provide the best additional insight into the relationship of disorder with both gender and race. This conclusion is based on the observation that disorder is manifest in different forms in various gender and racial groups. For example, Dohrenwend and Dohrenwend (1976) maintain that women are more likely to suffer from depression, while men are more likely to experience personality disorders, such as alcoholism (see also Weissman & Klerman, 1977). If these observations are correct, then researchers must use scales that are sensitive to variations in the manifestations of disorder in these groups.

Merely relying on scales that assess specific types of disorder will obviously not resolve all of the relevant problems. Indexes used to study psychological disorder must also possess desirable psychometric properties; they must be reliable and valid. Unfortunately, serious reservations are expressed in the literature concerning the reliability and validity of existing measures of psychological disorder. The controversy surrounding the DIS is an example of this problem. Information on the reliability of the DIS was obtained in part by computing the degree of agreement in community samples between DIS ratings and clinical diagnoses. Previous research on the DIS had suggested that the correspondence between these two ratings was generally high (see Helzer et al., 1985). However, a recent reexamination of these data by Shrout, Spitzer, and Fleiss (1987) indicates that serious data analytic errors were committed in computing reliability estimates and that the agreement between DIS ratings and clinical diagnoses in community samples is poor.

There are, however, even greater problems with the reliability and validity of scales that have been virtually ignored in studies of gender and racial differences in disorder. As Jackson, Tucker, and Bowman (1982) argue, many scales assessing psychological disorder have been developed on and for use in the study of middle-class, American, white populations. As such, there is no guarantee that minority respondents understand and interpret the items in these scales in the manner intended by researchers. To the extent that they do not, the reliability and validity of these studies will be in question when data are gathered on minority respondents. While sophisticated simultaneous confirmatory factor analysis procedures are available to assess the extent of this problem (see Liang & Bollen, 1985, for an application of these techniques), these procedures have rarely been used by researchers assessing gender and racial differences in disorder among older adults. This type of investigation is strongly recommended for future research.

There are no easy resolutions to these problems. Until better scales are available, however, researchers must be aware of existing limitations. They must also use data analytic procedures that take the effects of unreliability into account [e.g., LISREL analysis (see Jöreskog & Sörbom, 1986)].

GENDER AND RACIAL DIFFERENCES IN PSYCHOLOGICAL DISORDER

Although contradictory conclusions are reported in studies comparing rates of disorder in different gender and racial groups, some interesting findings emerge when differences within these groups are examined. By identifying these subgroup differences, existing studies may provide a useful foundation for future work by beginning to identify those aspects of gender- and racial-status positions that are responsible for differential rates of psychological and psychiatric disorder. Selected studies of the prevalence of psychological disorder in community populations of older adults do suggest potentially important directions for future research. Treated psychiatric disorder will not be examined here because ethnic and gender differences in the propensity to seek treatment are confounded with symptomatology and the need for treatment among members of lower-status groups (see, e.g., Kart &

Beckham, 1976). In the review that follows, research on gender differences will be presented first, followed by an examination of racial differences in psychological and psychiatric disorder.

Gender Differences in Disorder

The literature suggests possibly significant sex differences in specific forms of psychological and psychiatric disorder. The research reviewed below emphasizes those studies that assess gender differences in depressive symptoms, clinical depression, alcohol abuse, and suicide.

Depressive Symptoms

Six studies examining gender differences in depressive symptoms are reviewed in this section. Half show higher rates of depressive symptomatology among older women; half fail to support this conclusion. A thorough assessment of the methodology used in research reviewed as well as an application of a causal modeling perspective will demonstrate a greater consensus in the literature than appears to be the case initially.

Murrell, Himmelfarb, and Wright (1983) report findings from an impressive statewide survey of older adults in living in Kentucky ($N = 2,517$). Depressive symptoms were assessed in this study with the CES-D Scale. These researchers estimated the proportion of depressed elderly men and women with CES-D scores above a cutpoint value of 20. This is somewhat higher than the cutpoint of 16 that is typically used to indicate depression by investigators who use this scale (e.g., Radloff, 1977). Aged persons with scores of 20 or greater are thought to be "very likely at risk for a degree of psychological distress that would require intervention" (Murrell et al., 1983, p. 175).

Findings from this study reveal that 13.7% of the older men and 18.2% of the older women had CES-D scores above the designated cutpoint. This difference is statistically significant, suggesting that rates of depressive symptomatology are higher for older women than for older men.

Berkman and associates (1986) also report significant sex differences on CES-D scores for older adults. Based on a random community of 2,806 aged people in New Haven, Connecticut, they report that 11.3% of the elderly men had CES-D scores above a cutpoint of 16, whereas 19.2% of the elderly women had scores above this cutpoint.

O'Hara, Kohout, and Wallace (1985) examined depressive symptoms among 3,159 older adults residing in rural Iowa. Unlike the studies reviewed above, these investigators used a shortened, 11-item version of the original 20-item CES-D Scale. Based on responses to this shortened version, they projected the proportion of elderly people who would have scored above the cutpoint of 16 had the full scale been used. Consistent with the studies reviewed above, a higher proportion of elderly women than elderly men were found to have scores above the selected cutpoint value (10.0% versus 7.3%, respectively).

A study failing to find that older women were more depressed than older men, however, was conducted by Weissman and Myers (1978). These investigators report that among persons aged 55–70, men were more likely than women to suffer from depressive symptomatology. These contradictory findings can probably be explained by reviewing the sample as well as the measure of depression used in this study. The sample consisted of 938 individuals of all ages who were selected at random in New Haven, Connecticut. While the sample as a whole was fairly large, the number of persons in the 55–70 age range is inevitably small in a random sample. The authors do not provide the actual figures, but if the proportion is similar to that in the census, then there probably were fewer than 200 older adults in this study. This is considerably smaller than the sample sizes reported in the studies reviewed earlier.

Perhaps of greater concern is the measure of depressive symptoms. Five items were taken from a scale assessing nonspecific symptoms of mild psychological disorder developed by Gurin, Veroff, and Feld (1960). Three additional items were added from "similar scales" to form an eight-item composite. The sensitivity of this index was assessed by administering it to 10 acutely depressed outpatients. Since all of these patients scored beyond a cutpoint designating moderate symptomatology, the authors concluded that the scale assessed depression.

Another study that does not report significant gender differences in depression among the elderly was conducted by Blazer and Williams (1980). Data for this study of 997 older adults came from a random stratified sample of residents in Durham County, North Carolina. Depression was measured with 18 items abstracted from the mental health section of the OARS Multidimensional Functional Assessment Questionnaire (Duke University Center for the Study of Aging and Human Development, 1978).

Findings from the analysis of these data indicated that older women were more depressed than older men. However, the widowed were found to have higher depression scores than those in other marital-status categories. As will be argued below, the relationship between marital status and depression may be important in the study of sex differences in depression.

The third study failing to uncover significant gender differences in depressive symptoms was reported by Feinson and Thoits (1986). Data for this study came from a random community survey of 313 older adults residing in New Jersey. Psychological disorder was assessed with the Johns Hopkins Symptom Checklist (SCL-90-R) (Derogatis, Lipman, Rickles, Ulenhuth, &

Covi, 1973). This checklist measures nine specific forms of disorder, including depression. These researchers failed to find significant gender differences in depression, even at the bivariate level of analysis. However, further analyses revealed that both marital status and income were significantly related to depression. More specifically, those who were widowed and those with less income were more likely to be depressed.

It is noteworthy that Feinson and Thoits (1986) as well as Blazer and Williams (1980) found widowhood to be a significant predictor of depression and that Feinson and Thoits (1986) found that income was also a significant correlate of depression. Census data reveal that approximately half of all older women are widowed, whereas only 12.5% of older men have experienced the death of a spouse (U.S. Bureau of the Census, 1983a). Moreover, the income of elderly women is substantially below that of elderly men: Twice as many older white women and four times as many elderly black women are below the poverty level as their male counterparts (U.S. Bureau of the Census, 1983b).

If gender is associated with widowhood and poverty, and widowhood and poverty in turn affect depression, then we may conclude that gender exerts an indirect effect on depression through these factors. In effect, by specifying this intervening link we are getting closer to measuring explicitly the experiences confronting older women that contribute to the development of psychological disorder. When viewed from this perspective, the findings from the studies reviewed above are not as equivocal as they initially appear. Instead, some studies find direct effects of gender on depression, while others reveal only indirect effects through widowhood and poverty. In either case, gender still figures in the development of depressive symptoms.

Clinical Depression

The best data on clinical depression as it is defined in the *Diagnostic and Statistical Manual III* (*DSM-III-R*) (American Psychiatric Association, 1987) come from the recently completed Epidemiologic Catchment Area (ECA) studies (see Eaton, Regier, Locke, & Taube, 1986, for a detailed discussion of these surveys). Essentially, the DIS was administered to a large representative sample of adults of all ages in five selected sites around the country (approximately 3,000 respondents were interviewed per site).

Data on the six-month prevalence rates of depression for persons 65 years of age and older have been reported in four of the five ECA sites. At each of the four sites, rates of major depression were significantly higher among older women than among older men (for a detailed discussion of these results, see Blazer, Hughes, & George, 1987; Myers et al., 1984). It is important to point out that in addition to observing direct effects of gender on depression, potential indirect effects may also be present. Consistent with the research reviewed earlier, higher rates of major depression were found among the nonmarried and the poor (Blazer et al., 1987), suggesting once again that greater insight into the relationship between gender and depression may be gained by focusing on the experiences that differentially confront older women.

Alcohol Abuse

As part of the ECA research program, data were also gathered on alcohol abuse as it is defined in the *DSM-III-R* (American Psychiatric Association, 1987). As measured by the DIS, studies from all the ECA sites show that older men were more likely than older women to suffer from alcoholism.

Data on the six-month prevalence of DIS-rated alcohol abuse in the elderly were presented by Myers and associates (1984). Findings were reported in this study from three of the five ECA sites. Although rates of alcoholism are lower for the aged as a whole, these data suggest that in each study location, elderly men suffered from higher rates of alcohol abuse than elderly women. More specifically, the findings reveal that in New Haven, 3% of the older men but none of the older women suffered from alcohol abuse. Similarly, in Baltimore, 3.7% of the aged men could be classified as suffering from alcohol abuse, while none of the aged women were diagnosed in this manner. Finally, in St. Louis, 3% of the older men were alcohol abusers, while only .7% of the older women were so classified.

The findings from the ECA studies are supported by research on less severe alcohol problems (so-called heavy drinking). These studies suggest that heavy drinking occurs more frequently among elderly men (e.g., Barnes, 1979) and that it may be very rare among elderly women (Caetano, 1984).

Despite the apparent research consensus about gender differences in alcohol use among the elderly, these findings must be viewed cautiously. As discussed by Graham (1986) and others, researchers encounter numerous problems when they attempt to assess alcohol intake among the elderly. In addition to problems arising from the questionable validity of self-reported use, most measures of alcohol abuse have been standardized on younger persons, raising serious questions about their applicability in elderly populations. For example, part of the assessment of alcohol abuse in the DIS relates to employment problems created by alcohol use. This is clearly not an appropriate indicator of alcohol-related problems in populations consisting largely of retired persons.

Regardless of these measurement problems, the consistency of research findings should not be overlooked. While researchers are probably underestimating the extent of alcohol abuse among the elderly (Graham, 1986), the observation that elderly men abuse alcohol more frequently than elderly women is probably accurate.

Suicide

Unlike alcohol abuse, suicide rates have been shown to increase sharply with age (see Osgood, 1985, for a review of this research). Perhaps more important for the purposes of the present discussion, suicide rates are overwhelmingly higher among older men than among older women.

Rather than review an extensive array of studies here, discussion will be limited to a recent study by Manton, Blazer, & Woodbury (1987). The presentation is restricted in this manner because of the remarkably high consensus among studies on gender differences in suicide. The study by Manton and associates (1987) is singled out for discussion because it is based on an extensive data file and therefore is one of the better studies in the literature.

Manton and associates (1987) examined information provided in death certificates for all deaths of U.S. residents from 1962 through 1981. Although they assessed changes in suicide rates through time, the following comments will be largely limited to data bearing on gender differences in suicide.

The results of analyses involving suicide rates among white men and women aged 70–74 for the years 1979–1981 are typical of the magnitude of the gender differences that were observed in this study. Manton and associates (1987) report that the suicide rate for men in this age range was 35.59 per 100,000, whereas the corresponding rate for women was 6.96, a rate five times higher for older men than older women.

Manton and associates (1987) report a particularly sharp increase in suicides among white men aged 85 and over. Consistent with the theme developed earlier, the reason for this finding may become clear when the experiences confronting men in this age group are given careful consideration. Specifically, the experience of chronic illness may help explain these rates. Research reviewed by Osgood (1985) suggests that the disability associated with chronic illness plays a major role in suicides among the elderly. She cites several studies showing that up to 70% of those older adults who committed suicide were suffering from some illness at the time of their death.

If debilitating illness is related to suicide, and men commit suicide more frequently than women, then research should also show that elderly men suffer from more debilitating illnesses than elderly women. Research reviewed by Verbrugge (1985) provides such evidence. She reports that men have higher prevalence rates than women of life-threatening diseases. More importantly, however, long-term disability due to chronic health problems was found to be more prevalent among men, and this gender difference in disability was shown to increase with age.

The point to this discussion is straightforward: If we seek to understand gender differences in disorder, then we must examine the experiences of older men and women. With regard to suicide, we have argued that aged men are more likely to experience debilitating illness than aged women and that long-term disability associated with these chronic illnesses is a factor in the disproportionately high rate of suicide among older males.

Summary

Two findings have emerged from the review of gender differences in psychological and psychiatric disorder. First, observed differences in rates depend on the type of disorder under consideration. Elderly women generally appear to suffer from higher rates of depression, whereas older men are more likely to commit suicide or suffer from alcohol abuse. Although discrepancies were found in the findings with regard to depression, it was argued that the contradictions could be resolved if we examine the experiences women encounter as they age (e.g., widowhood and poverty). This point was further supported by examining the experiences of older men (e.g., chronic illness) and positing them as a potential explanation for differential rates of suicide.

Racial Differences in Disorder

Compared to the literature on gender differences in disorder, it is considerably more difficult to ascertain clear trends in the research on ethnic and racial differences in disorder among older adults. This is due in part to the fact that there is relatively little comparative, community-based research on psychological and psychiatric disorders of elderly whites versus elderly minority group members (Santos, Hubbard, & McIntosh, 1983). This is especially true for older Native Americans and older Asian-Americans. It is for this reason that discussion of the research reviewed below will focus exclusively on comparative rates of disorder among elderly whites and elderly blacks. These studies will be reviewed selectively, and discussion will be concerned solely with differences in depressive symptoms, cognitive disability, and suicide.

Depressive Symptoms

Studies of racial differences in depressive symptoms generally come to one of three contradictory conclusions: (1) there are no significant racial differences in depressive symptomatology, even at the bivariate level of analysis; (2) there are significant bivariate-level differences, but they tend to disappear once the effects of economic factors are controlled statistically; and (3) significant racial differences persist even after controls have been established for income and education. Studies reflecting each of these findings will be presented below, and an attempt will be made to reconcile the divergent findings.

In a study discussed earlier, Berkman and associates (1986) did not find significant bivariate-level differences in the proportion of older whites and nonwhites who scored above 16 on the CES-D Scale. However, these findings are somewhat confounded by the fact that members of all racial groups other than whites were included in the nonwhite category. Perhaps more importantly, Berkman and associates (1986) report that older adults with less income and education were more likely to have CES-D scores above the 16 cutpoint, indicating depression. Research reviewed by Schultz (1985) indicates that the income and educational levels of older blacks are substantially lower than those of older whites, suggesting that there may be significant indirect effects of race on depressive symptoms operating through these socioeconomic factors.

Comstock and Helsing (1976) examined depressive symptoms among blacks and whites of all ages in a random community survey of 1,154 persons residing in Kansas City, Missouri. However, a careful examination of these data reveal that only 43 black respondents were 65 years of age and older and that only 166 whites were in this age range. Based on a cutpoint of 16 on the CES-D Scale, Comstock and Helsing (1976) report that at the bivariate level of analysis, rates of significant depressive symptomatology among older blacks exceeded those of older whites (the rates were 25.6% and 18.1%, respectively). However, the rates among elderly whites were found to exceed those of elderly blacks once the effects of a number of demographic factors (including income and education) were controlled statistically.

The final study reviewed here was conducted by Eaton and Kessler (1981). Data for this study came from a nationwide survey conducted by the National Center for Health Statistics and is known as the Health and Nutrition Examination Survey (HANES). This sample included subjects aged 18–74. Depressive symptoms were assessed with the CES-D Scale, and these researchers used the standard cutpoint score of 16 to create a binary variable designating those suffering from significant depressive symptomatology.

Findings from this study revealed that older blacks (i.e., those aged 65–74) had higher rates of significant depressive symptomatology than older whites even after controlling for the effects of a number of factors, including education and income. Consistent with the earlier studies, lower education and lower income were found to be strongly related to elevated depressive symptom scores. However, a careful examination of these data reveals that only 40 blacks were aged 65–74, while 307 whites were in this age group. The discrepancy between the studies reviewed in this section could, therefore, easily be attributed to instability arising from the small number of elderly blacks in the studies by both Comstock and Helsing (1976) and Eaton and Kessler (1981).

These studies are typical of the kind of comparative information that is available in older whites and blacks. As this review reveals, data from studies of the general population inevitably result in small numbers of elderly blacks in random samples. This seriously compromises the quality and generalizability of the existing knowledge base. Nevertheless, available data suggest that race may play an indirect role in the genesis of depressive symptomatology in that education and income are consistent predictors of depression and that race, in turn, is associated with these socioeconomic factors.

Cognitive Disability

Three studies in the literature that use community-based data to assess racial differences in cognitive disability among the aged were identified. Palmore and associates (1985) examined data from 287 survivors of a longitudinal community study of the aged in North Carolina. Cognitive disability was assessed with the OARS Multidimensional Functional Assessment Scale (Duke University Center for Aging and Human Development, 1978). These researchers report that compared to elderly whites, elderly blacks were significantly more likely to suffer from cognitive disability. It is significant that these effects were observed after the impact of a number of variables (including income and education) had been controlled statistically.

Support for these findings at Duke is provided by a study of older adults in New York and London conducted by Gurland and associates (1983). Based on bivariate-level analyses, these investigators found significantly higher rates of dementia among older nonwhites in New York ($N = 67$) than among older whites ($N = 378$). Meaningful results could not be obtained in the London sample because it did not contain a sufficient number of nonwhites. However, the findings from this study are difficult to interpret because the category "nonwhite" contained members of all nonwhite racial groups, including blacks and Hispanics.

The third study reviewed in this section is based on data from the ECA Program of NIMH reported by Weissman and associates (1985). Although the probability sample included 2,588 persons aged 65 and over, only 117 of the study participants were older blacks. Bivariate-level analyses revealed that the rates of severe cognitive impairment were higher among elderly blacks (5.4%) than among elderly whites (3.1%). However, the effects of education on cognitive impairment were even more pronounced: 6.1% of those older adults with less than eight years of education had severe cognitive impairment, while less than 1% of those with nine or more years of education could be classified in this manner.

While data from these three studies suggest that older blacks may suffer from severe cognitive impairment more often than older whites, the findings are limited severely by the small number of older blacks in these samples. Moreover, the indirect effects of race on cognitive impairment that operate through education make it difficult to determine what the cognitive disability scales are really measuring. Does evidence of impairment reflect organic mental problems or the simple inability to comprehend scale items due to a limited educational background?

Suicide

While data on racial differences in depressive symptoms and cognitive impairment are inconclusive, findings regarding racial differences in suicide are considerably more clear. The study by Manton and associates (1987) shows that for all age groups over 65, suicide rates of white men are considerably higher than those of black men. Moreover, the suicide rates of white women also exceed those of black women in this age range, although the magnitude of the differences among black and white women is not as great as it is for men. Other studies reviewed by Osgood (1985) support the conclusions reported by Manton and associates (1987).

Summary

With the exception of studies on suicide, findings involving racial differences in disorder must be considered cautiously because of the small numbers of older blacks typically included in the samples. To the extent that any conclusions can be drawn from these data, it would appear that although older blacks may experience higher rates of depressive symptoms and cognitive disability, these effects are largely indirect. That is, potential racial effects on depressive symptoms and cognitive disability may be explained primarily by focusing on factors related to the educational and economic experiences of older blacks.

Conclusions

The findings reviewed in this section indicate that gender and racial differences in rates of disorder may be present. However, these relationships are not straightforward. There are at least two factors responsible for complicating the relationships: The first is associated with potential gender and racial differences in the manifestation of disorder; the second arises from the possibility that disadvantaged social positions may affect disorder indirectly through their association with gender and race.

If the inferences regarding these indirect effects are valid, then additional work needs to be done in two areas. First, although indicators such as marital status and education may identify more clearly the causal mechanisms that link gender and race with disorder, awareness of indirect effects may not be enough. This is because indicators such as marital status and education do not indicate the experiential dimensions of these roles directly; they remain proxy measures. If we are to understand how disadvantaged social statuses affect disorder, then we must adapt a theoretical perspective that highlights the experiential nature of the disadvantage and attempt to measure these experiences directly.

An appropriate model would also have to come to grips with the fact that not all persons in disadvantaged social positions suffer from disorder. The majority of disadvantaged persons are in good mental health. Some mechanism must, therefore, be reducing or buffering the deleterious effects of the negative experiences of women and minority group members. If further advances are to be made in the field, then a theoretical framework capable of identifying this mechanism is essential.

As will be argued below, the life-events perspective addresses these basic issues by both focusing directly on the stressful experiences associated with given social-status positions and by providing a conceptual framework for understanding why most older adults remain in good mental health despite exposure to these stressors over the life course. Researchers are now in a position to move beyond the analysis of demographic correlates of disorder and take advantage of the advance made in life-events research.

STRESSFUL EVENTS AND DISADVANTAGED SOCIAL POSITIONS

Proponents of the life-stress perspective assume that the experience of stressful life events increases the risk of developing psychological and psychiatric disorder (for reviews of this research, see Tennant, 1983; Thoits, 1983). They assume further that social resources (e.g., social support) and psychological resources (e.g., locus of control beliefs) enable individuals to cope effectively with the challenges presented by stressful events (for detailed discussions of these resources, see Pearlin, Menaghan, Lieberman, & Mullins, 1981; Sarason & Sarason, 1985).

The purpose of this section is to illustrate how developments in the life-stress field may be useful in clarifying the relationships among gender, race, and disorder. This section is divided into two parts. The first part is devoted to an examination of the differential exposure and differential vulnerability hypotheses proposed by Kessler (1979). These hypotheses link the risk of developing disorder with differences in exposure to stress and to differences in coping ability associated with various social roles. The second part reviews the literature on social support, emphasizing the role played by supportive social relations in differential vulnerability to stress.

Differential Exposure and Differential Vulnerability

Three topics will be discussed below. First, the differential exposure and differential vulnerability hypotheses will be examined in greater detail. Following this, a statistical procedure (the demographic mean decomposition technique) will be introduced as a useful tool for evaluating the contributions of these hypotheses to our understanding of gender and ethnic differences in disorder. A discussion of the limitations of this technique will also be provided. Finally, research applying the demographic mean decomposition procedure will be reviewed.

The differential exposure hypothesis states that higher rates of disorder arise in lower-status groups because disadvantaged persons experience greater exposure than others to disorder-provoking environmental experiences. Hence, gender and race may be viewed as proxy indicators for this differential exposure and its presumed effects.

Besides creating an increased risk of exposure to stress, lower-status positions can also influence the ability of disadvantaged persons to cope with or react to existing stressors. This aspect of the stress process is reflected in the differential vulnerability hypothesis, which states that a given event may exert a more adverse effect on persons in lower-status positions than individuals in higher-status groups. Presumably, variations in coping ability are a function of social position. This hypothesis is reflected in the classic work of Kohn (1976). Essentially, Kohn argues that the substantive complexity of one's job affects a number of facets in the adult personality, including the ability to manage life crises. In this view, lower-class jobs are characterized by lack of input into and control over the production process. As a result, such jobs are thought to diminish feelings of self-direction and foster a sense that problems are neither manageable nor solvable (see Antonovsky, 1979, for a discussion of related research).

It should be emphasized, however, that the differential exposure and differential vulnerability hypotheses are not mutually exclusive. Theoretically, it is possible for members of lower-status groups to be exposed to more stressful experiences and at the same time to be less effective in coping with them. The object is not to determine whether one hypothesis is right and the other is wrong. Instead, the goal is to estimate the relative contribution of each factor to the observed differences in disorder between the groups under consideration (e.g., older whites and nonwhites).

It is important for researchers to pay careful attention to the differential exposure and differential vulnerability hypotheses because clarification of these issues will help set the agenda for research in the future. If, for example, differences in disorder between members of disadvantaged groups and others can be attributed largely to greater exposure to stress, then research on coping with stress should be given a lower priority in the future. On the other hand, if most of the observed differences can be attributed to differential vulnerability, then more research emphasis should be placed on identifying the reasons for the differential impact of stress.

Demographic Mean Decomposition

Kessler (1979) introduced a statistical procedure into the life-stress literature that can be used to derive estimates simultaneously of the portions of the mean difference in disorder that may be attributed to differential exposure and differential vulnerability to stress. This procedure, which was adapted from the work of Iams and Thornton (1975), is referred to as the demographic mean decomposition technique. Iams and Thornton (1975) provide several different equations for deriving these estimates. One of these questions is described in detail below.

Suppose that a study was conducted with two goals in mind: (1) to determine whether elderly women suffer from higher rates of depression than elderly men and (2) to explain these differences from a life-stress perspective. Assume that preliminary data analyses revealed that the mean depression score of elderly women was higher than that of elderly men. The following formula may then be used to determine the proportion of the observed mean difference in depression scores that can be attributed to differential exposure and differential vulnerability to stress:

(1) $$\bar{D}_w - \bar{D}_m = \Sigma\ (b_w - b_m)\ (\bar{X}_w + \bar{X}_m)/2 \\ + \Sigma\ [(b_w + b_m)/2]\ (\bar{X}_w - \bar{X}_m) \\ + (a_w - a_m)$$

In Equation (1), mean depression scores are depicted by $\bar{D}$, mean stress scores are represented by $\bar{X}$, and the b_i denotes unstandardized multiple regression coefficients for the effects of the stress indicators on depression. Throughout, the subscripts m and w refer to the fact that estimates were derived from separate analyses of men and women respectively.

The first component in Equation (1) assesses differential vulnerability. It answers the following question: Assuming that men and women experience equal amounts of stress $[(\bar{X}_w + \bar{X}_m)/2]$, is the impact of comparable levels of stress greater for women than men $(b_w - b_m)$? Note that the summation sign (Σ) reflects the fact that the differential vulnerability and differential exposure components are computed for each stressor and summed to create a total score.

The second component in Equation 6.1 measures differential exposure. This portion of the equation answers the following questions: Assuming that a given stressor has the same impact on older men and women $[b_w + b_m)/2]$, how much of the observed difference in depression scores can be attributed to the fact that elderly women may experience more of that type of stress than elderly men $(\bar{X}_w - \bar{X}_m)$?

The last component in Equation (1) $(a_w - a_m)$ represents residual differences (i.e., differences in regression intercepts) that cannot be attributed to the indicators that were explicitly included in the equation.

Although the demographic mean decomposition technique provides a concise way of conceptualizing and testing two hypotheses that attempt to explain group differences in disorder, there are at least two problems with this procedure. The first arises from the fact that all mean and regression slope differences are taken into consideration whether or not they are statistically significant. Because of this problem, researchers should supplement the findings from these analyses with results from t-tests (for mean differences) and tests for statistical interaction effects (for differences in regression slopes across groups).

The second problem associated with the demographic mean decomposition procedure arises from the fact that it falls short of providing a comprehensive explanation of observed differences in disorder because it fails to directly assess the factors responsible for differential vulnerability to stress. Thus this procedure is a necessary, but not sufficient, step in exploring group differences in disorder. However, it is important to begin with this technique because it brings two important research issues into sharper focus and provides some indication of where further work should begin.

Applications of the Decomposition Procedure

Despite the intuitive appeal of the differential exposure and differential vulnerability hypotheses, there have been relatively few attempts to evaluate them fully with the demographic mean decomposition technique. This is unfortunate because, as the research reviewed below will reveal, this procedure can help identify areas in need of further research that might have been overlooked with conventional data analytic techniques.

Three studies using the demographic mean decomposition technique are examined below. Of these studies, two involved samples drawn from the general population; that is, they included subjects of all ages. Although data from the general population leave questions about age-specific changes unanswered, a review of findings based on such data is useful because it provides evidence of how the demographic mean decomposition technique can be applied to problems in gerontology.

The first study, which was conducted by Kessler (1979), examined social-class, race, gender, and marital-status differences in global symptoms of disorder (see Gurin and associates, 1960, for a discussion of this measure). The data from this study came from a survey of 720 persons of all ages who were interviewed in New Haven by Myers, Lindenthal, Pepper, and Os-trander (1972). Consistent with existing research, Kessler (1979) found that mean psychological disorder scores were higher for women than for men but that significant mean differences in disorder were not observed between whites and nonwhites. However, reanalysis of these data revealed that nonwhites were twice as likely as whites to have extremely high scores on the psychological disorder scale (i.e., scores above a selected cutpoint). Subsequent analyses with regard to race therefore focused on explaining why nonwhites had a higher proportion of extreme psychological disorder scores than whites.

In applying the demographic mean decomposition procedure to these data, Kessler (1979) found that differences in psychological disorder between men and women could largely be attributed to women's greater vulnerability to stress (see the first component of Equation 1). This means that at comparable levels of exposure, stress is more likely to have an adverse effect on women than on men. However, Kessler (1979) found that the differential exposure hypothesis provided the best explanation for the observed differences between whites and nonwhites. More specifically, findings from the demographic mean decomposition analysis revealed that differences between whites and nonwhites were found to be related to greater exposure to stress among nonwhites (see the second component of Equation 1).

Radloff and Rahe (1981) examined gender differences in depressive symptoms among members of the general population. The study design included a combined probability sample of men and women of all ages from Kansas City, Missouri ($N = 1,161$), and Washington County, Maryland ($N = 1,671$). Depressive symptoms were assessed with the CES-D Scale. Consistent with the work of Kessler (1979), these researchers found that the mean depressive symptom score for women was higher than the mean for men. Radloff and Rahe (1981) found that at similar levels of exposure to stress, life events had a more deleterious effect on women than on men. Thus the differential vulnerability hypothesis once again appeared to explain observed differences in disorder between men and women.

To date, only one study has examined the issue of differential exposure and differential vulnerability among the elderly with the demographic mean decomposition technique. This study, which was conducted by Krause (1986b), involved a random community survey of 351 older adults residing in Galveston, Texas. Psychological disorder was assessed with the CES-D Scale. Preliminary analyses revealed that the elderly women in this sample had higher mean levels of depressive symptoms than elderly men. Results from the decomposition analyses suggested that these mean differences could largely be explained by the differential vulnerability hypothesis. That is, given equal exposure to stress, life events exerted a more negative effect on aged women than on aged men. The analysis further revealed that greater vulnerability on the part of elderly women could be attributed largely to the effects of ongoing financial difficulties (i.e., chronic financial strain).

Taken as a whole, findings from studies using the demographic mean decomposition technique tend to suggest that higher mean levels of disorder may arise among nonwhites because they experience more stress than whites, while higher mean levels of disorder among women may be attributed to their greater vulnerability to the effects of life stress.

In spite of the apparent consistency of these findings, however, there are at least three reasons why these studies must be viewed with caution. First, these studies need to be replicated in community samples of older adults in order to determine whether age differences will influence the findings observed by Kessler (1979) and Radloff and Rahe (1981). Based on the work of Krause (1986b), it appears as though findings observed with regard to gender persist into late life, but no studies have been conducted to determine whether potential racial differences can be explained in terms of differential exposure to stress.

In addition, researchers need to examine a broader range of outcome measures when they attempt to study older adults. Earlier it was argued that gender and racial differences may exist in the expression and manifestation of disorder. If this is true, then researchers must test the differential exposure and differential vulnerability hypotheses with indices that assess a more complete range of psychological disorders. For example, studies investigating gender differences in disorder should also include measures of alcohol abuse as well as scales assessing depressive symptoms.

Finally, we must not lose sight of the fact that, in the end, the demographic mean decomposition procedure is a necessary but not entirely sufficient data analytic technique. Existing findings appear to suggest that women are more vulnerable to the effects of stress than men, but the reasons for this differential vulnerability cannot be determined with this statistical procedure. As discussed above, the main contribution of the decomposition technique lies in the fact that it brings salient research issues to the foreground and indicates where further work is needed.

The issue of heightened vulnerability on the part of older women needs to be examined in much greater detail. More specifically, the reasons for or sources of this increased susceptibility need to be identified and assessed directly. Such studies need to examine the resources that are available to and used by older adults in times of crisis. Many such resources have been studied in the life-stress literature, ranging from social-support to psychological-coping resources, such as locus of control beliefs.

Research on social support will be examined in the last portion of this chapter in order to illustrate further how the life-stress perspective can be useful for understanding gender and ethnic differences in disorder. Social support was selected from among several alternative resources because some investigators suspect that support provided by others becomes increasingly important with age, while biological and developmental factors tend to erode the efficacy of personal or psychological resources, such as locus of control beliefs (see Rodin, Timko, & Harris, 1985, for a discussion of the issues involved in this research).

THE ROLE OF SUPPORTIVE SOCIAL RELATIONS

To date numerous studies have attempted to examine the impact of social support on both psychological and psychiatric disorder (for reviews of this literature, see Alloway & Bebbington, 1987; Cohen & Wills, 1985). Essentially, researchers maintain that individuals with strong social-support systems are protected from developing symptoms of disorder. There is, however, considerable disagreement over how this is accomplished. One body of research suggests that supportive social relations affect disorder by buffering or reducing the negative impact of life stress (see Wheaton, 1985, for a discussion of these models). However, the findings from these studies are inconsistent; while some investigators provide evidence that support buffers the deleterious effects of stress (e.g., Krause, 1987a), others fail to observe significant effects (e.g., Simmons & West, 1985).

Undoubtedly, the inconsistencies in social-support research can be attributed to a host of problems in the measurement, conceptualization, and data analytic procedures used in this research (see Krause, in press, for a detailed discussion of these issues). It would be impossible to review all these methodological problems here. Instead, based on a reading of the literature as well as theoretical considerations, it is probably safe to assume that social support is to some degree an effective stress-buffering mechanism.

Given this assumption, the remainder of this chapter will be devoted to examining gender and ethnic differences in social support. Throughout, an attempt will be made to determine whether social support can be useful for explaining why differential vulnerability to stress may exist among older women but not older men, as well as why older nonwhites may not experience greater vulnerability to the effects of life stress. After examining gender differences in social support, research involving racial differences in support will be reviewed.

Gender Differences in Social Support

Research indicates that regardless of the type of measure used, elderly women appear to receive more social support than elderly men (see Antonucci, 1985, for a review of this research). With regard to social-network structure, studies consistently report that older women have significantly larger social networks than older men (see, e.g., Kahn & Antonucci, 1983) and that they report having greater access to relationships that are close, confiding, and emotionally intimate (e.g., Henderson et al., 1986). The same pattern of findings emerges when studies focusing on the actual receipt of supportive behaviors are considered. For example, research by Arling (1987) indicates that elderly women receive more instrumental support than older men, while a study by Krause (1987a) suggests that older women receive more informational, tangible, and emotional support than aged men.

If the findings from this research are valid, then we are faced with an interesting paradox: If it is true that social support buffers the effects of stress and that women receive more support than men, how can it be that women are also more vulnerable to the effects of stress than men? Three potential explanations for these unanticipated findings are considered below.

The first potential explanation has its basis in the literature, reviewed earlier, suggesting that, while older women may be more likely to suffer from certain types of disorder (e.g., depression), symptoms of disorder in older men may simply be manifest in other forms (e.g., alcoholism). To the extent that this is true, it might be argued that if we were to estimate the impact of stress on alcoholism, we might observe greater vulnerability to stress on the part of older men. As a result, women may not suffer from more disorder than men and the paradox discussed above may simply be caused by bias arising from the type of disorder selected for analysis.

However, this is not an entirely satisfactory explanation, because if support reduces the disorder and women receive more support, then women should not have higher rates of *any* type of disorder than men. The reason for the observed paradox must lie in some other explanation.

A more reasonable explanation may involve the costs that women pay because of their more extensive involvement in social relationships. As research by Lee (1985) suggests, social relations among older adults are governed by the norm of reciprocity, whereby elderly people strive to maintain a sense of equity in the exchange of supportive social behaviors. Stated simply, there may be a strong tendency among the aged to give to others in proportion to what they receive.

Thus, as the size of social networks increases, so does the burden of reciprocity. There is now a growing body of research to support this argument. To begin with, literature reviewed by Antonucci (1985) suggests that elderly women, in addition to receiving more support than elderly men, also report providing more support to others. More importantly, research presented by Kessler, McLeod, and Wethington (1985) indicates that women's greater involvement in the lives of others can be a source of psychological disorder. Presumably, worry and concern about others, as well as the provision of specific supportive acts, may at some point become overwhelming for women, resulting in increased psychological disorder. Thus higher rates of disorder among women in the face of greater social support may reflect the "costs of caring" (Kessler et al., 1985).

A final explanation of the unanticipated relationship among gender, social support, and disorder may be developed by extending the findings from a recent study by Krause (1987b). The purpose of this study was to suggest that social support affects disorder indirectly by influencing locus of control beliefs. A careful examination of the interplay between social support, feelings of control, and disorder, coupled with the findings from this study, may shed some light on the paradox discussed in this section.

One of the most frequently examined psychological coping resources is locus of control beliefs. A number of studies have shown that persons who believe that the events in their lives are under their own control (i.e., individuals with internal locus of control beliefs) are able to cope more effectively with life stress than people who feel that the events of their lives are determined by fate, luck, or chance (i.e., individuals with an external locus of control orientation) (see Blaney, 1985, for a review of this research).

Based on the work of Caplan (1981) and others, Krause (1987b) argues that social support affects well-being by bolstering internal locus of control beliefs. According to this view, supportive others help the stressed person evaluate the situation, formulate a plan of action, and implement this plan; they also provide feedback on the plan's progress. The net result of this feedback and assistance is an increased feeling of personal competence.

However, drawing on existing studies by Rook (1984) and others, Krause (1987b) further hypothesizes that there is a limit to the beneficial effects of social support. More specifically, he argues that excessive support may lead to feelings of dependence and enmeshment and that when older adults become overdependent on significant others, the support they receive from others tends to diminish rather than increase feelings of control.

Findings from this longitudinal study tend to support this hypothesis. More specifically, emotional support was found to initially bolster internal feelings of control through time. However, once a certain threshold was reached, additional increments in emotional support tended to foster more external locus of control beliefs. Similar findings were observed with respect to support provided by study participants to others.

As discussed earlier, research suggests that despite receiving greater amounts of social support, older women may be more vulnerable to the effects of stress than older men. The findings from the study by Krause (1987b) provide a potential explanation for this paradox. Older women may be more vulnerable to the effects of stress despite receiving more social support because the added levels of support tend to erode their feelings of personal control. These external feelings of control may, in turn, impede the ability of older women to cope with the effects of life stress.

Racial Differences in Social Support

Earlier, research was reviewed that indicates that nonwhites experience more extreme levels of psychological disorder than whites because nonwhites are differentially exposed to life stress (Kessler, 1979). If it is true that mean levels of stress are higher among nonwhites, then we need to know more about how nonwhites cope with stress and why we do not also observe a differential vulnerability effect among minority group members. Because women and blacks are members of disadvantaged groups, it is especially important to attempt to explain why women are more vulnerable than blacks to the effects of stress.

Greater insight into these issues may emerge from a careful review of the coping resources available to elderly blacks and women. Consistent with the previous section, the discussion below focuses on social support. In addition, only studies dealing with differences in support between older whites and older blacks will be examined. It will be argued that there are differences between aged blacks and aged women in both the quantity and nature of the support they receive and that this may in part explain why we do not find a differential vulnerability effect among nonwhites.

Although the existing literature consistently shows that women receive more social support than men, there is less consensus on whether older blacks receive more support than older whites. Focusing primarily on research conducted with older blacks and whites, Antonucci (1985) concludes that blacks may receive more support than whites. However, a careful examination of the studies reviewed by Antonucci (1985) reveals that many of them measure social support by assessing the frequency of social contact, primarily among family members. As Barrera (1986) and others have argued, measures of social contact are flawed because they only assess the potential for social support—not the actual receipt of supportive behaviors. These objections are based in part on the fact that there is no guarantee that contact with others is always supportive and that there is a negative or undesirable side to social interaction (see Rook, 1984).

A thorough review of existing studies that assess the frequency or receipt of actual supportive behaviors by older whites and blacks fails to consistently show significant differences. Three studies examining this issue are examined below.

The first study, which was conducted by Mindel, Wright, and Starrett (1986), examined differences in support received by 1,519 older blacks and whites in Cleveland, Ohio. Their measure of social support appears to assess instrumental support, which involves financial contributions, help with transportation, and assistance with household chores. As these authors conclude, the bivariate correlation between race and instrumental support was "remarkably small" (p. 281).

The second study, which also compares older whites and blacks, was conducted by Arling (1987). The data for this study came from a statewide survey of 2,146 older adults in Virginia. Unfortunately, Arling (1987) used a summary measure that aggregated emotional and instrumental assistance into the same global scale. As research by Krause (1986a) suggests, more interesting results might have been obtained if the effects of these different types of social support had been assessed individually. The results from the multivariate analyses performed by Arling (1987) nevertheless reveal no significant differences in the amount of social support received by older blacks and whites. However, these findings were observed after the effects of self-rated economic difficulties were controlled statistically. Arling (1987) fails to provide information on the relationship between race and economic problems, thereby missing an opportunity to assess potentially important indirect effects. As the next study shows, such indirect effects may provide valuable insight into the relationship between race and social support.

The final study to be examined here was performed by Mutran (1985). Data for this study came from a national study that included responses from 1,314 individuals who were 65 years of age and over. However, only 194 people in this sample were black, suggesting greater variation in responses to the survey items may have been obtained in the white sample than in the sample of black respondents. Like the studies discussed above, Mutran (1985) relied on a measure of instrumental support to assess supportive social relations. While preliminary data analyses revealed that older blacks received more instrumental support than older whites, these differences failed to remain statistically significant once the effects of income, education, self-rated health, and marital status were controlled statistically. Mutran (1985) concluded that, while aged blacks may receive more assistance than aged whites, the greater amount of assistance is the result of socioeconomic factors. This suggests that race may exert an indirect effect on social support through economic status.

Taken as a whole, the studies reviewed above fail to provide consistent evidence that older blacks receive more social support than older whites. At best, race may affect social support indirectly through economic factors. However, the studies examined here are limited because they focus almost exclusively on instrumental support, ignoring other dimensions of supportive social relations (e.g., emotional support). Nevertheless, it is clear that the consistent findings of gender differences in support may not exist regarding racial differences.

If further studies reveal that there are no major racial differences in support, then we may be in a better position to explain why older blacks do not experience differential vulnerability to the effects of life stress. Earlier, based on the work of Krause (1987b), it was suggested that large amounts of social support may have an adverse effect on older adults because they decrease feelings of personal control. If research continues to suggest that older blacks do not receive excessively large amounts of support, while elderly women do, then we may be able to use the rationale provided by Krause (1987b) to explain why elderly women experience differential vulnerability to stress, while elderly blacks do not.

A second reason why differences may exist in the response to stress of elderly blacks and women may be attributed to differences in the types of support received by members of these disadvantaged groups. Research by Kessler and associates (1985), as well as by Krause (1987b), seems to indicate that the negative effects associated with large amounts of social support are most likely to occur with emotional support. If further research reveals that elderly women receive much larger amounts of emotional support than elderly blacks, this may suggest that elderly women's greater vulnerability to stress may have something to do with the content as well as the quantity of support.

The conclusions reached in this section are clearly tentative, since they rely on an inadequate research base. Additional studies must be conducted. Since a number of older blacks are obviously also women, analyses must be performed by race and gender if we are to understand why women experience differential vulnerability to stress while blacks do not. However, the main contribution of existing studies of this time arises from the fact that they call our attention to the interplay between race and social support as a potential explanation for observed racial and gender differences in coping with stress.

SUMMARY

Are there significant gender and racial differences in disorder among older adults? This chapter has shown that the answer to this question is not straightforward. There are at least two reasons why a definitive answer cannot be provided at this time. First, researchers confront formidable problems in the measurement of psychological and psychiatric disorder. Measures must be developed that are appropriate for use with older women and minority group members. Moreover, investigators must make an effort to assess a complete range of specific types of disorder in the same study. As such studies are conducted, it is likely that no one group will emerge with consistently higher rates of disorder. Instead, we may find that disorder is simply manifest in different ways across the various social-status groups.

Researchers must also adopt a conceptual framework that is capable of directing our thinking beyond simple models that merely assess the direct effects of race and gender on disorder. Variables such as gender and race must be recognized as relatively crude proxy measures for the experiences confronting elderly women and nonwhites. The life-stress perspective represents a useful conceptual scheme that can focus attention on those specific experiences in lower-status life that create psychological and psychiatric disorder.

REFERENCES

Alloway, R., & Bebbington, P. (1987). The buffer theory of social support—A review of the literature. *Psychological Medicine, 17*, 91–108.

American Psychiatric Association. (1987). *Diagnostic and statistical manual of mental disorders* (3rd rev. ed.). Washington, DC: Author.

Antonovsky, A. (1979). *Health, stress, and coping.* San Francisco: Jossey-Bass.

Antonucci, T. (1985). Personal characteristics, social support, and social behavior. In R. Binstock & E. Shanas (Eds.), *Handbook of aging and the social sciences* (pp. 94–128). New York: Van Nostrand Reinhold.

Arling, G. (1987). Strain, social support, and distress in old age. *Journal of Gerontology, 42*, 107–113.

Barrera, M. (1986). Distinctions between social support concepts, measures, and models. *American Journal of Community Psychology, 14*, 413–445.

Barnes, G. M. (1979). Alcohol use among older persons: Findings from a western New York State general population survey. *Journal of the American Geriatrics Society, 27*, 244–250.

Berkman, L. F., Berkman, C. S., Kasl, S., Freeman, D. H., Leo, L., Ostfeld, A., Huntley, J. C., & Brody, J. A. (1986). Depressive symptoms in relation to physical health and functioning in the elderly. *American Journal of Epidemiology, 124*, 372–388.

Blaney, P. (1985). Stress and depression in adults: A critical review. In T. Field, P. McCabe, & N. Schneiderman (Eds.), *Stress and coping* (pp. 263–283). Hillsdale, NJ: Erlbaum, 1985.

Blazer, D. G., Hughes, D. C., & George, L. K. (1987). The epidemiology of depression in an elderly community population. *The Gerontologist, 27,* 281–287.

Blazer, D. G., & Williams, C. D. (1980). Epidemiology of dysphoria and depression in an elderly population. *American Journal of Psychiatry, 137,* 439–444.

Bohrnstedt, G. (1983). Measurement. In P. Rossi, J. Wright, & A. Anderson (Eds.), *Handbook of survey research* (pp. 69–121). New York: Academic Press.

Caetano, R. (1984). Ethnicity and drinking in northern California: A comparison among whites, blacks, and Hispanics. *Alcohol and Alcoholism, 19,* 31–44.

Caplan, G. (1981). Mastery and stress: Psychosocial aspects. *American Journal of Psychiatry, 138,* 413–420.

Cohen, S., & Wills, T. (1985). Stress, social support, and the buffering hypothesis. *Psychological Bulletin, 98,* 310–357.

Comstock, G., & Helsing, K. (1976). Symptoms of depression in two communities. *Psychological Medicine, 6,* 551–563.

Derogatis, L., Lipman, R., Rickles, K., Ulenhuth, E., & Covi, L. (1973). The Hopkins Symptom Checklist (HSCL): A self-report inventory. *Behavioral Science, 19,* 1–19.

Dohrenwend, B. P., & Dohrenwend, B. S. (1976). Sex differences in psychiatric disorders. *American Journal of Sociology, 81,* 1447–1454.

Dohrenwend, B. S., & Dohrenwend, B. P. (1970). Class and race as status related sources of stress. In S. Levine & N. A. Scotch (Eds.), *Social stress* (pp. 111–140). Chicago: Aldine.

Duke University Center for the Study of Aging and Human Development. (1978). *Multidimensional functional assessment: The OARS methodology.* Durham, NC: Duke University Press.

Eaton, W., & Kessler, L. (1981). Rates of symptoms of depression in a national sample. *American Journal of Epidemiology, 114,* 528–538.

Eaton, W., Regier, D., Locke, B., & Taube, C. (1986). The NIMH Catchment Area Program. In M. Weissman, J. Myers, & C. Ross (Eds.), *Community surveys of psychiatric disorders* (pp. 209–219). New Brunswick, NJ: Rutgers University Press.

Feinson, M. (1987). Mental health and aging: Are there gender differences? *The Gerontologist, 27,* 703–711.

Feinson, M. C., & Thoits, P. A. (1986). The distribution of distress among elders. *Journal of Gerontology, 41,* 225–233.

George, L. K. (1981). Subjective well-being: Conceptual and methodological issues. In C. Eisdorfer (Ed.), *Annual review of gerontology and geriatrics* (Vol. 2) (pp. 345–382). New York: Springer.

Gove, W. R., & Tudor, J. F. (1973). Adult sex roles and mental illness. *American Journal of Sociology, 98,* 812–835.

Graham, K. (1986). Identifying and measuring alcohol abuse among the elderly: Serious problems with existing instrumentation. *Journal of Studies on Alcohol, 47,* 322–326.

Gurin, G., Veroff, J., & Feld, S. (1960). *Americans view their mental health: A nationwide survey.* New York: Basic Books.

Gurland, B., Copeland, J., Kuriansky, J., Kelleher, M., Sharpe, L., & Dean, L. (1983). *The mind and mood of aging: Mental health problems of the community elderly in New York and London.* New York: Haworth.

Helzer, J., Robins, L., McEvoy, L., Stoltzman, R., Farmer, A., & Brockington, I. (1985). A comparison of clinical and DIS diagnoses: Physician reexamination of lay interviewed cases in the general population. *Archives of General Psychiatry, 42*, 657–666.

Henderson, A. S., Grayson, D. A., Scott, R., Wilson, J., Rickwood, D., & Kay, D. W. (1986). Social support, dementia, and depression among the elderly living in Hobart community. *Psychological Medicine, 16*, 379–390.

Iams, H. M., & Thornton, A. (1975). Decomposition of differences: A cautionary note. *Sociological Methods and Research, 3*, 341–352.

Jackson, J., Tucker, M., & Bowman, P. (1982). Conceptual and methodological problems in survey research on black Americans. In W. Liu (Ed.), *Methodological problems in minority research* (pp. 11–40). Chicago: Pacific/Asian American Mental Research Center.

Jöreskog, K., & Sörbom, D. (1986). *LISREL VI: Analysis of linear structural relationships by method of maximum likelihood.* Mooresville, IN: Scientific Software.

Kahn, R., & Antonucci, T. (1983). Social supports of the elderly: Family/friends/professionals. Final report to the National Institute on Aging, Bethesda, MD.

Kart, C. S., & Beckham, B. (1976). Black–white differences in the institutionalization of the elderly. *Social Forces, 54*, 901–910.

Kessler, R. C. (1979). Stress, social status, and psychological distress. *Journal of Health and Social Behavior, 20*, 259–272.

Kessler, R. C., McLeod, J. D., & Wethington, E. (1985). The costs of caring: A perspective on the relationship between sex and psychological distress. In I. G. Sarason & B. R. Sarason (Eds.), *Social support: Theory, research, and application* (pp. 491–506). The Hague, The Netherlands: Martinus Nijhoff.

Kohn, M. (1976). The interaction of social class and other factors in the etiology of schizophrenia. *American Journal of Psychiatry, 133*, 177–180.

Krause, N. (1986a). Social support, stress, and well-being among older adults. *Journal of Geronotology, 41*, 512–519.

Krause, N. (1986b). Stress and sex differences in depressive symptoms among older adults. *Journal of Gerontology, 41*, 727–731.

Krause, N. (1987a). Life stress, social support, and self-esteem in an elderly population. *Psychology and Aging, 2*, 349–356.

Krause, N. (1987b). Understanding the stress process: Linking social support with locus of control beliefs. *Journal of Gerontology, 42*, 589–593.

Krause, N. (in press). The measurement of social support in studies on aging and health. In K. Markides & C. Cooper (Eds.), *Aging, stress, social support and health.* New York: Wiley.

Langner, T. S. (1962). A twenty-two item screening score of psychiatric symptoms indicating impairment. *Journal of Health and Human Behavior, 3*, 269–276.

Lee, G. (1985). Kinship and social support of the elderly: The case of the United States. *Aging and Society, 5,* 19–38.

Liang, J., & Bollen, K. (1985). Sex differences in the structure of the Philadelphia Geriatric Center Morale Scale. *Journal of Gerontology, 40,* 468–477.

Manton, K. G., Blazer, D. G., & Woodbury, M. A. (1987). Suicide in middle age and later life: Sex and race specific life table and cohort analyses. *Journal of Gerontology, 42,* 219–227.

Mindel, C., Wright, R., & Starrett, R. (1986). Informal and formal health and social support systems of black and white elderly: A comparative cost approach. *The Gerontologist, 26,* 279–285.

Murrell, S. A., Himmelfarb, S., & Wright, K. (1983). Prevalence of depression and its correlates in older adults. *American Journal of Epidemiology, 117,* 173–185.

Mutran, E. (1985). Intergenerational family support among blacks and whites: Response to culture or to socioeconomic differences. *Journal of Gerontology, 40,* 382–389.

Myers, J., Lindenthal, J., Pepper, L., & Ostrander, D. (1972). Life events and mental status: A longitudinal study. *Journal of Health and Social Behavior, 13,* 398–406.

Myers, J. K., Weissman, M. M., Tischler, G. L., Holzer, C. E., Leaf, P. J., Orvaschel, H., Anthony, J. C., Boyd, J. H., Burke, J. D., Kramer, M., & Stolzman, R. (1984). Six-month prevalence of psychiatric disorders in three communities. *Archives of General Psychiatry, 41,* 959–967.

Neighbors, H. W. (1984). The distribution of psychiatric morbidity: A review and suggestions for research. *Community Mental Health Journal, 20,* 5–18.

O'Hara, M. W., Kohout, F. J., & Wallace, R. B. (1985). Depression among the rural elderly: A study of prevalence and correlates. *Journal of Nervous and Mental Disease, 173,* 582–589.

Osgood, N. J. (1985). *Suicide in the elderly: A practitioner's guide to diagnosis and mental health intervention.* Rockville, MD: Aspen.

Palmore, E. B., Nowlin, J. B., & Wang, H. S. (1985). Predictors of function among the old-old: A 10-year follow-up. *Journal of Gerontology, 40,* 244–250.

Pearlin, L., Menaghan, E., Lieberman, M., & Mullins, J. (1981). The stress process. *Journal of Health and Social Behavior, 22,* 337–356.

Radloff, L. S. (1977). The CES-D Scale: A self-report depression scale for research in the general population. *Applied Psychological Measurement, 1,* 385–401.

Radloff, L. S., & Rahe, D. S. (1981). Components of the sex difference in depression. In R. G. Simmons (Ed.), *Research in community and mental health* (Vol. 2) (pp. 111–137). Greenwich, CT: JAI Press.

Robins, L. N. (1986). The development and characteristics of the NIMH Diagnostic Interview Schedule. In M. M. Weissman, J. K. Myers, & C. E. Ross (Eds.), *Community surveys of psychiatric disorders* (pp. 403–427). New Brunswick, NJ: Rutgers University Press.

Rodin, J., Timko, C., & Harris, S. (1985). The construct of control: Biological and psychological correlates. In M. P. Lawton & G. L. Maddox (Eds.), *Annual review of gerontology and geriatrics* (Vol. 5) (pp. 3–55). New York: Springer.

Rook, K. S. (1984). The negative side of social interaction: Impact on psychological well-being. *Journal of Personality and Social Psychology, 46,* 1097–1108.

Santos, J. F., Hubbard, R. W., & McIntosh, J. L. (1983). Mental health and the minority elderly. In L. D. Breslau & M. R. Haug (Eds.), *Depression and aging: Causes, care, and consequences* (pp. 51–70). New York: Springer.

Sarason, I., & Sarason, B. (1985). *Social support: Theory, research, and applications*. The Hague, The Netherlands: Martinus Nijhoff.

Schulz, J. H. (1985). *The economics of aging*. Belmont, CA: Wadsworth.

Shrout, P., Spitzer, R., & Fleiss, J. (1987). Quantification of agreement in psychiatric diagnosis revisited. *Archives of General Psychiatry, 44*, 172–177.

Simmons, R., & West, G. (1985). Life changes, coping resources, and health among the elderly. *International Journal of Aging and Human Development, 20*, 173–189.

Tennant, C. (1983). Life events and psychological morbidity: Evidence from prospective studies. *Psychological Medicine, 13*, 483–486.

Thoits, P. A. (1983). Dimensions of life events that influence psychological distress: An evaluation and synthesis of the literature. In H. B. Kaplan (Ed.), *Psychosocial stress: Trends in theory and research* (pp. 33–103). New York: Academic Press.

U.S. Bureau of the Census. (1983a). *America in transition: An aging society* (Current Population Reports, Series P-23, No. 128). Washington, DC: U.S. Government Printing Office.

U.S. Bureau of the Census. (1983b). *Money, income, and poverty status of families and persons in the U.S.: 1982* (Current Population Reports, Series P-60, No. 128). Washington, DC: U.S. Government Printing Office.

Verbrugge, L. (1985). Gender and health: An update on hypotheses and evidence. *Journal of Health and Social Behavior, 26*, 156–182.

Weissman, M. M. (1987). Advances in psychiatric epidemiology: Rates and risks for major depression. *American Journal of Public Health, 77*, 445–451.

Weissman, M. M., & Klerman, G. L. (1977). Sex differences in the epidemiology of depression. *Archives of General Psychiatry, 34*, 98–111.

Weissman, M. M., & Myers, J. (1978). Rates and risks of depressive symptoms in a United States urban community. *Acta Psychiatrica Scandinavia, 57*, 219–231.

Weissman, M. M., Myers, J. K., Tischler, G. L., Holzer, C. E., Leaf, P. J., Orvaschel, H., & Brody, J. A. (1985). Psychiatric disorders (DSM-III) and cognitive impairment among the elderly in a U.S. urban community. *Acta Psychiatrica Scandinavia, 71*, 366–379.

Wheaton, B. (1985). Models of the stress-buffering functions of coping resources. *Journal of Health and Social Behavior, 26*, 352–364.

PART III

Some Policy Implications of Population Heterogeneity

Better Options for Work and Retirement: Some Suggestions for Improving Economic Security Mechanisms for Old Age

YUNG-PING CHEN

FRANK J. MANNING EMINENT SCHOLAR'S CHAIR
UNIVERSITY OF MASSACHUSETTS AT BOSTON

In his Kleemeier Lecture before the Gerontological Society of America, Maddox discussed three ideas about human aging that are central to his thought and research: heterogeneity of older adults, modifiability of aging processes, and choices regarding alternatives in constructing the future of aging (Maddox, 1987). Socioeconomic status, he reports, is one of the most powerful variables explaining the heterogeneity of older adults. Socioeconomic status, he argues, is the outcome of a society's differential allocation of resources, as indexed mainly by income and education. While he views income and education as consequences of society's differential allocation of resources, some may argue that uneven levels of income and educational attainment may result from other factors. Whether problems of adjustment to life are individually based or societally caused is an intriguing question. He does not discuss that controversy, however, since he recognizes that demonstrating the importance of soicoeconomic factors in human development does not require minimizing the relevance of biological factors. Regarding the question of what produces heterogeneity, he cites such factors as socioeconomic status of parents, personal ability, choices by self and others related to human-capital investments, learned adaptive skills, and randomness (or unpredictability of outcome) in the intersection of complex organisms with complex environments.

The author appreciatively acknowledges helpful comments and advice on earlier drafts by Francis J. Crowley, Helen Ginsburg, Stephen C. Goss, Edward Howard, Francis P. King, Robert J. Myers, Bruce D. Schobel, James H. Schulz, Wayne Vasey, Dean A. Worcester, Jr., and the editors of this volume. He is, however, solely responsible for the final product.

Concluding that much of the heterogeneity in later life is a product of how societies have allocated their material and social resources in the past, he challenges us to imagine alternative ways of allocating resources for an aging society. This chapter accepts the hypothesis that heterogeneity among the elderly results largely from society's differential allocation of resources and the proposition that policy can make a difference in people's lives. One of the hallmarks of a high quality of life, it may be argued, is accessibility to constructive options and opportunities. An index of a creative and just society, it may further be argued, is the availability of such options and opportunities to its members. Historically and contemporarily, for example, minorities (by gender, religion, or race and ethnicity) in various societies have been denied equal access to opportunities as well as to goods and services. That is morally wrong and socially destructive. And often a person's range of options narrows in late life. That, too, need not be the case.

Just as the present reflects the past, it also determines the future. The options for work and retirement in late adulthood, with their implications for income adequacy or inadequacy three or four decades from now, will be largely determined by current and future decisions in the private and public sectors. Careful thought should therefore be given now to ways of improving economic security mechanisms in order to provide better options regarding work and retirement in old age; that is, a better future for an aging society.

The first section of this chapter briefly describes the present old-age economic security system and offers different interpretations of the role of the individual, the employer, and the government. The second section discusses the several sources from which older persons curently derive income and the relative importance of these sources to various income groups. The third section reviews the role these sources have played in providing income to older persons during the last two decades and speculates on what these sources may contribute to the future income status of the aged if current laws and practices prevail. The fourth section suggests possible ways of dealing with certain important problems and issues in the existing old-age income security system. The fifth section emphasizes the relevance of health care financing to economic security. And some concluding remarks are made in the final section.

THE PRESENT OLD-AGE ECONOMIC SECURITY SYSTEM

Income Security Tripod

The old-age income security system in the United States may be seen as resting on a tripod, the three legs of which include government or social effort, group or corporate effort, and individual effort. Programmatically these three efforts are represented, respectively, by government-sponsored

Social Security—the old-age, survivors, and disability insurance program (OASDI), as well as the government-provided Supplemental Security Income program (SSI); employer-maintained occupational pensions (private and governmental) and other employer-sponsored capital accumulation programs; and individual saving and investment activities that result in home equity, holdings of insurance and stocks and bonds, individual retirement accounts, Keogh and 401(k) plans, and other similar arrangements. In addition to these sources, older persons may also receive income from employment, intrafamily transfers, and public charities.

Concept of Economic Security

The programs and activities cited above comprise the sources of income to older persons. They are, then, financial mechanisms or arrangements for providing income security in old age. But income security is not the same as economic security; economic security is a broader concept. A person is concerned not only with the receipt of income and holding of assets but also with the retention and disposal of income and assets, which are affected by a number of factors, such as accessibility and affordability of health care, housing and living arrangements, service delivery, and support networks. In an even broader framework, acquisition and retention of income and assets are influenced by the effects of macroeconomic stability or instability on employment, prices, economic growth, investment safety, property values, and the like. Of particular concern for older persons is the possibility of significant expenditures for health care, including long-term care. In this light, the economic security structure must recognize the roles of Medicare and Medicaid as well as of employer-paid postretirement health benefits.

Framework of Economic Security in Old Age

The framework of economic security in old age is wider than that of economic security in retirement. The former can include older persons' earnings from employment or self-employment, while the latter, which specifies retirement, by definition precludes most work-generated income.

Role of the Individual

Although Social Security, occupational pensions, and income from assets are generally regarded as representing the efforts of government, employer, and individual to provide income security to the elderly, the role of the individual in these efforts seems to have been underestimated.

Because Social Security is the mainstay of retirement income, one often hears that too much reliance is placed on the government. This view is correct only insofar as the sponsorship of Social Security is concerned. In terms of financing, however, individual workers and their employers jointly pay for the program and the government does not contribute general revenue to support it, except in minor ways. Moreover, there is the question of who ultimately bears the burden of the employer portion of the payroll tax; if employers reduce wages by the amount they pay in Social Security taxes, then workers are bearing nearly the entire cost of the program.

This interpretation of the individual's role in financing Social Security is not intended to dismiss the element of compulsion involved in the government's sponsorship of the program. It is intended, rather, to make clear the fact that it is the participants in the program who pay for it. In this interpretation, then, the "role" of the individual does not imply initiative on the part of each person. To the extent, however, that citizens vote in accord with their preferences for the program, the element of compulsion may be, to a degree, collectively self-imposed, thus demonstrating group initiative.

In the case of noncontributory occupational pensions under which the employer pays for pension contributions, individual workers may in fact be paying what the employer pays, if the employer would be paying higher wages in the absence of pension contributions. In addition, although uncommon, there are contributory plans under which workers pay at least part of the cost of their pensions. Therefore, the individual worker may well be a major provider for retirement income, even under occupational pension plans.

Private savings, whether in the form of home equity, insurance, stocks and bonds, Keogh plans, or individual retirement accounts, are by definition funded by the individuals themselves. Therefore, it is important to recognize that, despite governmental and employer sponsorship of various plans, the individual is a primary contributor to his or her income in old age.

Lest the role the individual plays be overemphasized, another interpretation of the role of the employer and of the government in providing economic security in old age could be introduced, an interpretation that casts the employer and the government in a broader framework for facilitating and generating economic security.

Role of the Employer

Employers' role in providing economic security for retired workers may extend beyond the creation and maintenance of occupational pensions, health benefit plans, and other savings mechanisms. The role of the employer, especially corporations, may include both preretirement and postretirement counseling, as well as the creation and maintenance of innovative work environments to accommodate an aging workforce.

Role of the Government

Through their influence on the overall economy, the federal government's fiscal, monetary, and regulatory policies significantly affect the elderly's economic security. For example, the high inflation and unemployment rates in the late 1960s and the 1970s (especially when inflation and unemployment coexisted) had major consequences on the financial status of Social Security. High inflation rates increase the outflow of benefit payments. High unemployment causes layoffs and reduces inflow of payroll tax revenues to the system. In addition, high unemployment also may reduce the hours of work and wage levels for many, or at least, some of the workers still employed. Moreover, high unemployment may increase Social Security expenditures by encouraging workers to retire earlier or seek disability benefits sooner than they might otherwise do.

Another example of the federal government's effect on old-age economic security is the result of the massive accumulation of national debt in the 1980s. Not only did budget cuts in expenditures for programs (other than OASDI) reduce economic security to older persons, the insistence on the "revenue-neutral" criterion in deliberations leading to the Tax Reform Act of 1986, for example, was also directly related to the succession of large budget deficits.

Moreover, since the federal government possesses an overarching influence on the economy, and since a productive and growing economy is the foundation of economic security (for older adults and young persons alike), considerations of ways to provide economic security in old age should go beyond designing, monitoring, and revising (in light of changing economic, demographic, and social circumstances) such economic security mechanisms as Social Security, occupational pensions, private savings, employment, and public assistance, as well as Medicare and Medicaid and other health care provisions. Concerns with economic security in old age should also include, at a minimum, how the government uses fiscal (taxing, spending, and borrowing), monetary (money supply and interest rates), and regulatory policies and, more broadly, the entire range of government activities, including war and peace, that impact the survival and vitality of the nation and all its people.

CURRENT SOURCES OF INCOME AND THEIR RELATIVE IMPORTANCE

Percentage of Older Persons with Specific Sources of Income

Older persons receive income from various sources: in 1984, 91% of couples and nonmarried persons aged 65 and over (hereafter referred to as aged units) received Social Security; 67% had income from assets; 27% derived income from private pensions; 20% had earnings from employment; 14% received government employee pensions; and 7% received public assistance (Upp, 1986).

Older Persons' Total Income by Income Source

These sources, however, were not equally important in providing the actual dollar amounts of income to older persons. In 1984, in terms of the percentage of total income of all aged units, the relative importance of the various income sources was as follows: Social Security, 38%; asset income, 26%; employment earnings, 17%; private pensions, 7%; government employee pensions, 7%; public assistance, 1%; and other sources, 4% (Upp, 1986).

Income Sources by Income Class

While highlighting the heterogeneity among older adults, the following discussion also serves to emphasize the relative importance of these sources to different income classes.

The most comprehensive data presently available for an analysis of the income status of the elderly by income class are the statistics for 1986 (Grad, 1988). In that year, there were approximately 21.6 million aged units in the United States, of which married couples constituted 8.7 million units and nonmarried persons, 12.9 units.

Aged units can be divided into four income classes (according to 1986 income) as follows: the lowest income class received less than $5,000; the second class, between $5,000 and $9,999; the third class, between $10,000 and $19,999; and the highest, $20,000 or more (Grad, 1988). Considerable variations existed in how much different sources of income contributed to the total income of the elderly in different income groups (Table 7.1). The distribution of the aged units by marital status among different income levels is shown in Table 7.2.

Lowest Income Group

To aged units in the lowest income group, Social Security benefits were of paramount importance, providing 77% of total income, with public assistance payments providing 14% of total income. In other words, more than 90% of the total income of the aged units in this group came from Social Security and public assistance. Other minor sources consisted of asset income (4%), other income (2%), private pensions (1%), and government employee pensions (1%). This group did not have any income from employment.

Table 7.1 Relative Importance of Various Income Sources in the Total Income of Aged Units[1] by Income Levels, 1986.

| | | | Income Levels | | | | | | |
| Lowest (less than $5,000) | | Second ($5,000–$9,999) | | Third ($10,000–$19,999) | | Highest ($20,000 or more) | | All units | |
Income sources	Percent of total income	Income sources	Percent of total income	Income sources	Percent of total income	Income sources	Percent of total income	Income sources	Percent of total income
1. Social Security	77%	1. Social Security	75%	1. Social Security	51%	1. Asset income	34%	1. Social Security	38%
2. Public assistance	14	2. Asset income	9	2. Asset income	19	2. Employment income	24	2. Asset income	26
3. Asset income	4	3. Government employee pensions[2]	4	3. Employment income	9	3. Social Security	21	3. Employment income	17
4. Other	2	4. Employment income	3	4. Private pensions	9	4. Government employee pensions[2]	9	4. Private pensions	7
5. Private pensions	1	5. Private pensions	3	5. Government employee pensions[2]	8	5. Private pensions	8	5. Government employee pensions[2]	7
6. Government employee pensions[2]	1	6. Public assistance	3	6. Other	2	6. Other	2	6. Other	2
7. Employment income	0	7. Other	2	7. Public assistance	0	7. Public assistance	0	7. Public assistance	1

Notes: [1]An aged unit, either a married couple living together or a nonmarried person, refers to one in which at least one member is 65 years of age or older. Nonmarried persons may be widows or widowers, divorced, never married, or persons married but living apart. [2]Railroad retirement pensions are included in government employee pensions. In 1986, they were received by persons in the second and third income classes, in both cases accounting for no more than 1 percent of total income.

Source: Grad, Susan, (in press).

Table 7.2 Aged Units by Marital Status and Income, 1986.

Income level	All Units	Married couples	Nonmarried persons
Less than $5,000	17%	3%	27%
	(3.7 million)	(0.3 million)	(3.5 million)
$5,000–$9,999	29%	13%	39%
	(6.2 million)	(1.2 million)	(5.1 million)
$10,000–$19,999	29%	37%	23%
	(6.2 million)	(3.2 million)	(2.9 million)
$20,000 or more	25%	46%	11%
	(5.4 million)	(4.0 million)	(1.4 million)
Total	100%	100%	100%
	(21.6 million units)	(8.7 million units)	(12.9 million units)

Source: Grad (in press).

Second Income Group

For aged units in the second income group, Social Security was still a very significant contributor, accounting for three-quarters of total income. Asset income was second in importance, providing 9% of total income. After Social Security and asset income came government employee pensions (4%), with employment, private pensions, and public assistance each at 3%. The rest, 2%, came from other sources.

Third Income Group

The relative importance of these income sources for the aged units in the third income group was quite different. Social Security, though still important, was less significant for this group, providing only 51% of total income. Nearly one-fifth came from assets. Next in importance were employment income and private pensions, each providing 9% of total income. The remaining sources of income were government employee pensions (8%) and other income (2%). This group did not receive any public assistance.

Highest Income Group

Aged units in the highest income group ($20,000 or more) derived their income from essentially the same sources, but the relative importance of these sources was significantly different. Asset income was the most important (about one-third of the total). Next was employment income (about one-quarter). Ranked third in importance, Social Security provided only about one-fifth of the total income. Of lesser importance were government employee pensions (9%) and private pensions (8%).

RELATIVE ROLE OF INCOME SOURCES
IN PAST AND FUTURE

During the last two decades, important developments have occurred in the relative contributions of the various income sources to the income status of older persons. This section reviews the changing importance of these sources in the past and discusses some of the more significant factors that will affect these income-generating mechanisms in the future.

Role of Social Security

The Social Security Act was passed in 1935. The collection of payroll taxes for old-age benefits was begun in 1937, and the first monthly Social Security benefits were paid in 1940. The original Social Security program was expanded to include survivors insurance in 1939 and disability insurance in 1956. These three components—old age, survivors, and disability insurance (OASDI)—are most often what is meant by Social Security.

During the last 20 years, Social Security continued to gain in importance (Upp, 1986). Whereas in 1962, 69% of aged units received income from it, 91% of them did in 1984. In terms of Social Security's role in the total income of aged units, its contribution has also grown, from accounting for 31% in 1962 to 38% in 1984. Social Security will continue to play a significant role in providing income to older persons.

Under the 1983 amendments, a portion of OASDI benefits is included in taxable income for taxpayers whose adjusted gross income, including otherwise tax-exempt interest income, combined with one-half of their benefits, exceeds $25,000 for an individual and $32,000 for a married couple filing a joint return. This provision reduces the relative importance of this income source to higher-income groups.

The normal retirement age for full benefits will be gradually raised to 66 by 2009 and to 67 by 2027. After the age for full benefit retirement is changed to 67, early retirement benefits commencing at age 62 will be reduced to 70% of full benefits, as compared to 80% at present. These provisions will combine to reduce Social Security benefits in the future from what they would be if the normal retirement age were not raised.

Role of Asset Income

During the past two decades, income from assets has increased its role in older persons' total income. While 54% of aged units received income from this source in 1962, 68% of them did in 1984. This income source also became a larger share of the total income of older persons, increasing from 16% in 1962 to 28% in 1984 (Upp, 1986). As noted earlier, asset income is the most important source of income among the highest income group.

Even though asset income represented an important percentage of the total income of the high-income aged, and even though a large proportion of the aged had income from this source, the median amounts of asset income were quite low in 1980: $1,700 for couples, $1,010 for single men, and $740 for single women, according to an unpublished tabulation by the U.S. Social Security Administration (Chen, 1985). One major reason for the relatively meager median asset income is that the value of liquid or financial assets in the hands of the aged is typically small or modest (Radner, 1988b).

Another problem is the nonliquid nature of home equity. In the context of private savings, home ownership requires special attention: Using home equity to augment current income poses a dilemma under existing circumstances. Although voluntary plans for converting home equity into spendable income have aroused interest and action, they still present a number of complex issues for home owners, lenders, and tax, welfare, and regulatory agencies of government.

There now exist some tax-induced mechanisms to encourage retirement savings, such as, the individual retirement account (IRA). Authorized in the Employee Retirement Income Security Act of 1974 (ERISA) and effective beginning in 1975, IRAs were created as tax incentives for generating retirement income to supplement Social Security and private pension benefits.

The current law permits anyone under age 70½ to contribute up to 100% of compensation (employment or self-employment income), with a maximum of $2,000 per year, to an IRA account. A person with a nonworking spouse may establish two IRAs with a combined maximum of $2,250 annually. When both spouses work, they may have two IRAs with a maximum of $2,000 each per year.

The federal income tax normally payable on the income placed into IRAs is deferred through a tax deduction. Under the Tax Reform Act of 1986, effective in 1987, such a tax deduction is allowed only to taxpayers who (1) do not have employer-maintained retirement plans (such as a qualified pension or profit-sharing plan) or (2) though covered by such plans, have adjusted gross income (AGI) below $25,000 (for individuals filing single return) or $40,000 (for married couples filing joint return). For individuals with AGI between $25,000 and $35,000 and couples with AGI between $40,000 and $50,000, tax deductions for IRA contributions will be phased out so that no deductions are allowed for single filers with AGI over $35,000 and joint filers with AGI over $50,000. For each $5 of AGI over these levels, $1 of IRA contribution will not be deductible.

However, taxpayers with employer-maintained retirement plans whose AGI is too high to qualify for tax deductions may still establish IRAs; these may be called *nondeductible* IRAs. These IRA deposits will accumulate interest income that is not taxed as it is earned but is subject to tax when withdrawn. Deposits into the IRAs will be tax-free when withdrawn because they were nondeductible when contributed. The interest income produced by IRAs is not currently taxed as income; the taxability of that income is deferred to the future, when it is withdrawn.

Although IRAs have been rather popular in the last several years, the Tax Reform Act of 1986, which imposed restrictions on their use to the categories of taxpayers described above, would dampen the interest in and reduce the use of this savings vehicle for retirement.

Role of Occupational Pensions

Occupational pensions refer to private pension plans as well as federal, state, and local government employee pension systems. Private pension plans are now a very important economic and social mechanism for providing income in old age. They have shown significant growth since 1950, when they first became accepted for collective bargaining (in the *Inland Steel* case, which was the result of a denial of *certiorari* by the United States Supreme Court in 1949).

Private retirement plans consist of pension plans and deferred profit-sharing plans. A private pension plan is generally defined as a plan established by an employer, union, or both that provides cash income for life to qualified workers upon retirement. Benefits are usually financed by regular contributions from employers (noncontributory plans) and, in some cases, from employees as well (contributory plans). Under deferred profit-sharing plans, on the other hand, contributions and benefits depend on the profits of the employer and are therefore not determinable in advance.

Private pension benefits have gained in relative importance in the last two decades. Whereas in 1962 only 9% of all aged units had private pension income, 24% had such income in 1984. The relative importance of such an income source is also evidenced by the fact that private pension benefits accounted for 3% of total income of all aged units in 1962 and 6% in 1984—though still a minor fraction of total income (Upp, 1986).

Private pension plans grew throughout the 1970s, but future growth in coverage for workers not yet covered is expected to rise at a slower pace for several reasons: (1) the most accessible groups of workers (such as those in the manufacturing, mining, and transportation industries, and in large establishments) have already been covered; (2) industries with traditionally high pension coverage are expected to employ a declining share of workers, whereas industries with traditionally low pension coverage are expected to increase their share of workers; and (3) the large proportion of workers, primarily in small- and medium-sized businesses, will continue to find it difficult to obtain coverage (Andrews & Mitchell, 1986; Chen, 1985).

In the future, government employee pensions as an income source will be reduced by the Social Security amendments of 1983, which mandate coverage for new federal employees beginning in 1984; the resulting supplementary civil service retirement plan naturally provides lower benefits than the plan applicable to "old" employees. This legislation also prohibits state and local governments, which had previously elected coverage, from terminating coverage under Social Security for their employees and allows state and local governments that had withdrawn from Social Security to rejoin.

Role of Earnings

Employment as a source of income for the elderly has clearly declined during the past two decades. Whereas 36% of aged units had earnings in 1962, only 21% of them did in 1984. While earnings represented 29% of total income of all older persons in 1962, they represented only 16% of their total income in 1984 (Upp, 1986).

Earnings may contribute less to the total income of the aged in the future if participation of older persons in the labor force continues to decline and the early retirement trend continues to accelerate. However, it is also possible that earnings may become a more important income source if the elderly remain in the workforce longer as a means of enhancing their income position during inflationary times. In addition, if the health status of older persons improves with the decline in the mortality rate, then they may wish to work longer. Finally, low birth rates in recent years and the low rates projected for the future will result in a smaller labor force (as defined by conventional ages) in the future. The aged may well be called on to work longer. The change in the normal retirement age under OASDI, scheduled to begin in the year 2000 for persons born in 1938 or later, is also consistent with this possibility.

Role of Public Assistance

Public assistance to older persons is implemented through Supplemental Security Income (SSI), a means-tested program that was created in 1972 and became operational in 1974. SSI was created to replace old-age assistance, aid to the blind, and aid to the permanently and totally disabled, previously operated by state governments with matching grants from the federal government. SSI is administered by the Social Security Administration and funded from general revenues. Most states provide additional SSI payments.

SSI's main objective is to provide income support to the needy aged, blind, and disabled according to nationally uniform eligibility standards and payment levels. SSI, like the programs it replaced, is an income source of last resort. Congress requires that those persons receiving SSI have needs that are not met by such sources as Social Security payments, payments by other agencies, and payments from private pension plans.

In 1984, 10% of all aged units received public assistance. Although it constituted only 1% of the aggregate income of all aged units, to those receiving welfare payments, it was a very important income source.

IMPROVING INCOME SECURITY MECHANISMS

This section discusses several ways in which the existing income security mechanisms could be improved in order to widen the options for work or retirement in old age, which in turn will help enhance the quality of life of older adults and, through them, of all society.

Improving the Role of Social Security: Provide More for Women

The social, demographic, and economic environments have undergone great changes in the last few decades. When Social Security first started making monthly payments in 1940, the traditional family unit consisted of a "bread-winning father, bread-baking mother, and bread-eating children." Most marriages lasted a lifetime, and only 17% of married women worked for pay. Today the typical family can no longer be characterized simply by a wage-earning husband with a dependent homemaker-wife and children. Separation, divorce, cohabitation, and single parenthood have become more prevalent, and women have entered the paid labor force in record numbers. Now more than half of all married women are in the labor force, although many of them are only occasional or part-time workers (Chen, 1983). In light of these changes, many have criticized Social Security for unfair treatment of women, pointing to penalties for working, divorce, widowhood, and homemaking and/or childrearing.

Since a working or nonworking (that is, homemaking) married woman receives benefits based on her husband's earnings credits, a working wife may feel that she is no better off for the taxes she pays into OASDI: Where the total earnings of the two couples are identical, a husband and wife who both work (a two-earner couple) receive less in benefits than a couple with only one working spouse. Similarly, the surviving spouse of a two-earner couple receives less in benefits than does the surviving spouse of a one-earner couple with identical total earnings. Thus arises the argument that Social Security penalizes women for working.

A divorced wife or a surviving divorced wife has no Social Security protection based on her ex-husband's earnings credits unless their marriage had lasted for at least 10 years. That is the basis of the argument of the penalty for divorce. That no benefits are payable to a widow under age 60 unless she is either at least aged 50 and disabled or is caring for a child or children of her deceased husband underlies the argument of the penalty for widowhood.

The charge of the penalty for homemaking and/or child care arises out of the fact that a nonworking or homemaking married woman is not insured against disability, and her survivors are not entitled to benefits when she dies. When a woman takes time out from paid work to raise a family, she loses disability income protection if she does not meet the recent-work requirement. Furthermore, her working career is shortened and thus her lifetime average earnings credits are reduced because of too many zero-earning years. As a result, her retirement benefits are less than what they would have been had she not raised a family.

In the past, OASDI did contain unfair discrimination by gender, against both men and women. The 1983 amendments, however, prospectively eliminated all gender-based differential treatment and included several changes in benefits that primarily affect women. For example, benefits will be payable to an eligible divorced spouse once the other spouse is eligible for benefits, even if he or she is not receiving them (because of nonfiling or because of substantial employment) (Myers, 1983).

With respect to the penalty for working, the argument of unfairness misses the fact that under the existing system working wives are earning valuable credits toward disbility benefits (in case of permanent and total disability), survivors benefits (for eligible survivors in case of her death), and retirement benefits (in case she retires earlier than her husband). But there remains an argument about the penalty to the two-earner family. Although the two-earner family has more disability, young-survivor, and early retirement benefit protection, a one-earner family has more retirement and aged-survivor benefit protection (Myers, 1983).

One popular reform idea is the earnings-sharing approach. Under it, a worker's Social Security benefits would be based on his or her earnings when single plus one-half of the combined earnings of the couple when married. At divorce, each spouse's wage record would be credited with half the couple's combined earnings during the marriage, regardless of the length of the marriage. Therefore each spouse would receive a Social Security retirement benefit in his or her own right (Congressional Budget Office, 1986; U.S. House of Representatives, 1985).

It is possible to solve some of these problems by reducing the duration-of-marriage requirement for a divorced spouse from 10 years to 5 years, by removing the age-50 requirement for receiving disabled widow's or widower's benefits, and by providing more chlid-care credit years (beyond the very limited provision of child-care credit in the form of drop-out years for disabled female workers) in determining average earnings for benefit calculations.

Improving the Role of Private Pensions: Strengthen Portability Provisions

Whether a retired worker receives private pension income depends on the coverage, vesting, and portability provisions of the pension plan. Unlike Social Security, which is virtually universal, the coverage under private pension plans is uneven among industries, businesses of different sizes, and types of work.

Even when a worker is covered by a private pension plan, his or her prospect of receiving a pension depends on the plan's vesting provision. Vesting refers to the right of a pension plan participant to the ownership of the accrued deferred retirement benefits or annuity accumulation whether or not the participant leaves the plan before becoming eligible to receive the benefit at a stated early or normal retirement age. Private pension plans differ in their vesting provisions. Workers who leave employment before meeting vesting requirements will lose all benefits they would have earned on the job had they remained in it for the requisite number of years. Vesting requirements have been shortened over the years. Under the Tax Reform Act of 1986, the three vesting standards permitted by the Employee Retirement Income Security Act of 1974 will be replaced, beginning in 1989, by two formulas: (1) full vesting after 5 years or (2) 25% vesting after 3 years and full vesting after 7 years. The 10-year vesting standard remains permitted for multiemployer plans.

Pension portability generally refers to the transfer of pension rights from one pension plan to another when changing employment. There are two important aspects: portability of credited services and portability of current values. Service portability refers to the arrangement under which years of service credited under one pension plan are transferred into the next employer's pension plan. For example, if an employee has not met the vesting standard under one plan, his or her years of participation would be transferred into the next employer's plan and would count toward the pension on the next job. This is accomplished through multiemployer pension plans (Employee Benefits Research Institute, 1986).

Portability of current values or cash distributions refers to the transfer of the cash value of vested benefits directly to the worker or to another retirement benefit arrangement upon leaving the job before retirement age. Lump-sum cash distributions before retirement have become a concern to policy makers because workers are likely to acquire a series of vested benefits in lump-sum distributions before retirement and because of the evidence that many workers have used such distributions for current consumption rather than retirement savings (Employee Benefit Research Institute, 1986).

To cope with this problem, two basic approaches have been suggested. The first approach would create a federal portability agency or a central clearinghouse that would receive cash distributions on behalf of the workers. The second approach would require that preretirement cash distributions be saved in existing retirement benefit arrangements by rollovers to an IRA or some other plan (Employee Benefit Research Institute, 1986).

It is essential to assist workers in protecting the cash distributions of their vested pension benefits from current consumption. However, if an IRA is to be used as a vehicle to facilitate or mandate rollovers of preretirement distributions, then the suggestions (as to the early withdrawal penalty and the minimum age at which withdrawal can be made without penalty) in the next section for improving the IRA as a retirement savings vehicle should be seriously considered.

Improving the Role of Private Savings: Reform Individual Retirement Account

Tax deductions for IRA contributions could be made available only to workers aged 50 and over with modified adjusted gross income (MAGI) of $25,000 or less (if single return) and $35,000 or less (if joint return), even though they already have employer pension coverage. MAGI is the sum of adjusted gross income (AGI) and tax-exempt interest income. To ensure that IRAs would be used for retirement, the early withdrawal penalty could be raised to 20% from the current 10% and the age at which withdrawals can be made without penalty could be increased to age 62 from the current 59½. This proposal is based on the following analysis.

During the debates prior to the adoption of the Tax Reform Act of 1986, one argument for limiting deductibility was that IRAs had become tax shelters for upper-bracket taxpayers. In 1983, for example, 9.8% of taxpayers with AGI of $40,000 or less filed for IRAs, in contrast to the 50.6% of those with AGI of $40,000 or more who filed (U.S. Department of the Treasury, 1985). However, removing this tax incentive simply because higher-income persons reap substantially greater tax benefits than lower-income persons is like throwing the baby out with the bathwater. The problem would be better solved by using a tax credit instead of a tax deduction as a tax incentive.

According to the May 1983 "EBRI/HHS Current Population Survey Pension Supplement" findings, although only 38% of all respondents said they established IRAs for retirement, more workers at lower earnings levels indicated retirement income as their motive: this motivation was greatest (48%) among those earning $10,000–15,000; next greatest (44%), among those earning $5,000–10,000; and third greatest (42%) among those earning $15,000–20,000 (Employee Benefit Research Institute, 1984). Persons with modest or low incomes ought to be encouraged to save for retirement, even if they have employer-maintained retirement plans.

Another argument used to advocate the repeal of IRA deductions was that the lowered tax rates would leave the taxpayer with more disposable income and thus a greater capacity to save. More disposable income also creates a greater capacity to spend, however, and without a tax incentive, especially one that is taken away after having been available, the urge to spend could overcome the desire to save for many persons. Moreover, even when people do save, there is a difference between general savings and retirement savings, a point not commonly appreciated. General savings may be used for any purpose at any time, and the need or temptation to tap these savings may occur before retirement. Instead, saving specifically for retirement should be encouraged.

The reason for advocating an IRA tax incentive for older workers with low and modest incomes is simple: they have not been contributing to IRAs only for the tax advantage, and they are the age group closest to retirement. Furthermore, some 62% of respondents aged 55 and over had spousal IRAs, according to the May 1983 "EBRI/HHS Current Population Survey Pension Supplement" (Employee Benefit Research Institute, 1984). This development is salubrious and should be encouraged.

The controversy over whether IRAs have added to total savings or have merely shifted the forms of savings is not central or even particularly important. So long as law can bring about a larger percentage of total savings in the form of IRAs dedicated to retirement use, we will have fulfilled the original intent of the 1974 ERISA legislation to strengthen retirement income provisions. Raising the early withdrawal penalty and increasing the eligible age for withdrawals without penalty, along with tax deductibility of initial contributions, would greatly assist in achieving this objective. Making deductible IRAs available to older persons at low and modest income levels would offer the greatest incentive to this group. Making nondeductible IRAs available to younger persons or those of greater means would still encourage them through the deferral of taxes on IRA earnings. Together, these two types of IRAs would accelerate the growth in retirement savings in general.

Improving the Role of Employment: Change Work Environment

To the extent that population aging results from declining birth rates, the labor force in the traditional ages will be smaller because fewer babies born implies a smaller potential pool of future workers. The ratio of the population aged 20–64 (who are considered potential supporters) to the population aged 0–19 and 65 and over (potential dependents) may be called the "supporter index." This index is an indication of the numerical relationship between the working-age (supporters) and nonworking-age (dependents) populations. Although a crude measure, it does highlight the directions of change (Chen, 1987).

The larger the supporter index, the greater the potential number of workers to support the dependents. As shown in Table 7.3, the increase in the supporter index from 1980 to 2010 results largely from the baby boom of the mid-1940s to mid-1960s. But this index begins to fall after 2010 and rapidly so after 2020, when it is estimated to be 1.36; it is projected to drop under 1.20 during the period 2030–2060. Low and declining fertility rates from the 1970s on, combined with the retirement of the baby boomers, explain this downward trend.

When the number of potential supporters relative to potential dependents declines, society may need to call on the old to remain in or reenter the workforce. Furthermore, to the extent that population aging arises out of the prolongation of life, better health among the elderly may increase their desire to work longer. Economically and emotionally, voluntary postponement of retirement will be beneficial to the elderly themselves, and their continued active contributions to production will also benefit the young and middle-aged.

A criticism of delayed retirement is that it will leave little or no room at the top for young persons, who will have to cope with slower promotions. In the context of declining supporter indexes, however, to the extent that later retirement takes place, it will occur during 2030–2040, when the workforce aged 20–64 will be declining in absolute numbers by as much as 6 million, according to current estimates. Therefore, those older persons who choose to work would not be displacing the younger workforce, but rather supplementing it.

Another issue concerning postponement of retirement is that it runs counter to the early retirement trends evident in recent decades. Complex forces govern an individual's decision to continue working or to retire and an employer's decision to retain older workers or induce them to leave. Physical, psychological, and economic reasons may lead a person to decide on early retirement. Declining health and boredom with work have led many to retire early. Sufficient financial incentives for early retirement are a strong factor as well. Labor-market conditions, the state of the economy, and productivity considerations are factors affecting employer policies.

Table 7.3 Supporter Index in the United States in Selected Years, 1980–2060[a].

Year	Potential supporters (in thousands)	Potential total dependents (in thousands)	Supporter index
1980	134,850	101,034	1.33
1985	145,614	101,810	1.43
1990	152,660	105,617	1.45
1995	158,802	109,428	1.51
2000	165,728	111,414	1.49
2010	178,091	115,588	1.54
2020	177,210	130,535	1.36
2030	172,213	145,152	1.19
2040	174,997	148,313	1.18
2050	176,638	150,170	1.18
2060	178,449	152,202	1.17

[a]Supporter index is the ratio of potential supporters (population aged 20–64) to potential total dependents (population aged 0–19 plus population aged 65 and over). Calculated from Table 16b in Wade (1985).

Other things being equal, it seems that labor-force participation by older persons could be encouraged by job redesign, job reassignment, and other modifications to the work environment. Examples include alternate work patterns, such as flextime (part-time work, including part-day, part-week, or part-year, or alternate days, weeks, or months); job sharing; compressed work weeks (such as three-day or four-day weeks); cottage industries; phasing out retirement (which includes rehearsal retirement and sabbaticals); preparing and training for second and third careers; and volunteer work. In addition, a morale-lifting managerial climate within an organization and a prosperous economy are environmental factors conducive to keeping older adults in the workforce.

Moreover, it is possible to revise the Social Security program in order to widen the range of options for work or retirement. In this regard, recent innovations in Norway and Sweden may lead to creative arrangements offering more choices to older persons. While some flexibility of retirement age is part of social insurance programs in many countries, including the United States, explicit programs for phased or tapered retirement are rare. In the 1970s, both Norway and Sweden introduced partial pension plans into their social insurance programs, but the two plans differ considerably. Swedish workers may begin partial retirement at age 60, before the normal retirement age of 65, while the Norwegian plan encourages partial retirement after attaining the normal retirement age of 67 (Ginsburg, 1985).

In Norway, flexible and partial pension possibilities now enable workers to choose a retirement age between 67 and 70 with the option of tapering off work gradually. Thus persons between 67 and 70 may take none, one-fourth, one-half, or three-fourths of their pension while still working; the pension plus earnings, however, cannot total more than 80% of previous earnings. Very few workers, especially blue-collar ones, use this plan.

Sweden's national pension system offers workers aged 60–70 a wide range of pension options. Disabled workers and those unemployed with no hope of work are given disability pensions. In addition to disability payments, the pensions available to Swedish workers are (a) a full old-age pension at age 65 without any earnings or retirement test; (b) a delayed old-age pension with benefit increases for deferring retirement past age 65 up to age 70; (c) an early old-age pension with permanently reduced benefits, available at age 60; (d) a split pension, allowing a worker to collect half of the old-age pension before age 65 at the reduced rate and to collect the other half at age 65 with no benefit reduction; (e) and a partial pension.

Sweden's partial pension, instituted in 1976, enables a worker aged 60–64 to reduce his or her working hours voluntarily, receiving pay only for the time worked but also receiving a partial pension that replaces part of the lost earnings. There is no actuarial reduction in their old-age pension at age 65, and the old-age pension is paid in full at that time, without any retirement test. The partial pension pays 50% of the lost earnings up to a monetary limit that covers the entire earnings of nearly all blue-collar workers and about 80% of the earnings of salaried employees. The partial pension is taxable income, as are all pensions in Sweden; it is financed by a payroll tax of 0.5% (higher than at the onset of the program). Additional funds come from general revenues. Partial pensioners are only one of several groups of 60-to-64 year-olds with some type of early retirement benefits. In 1983, about 21% of all persons eligible for the partial pension had opted to receive it.

Improving the Role of Public Assistance: Raise SSI Payment

During the last two decades, the income status of the elderly has improved substantially, with the incidence of poverty markedly reduced (Radner, 1988a). However, statistics on income distribution and poverty unmistakably point to the special problems faced by several low-income subgroups among the elderly: single persons, especially single women and widows; racial minorities; and the very old (Commonwealth Fund Commission for Elderly People Living Alone, 1987; National Association for Hispanic Elderly, 1987; National Council of La Raza, 1987).

As shown in Table 7.4, of the 26.8 million noninstitutionalized persons aged 65 or over in 1987, 10% had incomes below the federal poverty line

Table 7.4 Percentage of the Elderly in Poverty Among Various Subgroups in 1987.

Subgroups	Percent and number (in millions) in poverty	
All elderly	10%	(2.6 million)
Elderly couples	4	(0.6)
All elderly living alone	19	(1.7)
Elderly widows living alone	19	(1.1)
Elderly men living alone	15	(0.3)
Elderly women living alone	20	(1.4)
Nonwhite elderly living alone	43	(0.3)
Hispanic elderly living alone	35	(0.1)
White elderly living alone	16	(1.3)

Source: Compiled from Figure 2 in Commonwealth Fund Commission on Elderly People Living Alone (1987).

($5,393, or $104 per week). While only 4% of the elderly couples lived in poverty, the elderly living alone and elderly widows living alone both had much higher poverty rates—19%. The incidence of poverty among elderly men living alone was 15%, while that for elderly women living alone was 20%. Of the single elderly who lived alone, the poverty rate was the highest among minorities: 43% for nonwhites and 35% for Hispanics, compared to 16% for whites.

Of the 8.8 million elderly who lived alone in 1987, 80% were women and two-thirds of these were widows. Half of the elderly people living alone were over 75 years of age. Table 7.5 shows that the poverty rates are higher in the older age groups for nearly every category of marital status/living arrangements. For example, in the group aged 85 and over, 16% of them were poor. While 9% of the couples in this age group were poor, 16% of the single men and 20% of the single women were. Moreover, of the single persons living alone, men had an 18% poverty rate and women had a much higher rate of 27%.

A simulation study by the Commonwealth Fund Commission on Elderly People Living Alone (1987) suggests that over the next 25 to 30 years, the number of elderly people living alone will continue to rise. The poverty rate in this group will, however, decline by several percentage points after the turn of the century as a result of changes in the labor force and increases in pension benefits. Nevertheless, without further policy initiatives the income gap between elderly women living alone and all other elderly groups may widen over the next 30 years, and by 2020 poverty among the elderly could be confined primarily to women living alone.

Although SSI represents the major public assistance program for the elderly poor, only one-third of them receive SSI benefits and these payments accounted for only 14% of their total income. Despite their low income,

Table 7.5 Percentage of the Elderly in Poverty by Age, Sex, Marital Status/Living Arrangements in 1987.

Categories of older persons	Percentage[a] in poverty			
	65 and over	65–74	65–84	85 and over
All elderly	10	7	12	16
Married couples	4	3	6	9
Single males	13	10	18	16
Single females	18	16	19	20
Single males living alone	15	11	20	18
Single females living alone	20	18	21	27
Single males living with others	10	9	10	9
Single females living with others	11	12	11	4

[a]Percentages have been rounded off from the figures given in the commission's report.

Source: Compiled from Table A-1 in Commonwealth Fund Commission on Elderly People Living Alone (1987).

approximately half of SSI-eligible persons did not apply for benefits. The low participation rate, apparently reflecting lack of awareness of the program and aversion to the means-tested stigma, limits the program's usefulness. Another problem is the highly stringent eligibility rules, which contain a severe asset test.

The Commission suggests that a combination of public and private effort can reduce by half the number of elderly people living alone who are in poverty by the year 2020. In the short term, government initiatives, such as changes in the SSI program, would be the most effective means of improving the situation. The Commission believes that the federal SSI payment should be raised to the poverty level ($104 per week for a single elderly person). Such a recommendation deserves serious consideration. Over the long term, the Commission believes that pension coverage can be expanded and employment opportunities enhanced. The implementation of suggestions discussed throughout this section should help to raise the level of income security in old age.

INCOME SECURITY AND ECONOMIC SECURITY: THE ROLE OF HEALTH CARE FINANCING

One objective in providing economic security in old age is the preservation of a certain standard of living in retirement relative to that in preretirement

years. Since income is singularly important for the attainment and maintenance of living standards, there is almost an exclusive interest in the income
status of older persons. Indeed, in the literature, *income status* and *economic status* are terms that are often interchangeable.

Equivalent Retirement Income

Concerning the difference in preretirement and postretirement income needs
or expenditures, at least three estimates are available. First, the Bureau of
Labor Statistics (BLS) has developed an "equivalence scale" for estimating
income and budget costs among families of different size, type, and age
(U.S. Department of Labor, 1970). According to the BLS scale, a single
person aged 65 or over would need 28% as much income for the same level
of living as a four-person family with husband aged 35–54, wife, and two
children aged 6–15. An elderly couple aged 65 or over would require 51% as
much income to gain parity in the living standard with the younger family
just described.

Second, to establish a living standard that maintains the same level of
living in retirement as existed just prior to retirement, Schulz suggests that
the appropriate replacement is about 65–70% of gross income for a middle-
income worker (Schulz, 1985). He derives this ratio by taking into account
three factors: the reduced income tax burden in retirement due to special
federal and state income tax provisions for persons aged 65 and over;
discontinued need for retirement savings; and the expenditure difference
(for the equivalent level of living) between couples aged 55–64 and couples
aged 65 or older as estimated by BLS.

Third, a presidential commission proposed a set of target replacement
rates for income in retirement (President's Commission on Pension Policy,
1981). Arguing that preretirement living standards should be measured in
terms of preretirement disposable income, the commission suggests a series
of equivalent retirement incomes for persons at different income levels—
ranging from a high of 86% for a married couple retiring in 1980 with
preretirement disposable income of $5,922 to a low of 51% for a single
person retiring in the same year with a disposable income of $27,751.

The different methodologies for deriving equivalent scales of living for
different families have not adequately accounted for the different expenditure patterns among families of different sizes with household heads of
different ages. For example, the BLS equivalence scale assumes that families
spending the same proportion of income on food have attained equal levels
of living. However, a recent study of household expenditure patterns concludes that the age of the head of the family has a significant influence on

expenditures (Chen & Chu, 1982). Within each income class, the average budget shares (i.e., the proportions of a household's budget allocated) for medical care, personal care services, household utilities, and gifts and contributions are positively related to the age of the household head, increasing as that age increases. Noting that even with Medicare and Medicaid the aged still allocate more of their total budget to medical care than do other age groups, the study suggests that health care provisions should be an important consideration in assessing economic status of the aged, including the measure of poverty.

That older persons are at greater health risk and therefore spend more for medical and personal care services is well known. It is not well recognized, however, that the possibility of significant expenditures for health care, including long-term care, therefore needs to be explicitly included in the concept of economic security. As stated earlier, economic security is a broader concept than income security; thus provisions for financing accessible and adequate health care should be an integral part of the economic security structure.

Acute Medical Care

The quality and costs of health care are a concern to everyone, especially the elderly. Although enacting a Medicare catastrophic illness program is an important step forward, it falls short of addressing financial catastrophe due to illness. In a recent study, it was pointed out that the monetary burden of medical expenses should be evaluated as a function of people's incomes (Feder, Moon, & Scanlon, 1987). To people with limited means, even small medical bills can be catastrophic. Catastrophic spending is defined in the study as spending above 15% of income. In 1986, while the elderly spent an average of 11% of their per capita incomes on acute medical care, more than one-fifth of the elderly spent more than 15%, more than one-tenth spent more than 20%, and more than 7% spent more than 25%. This study concludes that a large number of elderly persons can experience sizable financial burdens from acute care expenses alone.

Another recent study points out that of 3.3 million poor elderly in 1987, 2.2 million were without Medicaid, although the program is designed to help pay most of their health care costs not covered by Medicare (Rowland & Lyones, 1987). In addition, one-third of the 4.3 million near-poor elderly were driven to poverty by out-of-pocket payments for medical care. For them, basic medical care can be financially catastrophic. Two-thirds of the poor elderly without Medicaid coverage spent, on average, more than 15% of their out-of-pocket income on medical expenses. Over 40% of the elderly poor without Medicaid paid an average of $500 per year for private insurance (Medigap plans) to fill the insurance gap not covered by Medicare. Minority elderly had considerably less overall health care coverage than white elderly. Minority elderly, the report points out, were twice as likely as elderly whites to have only Medicare coverage. Among the elderly poor, one-third of the minorities relied only on Medicare, compared to one-quarter of whites. Only 18% of poor minorities supplemented Medicare with private insurance, compared to 48% of poor elderly whites.

Long-Term Care

The preceding discussion concerned the financial impact of acute care alone. Long-term care expenses are simply a matter of graver proportion; while acute medical care costs for most people may be heavy in some years and light in others, long-term care costs are by definition recurring. According to a recent study group on long-term health care policies, in 1984 approximately one-fifth of the 28 million persons aged 65 and over had long-term care (LTC) needs (U.S. Department of Health and Human Services, 1987). Of those needing LTC, 29% were in nursing homes and 71% were in the community. Approximately 1.5 million persons (5% of the elderly population) were nursing home residents. The percentages of the elderly in nursing homes are projected to rise to 8.8% between 1986 and 2000 and then fall to 8% by 2018.

In 1985, 2% of the elderly aged 65–74, 6% of those aged 75–84, and 23% of those aged 85 and over were in nursing homes. By age 85, 61% of those with limitations in activities of daily living were in nursing homes. In addition, approximately 14% of the elderly living in the community had limitations in activities of daily living. Of these persons, 2.6% of those aged 65–74 and 31.6% of those aged 65 and over needed assistance with personal care.

The financial dimensions of health care expenditures and long-term care costs are staggering. In 1984 the total health care expenditures for the elderly exceeded $119 billion. In the same year, the expenditures for nursing home care amounted to $32 billion. Nearly one-half (49.4%) of this $32 billion total was paid out-of-pocket; the rest was paid by Medicaid (43.4%), other government programs (3.7%), Medicare (1.9%), private insurance plans (0.9%), and other sources (0.6%). Perhaps the most dramatic statistic is the estimate of $22,000 as the average cost of a year's stay for one person in a nursing home for private-pay patients. Despite the costly nature of providing medical and personal care for those who can no longer function independently, few persons are willing or able to set aside funds for future

LTC expenses in their financial planning for retirement (see, e.g., Boyd & Hoyos, 1987).

While enacting a program to protect against catastrophic costs of acute illness is a step in the right direction, the real challenge lies in creating ways to provide long-term custodial care insurance, using the tripod structure involving the individual, the employer, and the government, for without it few persons can feel economically secure with their incomes.

SUMMARY

After identifying the income security system as a tripod structure symbolizing the efforts of the individual, the employer, and the government, the first section of this chapter suggested that economic security is a broader concept than income security, since a person is concerned not only with the acquisition of income and assets but also with the retention and disposal of them. Factors such as health care expenditures, housing and living arrangements, service delivery, and support networks affect income and asset retention. Both acquisition and retention of income and assets, furthermore, are influenced by macroeconomic policies. This section also discussed the possibility that the role of the individual in providing economic security may be underestimated.

In the second section, the heterogeneity of older persons was demonstrated in terms of both income sources and the relative importance of these sources to persons in different income classes. Social Security declines in importance as income level rises, whereas assets and employment as sources of income increase with income levels. Occupational pensions are of minimal importance to persons in the lowest-income class. Though more important to persons in the higher-income classes, occupational pensions as a proportion to their total income lie between 10% and 20% for these groups. By definition, public assistance is important only to the lowest-income class. During the last two decades, the relative importance of these income sources has changed, as pointed out in the third section, which also speculated on their future roles.

The fourth section proposed possible ways of improving the five income security mechanisms: to provide more child-care credit for women under Social Security, to strengthen portability under private pension plans, to make IRAs more accessible and more meaningful for retirement purposes, to enhance the role of employment for adults, and to raise SSI so as to eliminate poverty.

The chapter concluded by emphasizing that, without accessible and adequately financed health care, few persons will feel economically secure with the incomes they have.

REFERENCES

Andrews, E. S., & Mitchell, O. S. (1986). The current and future role of pensions in old age economic security. *Benefits Quarterly, 2*(2), 27–35.

Boyd, B., & Hoyos, A. (1987). *Benefits Quarterly, 3*(4), 1–9.

Chen, Y.-P. (1983). *Social security in a changing society.* Bryn Mawr, PA: McCahan Foundation.

Chen, Y.-P. (1985). Economic status of the aging. In R. H. Binstock & E. Shanas (Eds.), *Handbook of aging and the social sciences* (pp. 641–665). New York: Van Nostrand Reinhold.

Chen, Y.-P. (1987). Make assets out of tomorrow's elderly. *The Gerontologist, 27*(4), 410–416.

Chen, Y.-P., & Chu, K.-W. (1982). Household expenditure patterns: The effect of age of family head. *Journal of Family Issues, 3*(2), 233–250.

Congressional Budget Office. (1986). *Earnings sharing options for the Social Security system.* Washington, DC: U.S. Government Printing Office.

Commonwealth Fund Commission on Elderly People Living Alone. (1987). *Old, alone and poor: A plan for reducing poverty among elderly people living alone.* Baltimore: Author.

Employee Benefit Research Institute. (1984). *Individual retirement accounts: Characteristics and policy implications* (EBRI Issue Brief No. 32). Washington, DC: Author.

Employee Benefit Research Institute. (1986). *Pension portability and benefit adequacy* (EBRI Issue Brief No. 56). Washington, DC: Author.

Feder, J., Moon, M., & Scanlon, W. (1987). Nibbling at catastrophic costs. *Health Affairs, 6*(4), 5–19.

Ginsburg, H. (1985). Flexible and partial retirement for Norwegian and Swedish workers. *Monthly Labor Review, 108*(10), 33–43.

Grad, S. (1988). Income of the population 55 or over, 1986. USDHHS, Soc. Sec. Admin. SSA Pub. No. 13-11871.

Maddox, G. L. (1987). Aging differently. *The Gerontologist, 27*(5), 557–564.

Myers, R. J. (1983). Inequities toward women in the Social Security system. Hearing before the Task Force on Social Security and Women of the Subcommittee on Retirement Income and Employment, Select Committee on Aging, House of Representatives, 98th Congress, September 22, 1983 (Comm. Publication #98-413, p. 137).

National Association for Hispanic Elderly. (1987). *Improving the quality of life for aged Hispanics and other older Americans.* Washington, DC: Author.

National Council of La Raza. (1987). *The Hispanic elderly: A demographic profile.* Washington, DC: Author.

President's Commission on Pension Policy. (1981). *Coming of age: Toward a national retirement income policy.* Washington, DC: Author.

Radner, D. B. (1988a). *Shifts in the aged–nonaged income relationship, 1979–85* (Office of Research and Statistics Working Paper Series, No. 35). Washington, DC: Social Security Administration.

Radner, D. B. (1988b). *The wealth of the aged and nonaged, 1984* (Office of Research and Statistics Working Paper Series, No. 36). Washington, DC: Social Security Administration.

Rowland, D., & Lyones, B. (1987). *Medicare's poor*. Baltimore: The Commonwealth Fund Commission on Elderly People Living Alone.

Schulz, J. H. (1985). *The economics of aging*. Belmont, CA: Wadsworth.

Upp, M. (1986). Fast facts and figures about social security. *Social Security Bulletin, 49*(6), 7–8.

U.S. Department of Health and Human Services. (1987). *Report to Congress and the secretary by the task force on long-term health care policies*. Washington, DC: U.S. Government Printing Office.

U.S. Department of Labor. (1970). *Revised equivalence scale: For estimating equivalent incomes or budget costs by family types* (BLS Bulletin No. 1570-2). Washington, DC: Author.

U.S. Department of the Treasury. (1985). *Office of tax analysis advance data for 1983 on individual retirement accounts (August)*. Processed.

U.S. House of Representatives. (1985). *Report on earnings sharing implementation study* (Committee on Ways and Means, 99th Cong., 1st Sess., WMCP: 99-4). Washington, DC: U.S. Government Printing Office.

Wade, A. H. (1985). *Social security area population projections, 1985* (Actuarial Study, No. 95, SSA Publication No. 11-11542). Baltimore: Social Security Administration.

CHAPTER 8

Planning Long-Term Care for Heterogeneous Older Populations

KENNETH G. MANTON

CENTER FOR DEMOGRAPHIC STUDIES,
DUKE UNIVERSITY,
and
DIVISION OF COMMUNITY & FAMILY MEDICINE,
DUKE UNIVERSITY MEDICAL CENTER

Any evaluation of the U.S. elderly and oldest-old populations, and their need for both acute and long-term care (LTC) services, must be designed to recognize the heterogeneity of these populations. This heterogeneity is represented across many dimensions. One such dimension is chronological age, with the typical needs of the oldest-old (those aged 85 and over) for long-term care being very different from those of the young-old (those aged 65–74). These populations are also quite heterogeneous in terms of the medical and functional problems that determine their service needs. For example, certain components of these populations, such as persons affected by arthritic and other degenerative joint conditions, can expect to have stable but relatively low-intensity LTC needs. Others, such as persons with hip fractures, may need high levels of care, but possibly for relatively short periods of time, some of them with good chances of rehabilitation and recovery. Some groups, such as those with degenerative neurological conditions (e.g., Alzheimer's disease), can expect to need permanent and high levels of LTC; others, with more acute, potentially lethal conditions (e.g., cancer), can expect to need high levels of LTC, but for moderate periods of time. For most populations at very advanced ages, heterogeneity is increased by the high prevalence of persons with multiple health and functional problems. Another major source of heterogeneity is the differential likelihood for males and females of surviving to very advanced ages and the consequent sex differential in the probability of surviving one's spouse—a major

Research reported in this paper was supported by HCFA Cooperative Agreement 18-C-98641, NIA Grant Nos. AG01159 and AG07198.

determinant of differences in the availability of informal care resources and in the risk of long-term institutionalization (Manton & Soldo, in press). Failure to account for the various types of heterogeneity in health policy planning produces difficulty in anticipating changes in the mix of acute and LTC services required by the elderly population, difficulty in evaluating the ability to substitute between different types of acute, post-acute, and LTC services, and difficulty in projecting the mixture and level of service demand.

This chapter evaluates the heterogeneity of the U.S. LTC population, using data from a major new resource—the 1982 and 1984 National Long Term Care Surveys (NLTCS). These surveys were sponsored by the Health Care Financing Administration (HCFA) and the Assistant Secretary's Office for Policy and Evaluations (ASPE). The surveys have a number of important features for studying the heterogeneity of the U.S. LTC population. They employed a very detailed instrument specially designed to elicit the health, functional, economic, and social characteristics of the LTC population residing in the community. In addition, the 1984 survey employed a longitudinal design that allowed changes in the health, functional, and economic status of a large, nationally representative sample of disabled elderly individuals to be tracked over a two-year period.

Another major advantage of the surveys is that the tracked individuals' Medicare Part A service use files for 1980 to 1986 have been linked to the survey records. Thus this population's Medicare-reimbursed use of acute hospital, skilled nursing facility (SNF), and home health agency (HHA) services can be related to the long-term changes in their chronic functional and health status charcteristics as recorded in the detailed survey interviews.

Using the 1982–1984 NLTCS and linked longitudinal Medicare Part A service records, we will examine a number of the dimensions underlying the heterogeneity of the U.S. LTC population. Specifically, we will examine heterogeneity in both functional and health status at fixed points in time, as well as heterogeneity in individual changes in functional and health status over the interval 1982–1984. We will examine the medical conditions reported as causing long-term disability. We will also examine the disability changes and the reported causes of disability stratified by major demographic factors, such as age and sex. Finally, we will examine how these characteristics relate to the use of Medicare Part A services by various population groups over a recent one-year time frame.

We begin by briefly describing the 1982–1984 NLTCS data sets and then present our analyses of the heterogeneity of the elderly U.S. LTC population. Finally, we discuss the ramifications of this diversity in planning federal and state reimbursement systems for LTC services.

DATA

The National Long Term Care Surveys were conducted in 1982 and 1984. The 1982 and 1984 survey designs had certain important differences. The 1982 NLTCS was a cross-sectional survey that was begun by selecting nearly 36,000 persons, stratified by age, sex, and race, from the Medicare master beneficiary file. These 36,000 persons were then screened by telephone (and, in about 20% of cases, personal visits) to determine if they had an impairment in at least one activity of daily living (ADL) or instrumental activity of daily living (IADL) that had lasted (or was expected to last) at least 90 days. At the time of the screening, proxy respondents were identified when necessary. Proxy respondents were frequently employed when the sample respondent manifested serious cognitive impairments. If the respondent answered affirmatively to the query about chronic impairment, he or she was interviewed in person in greater detail. The household interview was successfully administered to 6,088 of the 6,393 persons who screened into the survey. Though persons were identified as being in an institution in the 1982 survey, no detailed questionnaire was administered to institutionalized persons.

In 1984 several important changes were introduced, some because the 1984 survey was explicitly designed to be longitudinal. One change was that a sample of 4,916 persons who were aged 63 or 64 in 1982 were screened for long-term disability in 1984 so that the cross-sectional representativeness of the total U.S. population aged 65 and over could be preserved. Second, all persons who reported chronic disabilities in 1982 were automatically reinterviewed in 1984 in order to assess functional and health changes of both a positive and negative nature. In addition, about 50% of the 1982 elderly population who did not report chronic disabilities (about 12,000 persons) were rescreened in 1984 so that new cases of disability could be identified. Finally, in 1984 several new instruments were used. Most important, perhaps, was the instrument delivered to the sample component who were institutionalized at the time of the 1984 survey. In addition, a decedent questionnaire was delivered to the next-of-kin of respondents to the 1982 survey who had died over the intervening two-year period (Manton, 1987).

A linked file for 25,000 persons was created from the 1982 and 1984 surveys—22,000 persons who were alive in 1984 (including an "age-in" sample of nearly 5,000 persons) and a little more than 3,000 persons who had died in the interim. These 25,000 records were linked to all Medicare Part A service records for 1980 to mid-1987, thus defining a continuous record of more than seven years of Medicare service use, with exact date and amounts of reimbursed services. The timeline for the linked 1982-1984 survey file, and its extension for a planned 1988 survey, is represented in

Figure 8.1. The survey components conducted at each date are listed, as are the dates during which recent major changes in Medicare reimbursement of acute hospital services were instituted.

To utilize the data from the linked longitudinal files, a number of analytic manipulations are required. For example, to analyze Medicare service use it is necessary to define service episodes—that is, the period of time during which one is receiving a specific type of service (e.g., 10 days spent in an acute care hospital—that are linked to the person's characteristics as reported in the survey. These episodes can then be analyzed by life table and multivariate event history modeling techniques in order to adjust for differences in the duration of service use and the competing effects of various types of "censoring," such as mortality (Manton, Stallard, Woodbury, & Yashin, 1987; Tolley & Manton, 1987). In addition, a series of special adjustments must be made to the longitudinal sample weights in order to estimate transitions over the two-year interval (e.g., Manton, in press).

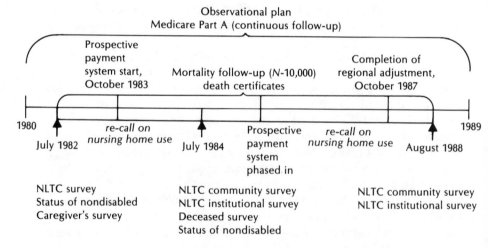

Figure 8.1. Timeline for 1982, 1984 and (planned) 1988 NLTCS linked to Medicare Part A records.

(1) Data on "state" of person at the three waves are multidimensional and involve both multiple functional and medical conditions.
(2) Data on service use and mortality are continuous with exact dates and with associated diagnostic data (e.g., hospital diagnoses after October, 1983; multiple medical conditions and service use).
(3) State can be expanded to include prior state characteristics (e.g., hospitalization or nursing home use in prior 12 months; Short Portable Mental Status Questionnaire).
(4) There are special one-time surveys (e.g., caregiver's help with cognitive assessments; deceased survey).

RESULTS

In this section we examine results from the 1982–1984 NLTCS population on both health and functional transitions over the period 1982 to 1984 and the Medicare Part A service use of the 1984 disabled elderly population.

Individual Transitions

The first type of diversity we examine are the changes between 1982 and 1984 in the functional and disability status of the U.S. elderly population. These changes are illustrated in Table 8.1, which presents the probability that a person in a given functional state in 1982 would end up in a given state in 1984.

Down the left side of the table we present the possible states of the population in 1982. The chronically disabled, community-resident population has been divided into four groups. The first, labeled "IADL only," represents persons with at least one impairment in the instrumental activities of daily living (e.g., cooking, laundering, traveling; see Table 8.9) but with *no* impairments in the more basic self-care functions (e.g., bathing, dressing, toileting; see Table 8.9). The next three groups represent the number of the six basic ADL impairments that a person has. Those with one or two ADL impairments have the lowest level of impairment (they may also have IADL impairments), while those with five or six ADL impairments are profoundly functionally impaired, often being fully bedfast or wheelchair-bound. In addition to the disabled elderly population, stratified by IADL and ADL disability level, we also present the two-year changes (1) in the nondisabled population, (2) for the subgroup who screened in but who were not interviewed in 1982, and (3) for the persons who were institutionalized at either the date of the screen or at the date of the attempted interview. Across the top of the table we describe the functional, institutional, and vital status of the population in 1984. Persons whose status was unknown in 1984 were reallocated on a proportional basis (always less than 3.5% of the total for any of the subpopulations).

An examination of the marginals showed that 78.1% of this population were *not* disabled in 1982. Of the remainder, 4.9% had only IADL impairments, 5.6% had one or two ADL impairments, 2.4% had three or four ADL impairments, 2.7% had five or six ADL impairments, 5.4% were institutionalized, and a negligible percent (0.85%) were nonresponders. The total 1982 population was estimated to be 26.9 million persons. Thus in 1982, 21 million persons were nondisabled, 730,000 persons living in the community had five or six ADL impairments, and about 1.5 million per-

Table 8.1 1982 Versus 1984 Disability Status Weighted Counts, National Long Term Care Survey.

1982 Functional institutional, and vital status	1984 Functional, institutional, and vital status							% Distribution in 1982
	Not disabled	IADL disability	1-2 ADL disabilities	3-4 ADL disabilities	5-6 ADL disabilities	Institutionalized	Deceased	
Not disabled[a]	81.59	4.02	2.96	0.99	0.86	1.48	8.09	78.1
IADL disability only	9.31	40.78	19.89	4.93	4.22	5.71	15.15	4.9
1-2 ADL disabilities	3.62	14.58	34.36	12.61	6.46	7.68	20.69	5.6
3-4 ADL disabilities	1.85	4.09	17.65	22.78	19.69	9.96	23.99	2.4
5-6 ADL disabilities	0.75	4.81	7.74	8.89	30.88	9.71	37.22	2.7
Institutionalized	0.96	1.07	1.98	1.14	1.09	54.18	40.58	5.4
Persons who did not complete household survey	5.04	7.47	8.86	6.61	7.59	16.51	47.89	0.9
% distribution in 1984	64.6	6.3	6.0	2.6	2.7	5.5	12.4	
% Distribution in 1984 adjusted for mortality	73.4	7.2	6.8	3.0	3.0	6.3		

[a]Includes those not disabled on screener or detailed interview.

sons were institutionalized at the time of the survey or benchmark date (about 1.25 million persons as of April 1, 1982).

By 1984 the transition probabilities had changed the distribution in several significant ways. Most significant were the 3.3 million deaths (12.4%) over the two-year period. Thus the surviving population in 1984 was about 23.6 million persons. To compare the distribution of disability among survivors to 1984 (who are now two years older), we must adjust the distribution for the mortality loss of 12.4%. This produces the bottom line in the table, where we see a small decline in the proportion in the community-dwelling non–disabled population and increases in the proportion in each disabled category (especially those with only IADL impairments) and in institutions. These shifts seem simply to reflect the aging of this population.

From the transition probabilities in the body of the table we see that the risk of mortality is strongly associated with disability level. There was a 4.5-fold difference in the two-year risk of mortality between persons in the community with impairment in five or six ADLs relative to persons who did *not* report any functional disability (i.e., 37.2% versus 8.1% two-year mortality). For institutionalized persons, we see that the mortality rate was about 41%. Interestingly, the mortality of the chronically disabled persons who had not completed the household survey in 1982 (48%) was higher even than that for institutionalized persons, suggesting that having serious health problems was a major reason for nonresponse. We report the changes in the disability status of the nonresponders to the 1982 survey as a separate category, since proportionally allocating them to the other categories could lead to serious bias in estimates of their transition probabilities (e.g., the nonresponders are more likely to be at high levels of disability).

The major figures of interest in the table are the changes in functional status. We see that, overall, 81.6% of the elderly who had not been disabled in 1982 remained wholly free of disability over a two-year period in this very elderly population (mean age, 77 years in 1982). The major forces of decrement for this nondisabled population were the loss of functional status (about 9%) and mortality (8.1%). Only 1.48% of the nondisabled population in 1982 became institutionalized over the two-year period.

Of persons who had been chronically disabled in 1982, a large proportion manifested significantly improved functional status two years later. For example, 22.2% of persons with five or six ADL impairments and 23.7% of the persons with three or four ADL impairments showed some improvement in functional status two years later. It is also interesting to note that persons with three or four ADL impairments were the most "unstable" group, with only 22.8% remaining at that level of impairment two years later (compared with 30.9% of persons with five or six ADL impairments in 1982). Thus this appears to be a transition group, with the highest risks of any of the groups for a change in status.

The 22.2% improvement of persons with five or six ADL impairments in 1982 can be compared with their 9.7% chance over two years of entering a nursing home. This highly impaired group was also nearly four times as likely to experience mortality as to enter a nursing home. Thus for persons in this highly impaired state living in the community, there was more than twice as much chance of improving and nearly four times as much chance of dying as there was of entering an institution. These dynamics seem somewhat at odds with the popular perception of the risk of institutionalization of highly impaired elderly persons. Specifically, it appears that a majority of highly impaired persons are resident in the community, not in institutions, at any given time and that mortality and functional improvement are stronger forces in the dynamics of these individuals than their institutionalized peers. Thus while the process of institutionalization in the LTC system is clearly important, these figures suggest that inadequate attention has been paid to processes of home care and to the effects of short- and medium-term illness and rehabilitative conditions that caused a certain proportion of the disability observed among community residents in 1982. It also emphasizes that, when discussing the heterogeneity of the elderly population, we must consider the heterogeneity of individuals over both short and long periods of time, as well as the population heterogeneity observed at any given period in time.

Among institutionalized persons, 54.2% remained in institutions while 40.6% died. Thus there was relatively little return to the community over the long term of persons institutionalized in 1982.

The figures in Table 8.1 show that analyses that do not take into account long-term functional improvement can seriously misrepresent individual trajectories of health and functional change. In particular, they emphasize the fallacy of viewing the process of functional change among the elderly as being unidirectional, with only functional decline. Clearly, there are a large number of cases in which long-term improvements in functional status occur. Such findings, in a nationally representative survey, validate similar observations made in local community surveys, such as the Cleveland GAO study (Maddox, Fillenbaum, & George, 1979). The fact that currently, without specialized programs, a large proportion of even profoundly impaired (i.e., five or six ADLs impaired) elderly persons show long-term improvements and remain in the community raises important questions about whether appropriate public health and medical interventions could significantly increase the rate of long-term functional improvements—and about the significance of any such improvements for our ability to finance LTC services. Clearly, a failure to accurately characterize the dynamics of individuals can lead to serious errors in policy judgments about systems for reimbursing and providing LTC services—especially for very elderly populations, where the rates of health and functional status change and the risks of mortality are so high.

An alternative way of examining these figures, one that highlights the significance of their dynamics, is to look at the risks of change in functional status only among the *survivors* to 1984. These figures, presented in Table 8.2, show that more than 35% of persons with five or six ADL impairments who *survived* two years (and 31% of those with three or four ADL impairments) showed some significant long-term improvement in functional status. Of survivors who were nondisabled in 1982, nearly 89% remained nondisabled in 1984.

Also striking is the large proportion (91.2%) of persons institutionalized in 1982 who survived to 1984 and remained in institutions. With the adjustment for survival, we also see that 31.7% of the nonresponders would be institutionalized in two years. Again after adjustment for survival, we see that, of the disabled subgroups in 1982, those with five or six ADL impairments were more likely to enter institutions by 1984 (15.5%) than those with three or four ADL impairments (as is the case in Table 8.1). The adjustment for mortality also makes those with five or six ADL impairments the group most likely to improve over the long term. Thus the functional dynamics among these two-year survivors appear quite different from the overall dynamics (which include the effects of mortality) of the total disabled population.

To better understand the diversity in these transitions, it is useful to decompose those transitions by sex and age. These transitions, decomposed into three age groups (65–74; 75–84, and 85 and over), are presented in Table 8.3.

The age differences in the transitions are dramatic. While 87.5% of persons 65 to 74 remained nondisabled after two years, only 47.3% of the oldest-old remained nondisabled. Interestingly, about 16 percentage points of the more than 40-point difference was due to the higher mortality rates of those aged 85 and over. Only 8.1% of the nondisabled oldest-old in 1982 were in nursing homes two years later. The most frequent disability transitions of the oldest-old who remained in the community were to the two lowest disability levels (i.e., IADL disability and one or two ADL impairments).

For persons who were chronically disabled in 1982, we also see major age differences in health and functional changes. For example, while almost 29% of persons aged 65–74 with five or six ADL impairments in 1982 showed functional improvement, only 13.5% of the oldest-old with that level of impairment showed long-term functional improvement. Clearly, though improvement in functional status was less likely for the oldest-old, it was not insignificant—especially if one examines the functional improvement specif-

Table 8.2 1982 Versus 1984 Disability Status Weighted Counts Eliminating Deceased Persons.

1982 Functional, institutional, and vital status	1984 Functional, institutional, and vital status						
	Not disabled	IADL disability	1-2 ADL disabilities	3-4 ADL disabilities	5-6 ADL disabilities	Institutionalized	% distribution in 1982
Not disabled[a]	88.77	4.37	3.22	1.08	0.94	1.61	78.1
IADL disability only	10.97	48.06	23.44	5.81	4.97	6.73	4.9
1-2 ADL disabilities	4.56	18.38	43.32	15.90	8.15	9.68	5.6
3-4 ADL disabilities	2.43	5.38	23.22	29.97	25.90	13.10	2.4
5-6 ADL disabilities	1.19	7.66	12.33	14.16	49.19	15.47	2.7
Institutionalized	1.62	1.80	3.33	1.92	1.83	91.18	5.4
Persons who did not complete household survey	9.67	14.34	17.00	12.68	14.57	31.68	0.85
% distribution in 1984	73.74	7.19	6.79	2.99	3.04	6.27	

[a]Includes those not disabled on screener or detailed interview.

ically among survivors (25.2%). In examining the risk of death for community-dwelling functionally impaired persons, we see that it increased relatively more rapidly for persons aged 65–74 (i.e., from 5.7% to 32.6%, or more than fivefold) than for those aged 85 and over (i.e., from 21.7% to 46.6%, more than double). Thus serious disability is a relatively graver prognostic risk for the young-old than the oldest-old. Stated differently, the risk of death for the healthy oldest-old (21.7%) is far lower than for the highly impaired young old (32.6%), suggesting that serious impairment is a stronger mortality risk factor than chronological age per se—*even* at very advanced ages.

The risk of being institutionalized also shows some interesting patterns. The highest risk of institutionalization for persons aged 65–74 was for the most seriously impaired persons. This was not the case for the oldest-old (or those aged 75–84). For the oldest-old, the highest risks were for those with three or four ADL impairments, with the second highest risk for those with one or two ADL impairments. Even for oldest-old persons with the highest level of risk (i.e., those with three or four ADL impairments), only 16% were in institutions two years later (approximately 24%, after adjustment for mortality). This pattern probably reflects differences in the motivations for institutionalization among the young-old and oldest-old. It is probable that institutionalization for the young-old, given the greater likelihood of spouse survival, is more medically motivated than for the oldest-old. The oldest-old are more likely to enter nursing homes at lower levels of impairment because they are likely to have fewer informal care resources. The highly impaired oldest-old probably disproportionately include persons with unusually rich social and economic resources, such that they tend to remain in the community. The mix of medical conditions causing impairments at different levels at different ages is probably also a determinant of these different institutional risks. We will analyze some of these factors in subsequent sections.

We find that few institutionalized persons returned to the community. Among the oldest-old, only about 3% returned; among those aged 65–74, only about 10%. Two-year mortality in institutions ranged from 30% (aged 65 to 74) to more than 48% (aged 85 and over). Thus long-institutionalized persons seldóm returned to the community at any age.

At the bottom of Table 8.3 we see the age-specific distributions for disability, institutionalization, and vital status in 1984. We see that the percentage of those not disabled varied from 77.1% at ages 65–74 (age in 1982) to 19.9% for persons aged 85 and over. The proportion institutionalized varied from 2.1% at ages 65–74 to 20.1% at age 85 and over (not adjusted for mortality). The percentage who died over the two years varied from 7.6 to 31.5%. Adjustments for mortality would increase the two-year transition probabilities for oldest-old survivors by about 46%.

Table 8.3 1982 Versus 1984 Disability Status Weighted Counts by Age Groups.

1982 Functional, institutional, and vital status	1984 Functional, institutional, and vital status						
	Not disabled	IADL disability	1-2 ADL disabilities	3-4 ADL disabilities	5-6 ADL disabilities	Institutionalized	Deceased
Not disabled[a]							
65-74	87.53	3.07	1.81	9.76	0.55	0.55	5.73
75-84	73.40	5.75	4.48	1.29	1.21	2.51	11.36
85+	47.28	7.04	10.18	2.64	3.03	8.14	21.68
IADL disability only							
65-74	13.72	46.82	17.19	3.75	3.67	3.21	11.63
75-84	7.08	37.26	21.62	6.03	4.39	7.36	16.27
85+	0.87	30.52	23.99	5.71	5.58	9.37	23.94
1-2 ADL disabilities							
65-74	6.25	118.17	36.68	12.78	5.65	4.61	15.55
75-84	2.65	14.02	34.80	11.46	5.39	7.85	23.83
85+	0.48	8.15	228.99	14.56	10.11	13.30	24.40
3-4 ADL disabilities							
65-74	3.58	5.79	24.42	25.74	12.07	4.75	18.65
75-84	1.16	3.51	16.87	22.24	19.84	11.76	24.61
85+	0.00	2.10	7.08	18.48	24.08	15.99	32.28

5-6 ADL disabilities							
65–74	1.16	7.49	9.61	10.14	32.29	6.74	32.57
75–84	0.80	4.54	7.07	8.81	31.64	10.97	36.17
85+	0.00	0.85	5.81	6.94	27.30	12.51	46.60
Institutionalized							
65–74	2.77	1.48	1.91	2.29	1.39	60.20	29.96
75–84	0.91	1.60	1.40	1.02	1.31	55.69	38.06
85+	1.00	0.35	0.12	0.71	0.70	49.72	48.28
Persons who did not complete household survey							
65–74	6.45	11.46	11.35	10.35	6.36	6.29	47.74
75–84	6.63	6.76	9.11	4.98	9.12	17.48	45.94
85+	0.00	3.19	4.67	4.42	5.89	27.03	47.94
% distribution in 1984 (age in 1982)							
65–74	77.13	5.41	4.17	1.92	1.69	2.09	7.58
75–84	53.38	7.98	8.09	3.26	3.42	7.75	16.12
85+	19.94	6.48	10.45	5.08	6.43	20.10	31.51

[a]Includes those not disabled on screener or detailed interview.

In order to better understand these transitions, we can decompose them by sex. In Table 8.4 we present a table analogous to Table 8.3, but with additional stratification by sex.

We see that there are two highly significant features regarding the transition of males compared to that of females. First, we see that the probability of remaining free of disability was quite similar for males and females. If anything, females had a lower risk than males of becoming chronically disabled in the two-year period. This is an interesting observation, given the finding that disability tends to be more prevalent among females (Verbrugge, 1984). The second is that there were very large differences in the mortality rates for males and females, even at corresponding levels of disability. For example, for those with five or six ADL impairments, the male mortality rates were from 5 to 16 percentage points higher than those for females. This means that cross-sectional data showing a higher prevalence of long-term disability among females are *not* a result of females' increased risk of becoming chronically disabled; rather they are due to females' greater longevity with the same level of disability. This effect becomes more pronounced with age, as the mortality advantage for females becomes more pronounced. For example, at age 85 and over, 24.2% of males were free of disability, as opposed to 18.2% of females. Females had higher proportions of disabled persons than males for almost all ADL-impaired categories and much higher rates of institutionalization. This will be addressed further in the next section, where we examine sex differences in the medical conditions reported as causing long-term disability.

In the body of Table 8.4 we see that there are striking sex differences for persons with one or two and three or four ADL impairments. Specifically, the likelihood of community-dwelling females at this level of impairment remaining so impaired was much higher than for males, in spite of females also having higher institutionalization rates. This is partly because of extremely large sex differentials in mortality for persons at this level of impairment, with females showing up to 23 percentage points greater survival rates (e.g., 47.9% versus 24.8% mortality for females and males aged 85 and over with three or four ADL impairments). For persons with only IADL impairment, or with five or six ADLs impaired, the difference in the proportion of males and females remaining at that level was less, though institutionalization and mortality risks remained elevated for males.

Again we find, for both males and females, that few institutionalized persons returned to the community—they either remained in institutions or died, with male mortality rates in institutions being much higher than female rates.

Table 8.4 1982 Versus 1984 Disability Status Weighted Counts by Males and Females by Age Group.

							1984 Functional, institutional, and vital status						
	Not disabled		IADL disability		1-2 ADL disabilities		3-4 ADL disabilities		5-6 ADL disabilities		Institutionalized		Deceased
1982 Functional institutional, and vital status	Male	Female	Male	Female	Male	Female	Male	Female	Male	Female	Male	Female	Male	Female
Not disabled[a]														
65–74	86.0	88.7	2.5	3.5	1.4	2.1	0.8	0.8	0.6	0.6	0.6	0.5	8.2	3.8
75–84	71.7	73.7	,48	6.4	3.7	5.0	0.7	1.7	1.4	1.1	1.6	3.1	14.9	9.1
85+	48.8	46.5	6.7	7.2	8.8	10.9	3.1	2.4	2.1	3.6	4.3	10.2	26.3	19.3
IADL disability only														
65–74	14.6	13.1	48.6	45.6	12.5	20.5	1.0	5.7	4.9	2.8	1.9	4.1	15.5	8.2
75–84	11.0	4.9	36.6	37.6	13.9	25.9	6.5	5.7	7.2	2.9	6.7	7.7	18.1	15.3
85+	1.4	2.7	33.4	15.1	15.4	37.0	6.7	12.8	4.0	4.3	5.7	10.1	33.4	18.1
1-2 ADL disabilities														
65–74	3.4	7.9	16.0	19.9	31.2	39.8	16.2	10.8	7.2	4.8	5.3	4.2	20.7	12.6
75–84	2.6	2.7	11.5	15.1	29.6	37.0	8.3	12.8	8.1	4.33	2.5	10.1	37.5	18.1
85+	0.0	0.7	6.6	8.8	20.9	32.4	11.0	16.1	13.8	8.6	15.7	12.3	32.1	21.2
3-4 ADL disabilities														
65–74	4.6	2.9	5.4	6.0	19.9	27.6	22.2	28.3	17.2	17.0	2.4	6.4	28.3	11.9
75–84	3.1	0.4	3.1	3.7	8.6	20.1	18.5	23.7	18.2	20.5	10.5	12.3	38.1	19.3
85+	0.0	0.0	1.8	2.2	5.5	7.9	12.1	21.5	20.0	26.0	12.7	17.6	47.9	24.8

(continued)

Table 8.4 (*continued*)

1982 Functional institutional, and vital status	1984 Functional, institutional, and vital status												
	Not disabled		IADL disability		1-2 ADL disabilities		3-4 ADL disabilities		5-6 ADL disabilities		Institutionalized		Deceased	
	Male	Female	Male	Female	Male	Female	Male	Female	Male	Female	Male	Female	Male	Female
5-6 ADL disabilities														
65-74	1.3	1.1	6.2	8.6	9.9	9.4	10.1	10.2	31.9	32.7	5.7	7.7	35.1	30.4
75-84	1.4	0.5	4.7	4.4	5.0	8.4	8.1	9.3	26.4	35.0	8.1	12.8	46.3	29.6
85+	0.0	0.0	0.0	1.1	4.3	6.3	8.6	6.4	27.1	27.4	6.4	14.3	53.6	44.5
Institutionalized														
65-74	2.8	2.8	1.4	1.6	2.1	1.8	2.4	2.4	1.9	1.2	54.1	64.6	35.7	25.8
75-84	0.4	1.1	1.5	1.7	1.4	1.4	1.3	0.9	0.9	1.5	47.3	58.8	47.3	34.7
85+	0.0	0.2	0.0	0.5	0.6	0.0	0.6	0.7	0.0	0.9	36.7	53.0	62.1	44.9
Persons who did not complete household survey														
65-74	4.6	8.7	6.7	17.5	4.6	19.8	9.4	11.5	4.5	8.7	9.1	2.8	61.1	30.9
75-84	6.7	6.6	9.33	5.3	6.7	10.5	2.2	6.6	9.0	9.2	4.5	25.0	61.5	36.9
85+	0.0	0.0	5.6	2.3	5.6	4.7	0.0	7.0	0.0	9.3	16.7	34.7	72.2	42.0
% distribution in 1984 (age in 1982)														
65-74	76.3	77.8	4.7	6.0	3.2	5.0	1.8	2.0	1.8	1.6	1.9	2.2	10.5	5.4
75-84	56.3	51.7	7.0	8.6	5.9	9.4	2.3	3.9	3.5	3.4	4.8	9.5	20.3	13.7
85+	24.2	18.2	7.1	6.2	8.9	11.1	4.8	5.2	5.7	6.7	12.1	23.5	37.3	29.1

[a]Includes those not disabled on screener or detailed interview.

Medical Conditions Causing Disability

In order to understand the disability and mortality transitions presented in the prior section, it is necessary to decompose the risks of disability by the medical conditions that caused them, since, holding disability level constant, there will be different durations of disability (and probabilities of functional improvement) and different mortality risks, depending on the conditions causing the disability. For example, if persons with five or six ADL impairments are primarily bedfast, with previous relatively acute medical problems (e.g., cancer or heart disease), we would expect them to either die or improve rather than enter nursing homes. Alternatively, if chronic medical problems (e.g., Alzheimer's disease) are the major cause of profound disability, it will be more difficult to explain relatively lower institutionalization rates.

In Table 8.5 we present a listing of the conditions reported by chronically disabled persons in 1984 as causing their disability. Since these conditions are self-reported, care should be exercised in evaluating these patterns—especially for conditions implying serious cognitive impairment, which have a high proxy response rate. The conditions are crudely grouped into several general medical categories (e.g., the first category represents major lethal conditions and conditions contributing to the risk of lethal conditions, the second category refers to neurological problems, etc.). Note that, in the survey, a person could report up to four causes of disability.

In Table 8.5 we see immediately that a number of medical problems not usually identified as lethal were frequently reported as causes of long-term disability. For example, the five most prevalent causes of disability were, in descending order, arthritis, skeletal problems, other circulatory diseases, senility, and visual disorders. By far the most prevalent causes of disability—degenerative skeletal problems, peripheral vascular disease, and senility—are conditions for which we have not yet confirmed the identity of major risk factors in large epidemiological studies. In any case, because the risk factors for these conditions are probably very different from those for many important causes of death, the effort to reduce disability at advanced ages will often involve very different mechanisms and interventions than does the effort to reduce mortality at those ages. For example, our best understanding of the mechanisms causing arthritic and degenerative joint and skeletal problems implicates the cumulative effects of trauma, metabolic disorders (e.g., the effects of hormonal status and other factors on osteoporosis), and immunological mechanisms (e.g., rheumatoid arthritis and complications of systemic lupus erythematosus). Our understanding of the mechanisms and risk factors of neurological problems such as Alzheimer's disease is even less complete. This will be a major area of research on aging in coming years.

Table 8.5 Weighted Proportion of Disabled Sample Persons Reporting Disabling Medical Conditions by Condition, 1984 NLTCS, by Disability Level.

	1-2 IADL disability	3-4 ADL disabilities	5-6 ADL disabilities	ADL disabilities	Total
Cancer	3.7	3.7	5.9	7.8	4.7
Ischemic heart disease	4.2	2.9	4.6	5.8	4.1
Hypertension	9.3	8.7	11.3	9.5	9.4
Other circulatory disease	27.7	25.6	30.8	43.6	29.9
Diabetes	5.8	5.8	7.0	8.7	6.4
Senility	14.0	13.8	15.9	22.2	15.4
Mental disorders	3.9	4.2	5.0	5.9	4.5
Parkinson's disease	6.0	6.4	9.5	16.1	8.2
Visual disorders	16.8	14.6	14.4	13.1	15.1
Deafness	7.0	4.9	3.2	5.5	5.5
Ulcers	0.8	0.9	1.1	0.7	0.9
Hernia	2.1	2.1	1.5	1.6	1.9
Other digestive disorders	4.0	4.1	4.1	4.9	4.2
Kidney & bladder disease	2.5	2.7	3.3	3.4	2.8
Genitourinary disease	1.0	1.2	1.0	0.9	1.1
Emphysema & bronchitis	6.0	4.4	3.2	5.1	4.9
Acute respiratory disease	6.0	5.1	4.2	3.5	5.1
Skin disease	1.3	1.3	1.6	1.2	1.3
Arthritis	30.5	41.4	43.8	28.6	35.9
Other skeletal problems	19.1	26.0	29.9	20.7	23.3
Residual	11.6	15.1	18.7	15.0	14.4
Mean Number of Conditions	1.8	1.9	2.2	2.2	2.0

An increase in the prevalence of a condition occurs sometimes with an increase in impairment and sometimes a decrease. For example, senility was reported as a cause of disability for 14.0% of those with only IADL impairment but for 22.2% of those with five or six impaired ADLs. Visual disorders, in contrast, decreased from 16.8% for those with IADL impairment only to 13.1% for those with five or six ADL impairments. It may be that those with five or six ADL impairments no longer view these conditions as important causes of their higher levels of impairment, though, overall, persons with five or six ADL impairments reported significantly more medical conditions causing their disability (2.2) than those reporting only IADL impairments (1.8).

In order to better understand these associations, we decompose Table 8.5 by sex. The sex-specific probabilities are reported in Table 8.6.

Regarding community-dwelling persons with long-term functional impairment, the data in this table confirm some well-known epidemiological differences in disease risk for males versus females in the total U.S. population. For example, the overall risk of cancer was greater for chronically impaired males (5.7%) than for similarly limited females (4.2%), while the risk of diabetes was greater for females (6.9%) than for males (5.4%). In both cases, the risk of the condition increased with disability level. Senility was more prevalent among females (16.2%) than males (13.7%), although Parkinson's disease was more prevalent among males and more prevalent than senility among males with five or six ADL impairments. While diabetes was reported as a more prevalent cause of disability among females, circulatory disease and heart disease were more prevalent as causes of disability among males. In contrast, hypertension was more prevalent as a reported cause of disability among females. Sensory impairments (visual and hearing) were more prevalent among males, while arthritis, a set of diseases often with an immunological basis, was more prevalent among females. Thus the general epidemiological pattern of disease risk found among males and females in the total U.S. population is not markedly different from the patterns of diseases reported as causing disability in this community-dwelling chronically disabled subpopulation. This suggests an intimate relation between the pattern of long-term disability risks and the population risks of major chronic disease such as would be produced if disability emerged as stages in the natural history of these disease processes. This again evidences the need to jointly examine disease risks (and their risk factors) and level of functional impairment when evaluating determinants of LTC service requirements.

In general, it appears that the higher prevalence of female disability is at least partly due to the different medical causes of serious disability for males and females. Males tend to have a higher prevalence of lethal conditions (e.g., cancer, heart disease) causing their disability than females. Thus the greater longevity of females in comparable disability states is apparently due to the different male/female mix of disabilty-causing medical conditions. This suggests that appropriate case-mix adjustments will be necessary in any system to reimburse for postacute and long-term care services because of the need to control for differentials in duration and survivability for persons with the same level of impairment but different underlying medical profiles (Manton & Hausner, 1987).

A final dimension across which these relations are stratified is age. Age-specific and sex-specific patterns are presented in Table 8.7. To keep the

Table 8.6 Weighted Proportion of Disabled Sample Persons Reporting Disabling Medical Conditions by Condition, 1984 NLTCS, by Sex.

	IADL disability		1–2 ADL disabilities		3–4 ADL disabilities		5–6 ADL disabilities		Total	
	Males	Females	Males	Females	Males	Females	Males	Females	Males	Females
Cancer	4.6	3.3	4.8	3.3	7.2	5.3	8.3	7.4	5.7	4.2
Ischemic heart disease	5.8	3.4	2.4	3.2	5.1	4.4	8.0	4.5	5.0	3.6
Hypertension	7.4	10.2	6.0	9.7	6.2	13.7	5.9	11.6	6.6	10.8
Other circulatory disease	29.9	26.5	29.4	24.0	34.1	29.3	48.4	40.8	33.6	28.1
Diabetes	4.9	6.2	4.1	6.5	7.0	7.0	7.1	9.7	5.4	6.9
Senility	12.3	14.9	10.5	14.8	16.9	15.5	19.5	23.8	13.7	16.2
Mental disorders	3.7	4.1	4.3	4.2	3.4	5.8	5.5	6.2	4.1	4.7
Parkinson's disease	4.3	6.9	8.7	5.5	8.9	9.6	20.4	13.5	9.1	7.8
Visual disorders	17.4	16.5	17.8	13.3	14.3	14.5	13.3	13.0	16.4	14.6
Deafness	12.4	4.2	8.7	3.3	4.3	2.6	4.7	6.0	8.7	3.9

Ulcers	1.2	0.6	0.6	1.1	2.1	0.7	0.9	0.5	1.2	0.8
Hernia	1.5	2.4	2.1	2.0	1.2	1.7	1.1	1.9	1.5	2.1
Other digestive disorders	4.4	3.9	3.4	4.4	4.4	4.0	4.9	4.9	4.2	4.2
Kidney & bladder disease	2.6	2.4	3.5	2.4	2.9	3.4	3.9	3.1	3.2	2.7
Genitourinary disease	2.5	0.3	2.0	0.9	2.5	0.3	2.2	0.2	2.3	0.5
Emphysema & bronchitis	10.8	3.6	8.4	2.8	5.5	2.1	10.2	2.1	9.2	2.9
Acute respiratory disease	7.9	5.0	7.1	4.3	5.0	3.8	5.3	2.5	6.8	4.2
Skin disease	0.7	1.6	0.6	1.5	0.6	2.0	0.3	1.7	0.6	1.7
Arthritis	22.0	34.8	35.7	43.8	32.6	48.9	19.7	33.8	27.3	40.0
Other skeletal problems	17.8	19.8	26.8	25.7	35.0	27.5	22.3	19.7	23.8	23.1
Residual	4.1	15.5	8.4	17.8	12.7	21.4	6.1	20.2	7.0	17.9
Mean Number of Conditions	1.8	1.9	2.0	1.9	2.1	2.2	2.2	2.3	2.0	2.0

Table 8.7 Weighted Proportion of Disabled Sample Persons Reporting Disabling Medical Conditions by Condition, 1984 NLTCS, by Age and Sex.

	65–74 years										85+ years										
	IADL disability		1–2 ADL disabilities		3–4 ADL disabilities		5–6 ADL disabilities		Total		IADL disability		1–2 ADL disabilities		3–4 ADL disabilities		5–6 ADL disabilities		Total	
	Males	Females	Males	Females	Males	Females	Males	Females	Males	Females	Males	Females	Males	Females	Males	Females	Males	Females	Males	Females
Cancer	5.0	4.6	3.3	3.8	6.7	7.9	8.5	8.1	5.3	5.2	0.0	4.4	3.8	3.3	19.1	2.6	10.4	5.5	7.1	3.3
Ischemic heart disease	7.2	3.9	3.9	4.4	0.8	4.8	10.0	4.5	5.7	4.3	1.9	0.0	1.3	1.1	9.5	3.7	8.5	6.8	4.5	2.7
Hypertension	11.9	13.9	7.2	13.9	7.6	21.2	7.2	16.4	9.2	15.2	1.4	2.6	5.8	6.3	5.6	3.6	1.9	8.3	3.8	5.5
Other circulatory disease	32.5	27.4	29.1	23.8	33.9	30.5	52.6	42.4	34.9	28.4	18.7	28.4	23.8	20.5	37.5	20.7	34.6	35.8	27.4	25.8
Diabetes	6.2	8.7	4.5	9.3	8.1	8.8	12.2	11.0	7.0	9.2	0.0	1.9	2.5	3.6	0.0	1.7	1.7	4.1	1.2	3.0
Senility	6.5	5.8	2.7	4.5	5.4	3.8	7.9	9.3	5.5	5.5	27.2	41.4	26.3	36.3	45.4	45.0	51.9	50.1	35.6	42.2
Mental disorders	4.5	4.6	4.2	6.2	4.6	9.1	6.1	8.9	4.6	6.3	1.4	2.2	2.5	2.3	0.0	3.3	2.5	1.7	1.7	2.3
Parkinson's disease	5.5	8.7	7.3	6.9	14.1	12.4	24.5	19.5	10.3	9.9	1.8	5.9	5.1	5.2	4.7	5.6	8.6	6.4	4.9	5.7
Visual disorders	12.2	11.4	11.0	9.3	8.8	10.7	11.7	5.7	11.2	10.0	32.1	25.7	27.2	17.0	22.4	23.4	25.1	23.9	27.1	21.6
Deafness	7.0	2.6	4.2	1.4	2.5	1.1	1.4	4.0	4.7	2.1	23.2	8.2	13.5	8.1	10.4	8.9	4.2	13.4	13.4	9.5
Ulcers	1.1	0.9	0.0	1.2	0.6	0.9	1.4	0.0	0.8	0.9	3.7	0.0	1.3	0.3	4.8	0.0	0.0	0.8	2.3	0.3
Hernia	2.2	3.8	2.7	1.6	2.2	0.8	0.8	2.6	2.1	2.5	0.0	1.1	3.8	1.2	0.0	1.7	2.1	0.8	1.7	1.2
Other digestive disorders	5.9	5.0	4.2	4.2	2.6	4.3	3.0	7.0	4.4	4.8	1.6	0.6	7.0	2.2	2.1	1.9	3.8	1.6	4.0	1.7
Kidney & bladder disease	3.0	2.5	4.2	4.0	1.2	3.7	2.7	2.7	3.0	3.2	0.0	0.6	1.1	0.3	4.7	1.0	3.4	1.8	2.0	0.9
Genitourinary disease	.26	0.3	2.8	0.6	2.0	0.4	0.0	0.5	2.2	0.4	0.0	1.4	1.0	1.2	2.4	0.0	2.5	0.0	1.3	0.7
Emphysema & bronchitis	12.0	5.2	12.2	3.5	7.0	3.1	12.2	2.9	11.3	4.1	5.3	1.5	4.1	0.4	0.0	1.3	3.6	1.1	3.5	1.0
Acute respiratory disease	8.6	5.8	9.3	6.8	6.5	4.0	6.6	1.0	8.1	5.3	9.2	2.5	8.1	1.8	0.0	2.9	7.4	2.4	6.7	2.3
Skin disease	1.0	2.7	0.0	3.3	0.0	3.4	0.7	2.7	0.5	3.0	0.0	0.0	0.0	0.8	0.0	0.0	0.0	1.0	0.0	0.5
Arthritis	23.0	36.4	36.3	47.4	25.5	49.7	19.4	35.0	26.5	41.8	19.3	30.0	38.7	35.4	34.3	39.8	27.5	28.8	30.4	33.5
Other skeletal problems	20.1	21.3	33.2	27.6	39.7	26.0	26.0	19.5	27.7	23.8	18.7	11.5	18.9	27.1	27.0	20.7	13.3	13.7	19.2	19.5
Residual	4.7	23.3	11.9	28.9	11.1	32.4	7.2	35.4	8.1	27.9	1.5	8.5	2.5	7.8	13.1	15.8	10.2	15.4	5.9	11.2
Number of conditions	1.8	2.0	1.9	2.1	1.9	2.4	2.2	2.4	1.9	2.1	1.7	1.8	2.0	1.8	2.4	2.0	2.2	2.2	2.0	1.9

table at a manageable size, the intermediate age group, 75-84, has been deleted from the table.

In this table we see that only a few conditions are more highly prevalent at advanced ages. Most notable are senility and sensory impairments. More than 35% of disabled males and 42% of disabled females over age 85 reported senility as a cause of disability. Strikingly, this percentage was even higher at high levels of impairment, with more than 50% of both community-dwelling males and females with five or six ADL impairments having this condition. Heart disease, hypertension, other circulatory diseases, diabetes, arthritis, and skeletal problems were more prevalent at ages 65-74 than above age 85.

Medicare Part A Service Use

Medicare service use is administratively divided into two major components: Part A and Part B. Part A reflects the use of acute care hospitals, Medicare skilled nursing facilities (SNFs), and Medicare-reimbursed home health agency (HHA) use. Medicare Part B reflects the use of outpatient services. In this section we examine the use of Medicare Part A services by the 1984 NLTCS sample population. To examine this service use, we employ life tables calculated for different types of service episode (i.e., for acute care hospital, SNF, and HHA service episodes) occurring in the period October 1, 1984, to September 30, 1985. By using life tables to describe the service episodes we can (1) examine the duration-specific probabilities of terminating a service episode (rather than just the average duration of an episode), (2) describe the different modes of terminating an episode, and (3) adjust for different types of censoring. In addition to the three different types of service episodes, we also calculate a life table for "community" episodes, that is, episodes during which no Medicare-reimbursed service was provided.

The service episodes are calculated for four different types of sample components. The first component is the chronically disabled community-dwelling population (CDP) who were identified as chronically disabled in the NLTCS screen and who received the detailed questionnaire. The second component (NR) is the set of 1984 survey nonresponders who, if they are like the nonresponders in 1982 (see Table 8.1), would be seriously impaired and at high risk of death and institutionalization. The third group (INST) is comprised of persons identified as being in institutions in 1984. The fourth group (CNP) was identified in the survey screen as *not* chronically impaired.

In Table 8.8 we present both the average duration and the percentage of episodes that terminated in one of five ways (i.e., in SNF, HHA, hospital or community episode, or death). The table has two panels. The first, panel A,

Table **8.8** Duration in Days and Percent of Persons in a Given Type of Episode for Elderly Community Nondisabled Persons (CNP), Community Disabled Persons (CDP), Nonresponders (NR), and Institutionalized Persons (Inst), 1984 National Long Term Care Survey.

A. Duration

	All causes	Nursing home	Hospital	Home health agency	Community	Deceased
Skilled nursing home episode						
CNP	33.2	—	21.0	29.7	36.9	28.7
CDP	35.3	—	44.0	28.1	32.5	30.4
NR	62.4	—	70.2	75.0	66.6	14.1
INST	103.2	—	87.7	0.0	83.3	105.2
Home health agency episode						
CNP	37.2	32.8	30.7	—	36.7	29.5
CDP	45.5	38.1	48.8	—	41.3	40.0
NR	37.0	0.0	34.8	—	33.3	35.2
INST	47.2	10.5	35.4	—	49.2	36.5
Hospital episode						
CNP	8.8	20.0	—	14.3	7.7	12.4
CDP	10.4	14.3	—	12.2	9.6	11.4
NR	10.5	20.5	—	9.5	9.1	12.5
INST	10.0	14.4	—	12.6	9.1	10.0
Community episode						
CNP	288.3	102.7	136.3	43.8	—	133.3
CDP	206.4	105.9	119.4	49.3	—	98.2
NR	208.8	49.1	122.3	47.1	—	113.8
INST	238.3	101.4	122.3	47.4	—	136.5

B. Percent

	All causes	Nursing home	Hospital	Home health agency	Community	Deceased
Skilled nursing home episode						
CNP	89.2	—	7.1	10.3	63.0	8.8
CDP	92.7	—	15.7	10.7	58.3	8.0
NR	100.0	—	33.5	3.5	52.2	10.8
INST	89.8	—	30.4	0.0	39.1	20.3
Home health agency episode						
CNP	91.8	.5	8.8	—	80.3	2.2
CDP	96.3	5.3	9.6	—	78.1	3.3
NR	95.7	0.0	22.1	—	67.4	6.2
INST	98.7	1.7	11.1	—	84.8	1.1
Hospital episode						
CNP	97.7	2.4	—	7.6	82.5	5.2
CDP	97.6	4.5	—	14.5	70.5	8.1
NR	97.8	8.0	—	12.8	65.4	11.6
INST	97.4	10.0	—	2.5	71.7	13.2
Community episode						
CNP	22.1	0.2	18.6	2.3	—	1.0
CDP	45.9	0.5	30.1	12.6	—	2.7
NR	45.8	0.9	31.6	9.1	—	4.2
INST	40.8	1.2	26.1	2.0	—	11.5

contains the average duration (in days) of episodes observed to end during the follow-up interval according to one of five specific ways. In addition, certain episodes ended because the follow-up interval (i.e., the 12-month period from the end of September 1984 to the beginning of October 1985) ended. As a consequence, the average duration of episodes ending from all causes can be longer than for each of the five specific termination types, since the average includes those episodes that ran to the end of the observation period without one of the five specific modes of termination. The effect of truncation by the end of the study period is strongest for the longest episodes (i.e., community episodes) and weakest for the shortest episodes (i.e., hospital visits). The average duration for termination from all causes indicates the actual amount of time expected to be spent in a given type of episode during the 12-month interval. Thus the average hospital stay during the 12-month follow-up was 10.4 days for chronically disabled persons, while the average community stay was 206.4 days. One can obtain estimates of what the average duration of each type of episode would have been if the stays had not been truncated at the end of the observation period by making certain competing risk adjustments. Thus for hospital stays among chronically disabled persons who were discharged to home health agencies, the observed stay in the follow-up interval was 12.2 days, while, after adjusting for the truncation of stays, the new estimate is 12.4 days. The adjustment is small because only 2.4% of hospital stays were truncated due to the end of study. For home health episodes the truncation effect is greater, with the average use of home health agencies for chronically disabled persons who returned to the community being 41.3 days, while with adjustments for truncation the estimate is 49.2 days. The larger adjustment is due to the fact that a greater proportion of home health episodes, 3.7%, were truncated.

In Panel B we present the proportion for episodes that terminated in a given way. The proportions do not add to 100% because some episodes were truncated; for example, 8.2% of the home health agency episodes among the community-dwelling nondisabled and 77.9% of the community episodes had not ended by the close of the follow-up period. In effect, these estimates are similar to the proportions of persons making transitions reported in Table 8.1 before adjusting for the effects due to different groups having different mortality rates.

What these adjustments for truncation due to the fixed length of the follow-up period suggest is that one can get severely biased estimates of the duration of the longer service episodes if truncation is ignored. Actually, the existence of "bias" has to be evaluated according to the type of estimate desired. The values presented in Table 8.8 are the *observed* durations of episodes of different types within the observation period. Thus, if one wished to examine the amount of service use in a 12-month interval, these estimates would be appropriate. To generate *estimates* of the actual length of a service episode requires adjusting for the truncation of the observation window. In Table 8.8 we have opted to examine the observed service use duration in the 12-month follow-up because this better represents service use in a fixed interval.

In this table we see that the community-dwelling nondisabled generally had the lowest mortality rates, followed by the community-dwelling disabled, the nonresponders, and finally the institutionalized. The nondisabled also had the lowest hospitalization rates (e.g., 18.6% from community episodes), low rates of HHA and SNF use, and, consequently, the highest rates of return to the community of all groups.

Consistent with the findings in the prior section, institutionalized persons showed the lowest rates of return to the "community" (39.1%; community episodes represent non-Medicare service use periods and could reflect use of Medicaid-reimbursed and private-pay nursing home services) and the highest hospitalization and mortality rates when in a SNF. Such transitions can occur, because, obviously, persons in institutions at the time of the survey may have been discharged. Such persons who were discharged in the 12 months following the survey date may have had other types of service use episodes. We see that such persons were very likely to return to the "community" (which might include a Medicaid-reimbursed or private-pay nursing home) at the end of a hospital of HHA episode.

The community-dwelling disabled elderly had fairly high rates of hospital entry (30.1%) from community episodes. They had only a small likelihood of institutionalization from either HHA, hospital, or community episodes. These persons had the highest rates of home health service use.

In addition to seeing how different episodes end, it is useful to examine the duration of each episode. These figures are presented in the upper half of Table 8.8. For example, we see that the community-dwelling nondisabled elderly had shorter hospital stays (8.8 days) than any of the other groups. Institutionalized persons had the longest stays (20.5 days). Community-dwelling disabled elderly averaged hospital stays 1.6 days longer (10.4 days) than the community-dwelling nondisabled elderly. The length of stay (LOS) of hospital episodes varied by discharge status, with hospital discharges to the community having the shortest duration and those to SNFs the longest.

The data presented in Table 8.8 are organized by very crude groupings of the elderly population based on the definition of major sample components. For the community-dwelling disabled elderly, we can conduct multivariate analyses of their variation on a wide battery of functional and health measures. Such an analysis was conducted using an analytic procedure called Grade of Membership (GOM) analysis (Woodbury & Manton, 1982). In this analysis, the variation of individuals on a wide battery of functional and health measures is predicted as a function of two types of coefficients.

The first type of coefficient describes each of K analytically defined profiles in terms of the battery of measures introduced to the analysis. These coefficients, of which there are K sets, represent the probability that a person characterized by the Kth profile will have one of the attributes entered into the analysis. The substantive content of each of the K profiles can be determined by identifying which of the attributes have high probabilities of occurring in a given profile relative to the probability that the attribute occurs in the total sample (column marked "sample proportion"). These coefficients are presented in Table 8.9, which should be read by column. This characterization of each of the analytically generated profiles proceeds much in the same way that one examines patterns of factor loadings to label factors in factor analysis. The GOM profiles have the advantage that the model used to generate them makes no assumption about the distribution of cases, while factor analysis assumes multivariate normality.

The second set of coefficients relates each person to the attributes defined by each of the K profiles. In this model a person can be "like" or "partially resemble" more than a single profile, so that he or she may have scores, which sum to 1.0, that define how closely the person resembles each of the analytic profiles. Since no assumption is made about the distribution of these scores, the model is more general than most forms of factor analysis. There are as many of these coefficients as there are persons in the analysis times the number (K) of profiles. As a consequence, we do not present tables for these coefficients. The effects of the second type of coefficient are manifest, however, in the coefficients presented in Table 8.9, since they allow these coefficients to be estimated without making assumptions about the distribution of cases.

In addition, it is possible to calculate the probability that persons in one of the K groups will have an attribute that was not used in the analysis to define the groups. This was done in subsequent analyses for demographic (e.g., age, sex) and service use variables.

The GOM analysis was applied to cases from the 1982 and 1984 NLTCS such that the profiles generated are representative of both survey dates. The value of K was determined by running analyses with different numbers of profiles and selecting a value of K (i.e., a number of profiles) that reproduced the data within acceptable statistical error. The probabilities for each of the 17 ADL, IADL, and IADL2 (i.e., direct measures of functional loss, such as problems in holding packages) impairments, as well as 29 measures of medical condition employed in the analysis, are presented in Table 8.9 for each of the four analytically defined profiles. The size of these probabilities may be compared with the frequency of occurrence of the attribute in the total population. These probabilities are presented in the column marked

Table 8.9 Probabilities for ADL, IADL, and IADL2 Limitations and Medical Conditions, 1982 and 1984 National Long Term Care Survey, Community Disabled Persons.

	Sample proportion	"Mildly disabled"	"Oldest-old"	"Heart-lung" problems	"Severe ADL" dependency
ADL limitations					
Respondent needs help with:					
Eating	10.8	0.0	0.0	0.0	59.8
Getting in/out of bed	38.7	0.0	71.8	0.0	100.0
Getting about inside	52.2	0.0	100.0	0.0	100.0
Dressing	32.3	0.0	0.0	0.0	100.0
Bathing	57.9	0.0	100.0	35.7	100.0
Using toilet	33.5	0.0	49.6	0.0	100.0
Bedfast	2.3	0.0	0.0	0.0	10.6
No inside activity	3.7	0.0	0.0	0.0	17.1
Wheelchair fast	7.2	0.0	0.0	0.0	32.8
IADL limitations					
Respondent needs help with:					
Heavy work	84.5	33.3	100.0	100.0	100.0
Light work	38.3	0.0	100.0	0.0	100.0
Laundry	60.4	0.0	100.0	50.6	100.0
Cooking	47.6	0.0	100.0	0.0	100.0
Grocery shopping	75.2	0.0	100.0	100.0	100.0
Getting about outside	74.9	3.3	100.0	100.0	100.0
Traveling	74.1	0.0	100.0	100.0	100.0
Managing money	38.8	0.0	41.8	3.7	100.0
Taking medicine	36.3	0.0	0.0	0.0	100.0
Telephoning	24.0	0.0	0.0	0.0	100.0
IADL2 limitations					
How much difficulty does respondent have:					
Climbing 1 flight of stairs					
No difficulty	10.7	31.8	0.0	0.0	0.0
Some difficulty	24.9	68.2	0.0	0.0	11.0
Very difficult	34.1	0.0	44.7	88.0	0.0
Cannot	30.3	0.0	55.3	12.0	89.1
Bending for socks					
No difficulty	33.8	92.5	0.0	0.0	0.0
Some difficulty	26.6	7.5	53.1	56.5	0.0
Very difficult	20.9	0.0	46.9	43.5	8.4
Cannot	18.8	0.0	0.0	0.0	91.6

(*continued*)

Table 8.9 (*continued*)

	Sample proportion	"Mildly disabled"	"Oldest-old"	"Heart-lung" problems	"Severe ADL" dependency
Holding 10 lb. package					
No difficulty	17.6	58.7	0.0	0.0	0.0
Some difficulty	14.4	37.5	4.5	9.0	0.0
Very difficult	16.5	3.8	20.9	43.0	0.0
Cannot	51.5	0.0	74.7	48.1	100.0
Reaching over head					
No difficulty	45.8	96.4	77.4	0.0	0.0
Some difficulty	22.9	3.6	22.6	47.4	18.5
Very difficult	17.5	0.0	0.0	39.6	32.8
Cannot	13.8	0.0	0.0	12.9	48.7
Combing hair					
No difficulty	60.3	100.0	100.0	0.0	0.0
Some difficulty	18.0	0.0	0.0	75.5	17.7
Very difficult	10.8	0.0	0.0	24.5	29.9
Cannot	10.8	0.0	0.0	0.0	52.4
Washing hair					
No difficulty	39.8	100.0	31.9	0.0	0.0
Some difficulty	14.5	0.0	8.2	61.9	0.0
Very difficult	11.0	0.0	12.3	38.1	3.2
Cannot	34.7	0.0	47.6	0.0	96.8
Grasping small objects					
No difficulty	59.4	100.0	100.0	0.0	0.0
Some difficulty	21.7	0.0	0.0	73.0	31.1
Very difficult	12.0	0.0	0.0	27.0	32.1
Cannot	7.0	0.0	0.0	0.0	36.8
Respondent can see well enough to read newsprint	67.5	89.8	77.6	64.9	28.9
Medical conditions					
Rheumatism/arthritis	71.8	57.7	47.2	100.0	76.0
Paralysis	12.3	0.0	0.0	0.0	54.0
Permanent stiffness	26.5	5.4	0.0	61.5	47.2
Multiple sclerosis	1.3	0.0	0.0	0.0	5.5
Cerebral palsy	0.6	0.0	0.0	0.0	2.4
Epilepsy	1.1	0.8	0.0	0.7	3.0

(*continued*)

Table 8.9 (continued)

	Sample proportion	"Mildly disabled"	"Oldest-old"	"Heart-lung" problems	"Severe ADL" dependency
Parkinson's disease	4.4	1.9	0.0	0.0	16.3
Glaucoma	9.2	6.4	14.8	3.9	11.9
Diabetes	21.2	11.9	0.8	45.4	30.5
Cancer	8.2	6.0	10.8	8.9	7.6
Constipation	36.7	14.2	0.0	84.4	62.2
Insomnia	41.9	19.2	0.0	100.0	54.3
Headache	18.9	0.0	0.0	63.9	26.4
Obesity	17.7	13.5	4.0	51.6	5.5
Arteriosclerosis	36.5	12.4	0.0	80.5	71.8
Mental retardation	2.3	0.0	0.0	0.0	10.2
Senility	13.2	0.0	0.0	0.0	59.5
Heart attack	9.1	0.0	0.0	31.4	9.7
Other heart problems	33.8	8.9	0.0	100.0	41.6
Hypertension	44.0	33.4	2.9	100.0	47.6
Stroke	11.4	4.2	0.0	7.6	38.6
Circulation trouble	56.2	23.1	0.0	100.0	100.0
Pneumonia	7.5	0.0	0.0	21.9	10.9
Bronchitis	12.8	0.0	0.0	43.6	13.5
Influenza	15.0	6.8	0.0	41.4	15.8
Emphysema	12.9	6.1	5.0	29.6	12.9
Asthma	7.9	1.7	0.0	25.2	8.1
Broken hip	2.5	0.0	8.8	0.0	1.4
Other broken bones	6.1	2.8	13.4	2.6	6.0

"sample proportion." In describing each group below, we also report certain patient attributes that were found to be strongly discriminating of each type (e.g., age and sex), even though they were not employed in the multivariate analysis to identify the profiles.

The four analytically defined profiles may be roughly characterized as those who are mildly disabled, the oldest-old, those with acute heart and lung problems, and those with severe ADL dependency (Liu & Manton, 1987).

The mildly disabled group was characterized by rheumatism and arthritis and little IADL or ADL impairment. On the demographic variables, not reprinted in the table, the group was found to be relatively young, with only 10% over age 85; 50% were married; 54% were males; 67% had good to excellent health; only 3% had been previously institutionalized, while 47% required no informal care.

In contrast, 47% of those over age 85 (19.4% of whom were over age 90) had significant IADL problems, as well as mobility, toileting, and bathing limitations. This group had significant risk of hip and other fractures and the highest risks of cancer but fewer reported medical conditions than the first group. In this group 70% were unmarried; 69% were females; and 22% had had a prior nursing home stay.

The group with heart and lung problems had IADL and IADL2 problems as well as trouble bathing. This group was predominantly female, with a 45% prevalence of diabetes, a 50% prevalence of obesity, and very high levels of impairment due to arthritis. It had the highest risks of cardiovascular and lung disease and was predominantly (84.3%) under age 80.

The group with severe ADL dependency had a 60% prevalence of limitation in eating and was impaired on all other ADLs, IADLs, and IADL2's. Eleven percent of this group were bedfast; 33%, chairfast; 70%, incontinent, with 27% having a catheter or having had a colostomy. This group was strongly characterized by some form of neurological disorder (e.g., senility for 60% and paralysis for 54%). It had significant circulatory problems, with 80% reporting poor subjective health. This group was 48% male and 58% married—probably because any person with this level of impairment requires large amounts of informal care in order to stay out of an institution.

In contrast to Table 8.8, which presented estimates of the duration (and prevalence) of different types of service episodes ending in different ways, Table 8.10 presents duration and prevalence estimates for different service episode types for each of the four multivariate-defined subgroups. In Table 8.10 we present the duration and prevalence of each of the four analytically defined group's use of three types of Medicare Part A services in the community-dwelling disabled population. The estimates, in contrast to the empirical values in Table 8.8, *have* been adjusted for truncation.

In the bottom panel of Table 8.10, which contains statistics for all types of episode endings, we see considerable variation in the hospital LOS of the four groups, ranging from 8.2 days for the mildly disabled to 13.5 days for the oldest-old. The mildly disabled group also had the shortest SNF episodes (28.6 days), though the heart–lung group had the shortest HHA episodes (35.9 days). The mildly disabled group had the longest community episodes (suggesting the least Medicare service use), while the severely disabled had the shortest community episodes (suggesting a higher prevalence of multiple service episodes). While not different from two of the three other groups in SNF episode duration, the oldest-old group had the longest HHA episodes (73.5 days). The severely disabled group had the second longest HHA episodes.

These service episodes can also be broken down by the nature of the discharge from each episode, as shown in the separate panels of the rows of

Table 8.10 The Duration in Days and Probability of Transitions to Various Services Following Initial Service Use for Four Elderly Subgroups.

	Initial assignment							
	A. Duration in days				B. Transition probability			
Place of discharge	Hospital	SNF	HHA	Community	Hospital	SNF	HHA	Community
To hospital								
Mildly disabled	—	3.5	62.4	287.9	—	5.2	10.1	70.4
Oldest-old	—	62.9	50.4	248.2	—	19.5	9.9	56.4
Heart and lung	—	28.9	42.8	217.9	—	27.4	14.3	85.6
Severely disabled	—	49.4	85.4	199.9	—	25.4	9.5	45.3
To SNF								
Mildly disabled	10.1	—	103.8	309.2	2.9	—	0.2	2.1
Oldest-old	14.3	—	85.6	235.4	10.7	—	0.3	1.0
Heart and lung	21.5	—	52.5	140.5	1.6	—	0.2	0.5
Severely disabled	21.1	—	33.2	215.2	6.4	—	1.3	1.7
To HHA								
Mildly disabled	14.9	35.3	—	290.8	6.3	7.2	—	19.7
Oldest-old	16.7	13.0	—	127.2	15.6	13.3	—	24.3
Heart and lung	11.5	55.5	—	67.6	18.9	20.1	—	12.2
Severely disabled	9.6	22.2	—	94.8	29.7	1.5	—	45.8

To community								
Mildly disabled	7.6	30.0	36.9	—	84.8	83.7	86.9	—
Oldest-old	13.0	41.3	73.7	—	61.6	63.6	85.8	—
Heart and lung	9.6	35.7	30.0	—	75.7	38.7	81.1	—
Severely disabled	7.7	53.7	61.2	—	44.9	46.6	85.4	—
To death								
Mildly disabled	9.7	18.0	25.2	316.7	6.0	3.9	2.9	7.7
Oldest-old	12.0	31.6	124.2	264.4	12.0	3.6	4.0	18.3
Heart and lung	20.1	63.5	123.9	266.1	3.9	13.8	4.3	1.7
Severely disabled	9.9	32.5	58.0	89.6	19.0	26.5	3.9	7.2
All episodes								
Mildly disabled	8.2	28.6	39.2	291.2				
Oldest-old	13.5	41.4	73.5	221.7				
Heart and lung	10.6	41.6	35.9	200.1				
Severely disabled	9.5	46.5	63.3	144.1				

Table 8.10 (e.g., the panel where persons go "to hospital" or "to SNF"). Again we see considerable heterogeneity in the various groups. For example, among the mildly disabled, the hospital LOS ranged from 7.6 days for community discharges to 14.9 days for discharges to HHAs. Considerable variability also existed across the health and functional groups for discharges of a given type. Hospital episodes ending in return to the community ranged in length from 7.6 days for the mildly disabled to 13.0 days for the oldest-old. The probabilities of death varied widely, with the severely disabled (19%) and oldest-old (12%) having the highest hospital mortality. The severely disabled had extremely high mortality rates for SNF episodes, while the oldest-old had the highest death rate for community episodes. Interestingly, there was relatively little variation in the death rates for HHA episodes.

The sets of transition probabilities and duration estimates in Table 8.10 fully describe the pattern of Medicare-reimbursed Part A service use for the disabled, elderly, community-resident population. As a consequence, it is these transition probabilities and duration estimates for medically and functionally distinct populations that we will wish any proposed LTC service policy changes to affect. The distribution of persons in each of the four analytic subgroups should be the targets for change by public health policies and clinical management directed to improving the functional and health status of the U.S. elderly population.

DISCUSSION

Above we exmained the heterogeneous health, functional status, and service use of a national sample of elderly persons. In examining that heterogeneity, we were able to examine individual changes in functional status using data from the 1982 and 1984 NLTCS. These longitudinal data helped us identify individual diversity in change that is not directly manifest in cross-sectional or prevalence data. In addition to exploring differences in individual changes in functional status, we used a multivariate procedure, the Grade of Membership (GOM) classification procedure, to study heterogeneity in terms of a large number of variables simultaneously.

In particular we saw that females have a lower probability than males of becoming disabled over a two-year period. This finding is superficially inconsistent with the observation in cross-sectional surveys (e.g., Verbrugge, 1984) that females have a higher prevalence of chronic disability. The explanation of why females had a high prevalence of disability was found in the individual transition data—females had much lower mortality, and hence longer life expectancy, in functionally disabled states than did males. The sex differences in these disability-specific mortality risks were explained by examining the different patterns of medical conditions that caused disability for males and females. Among males there was a higher prevalence of highly lethal conditions, such as cancer and heart disease. Among females, less lethal conditions were more prevalent, although, interestingly, females exhibited a higher prevalence of conditions causing such disabilities as hypertension, diabetes, and obesity, which are viewed as risk factors for heart disease, the largest single cause of death in the United States. In males these conditions were associated more strongly with ischemic heart disease, whereas in females they were the direct causes of disability.

These observations about sex differences in the age trajectories of the risks of mortality, institutionalization, functional loss, and the medical conditions causing disability have a number of implications for both U.S. public health policy and for federal and state policies governing the provision of and reimbursement for LTC services.

These data have public health implications for monitoring changes in "active life expectancy" (WHO, 1984) and in the "compression of morbidity" (Fries, 1980, 1983). Actually, the current data can only be suggestive about trends in these factors, since we have only two points of measurement. We need to await the data from the 1988 survey in order to compare the transition for the 1982–1984 interval with the transitions for the 1984–1988 interval. Nonetheless, the data do tell us about aspects of the mechanisms underlying the linkage of morbidity, disability, and mortality that determine both active life expectancy and the compression of morbidity. One clear fact is that females, with their greater life expectancy, also spent longer periods of time in disabled states than did the shorter-lived males. Furthermore, disability among males was more strongly related to more lethal conditions than among females. These two observations suggest that life expectancy can be increased more rapidly than the age at onset of disability can be delayed, implying that, with recent increases in life expectancy at advanced ages, there could be an increase in the amount of time spent in a disabled state (e.g., Wilkins & Adams, 1983). It also appears that there are strong sex differences in how certain chronic disease risk factors and conditions relate to the risk of death. For example, though diabetes, obesity, and hypertension are all risk factors for heart disease, females survived longer with those conditions (and with those conditions severe enough to cause disability) than did males, for whom the conditions appeared to be more lethal. This suggests that the linkage of morbidity, disability, and mortality at advanced ages is complex and involves the interaction of specific disease states and that these interactions vary strongly by sex. It suggests that a simple model in which death is due ultimately to "biological senescence" is neither very useful scientifically nor consistent with the evidence; for example, the longer-lived females had a higher prevalence of multiple chronic conditions that coexisted for a longer period of time. This suggests that the study of mortality at advanced ages requires qualitatively different concepts than those that can be used to describe mortality at younger ages—and that those concepts require the analyses of the interaction of multiple conditions, not a unified mortality force due to biological senescence.

In addition, these findings suggest that we must employ very different interventions to improve the aggregate functional status of the U.S. population at a given age than we employ to reduce the mortality risks of major causes of death at those same ages. Although many major risk factors have been identified for diseases like cancer, heart disease, and stroke, and although their effects on mortality have been conclusively demonstrated in community studies and clinical trials for at least certain types of interventions (e.g., the reduction of smoking on lung cancer risks; the reduction of hypertension on heart disease and stroke risks; the reduction of cholesterol on heart disease risks), we possess far less knowledge about the risk factors for causes of disability and the possible mechanisms for controlling those risk factors.

For example, hip fractures are usually due to trauma in persons with osteoporosis. We know how to mechanically intervene in the risk for certain types of in-home falls by redesign of the environment, but there is controversy over the efficacy of dietary calcium supplementation and exercise in controlling the rate of osteoporotic changes—the underlying physiological condition that heightens the risk of elderly persons to such in-home hazards (Radebaugh, Hadley, & Suzman, 1985; Russell, 1987). Indeed, the metabolic mechanisms involved in osteoporosis probably involve a number of factors, such as vitamin supplements to utilize dietary calcium, exercise, and such co-risk factors as smoking and hormonal status. Currently our knowledge of these factors, and how to manipulate them, is not adequate to confidently design intervention strategies. We can also partially control certain types of arthritic conditions through the use of anti-inflammatory agents, but we still lack much basic knowledge about the basic physiological mechanisms causing arthritic degeneration—many of which, recent evidence suggests, may be involved in complex ways in sex-specific age changes in immunological functions. Alzheimer's disease is a complex neurological degenerative process whose physiological mechanisms we are just beginning to understand.

What this complexity suggests is that, while control for the causes of disability could yield large benefits for the well-being of the elderly population, we are just beginning to assemble the basic biomedical understanding of the disease and degenerative processes involved. Once the scientific base is established, we then need epidemiological studies to assess the population distribution of risk factors and carefully controlled clinical and community intervention studies to assess the efficacy of intervention strategies. Thus we have much basic scientific and epidemiological work to do before we can influence the causes of disability as effectively as we can manipulate, for example, hypertension.

These studies also have implications for the provision of LTC services to the elderly population—and this is an area we can more directly manipulate. They suggest that an evaluation of the LTC service requirements of the elderly population must be at least bidimensional; that is, they must involve the interaction of the level of functional impairment (a major determinant of the intensity and type of LTC service) and medical condition (a major determinant of the duration of the functional impairment). Any reimbursement mechanism designed to provide for LTC services must also therefore reflect such case-mix differences. For example, in a recent study of the design and use of case-mix-based reimbursement for Medicare home health services, we found that measures of both functional status and medical condition had to be included in the definition of case mix. The functional measures determined the level of services required by the person, but the medical condition causing the impairment was important in determining the overall use of home health services by determining the duration of service need. Thus cancer and heart disease patients required medically intensive services, but the total use of home health services was moderate due to the acute nature of these conditions (or condition episodes). In the extreme, certain service use periods were terminated due to death. In contrast, cognitively impaired persons required lower levels of service but for much longer periods of time. As a consequence, neurologically impaired persons had by far the greatest service use (Manton & Hausner, 1987).

With the 1982–1984 NLTCS we could not only study health and functional changes but also examine the differential service use of persons with different health and functional characteristics. In particular, in our first set of analyses we examined the rate at which persons with different disability levels utilized both acute hospitals and Medicare SNFs and HHA services. Unfortunately, the Medicare data did not permit us to examine the continuous record of the use of non-Medicare LTC institutions, although we could evaluate long-term changes in the population of such institutions using data from the two sets of survey records. We found dramatic differences in the use of Medicare services by persons in LTC institutions and in four analytically defined disability subgroups of community-dwelling elderly. In other, more extended analyses of service use patterns for periods before and after the introduction of Medicare PPS, we found major shifts in the pattern of use of such services by people with similar medical and functional status profiles—suggesting considerable flexibility in the way in which various types of LTC and posthospital care may be delivered (Liu & Manton, 1987).

In particular, we found that the largest portion of the demand for LTC services involved disabled persons resident in the community. The actual rates for institutionalization when compared to the rates of functional loss in community-resident persons suggested the importance of home health options to support and extend informal care services. We also saw a high rate of improvement of functional status for persons in the community, suggesting that we need strategies that can provide services for specific amounts of time for disability caused by specific conditions. In effect, this involves generating some definition of in-home LTC service episodes based on the natural history of the underlying disease process in different age and sex groups. We also saw that persons who were institutionalized were seldom in the community two years later, suggesting the absorbing nature of this type of service use and challenging us to identify ways to ameliorate the physical and social conditions enforcing institutionalization—even though such strategies may not be cost effective in purely economic terms.

These observations suggest that we need reimbursement policies for LTC services that have a number of features. First, they must supplement rather than replace informal care services. Second, it appears that home health services, combined with appropriate informal care, may successfully maintain extremely disabled persons at home. Thus it is probably only for persons with inadequate social resources, or with very select conditions with special management problems (e.g., Alzheimer's disease), that institutionalization is appropriate. A careful assessment of persons in institutions might identify many persons who could successfully live in the community. Third, and as a consequence of these observations, LTC service mechanisms must involve the integrated management of a range of home and institutional care options. That is, separate policies for home health and institutional care enforce arbitrary service boundaries that are potentially both cost ineffective and inefficient. Finally, a successful reimbursement strategy must be bidimensional, involving both case-mix adjustments for medical conditions and the scaling of the intensity of services for degree of functional impairment. Based on these principles, a successful LTC service policy could be created and further developed by monitoring with the types of data systems used above.

REFERENCES

Fries, J. F. (1980). Aging, natural death, and the compression of morbidity. *New England Journal of Medicine, 303*, 130–135.

Fries, J. F. (1983). The compression of morbidity. *Milbank Memorial Fund Quarterly, 61*, 397–419.

Liu, K., & Manton, K. G. (1987). Effects of Medicare's hospital prospective payment system (PPS) on Medicare service utilization. Washington, DC: The Urban Institute.

Maddox, G. L., Fillenbaum, G., & George, L. (1979). Extending the uses of the LRHS data set. *Public Data Use, 7*, 57–62.

Manton, K. G. (1987, May). *The 1982 and 1988 National Long Term Care Surveys: Their structure and analytic uses.* Paper presented at Health and Human Services Conference on Long Term Care Data Bases, Washington, DC.

Manton, K. G. (in press). A longitudinal study of functional change and mortality in the U.S. *Journal of Gerontology.*

Manton, K. G., & Hausner, T. (1987). A multidimensional approach to case-mix for home health services. *HCF Review, 8,* 37-54.

Manton, K. G., & Soldo, B. J. (in press). Disability and mortality among the oldest-old: Implication in long term care service needs. In R. Suzman & D. Willis (Eds.), *The oldest-old.* New York: Oxford University Press.

Manton, K. G., Stallard, E., Woodbury, M. A., & Yashin, A. I. (1987). Grade-of-Membership techniques for studying complex event history processes with unobserved covariates. In C. Clogg (Ed.), *Sociological methodology 1987* (pp. 309-346). San Francisco: Jossey-Bass.

Radebaugh, T. S., Hadley, E., & Suzman, R. (Eds.). (1985). *Symposium on falls in the elderly: Biological and behavioral aspects.* (Clinics in Geriatric Medicine, Vol. 1, No. 3). Philadelphia: Sanders.

Russell, L. (1987). *Evaluating preventive care.* Washington, DC: The Brookings Institution.

Tolley, H. D., & Manton, K. G. (1987). A Grade of Membership approach to event history data. In *Proceedings of the 1987 Public Health Conference on Records and Statistics* (pp. 75-78) (DHHS Publication No. (PHS) 88-1214). Hyattsville, MD: U.S. Government Printing Office.

Verbrugge, L. M. (1984). Longer life but worsening health? Trends in health and mortality of middle-aged and older persons. *Milbank Memorial Fund Quarterly, 62,* 475-519.

Wilkins, R., & Adams, O. (1983). *Healthfulness of life.* Montreal: The Institute for Research on Public Policy.

Woodbury, M. A., & Manton, K. G. (1982). A new procedure for analysis of medical classification. *Methods of Information in Medicine, 21,* 210-220.

World Health Organization. (1984). The uses of epidemiology in the study of the elderly: Report of a WHO scientific group on the epidemiology of aging (Technical Report Series No. 706). Geneva, Switzerland: Author.

CHAPTER 9

Insuring Long-Term Care

ALICE M. RIVLIN, JOSHUA M. WIENER,
and DENISE A. SPENCE
THE BROOKINGS INSTITUTION

INTRODUCTION

Paying for long-term care has become a major problem for older people, their families, and society and will be an increasingly serious problem in the future. With increased longevity, many more people face a period of serious disability in old age. Most are cared for informally by relatives and friends, albeit often at great emotional and sometimes financial cost. When the disabled elderly and their families seek more formal home care or nursing home services, they find, often to their surprise and dismay, that long-term care is not covered to any significant extent by Medicare or private insurance. Frequently nursing home patients must use their entire life savings to pay for their care, and once totally impoverished, they must depend on Medicaid, a severely means-tested welfare program.

Over the next several decades, this financing and delivery system will become increasingly strained as the number of older people increases. Medical advances that reduce disability in old age are highly desirable but cannot be counted on. Both public and private spending for long-term care are likely to increase substantially. The question is not whether spending for long-term care will increase, but how and by whom these costs will be borne. How will costs be divided between the public and private sectors? Will they be borne largely by people unlucky enough to need expensive care or more broadly by society?

Public policy debate on the financing of long-term care increasingly reflects consensus around two issues: First, long-term care should be treated as a normal risk of growing old. The cost of long-term care should not come as an unpleasant surprise, causing severe financial distress to individuals

The views expressed in this chapter are those of the authors and should not be attributed to other staff members, officers, or trustees of the Brookings Institution.

and families or forcing normally self-sufficient people to depend on public charity. Both private-sector and public-sector advocates argue that the current system that impoverishes the elderly is unacceptable.

Second, risk pooling is an appropriate approach to paying for long-term care. A substantial majority of the elderly will never incur catastrophic long-term care expenses. Thus pooling the risk of high long-term care expenses through private or public insurance or some other risk-pooling mechanism provides financial protection against unforeseeable individual need for long-term care at a far lower cost than having each family bear the risk itself. Public policies that seek to have each individual save for his or her own catastrophic long-term care costs require annual levels of contributions far beyond those most people are likely to find affordable. They are also inefficient, since most people will end up saving for long-term care expenses they will never incur.

The policy consensus breaks down over the relative roles of the private and public sectors. This chapter examines two approaches to risk pooling for long-term care—private and public insurance—that differ on this dimension.[1] Partly using simulations from the Brookings-ICF Long-Term Care Financing Model, we examine the potential effect of these insurance options on public and private expenditures. In brief, we find that private insurance can play a much larger role than it does now, but that it is unlikely to be affordable by the majority of elderly or to finance a very large proportion of total long-term care expenditures. In contrast, public insurance virtually guarantees universality of eligibility but, depending on the design, could be quite expensive. However, the costs to society of a full-fledged private insurance program are unlikely to be much different than for a full-fledged public insurance program.

BROOKINGS-ICF LONG-TERM CARE FINANCING MODEL

The quantitative data in this chapter are from simulations using the Brookings-ICF Long-Term Care Financing Model. Detailed projections are made from 1986 to 2020; more aggregate projections are made to 2050. Since a detailed description of this computer simulation model is available in Rivlin and Wiener (1988), we only briefly summarize the structure and assumptions of the model here.

---

[1]Other examples of risk pooling include social/health maintenance organizations, which extend the principles of prepaid, capitated financing to include long-term care, and continuing care retirement communities, which combine residential settings with an array of services on the premises. For a variety of reasons, social/health maintenance organizations and continuing care retirement communities are likely to play a fairly small role in the financing of long-term care.

As shown in Figure 9.1, the detailed model consists of six major components:

1. *Population database.* Using data from the *Current Population Survey*, the first part of the model contains extensive information on a representative sample of adult individuals of all ages in 1979. This 1979 database was chosen because it has been merged with Social Security earnings histories for each individual in the sample.
2. *Income simulator.* Using ICF Incorporated's Pension and Retirement Income Simulation Model (PRISM), the second part of the model simulates labor-force activity, marital status, income, and assets for each individual. The model estimates retirement income from private-sector–defined benefit pension plans, private-sector–defined contribution plans, public pension plans, individual retirement accounts, and Keoghs. Using data from the Survey of Consumer Finances, the model also simulates the assets of the elderly individuals, including the value of home equity.
3. *Disability of the elderly.* Using probabilities estimated primarily from the 1982 National Long Term Care Survey and the 1977 National Nursing Home Survey, this part of the model simulates disability for persons aged 65 and over. The model simulates both development of and recovery from disability.
4. *Use of long-term care services.* This part of the model uses probabilities estimated primarily from the 1977 National Nursing Home Survey to simulate admission to and length of stay in a nursing home. For persons in the community, it also simulates admissions to and the number of paid home care services using probabilities derived from the 1982 National Long Term Care Survey.
5. *Sources and levels of payment.* The next part of the model simulates the sources of payment and the levels of expenditures for every individual receiving nursing home or home care services. The model incorporates the eligibility and coverage provisions of Medicare and Medicaid and the spend-down of individuals onto Medicaid.
6. *Aggregate expenditures and utilization.* The final part of the model accumulates Medicare, Medicaid, and private expenditures as well as use of long-term care services for the simulated individuals for each year.

The model uses Monte Carlo simulation methodology. It simulates changes for each individual in each year using estimated probabilities. Changes in each individual's marital, employment, retirement, and disability status, as well as nursing home and home care use, from one year to the next are simulated using probabilities that depend on the demographic and economic characteristics of the individual. The model simulates each of these changes in status for an individual by drawing a random number between 0 and 1 and comparing it to the probability of that event's occurring to an individual based on his or her socioeconomic characteristics.

The assumptions in any model play a key role in determining the results; this is especially true for models that project into the future. In general, the model follows the Social Security Administration's (SSA) midrange (Alternative II-B) economic and mortality assumptions. Behavioral relationships in the long-term care system are assumed to remain constant.

Projected mortality rates assume substantial declines over time, especially in the older age groups. Disability rates are assumed to remain constant over time on an age, sex, and marital-status basis. Controlling for these variables, the population becomes neither sicker nor healthier.

Over the long run, the Consumer Price Index (CPI) is assumed to increase at 4.0% per year. Real wage growth (i.e., net of inflation) is 1.6% per year, and real growth in "other compensation" (i.e., fringe benefits) is 0.2% per year. It is assumed that nursing home and home care compensation must increase at a rate roughly comparable with the rest of the economy. Reflecting the heavy labor component of long-term care services, nursing home and home care reimbursement rates increase by the CPI plus SSA's projection of real wage growth and other compensation. Over the long run, this cost increase is 5.8% per year.

Finally, nursing home and home care utilization rates remain constant on an age, sex, marital-status, disability, and (for home care) income basis. Despite recent efforts by states to control the nursing home bed supply, it is assumed that the long-run increase in demand will be so great as to make this strategy untenable. Thus nursing home and home care supply is assumed to keep pace with demand.

Examining the effects of different options through 2020 is sufficient to evaluate their relative importance and to provide an order of magnitude estimate of their impact on public and private expenditures. It is, however, well before the baby-boom generation's peak demand for long-term care. It is not adequate to develop estimates of the financing necessary to pay for various public insurance options. Thus a simple methodology was developed to extrapolate long-term expenditures in each year through 2050. Basically, inflation-adjusted, age-specific long-term care costs are multiplied by the number of elderly in each age category for each year through 2050. To estimate the payroll taxes required to finance various programs, total payroll was estimated by multiplying inflation-adjusted data on wages and salaries by the number of projected workers in various age and sex categories for each year through 2050. To estimate the additional income tax required to finance various programs, federal personal income tax revenues were assumed to increase at SSA's Alternative II-B assumption of real wage growth.

Figure 9.1 Brookings/ICF Long-Term Care Financing Model.

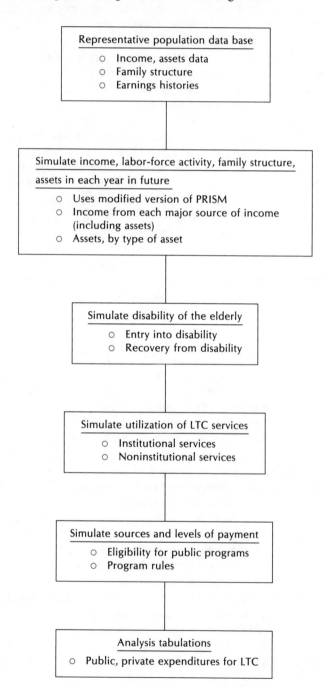

Figure 9.1 (*continued*)

Assumptions for LOWBEN Insurance Simulation
- The policy is similar to a currently marketed policy with a 100-day deductible period and a $30, $40, or $50 per day indemnity benefit, depending on what the individual can afford. The benefit is increased by $1.50, $2.00, and $2.50 per year for 10 years for the $30, $40, and $50 benefit, respectively. The maximum length of covered nursing home stay is 6 years. Seventy-five percent of insureds who use nursing home care are assumed to meet the 3-day prior hospitalization requirement. The policy also provides individuals with a limited home care indemnity benefit after a nursing home stay.
- Individuals and couples will buy the insurance only if they can afford it for less than 5% of their income and if they have $20,000 or more in assets. Couples will purchase policies only if they can afford two policies.
- In 1986, individuals aged 67–81 will be eligible to purchase the policy. After 1986, individuals will purchase the policies starting at age 67.
- Only the physically fit will be allowed to start to purchase the policy. People who become disabled after buying the policies will be able to keep them.
- In the years following 1986, the initial premium and indemnity level are increased by 5.8% per year to reflect nursing home and home care inflation.
- The premium for the policy is based on the age of initial purchase. In 1986 the annual premiums for the $50 indemnity benefit vary from $584 for persons aged 67 to $1,642 for persons aged 81. Premiums for the $30 and the $40 indemnity benefit are 60% and 80%, respectively, of the $50 indemnity benefit premiums.
- If an individual's income declines after purchasing the policy, the individual will keep purchasing the policy as long as the premium is less than 7% of income and the individual/couple has $10,000 in assets.

In interpreting the results from the simulations, several features of the model must be kept in mind. First, all tables present *only* information on the elderly population. Nursing home and home care expenditures for and utilization by the nonelderly population are not included, nor are expenditures for and utilization by residents of intermediate care facilities for the mentally retarded. Second, all expenditures are in constant 1987 dollars. Nominal amounts would be dramatically higher. Third, most tables are presented for the period 2016–2020. This period, which is the latest to which the full model projects, presents the option being analyzed in a relatively mature period and takes advantage of the projected increased income of the elderly between 1986 and 2020.

PRIVATE LONG-TERM CARE INSURANCE

For many financially catastrophic events, such as hospitalization, automobile accidents, home fires, theft, and early death, Americans rely heavily on private insurance to provide protection against such costs at an affordable price. For long-term care, however, private insurance currently plays a very small financing role. To date, only about 423,000 policies have been sold; only 1% of total nursing home expenditures were covered by private insurance in 1985 (U.S. Department of Health and Human Services, 1987; Waldo, Levit, & Lazenby, 1986). Despite these small numbers, private long-term care insurance is a rapidly changing and expanding market.

Advocates of private insurance argue that this approach has many advantages. First, it builds on the well-known willingness of the elderly to purchase Medigap insurance. Approximately two-thirds of all elderly persons own a Medigap policy, and high levels of coverage persist even at relatively low income levels (Cafferata, 1984). Second, since it does not require the development of a complicated new service-delivery system, it could be expanded relatively quickly into a major financing source. Third, private insurance is a noncompulsory alternative that provides the consumer greater flexibility in meeting individual needs.

Barriers to Growth

Private insurance, however, faces several problems in becoming a major source of long-term care financing. In general, insurance companies cautiously restrict policies in ways that reduce their financial risks. From the consumer's perspective, however, this limits the degree of financial protection that can be obtained from these policies.

Insurers see their risks as follows. The first problem is the danger of adverse selection; that is, the possibility that insurance will be purchased disproportionately by people who are likely to use services, thus driving up service use and policy prices. Insurers typically try to protect themselves against this possibility by screening for health problems, prohibiting coverage for preexisting conditions, excluding coverage of mental illnesses that are not organically caused, and not selling to individuals above age 80 (Weiner, Ehrenworth, & Spence, 1987). Unfortunately, to the extent that insurers succeed in screening out high-risk individuals, they exclude the people most in need of coverage.

A second problem is that insurance coverage might induce "moral hazard," or increased demand and utilization. One of the consequences of insurance is to lower the out-of-pocket cost of services. People generally buy more of a good or service when the price is lower. Increased demand could be a particular problem if the insurance covers home care, which is an attractive addition to the informal care provided by the family. Insurers try to protect themselves against moral hazard by using large deductibles, primarily covering only the most medically intense level of nursing home care, requiring a prior hospitalization before nursing home coverage, and covering very limited home care. Unfortunately, these policies exclude many persons in need of nursing home care, and the lack of home care may exacerbate the already strong institutional bias of the current financing system.

A third problem is the uncertain market interest in private long-term care insurance. Most elderly and virtually all nonelderly persons underestimate their chance of long-term disability. In addition, there is a widespread misunderstanding of what Medicare and supplemental private insurance covers, leading some people to think that they already have insurance that covers long stays in a nursing home or home care (American Association of Retired Persons, 1984; Equicor, 1986; Gendel, Strachen, & Lopatin, 1986; Louis Harris & Associates, 1986; Meiners & Tave, 1984; RL Associates, 1987).

Finally, insurance premiums are high, thus limiting the market. For example, in 1986 the cost of an Aetna $60-a-day long-term care insurance indemnity policy was $516 a year for those age 65 and $2,208 for those age 80. At these prices, long-term care insurance would represent a substantial increase in out-of-pocket health care expenditures for most elderly persons and a doubling or more of their Medigap premiums.

Potential of Private Insurance

What is the potential of private insurance as a long-term care financing mechanism? This is a key question because if it were demonstrably possible to market private long-term care insurance that would protect a large majority of the elderly population from hardship in the face of long-term care costs and reduce dependence on Medicaid, then new kinds of government intervention might not be needed.

To help answer this question, the Brookings-ICF Long-Term Care Financing Model was used to answer the following questions: What proportion of the elderly could conceivably participate in private insurance? What proportion of total nursing home expenditures could private insurance pay? What is the potential effect on Medicaid expenditures? What is the impact on out-of-pocket expenditures by nursing home patients? Detailed assumptions of the policies we modeled are presented in Table 9.1. In general, our assumptions about participation are very favorable to private insurance. Thus the estimates presented below represent the maximum potential effect of private insurance.

Description of the Simulated Policies

The first two policy alternatives, BIGBEN and LOWBEN, are based on a recently marketed policy. LOWBEN is described in detail in Figure 9.1. Both policies cover up to six years of nursing home care after a 100-day

Table 9.1 Coverage and Purchase Criteria for Alternative Private Long-Term Care Insurance Models.

Alternative insurance model	Start age	Indemnity benefit ($/day)	Indemnity inflation index	Coverage criteria				Purchase criteria
				Deductible period (days)	Coverage period (years)	Prior hospitalization		
BIGBEN	67	$50	A	100	6	yes		5% or less of family income + $10,000 in assets
LOWBEN	67	30/40/50	B	100	6	yes		5% or less of family income + $10,000 in assets
MEDIGAP	67	50	C	90	1	no		Same proportion of elderly population as now purchases Medigap insurance
YOUNGINS	30	50	C	90	1, 2, 4, 6, or unlimited	no		Age 65 or less or as much as 1% of income buys Age 65–80: 3% of income + $10,000 in assets
PENSIONS	65	50	C	90	2	no		$500 minimum annual pension

A For 10 years after purchase, indemnity increases 5% of initial coverage, or $2.50 per year.
B For 10 years after purchase, indemnity increases 5% of initial coverage, or $2.50 per year for $50 indemnity, $2.00 per year for $40.00 indemnity, and $1.50 per year for $30.00 indemnity.
C Increases yearly by nursing home inflation of 5.8%.

deductible and a prior hospitalization, as well as home care after an initial nursing home stay, and provide a fixed indemnity payment with a limited inflation adjustment. The initial nursing home indemnity level of BIGBEN is $50 a day, and for LOWBEN it is $30, $40, or $50 a day, depending on what the person can afford.

To estimate maximum affordability and impact of this approach, all individuals or couples who can afford the policy for 5% or less of their income and who have at least $10,000 in nonhousing assets are assumed to purchase a policy at age 67.

In 1986, the BIGBEN premiums for a $50 nursing home indemnity level ranged from $584 for those aged 67 up to $1,642 for those aged 81. LOWBEN's additional $40 and $30 indemnity levels require premiums that are 80% and 60%, respectively, of the $50 indemnity-level premium. In both options, once a policy is purchased, premiums remain constant over the years.

A third simulation, MEDIGAP, tests the idea that the elderly who have purchased Medicare supplemental insurance would also buy insurance for long-term care. The objective of this alternative is to introduce a potential link between acute care and long-term care insurance. Individuals who purchase Medigap insurance are assumed to buy a policy that covers one year of nursing home care after a 90-day deductible and pays $50 a day (indexed for inflation). This option primarily extends Medigap insurance to encompass short- or medium-term nursing home care. Social Security Administration actuaries estimate that these policies would cost $362 in 1986 (U.S. Department of Health and Human Services, 1986).

The fourth policy alternative, YOUNGINS, attempts to mitigate the problems of adverse selection and affordability by including insureds of working age. Starting at age 30 and over, individuals are assumed to buy as much (in terms of number of covered years) nursing home insurance as they can afford for 1% of their income. Again, premiums were estimated by Social Security Administration actuaries and range from $115 a year at age 30 for a policy that covers one year of nursing home care, to $2,530 a year at age 80 for a policy that covers unlimited nursing home care (U.S. Department of Health and Human Services, 1986).

The final policy simulated, PENSIONS, assumes that private long-term care insurance is provided to all individuals aged 65 and over receiving at least $500 in annual pension benefits. Qualifying individuals receive a long-term care insurance policy that provides a $50-a-day inflation-adjusted two-year nursing home benefit after a 90-day deductible. The objective of this alternative is to test the addition of long-term care insurance as a retiree benefit for those receiving at least a minimal pension.

Model Results

The results of the simulations for the time period 2016–2020 are presented in Table 9.2. In all of the simulations, private insurance can be purchased by far more elderly than currently have policies. The proportion of elderly projected to buy long-term care insurance in 2016–2020 ranges from a quarter of the elderly for BIGBEN to nearly two-thirds of the elderly for MEDIGAP. The freestanding, relatively comprehensive nursing home policy, LOWBEN, is affordable by only a minority of the elderly. With the exception of YOUNGINS, the policy that people can buy when they are young and working, the less comprehensive the benefits, the higher the participation in policies.

In the future, private insurance will play a far larger role in paying for nursing home care than it does now. However, under the policies simulated, private long-term care insurance will only account for between 7% and 18% of total nursing home expenditures. Thus the simulations suggest that private insurance will play a relatively modest role in paying for nursing home care.

The simulations also suggest that the effect of private long-term care insurance on Medicaid expenditures is likely to be fairly modest. Medicaid nursing home expenditures under different insurance options are between 1% and 18% less than they would be under the base case. Thus even with generous assumptions about participation, Medicaid expenditures are still likely to roughly triple over the simulation period.

Although private insurance does not substantially reduce public expenditures, it has a greater impact on private out-of-pocket payments. Not counting premium payments, private long-term care insurance reduces out-of-pocket payments for nursing home care by 12% to 18%.

To become eligible for Medicaid, nursing home patients must deplete virtually all of their income and assets. Hence the number of Medicaid nursing home patients is a rough proxy of the number of people who incur catastrophic costs and are impoverished by paying for their nursing home care. Compared to the base case, private insurance reduces the number of Medicaid nursing home patients by between 1% and 9%. Thus the overall impact of private insurance on the number of people who impoverish themselves is fairly small.

Implications of the Simulations

Private-sector options have a relatively limited effect on public and private expenditures for two main reasons. First, private insurance is too expensive to be affordable by most elderly persons. Since total long-term care expenditures per capita for the elderly exceed $1,200 a year, this is hardly surprising. Total (public and private) long-term care costs roughly equal Medicare

Table 9.2 The Effects of Private Long-Term Care Insurance on Participation, Proportion of Total Nursing Home (N.H.) Expenditures, Medicaid Expenditures, Out-of-Pocket Expenditures (Billions of 1987 Dollars), and Medicaid Nursing Home Patients: 2016–2020[a].

	Participation (% of elderly buying insurance)	N.H. expenditures paid by option (% of total expenditures)	Medicaid N.H. expenditures (% change from B.C.)	Out-of-pocket N.H. expenditures (% change from B.C.)	Medicaid N.H. patients (millions) (% change from B.C.)
Base case (B.C.)	N.A.	$98.1	$46.2	$50.3	2.34
BIGBEN[b]	25.4%	6.9	$45.8	$44.3	2.31
		(7.0%)	(−1.2%)	(−12.0%)	(−1.3%)
LOWBEN[b]	45.0%	11.7	$43.9	$42.9	2.24
		(11.7%)	(−5.0%)	(−14.8%)	(−4.3%)
MEDGAP[b]	63.7%	17.9	$37.7	$44.4	2.14
		(17.6%)	(−18.4%)	(−11.7%)	(−8.5%)
YOUNGINS[c]	62.5%	17.0	$40.5	$41.4	2,15
		(16.9%)	(−12.4%)	(−17.7%)	(−8.1%)
PENSIONS[c]	41.3%	14.8	$40.5	$43.6	2.14
		(14.7%)	(−12.3%)	(−13.3%)	(−8.5%)

[a]Each option is separate; the columns cannot be added.
[b]Ages 67 and older.
[c]Ages 65 and older.

Source: Brookings-ICF Long-Term Care Financing Model.

physician expenditures and exceed one-half of Medicare hospital expenditures. Thus costs never become trivial, even when spread over a large population.

Second, private insurance has restrictions that limit the amount of financial protection that it offers. For example, private long-term care insurance policies have prior hospitalization requirements, preexisting condition exclusions, age limitations on who may purchase policies, and limits on the levels of nursing home care covered. Very little home care is covered. Reimbursement levels almost never increase with inflation.

The problem is that improved coverage and affordability are trade-offs; that is, coverage improvements are likely to make products more expensive, thus reducing affordability. For example, indexing the indemnity level to inflation would probably increase premiums for the elderly by about 30% to 50%.

PUBLIC LONG-TERM CARE INSURANCE

A public insurance program is the most far-reaching option for restructuring the financing of long-term care. The United States already employs this financing mechanism to cover most acute health care costs for the elderly through Medicare. Indeed, most Western European countries and Canada cover long-term care through their national health insurance or national health sevice (Nusberg, Gibson, & Peace, 1984; Wilensky, Grana, & Dunlop, 1984).

The rationale for public insurance is that long-term care is a normal, insurable risk for the elderly but that for various reasons the private insurance market is unable to provide adequate coverage at a price that most elderly persons can afford. Covering long-term care under a universal public program avoids the problems of adverse selection and the tendency of insurance companies to react by screening out disabled applicants. It eliminates the high marketing costs of private insurance and makes it easier to spread the cost of long-term care over the working-aged population and the elderly. It also reduces the problems of equal access and quality of care inherent in the current distinction between private-pay and welfare patients.

This strategy involves risks, principally financial ones. Any public insurance program would require significant additional public expenditures and could grow substantially beyond initial estimates. The original gross underestimates of the costs of the Medicare and Medicaid programs are sober reminders of this possible problem. With most disabled elderly not receiving any paid services, a large increase in demand, which could result in expenditures outstripping the most conservative cost estimates, is clearly possible.

A social insurance program for long-term care would involve some form of contributory financing and entitlement to benefits, but many variations in design are possible. The most important program design issues are the level of cost-sharing and the means of financing the program.

Level of Cost-Sharing

A public insurance program could be designed either to provide long-term care services at little or no cost to eligible patients or to require cost sharing through coinsurance or deductibles at various levels. A program requiring relatively little cost sharing would benefit the elderly financially and emotionally. No one, not even the poorest of the elderly, would have to worry about the financial burden of care. This approach would also give the government maximum power to exert its buying power to control the price of services (Kane & Kane, 1985).

Covering virtually all costs would avoid creation of a Medigap-like supplemental insurance market, because no one would require supplemental insurance to receive adequate financial protection. Most current Medicare supplemental insurers, with the exception of Blue Cross-Blue Shield and Prudential, spend more than 40% of Medigap premiums for marketing, administrative expenses, and profits (U.S. General Accounting Office, 1986). These costs would be minimized with comprehensive government coverage of the entire elderly population.

On the other hand, by removing any financial disincentive for the consumer to use services, low cost-sharing would likely increase use of services and provider costs. Such a program could be very expensive and, in an environment in which policy makers fear rising costs, lacks political credibility and feasibility. Moreover, the high cost of this approach would likely impose a significant tax burden on moderate- and lower-income persons.

Another possibility would be to establish fairly substantial coinsurance and deductibles, uniform for all beneficiaries, as in the acute care Medicare program. The rationale for substantial cost-sharing is more cogent for long-term care than for acute care, since a substantial part of the nursing home bill is for room-and-board expenses that people would have even if they were healthy. While this approach would foster a substantial role for the private sector through gap-filling insurance, it would not depend wholly on massive expansion of private insurance for its success.

The difficulty is setting the proper level of cost-sharing. If it were set high enough to reduce the cost to the government substantially and deter middle- and upper-income people from overusing services, it would impose excessive burdens on the relatively low-income elderly. Hence, a large residual welfare program might have to be retained, partially defeating the goal of a public insurance program. Making coinsurance and deductibles income-related would reduce the need for a residual Medicaid program but would also risk making the long-term care insurance extremely complex to administer. Many social insurance advocates oppose this approach because it seems only one step away from a means test.

Another variety of cost-sharing would be for the government to cover long-term care after a very long deductible period—two years, for example. The government benefit would be limited to the relatively few people who incur catastrophic long-term care expenses. For this deductible period, the elderly would be encouraged to purchase private long-term care insurance. This catastrophic approach would encourage private-sector involvement by making marketing easier and by limiting the benefit period during which private insurance would be needed, thus reducing insurers' financial risks, insureds' premiums, and incremental public costs.

The principal problem with the catastrophic-only approach is that it places a great deal of faith in the ability of individuals and the private sector to carry the financial burden for the large front-end deductible. Most people incur catastrophic out-of-pocket costs well before they have spent two years in a nursing home. This approach would require a very strong private-sector response, but it is not certain that the insurers would flock to this market. Moreover, individuals unable to obtain insurance because they are either disabled or too poor would be left with no option other than spending down to Medicaid eligibility levels. Even with insurance, individuals might be faced with substantial out-of-pocket costs because current policies have significant restrictions that substantially reduce the level of financial protection that they offer (Wiener et al., 1987).

Sources of Financing

An essential feature of public insurance is that financing be contributory, meaning that beneficiaries have earned their entitlement to services by paying into the program. Pure public insurance is self-financing. The contributory taxes or premiums, generally paid into a trust fund, are set at a level adequate to pay the full costs of the program, as they are in Social Security and the hospital portion of Medicare. In less pure insurance, such as the physician part of Medicare, a portion of the cost of benefits is paid out of general revenues. The fact that the federal government is currently running large annual deficits makes it politically imperative that any new social insurance program pay for itself, not add to the deficit.

The United States currently uses the payroll tax to finance its social insurance programs, including Social Security, disability insurance, and Medicare hospital insurance. However, payroll taxes are regressive; that is, lower-income groups pay a higher proportion of their income in taxes than do higher-income groups. This is both because ceilings are placed on taxable earnings and because higher-income groups have asset and other nonsalary income that is not subject to the payroll tax. The federal income tax is more progressive than the payroll tax, but Americans have never used it to fund social insurance programs. Moreover, dedicating income tax funds to specific programs might set an undesirable precedent that could leave many general government functions underfunded.

As an alternative or addition to a payroll or income tax, insurance premiums could be paid by the elderly. As the primary beneficiaries of the program, the elderly could reduce the burden on the working population by helping to pay for the program. This contribution could be in the form of premiums, or through increasing income taxes either by changing the tax rates or by treating part of the actuarial value of benefits as income.

Any of these forms of contribution could be related to income in order to avoid a net income redistribution from low- and moderate-income workers to the upper-middle-income and wealthy elderly. While elderly advocacy groups have strongly opposed Medicare benefits that vary with income, financing the program through a progressive tax appears to be politically more palatable to them. The problem with progressive financing is that it explicitly introduces welfare elements into a social insurance program. Some redistribution from higher- to lower-income groups already occurs under Medicare, since even with a flat payroll tax, people with higher lifetime earnings pay more for the same Medicare benefits than do people with lower earnings. Financing benefits with a progressive tax, however, would increase the redistribution and might compromise the claim that the insurance is an "earned right" rather than welfare and cause upper-income individuals to oppose the program. Similar arguments about the future rate of return for upper-income groups under Social Security have already proved to be politically divisive.

There is little doubt that financing a public insurance program exclusively through a payroll tax, income tax surcharge, or elderly premiums would require fairly substantial increases in these taxes. Thus it would be desirable to include some general revenue funds to lower the incremental contributory tax or premium. Possible sources of revenue could include maintaining some state financial participation (although less than would be expected if the current Medicaid program was continued), excise taxes, and estate taxes.

Model Results

To estimate the costs and financing necessary for public long-term care insurance, four different programs were modeled. Table 9.3 summarizes eligibility criteria, benefits provided, cost-sharing, and other program characteristics of the different options. Since none of the programs provides free long-term care, some means-tested program for the poor must be retained.

The first option, CATINS, provides catastrophic nursing home coverage with a 10% coinsurance after a two-year deductible. Individuals are encouraged to purchase private insurance to finance their long-term care expenditures during the long deductible period. Medicaid is retained as a separate program to cover nursing home care for those poor enough to meet current Medicaid financial eligibility criteria. Home care benefits are not covered beyond what is currently available.

A second option, HIGHCO, provides a minimal long-term care insurance benefit to all elderly, imposing a high 50% coinsurance after a 100-day deductible. In addition, Medicaid is substantially liberalized as the means-tested component of the insurance program. The improved financial protection for the means-tested component includes raising the Medicaid personal needs allowance and level of protected assets, removing all pressure to sell the home to pay for nursing home expenses, and allowing the home-based spouses of nursing home patients to retain a much higher level of protected income. Home care is available only for persons with three or more deficiencies in activities of daily living.

The third option, MODCO, roughly replicating the level of cost-sharing of the current Medicare program, provides nursing home benefits with a moderate coinsurance of 25% after a 100-day deductible. The current Medicaid program is retained as a separate program with no improvements. Home care is available only to persons with three or more deficiencies in activities of daily living.

The final option, COMPUB, provides comprehensive public insurance. Coinsurance and deductibles for benefits vary with income but are low at all but the highest-income level. This program also liberalizes Medicaid financial eligibility by raising the personal needs allowance and level of protected assets as well as allowing the home-based spouses of nursing home patients to retain a much higher level of protected income. Home care is available for all disabled elderly.

Public insurance would almost certainly increase utilization of nursing homes and home care, but it is not clear by how much. Indeed, meeting some of the unmet demands for care is one of the goals of a public insurance program. The analysis below assumes a 20% across-the-board increase in nursing home use and expenditures and a 50% increase in home care use and expenditures. None of the estimates include administrative costs. Since

Table 9.3 Eligibility Criteria, Benefits, and Program Characteristics of Alternative Public Long-Term Care Insurance Programs.

Option	Medicaid & Medicare benefits	Nursing home benefits	Home care benefits	Reimbursement rates
CATINS[c] (including private insurance)	Medicaid separate program; no improvements Medicare LTC benefits maintained	Unlimited coverage of skilled nursing and intermediate care facilities Deductible 2 years Coinsurance 10%	Current Medicare and Medicaid home health benefits No new benefits	N.H: 115% of Medicaid rate H.C: same as current rates
HIGHCO	Medicaid improved: PNA $200/month $15,000 protected assets Home protected At-home spouse keeps 2 × SSI level of income Medicare LTC benefits maintained	Unlimited coverage of skilled nursing and intermediate care facilities Deductible 100 days Coinsurance 50%	Must have 3+ ADL disabilities Skilled & unskilled Deductible 1 mo. Coinsurance 20%	N.H: 115% of Medicaid rate H.C: 115% of weighted average cost/visit for all noninstitutional services
MODCO	Medicaid separate program; no improvements Medicare LTC benefits maintained	Unlimited coverage of skilled nursing and intermediate care facilities Deductible 100 days Coinsurance 25%	Must have 3+ ADL disabilities Skilled & unskilled Deductible 1 mo. Coinsurance 20%	N.H: 115% Medicaid rate H.C: 115% of weighted average cost/visit for all noninstitutional services

(continued)

Table 9.3 (*continued*)

Option	Medicaid & Medicare benefits	Nursing home benefits	Home care benefits	Reimbursement rates
COMPUB	Medicaid improved: Pays for coinsurance & deductibles for those who cannot afford PNA $60/mo. Assets protected except for paying deductible ($1800) At-home spouse keeps $3 \times$ SSI level of income Medicare LTC benefits maintained	Unlimited coverage of skilled nursing and intermediate care facilities Deductible & coinsurance vary with income[a]	All disabled elderly Skilled & unskilled Deductible 1 mo. Coinsurance varies with income[b]	Nursing Home (N.H): 120% of Medicaid rate Home Care (H.C): 120% of weighted average cost/visit for all noninstitutional services under base-case

[a]For income less than or equal to 200% poverty and assets less than or equal to $5000, no deductible and 10% coinsurance. For income less than or equal to 200% of poverty and assets more than $5000, 1-month deductible and 10% coinsurance. For more than 200% poverty, 30% coinsurance and 1-month deductible.

[b]For income less than poverty, no coinsurance. At 100–125% poverty, .05% coinsurance. At 125–150% poverty, 10% coinsurance. At 150–200% poverty, 15% coinsurance. At more than 200% poverty, 20% coinsurance.

[c]Eligibility for purchasing private insurance less than 5% of income, at least $10,000 in assets and nondisabled. Private insurance covers 2 years of nursing home care after 20 day deductible. Pays $50 per day, not indexed for inflation.

Medicare rates are higher than Medicaid rates for almost all services, the nursing home and home care reimbursement rates under the public insurance programs are assumed to be 15% to 20% higher than the expected Medicaid rate.

Results of the simulations are summarized in Table 9.4. Total long-term care (nursing home and home care) expenditures for the four different options range from $144 billion for CATINS to $166 billion for COMPUB in 2016–2020. This represents a 20% to 40% increase from the base case total expenditures of $120 billion and mostly reflects higher expenditures due to increased utilization. This is probably not very different from what total costs would be if private insurance were to spread to the vast majority of the elderly population. Private insurance would also be subject to increased service use, and total costs might even be higher because of higher administrative costs and profits.

One of the most important considerations in choosing a public long-term care insurance program is the effect on total public expenditures for nursing home and home care. Assuming a significant increase in service use, near-term public costs (federal, state, and local for all long-term care programs) in 1986–1990 range from $33 billion for CATINS to $47 billion for COMPUB, compared to $22 billion for the base case. Longer-run cost estimates in 2016–2020 range from $94 billion for CATINS to $130 billion for COMPUB—44% to 100% more than in the base case.

In all options, the vast majority of public expenditures are for nursing home rather than home care services. Almost three-quarters of total long-term care expenditures under the base case are for nursing home care. Home care expenditures represent only 18% to 26% of total public costs in 2016–2020, even with expanded coverage of home care services. Thus even with generous coverage of home care services and higher projected use of home care, home care costs remain a relatively small part of total expenditures. If home care utilization or reimbursement rates were higher than assumed or if increased coverage of home care resulted in fewer people using nursing homes, then the proportion of expenditures going for home care would be higher.

Given the expanded public role in all of these options, out-of-pocket expenditures for long-term care decline. The reduction in total out-of-pocket long-term care costs from the base case in 2016–2020 ranges from 34% for MODCO to 48% for CATINS (including the effect of private insurance).

Tax Burden

The payroll tax and income tax surcharges required to finance various public long-term care insurance programs were estimated for the four public programs we modeled. Table 9.5 presents the gross payroll tax rate required

Table 9.4 Total and Out-of-Pocket Long-Term Care Expenditures and Public Nursing Home and Home Care Expenditures by Base Case and Each Public Insurance Program, Assuming "Moral Hazard"[a]: 1986–1990 and 2016–2020 (Billions of 1987 dollars).

Option	Total	Out-of-pocket[c]	Public expenditures[b]		
			Total	Nursing home	Home care
1986–1990 expenditures					
CATINS[d]	$49.094	$14.769	$33.373	$26.383	$6.989
% change	18.01%	−25.72%	53.66%	79.11%	0.00%
HIGHCO	$55.549	$11.482	$44.064	$31.635	$12.429
% change	33.52%	−42.25%	102.88%	114.77%	77.84%
MODCO	$55.057	$12.880	$42.175	$29.746	$12.429
% change	32.34%	−35.22%	94.18%	101.94%	77.84%
COMPUB	$57.571	$10.978	$46.589	$35.734	$10.855
% change	38.39%	−44.78%	114.51%	142.59%	55.32%
BASE CASE	$41.602	$19.882	$21.719	$14.730	$6.989
2016–2020 expenditures					
CATINS[d]	$144.174	$28.461	93.465	76.233	17.292
% change	20.14%	−48.16%	43.58%	59.47%	0.00%
HIGHCO	$159.611	$35.913	123.690	92.071	31.619
% change	33.01%	−34.59%	90.01%	92.60%	82.85%
MODCO	$158.250	$36.285	121.959	90.340	31.619
% change	31.87%	−33.91%	87.35%	88.98%	82.85%
COMPUB	$166.409	$36.237	130.164	103.093	27.071
% change	38.67%	−34.00%	99.96%	115.66%	56.55%
BASE CASE	$120.003	$54.904	$ 65.096	$ 47.804	$17.292

[a]Assumes 20% increase in nursing home expenditures and 50% increase in home care expenditures.
[b]Public includes Medicaid, Medicare, public insurance, and other payer.
[c]Out-of-pocket includes cash income and assets.
[d]CATINS includes the effects of both public insurance and private insurance. There is no expansion of home care and no assumed increase in use of home care. In 2016–2020 there is an additional $22.244 billion in private insurance expenditures for long-term care.

Source: Brookings/ICF Long-Term Care Financing Model.

to finance the current base case long-term care expenditures and the four simulated public long-term care insurance programs in 1988–2050. The payroll tax estimated is based on total payroll unconstrained by current Social Security salary limits and represents both employer and employee contributions. Assuming a 20% increase in nursing home use and a 50% increase in home care expenditures, the average annual payroll tax required to finance various programs from 1988 through 2050 ranges from 2.22% for CATINS to 3.11% for COMPUB.

By means of comparison, if current public long-term care benefits were financed through 2050 by a payroll tax rather than general revenue, it would require an average annual payroll tax of 1.6%. If total (public and private) long-term care expenditures were financed on a payroll tax basis, it would require 2.84% of payroll. Although total tax rates would not be that high in absolute terms, the payroll tax required would be larger than the tax currently required for Medicare Part A benefits.

Increasing federal income tax rates or imposing a tax surcharge is another way to finance the program. From 1988 through 2050, an average income tax surcharge of between 12.97% for CATINS and 18.19% for COMPUB would be required (Table 9.5). This compares to an income tax surcharge of 9.31% for public costs over the 62 years for the base case. Including corporate income taxes would reduce the tax burden on individuals, but not by very much. In 1986, corporation income taxes accounted for only 15% of total federal income taxes (Pechman, 1987).

CONCLUSION

Devising a way to finance long-term care is one of the major challenges that society faces in caring for the elderly. Two of the most promising strategies for reform are private and public insurances. Simulations using the Brookings-ICF Long-Term Care Financing Model, as well as other data, suggest that the role of private long-term care insurance in the future could be far greater than it is today. Clearly, there is great potential for growth, with a multibillion-dollar market that is now virtually untapped. From an investment perspective, there are major opportunities for growth. Persons who participate in these options would be better protected against catastrophic costs.

While major growth is anticipated, private long-term care insurance will not be a panacea to the problems of long-term care. Results from the Brookings-ICF Long-Term Care Financing Model suggest that fairly comprehensive private insurance will be beyond the financial reach of the majority of the elderly, especially those who have traditionally been a public concern. Thus even with an expansion of private insurance, public financing of long-term care will increase substantially far into the next century. Given that public expenditures will not fade away, the critical public policy issue is how to structure public expenditures. Do we, as a society, wish to retain a severely means-tested welfare program as our principal mechanism for financing long-term care? Or do we wish to move to more of a social insurance strategy?

Table 9.5 Public Program Costs as a Percentage of Payroll and Federal Personal Income Tax, Assuming "Moral Hazard"[a]: 1988–2050.

	Payroll tax[b]			Income tax surcharge		
Public program	1988	2050	Average 1988–2050	1988	2050	Average 1988–2050
BASE CASE						
Total costs	1.57%	4.71%	2.84%	9.87%	26.51%	16.63%
BASE CASE						
Public costs	0.82%	2.93%	1.59%	5.15%	16.51%	9.31%
CATINS[c]	1.24%	3.70%	2.22%	8.42%	21.79%	12.97%
HIGHCO	1.67%	4.97%	2.96%	10.51%	27.98%	17.36%
MODCO	1.60%	5.02%	2.94%	10.03%	28.23%	17.19%
COMPUB	1.76%	5.15%	3.11%	11.08%	28.97%	18.19%

[a]Assumes a 20% increase in nursing home use and expenditures and a 50% increase in home care use and expenditures.
[b]Combined employee and employer contributions. No ceiling on taxable salaries.
[c]Under CATINS, there is no expansion of home care coverage and no assumed increase in home care use.

Source: Brookings/ICF Long-Term Care Financing Model.

A social insurance program in conjunction with private-sector initiatives could be used to meet the basic needs of the overwhelming majority of elderly. The public costs of such a program would be quite large, but society as a whole would incur most of the expenditures associated with a public insurance program even if it relied on private insurance in conjunction with Medicaid. The fundamental issue is whether these costs will be borne largely by those who need nursing home and home care or spread more broadly over the entire population.

REFERENCES

American Association of Retired Persons. (1984). *Long-term care research study.* Washington, DC: Author.

Cafferata, G. L. (1984). Private health insurance coverage of the Medicare population (Data Preview 18, National Health Care Expenditures Survey, National Center for Health Services Research). Rockville, MD: U.S. Department of Health and Human Services.

Equicor. (1986). *The Equicor health care survey–VI: Looking to the future of retiree health benefits.* New York: Author.

Gendel, T., Strachen, D., & Lopatin, P. (1986). The Blue Cross and Blue Shield Association long-term care project. Chicago: Blue Cross and Blue Shield.

Harris, Louis and Associates, Inc. (1986). *Problems facing elderly Americans living alone*. New York: Author.

Kane, R. L., & Kane, R. A. (1985). *A will and a way: What the United States can learn from Canada about caring for the elderly*. New York: Columbia University Press.

Meiners, M. R., & Tave, A. K. (1984). Consumer interest in long-term care insurance: A survey of the elderly in six states. Rockville, MD: National Center for Health Services Research.

Nusberg, C., Gibson, M. J., & Peace, S. (1984). *Innovative aging programs abroad: Implications for the U.S.* Westport, CT: Greenwood.

Pechman, J. A. (1987). *Federal tax policy* (5th ed.). Washington, DC: Brookings Institution.

Rivlin, A. M., & Wiener, J. M., with Hanley, R. J., & Spence, D. A. (1988). *Caring for the disabled elderly: Who will pay?* Washington, DC: Brookings Institution.

RL Associates. (1987). *The American public views long-term care*. Princeton, NJ: Author.

U.S. Department of Health and Human Services. (1986). *Report to the Secretary on private financing of long-term care for the elderly*. Washington, DC: Author.

U.S. Department of Health and Human Services. (1987). Survey of policies in force. In *Report to Congress and the Secretary* (pp. 72–74). Washington, DC: Author.

U.S. General Accounting Office. (1986). *Medigap insurance law has increased protection against substandard and overpriced policies*. Washington, DC: Author.

Waldo, D. R., Levit, K. R., & Lazenby, H. (1986). Nursing home expenditures, 1985. *Health Care Financing Review, 8*, 1–21.

Wiener, J. M., Ehrenworth, D. A., & Spence, D. A. (1987). Private long-term care insurance: Cost, coverage and restrictions. *The Gerontologist, 27*, 487–493.

Wilensky, G., Grana, J., & Dunlop, B. (1984, July). *Long-term care in Western Europe and Canada: Implications for the United States*. Report prepared for U.S. Senate Special Committee on Aging, Washington, DC.

Index

Index

Contents of Previous Volumes

Contents of Previous Volumes

295

VOLUME II

VOLUME III

VOLUME IV

VOLUME V

VOLUME VI

VOLUME VII

DATE DUE

GAYLORD			PRINTED IN U.S.A.